# No Black Heroes

Jackie,
Love you very much, Sis!

Ron Berry

## About the Author

Ron Bailey is a highly decorated African American police officer who served in a major metropolitan U.S. city. Having lived in the very projects where he later worked provided him insight most officers could never have. His experiences include five shooting incidents; he's also credited with saving six lives; and served 18 years of his lengthy career undercover.

Through his experiences, every police officer can benefit from reading about the struggles of black officers, their relationships with white officers, and the stories about the unanswered calls for justice from the communities they serve.

# No Black Heroes

The true story of a black police officer's struggle with racism, corruption and crime

Ron Bailey

I Roc Publishing, LLC

Copyright © 2017 by I Roc Publishing, LLC

Published by I Roc Publishing, LLC

All rights reserved. No part of this publication may be reproduced or utilized in any form or by any means, electronic or mechanical, including photocopying, recording, or by any information storage or retrieval system, without the prior written permission of the Author, except by a reviewer who may quote brief passages in a review.

For book signings, bulk purchases and inquiries, contact the author at ronbailey@snet.net.

To order *No Black Heroes* visit createspace.com/7568547

Any events, names, or other information that may appear to be that of any entity and/or specific person are coincidental.

Publisher's Cataloging-in-Publication Data
Bailey, Ron
    no black heroes : the true story of a black police officer's struggle with racism, corruption and crime / by Ron Bailey.—1st ed.
      p. cm.
ISBN 10: 0-9993992-0-9
ISBN 13: 978-0-9993992-0-0
1. Autobiographies. 2. Racism. 3. Law enforcement. 4. Police corruption. 5. Drugs and crime. I. Bailey, Ron. II. Title.

Printed in the United States of America
First Edition, 2017

Credits:
Cover design by Ron Bailey
Cover layout and interior design and layout by
Ray Fusci, rayfusci@momentumtime.com

Picture credits:
Except where otherwise credited, courtesy Bailey family collection.

To my parents Lizzie Lucy Bailey and Willie Bailey, thank you. This book is in dedicated to both of you for instilling in me honesty, integrity, determination, and the courage to fight for what I believe in. You are my heroes.

*Your son eternally,*

*Ronnie*

# Contents

Preface ............................................................. ix
Acknowledgments ............................................. xi
Prologue .......................................................... xiii
My Early Years ................................................... 1
    COATESVILLE, PENNSYLVANIA ........................................ 1
    WHITE DAYS ONLY ...................................................... 2
    BRIDGEPORT, CONNECTICUT ......................................... 6
Police Recruit Bailey ........................................ 13
Father Panik Early Days ................................... 21
Race a Problem, So is Crime ............................ 41
    I'M ALONE; GUARDIANS CHALLENGED ......................... 57
New Assignment ............................................... 63
Girls; A Stranger .............................................. 71
The Informant .................................................. 77
First Shooting; Black Officers Denied .............. 87
Informant Out of Control ................................. 99
The First Tactical Narcotics Team .................. 111

Mariano Sanchez and More ................................. 119
Cruz Makes His Move ............................................ 141
The Legal Battles .................................................. 165
Federal Court/Race Issues .................................... 181
Back on the Streets .............................................. 197
TNT Out of Control ............................................... 207
Police Board Cited for Racism ............................. 221
TNT Team Three .................................................. 227
Chief Ignores Racism ........................................... 239
    PROTESTS/CIVIL DISOBEDIENCE ................................. 245
Cruz Dead; A Shooting; The Fox and News ............ 255
My Arrest; Lost It; Shots Fired .............................. 273
Chief's Slipping and The Kings.............................. 285
    EXPLOSION; K-5; CHIEF IS OUT................................... 292
Major Drug Gangs................................................ 307
    K-5; JONES; ESTRADA; CORRUPTION?......................... 327
    TNT FINAL RAIDS; COURT; PROMOTION ...................... 340
Community Distrust/Institutionalized Hate .......... 355
The Fix; I Am Somebody; A National Problem........ 379
Court is Out; Union Deceit; Hope? ........................ 409
Cops Gone Wild; Hey Nigger; A Human Skull ......... 419
Education; Cancer; Two Miracles .......................... 439
Hangman's Noose/Shot in the Back ...................... 447
Cops on Drugs; The Struggles................................ 457
Conclusion No One Saw Coming............................ 467
Afterword .............................................................. 479

# PREFACE

April 6, 2010

What is it like to be a black police officer in America? How do we as African American officers serve our communities that, in many ways, hate us? What does it feel like to be distrusted by the very culture you came from? And how can we address the hatred of those in policing who don't want us involved in law enforcement?

Many of those answers will be revealed in what I have endured and documented as an African America police officer with 30 years of service. The material in this memoir is inspired by true events, supported by court cases, police files, newspaper articles, various documents and personal recollections. The names of individuals, including my informants and witnesses and/or the time frames and circumstances may have been changed for protection purposes. Some of the material herein is based on the opinions, views, and best recollections of others. Many of the characters in this book may have been combined, changed or altered, including some descriptions to prevent the identity(s) of anyone from being disclosed, or thought to be that of a particular person. Any events, names, or other information that may appear to be that of any entity and/or specific person are coincidental.

## No Black Heroes

As the author, I wanted you to be able to imagine enduring the indignation of racism, intimidation, harassment, and the pain associated with being a black officer in a predominately white police department. I must warn you, you may find some of the events and details hard to believe. You may say "No way," but trust me, I lived it. Those who know me would tell you, I'm exactly the kind of person you're going to read about.

Not surprisingly, officers who refuse to tolerate racism become targets. We endanger ourselves the moment we mention the words discrimination, or civil rights violations in the police department. And black officers who seek to protect people of color in a community are aware they can be labeled by white officers as turncoats and many times left to defend themselves in the streets alone. So there should be no surprise that the underlying motivation that almost got my family and me killed was driven by racism! What will likely surprise you are those who maneuvered purposefully in the hopes of my death.

I want to apologize to you in advance, because the words black and white are mentioned many times throughout this book. These references are inherent in pointing out the injustices we all experience due to color, and helping my readers understand what both races are facing.

Now, let me provide you with the true workings of a police department. I will place you in my shoes. Welcome to the Bridgeport Police Department (BPD).

# ACKNOWLEDGMENTS

With very special thanks to the founding members of the Bridgeport Guardians, retired Officer Ted Meekins, Lieutenant Dave Daniels III, Bishop J.C. White, Lennie Grimaldi, Professor Richard Andersen, my wife Yvette Bailey, and always first in my life, God.

## Prologue

People have asked me, "What would make anyone want to be a cop?" In the black community the question was, "Why would a black man want to join an organization that hates black people?" These questions cannot be answered by anyone who has not spent real time on the streets. If you have never fought the powers that be in a police department for your rights, you cannot answer these questions. The answers will come by way of how my life unfolds.

First, you need to know that most police departments do not readily accept minority police officers. The mistake people make is in thinking black officers join the police department and become one of them. Although some do become one of the good old boys, that was not the case for me. And African American officers should recognize the fact that it is undignified to fetch coffee, run errands, or be limited to menial tasks. You would be better suited in striving for what you are entitled to, a dignified part and position in your profession.

Looking at the facts, whether unintentional or not, police departments in America are majority white while black officers are constantly being challenged and denied their place in the ranks. That is especially true for police management positions. The system has always found some reason as to why we don't belong, or can't do a job.

Speaking as an officer in America, let me say this, the minority communities have suffered at the hands of abusive cops, mostly white officers. I say this with confidence, experiencing it as a young black man from the housing projects where I once lived and later worked. I too suffered at the hands of irate cops as a kid. Don't tell me it wasn't because of the color of my skin. I was there. How ironic; as an African American police officer, I suffered from, and then joined, the very police department that caused me so much pain in my youth.

The news accounts about crooked and abusive cops today is just the tip of the iceberg. That has been ongoing since the time organized police departments were first formed. And you should know the racist remarks, beatings, misuse of authority and shootings of unarmed blacks in America are, and have been, commonplace. Today's cell phones are now catching what has been going on for far too long. What really really hurts, many police shootings were executions by officers who justified those killings with the "I feared for my life" statement. That in itself is disgraceful.

In my experience, a great many white officers hold the perception that black officers are not qualified and just taking positions that were unfortunately held exclusively for their friends and family. Now, let me add a little tidbit of information; white supervision is in control of most police departments in our country. Under those conditions, it's almost assured that we cannot move forward or excel.

What's absolutely crazy is, no matter how much you fight for what's right, no matter how many times you expose the racism in a police department, no one will ever admit to it. The rule of thumb is to deny it, unless ultimately forced to address it by the court. They then pay monetarily for it, but don't actually acknowledge the racism. Black police officers across America who have challenged racism in court know what I'm talking about. You may get a settlement, but

# Prologue

the person who treated you differently didn't have to pay one cent. So basically, citizens' tax dollars pay for the racism we've suffered while the culprits get away with it. Talk about a warped sense of poetic justice.

Some of you may think, as you read, that my views on policing are due to my own prejudices. My facts come from over 30 years of federal court intervention at the police department I was a plaintiff to. Not to be one-sided, I also had opportunities to fight for white officers' rights, and did! Surprised? Well read on.

To all my readers, please try to understand why black officers not only feel disadvantaged, we are. The saddest lesson that will be revealed to you is after decades of federal court oversight and countless lawsuits won on discriminatory matters, the Bridgeport Police Department culture never really changed. The ones who hated us found creative ways that maintained their views. That is also a pattern that is reflective in our society today!

For many, the true source of our strength stems from our God, so thank you Mom for raising me in church. It has been through faith that I survived what you will now read about. I can honestly say there is no place worse to make a stand as a black person than in the middle of 450 cops with guns and badges. But my mother had told me this, "Ronnie, someday you will have to take a stand for what you believe in. We raised you right. You will make us proud."

So let me begin where my life first took shape.

Chapter 1

# MY EARLY YEARS

## Coatesville, Pennsylvania

The history of Coatesville, Pennsylvania, is somewhat shameful to me. It's a small town in a valley 40 miles from the city of brotherly love, Philadelphia. Coatesville had a dark history that made national news in 1911. That was the year several townspeople killed Zachariah Walker, a black laborer at Lukens Steel Mill. He was burned alive for killing a white security guard in what was said to be self-defense. Walker was caught by the police and held in Coatesville Hospital, the very place where I was born.

Some in Coatesville say the police turned Walker over to the populace for killing one of their own. History reflects the townspeople stormed the hospital and dragged Zachariah Walker to an open field where he was thrown into a huge bonfire. It was said Walker's screams could be heard a half mile away as he attempted to jump out of the fire three times. He was pushed back in with rakes and shovels. Walker's execution by fire brought about the NAACP movement to end lynching in the United States. Fifteen men were indicted for the lynching of Walker by fire but none were convicted of his murder. Irony at its best, I was born in a town with such a morbid history of racism, police abuse, and Walker's death without due process. Who would have known I was destined to become a police officer, the very thing that has historically caused so much pain to a race of people, even today.

## White Days Only

Imagine a little boy learning about racial hatred at such a young age, in the year 1959. My father Willie Bailey had just gotten up for his usual Saturday morning shift at Lukens Steel Mill. That was his day to make extra money for the family. He peered over at my bed and shook me. Still a little sleepy, I heard him say he wanted to take me out to eat, and to meet him at the mill gate by 12. I then woke up thinking I must have done something good.

"Dad, what did I do?" "Nothing, boy; I just wanted to take you out to eat with me for your first time." I looked over and saw Mom standing there smiling at us. She looked so happy. Dad put his hand on my head and swiped my hair with his fingers. He said he would see me later, turned and walked out of the room. Mom told me I should get up and dressed so I could get there on time. My father only worked four hours on a Saturday.

I got up slowly like always on a Saturday morning, but with excitement, knowing I was going to meet Dad for our first time out together. Of course, Mom was happy but a little cautious as always. I had to walk to Lukens Steel Mill about two miles away from home. Coatesville was a small, quiet town. Kids back then were safe and could go just about anywhere. Parents didn't have to worry, unlike today. Still, I was very young and Mom was always concerned when it came to me, her only child.

## My Early Years

"Ronnie, I want you to stay on this side of the street when you get to the gate, you hear? And don't stop 'til you get to Willie's job. You're only seven." "Ma, I'll be eight soon, and the gate is closer than the walk to school." Her response was clear, "You hear me, Ronnie?" "Yes Ma'am." I finished getting dressed, smiled at her and walked out the door. I was so excited to meet with Dad. I walked a little, and then ran some. I got to the mill gate in about 15 minutes but didn't cross the street like Mom told me to.

Dad was just coming out of the gate with that big black metal lunch pail he always had in his hand. He saw me waiting, smiled and motioned with his other hand for me to stay there. He crossed the street and looked down at me. He said he was a little tired but we were still going out. Today was our day. He pointed to the small cafe where most of the workers went after work. "Now Ronnie, you can't go in there because they sell liquor too. So you wait by the door. I'll get us two submarine sandwiches." He said they had the best subs in town. So he walked me over to the sub place where I stood by the door.

My father walked over to the bar. He spoke to some guy standing on the other side who must have been the owner. After a few words with my father the owner looked over at me from behind the bar and turned back to my father. That's when he spoke. "Get that shit-colored kid out my place." At first I was confused. There was no swearing in our house. Then I became afraid. What did I do wrong? Was I too far in the doorway? My father, who had never raised his voice in my entire life, was now yelling at this man.

I couldn't understand why they were arguing. All we wanted was a couple of sandwiches. I heard the man say to my father, "You know today ain't your day." I knew in my heart we were not being treated right. Although I was too young to understand then, my mother did tell me years later what happened that day. The owner of that bar was ignorant but knew how to make a buck. He had days for whites only, and days for blacks only. The only place close to get a sandwich, or something to drink for the workers,

## No Black Heroes

was his place, across the street from the mill. Whites and blacks had to be separated according to the owner.

I could hear Dad, "He's just a boy," when suddenly the voices got even louder. Several men behind my father got up from their seats and moved towards him. I remember seeing a smoke-clouded group of white men moving towards Dad. He was pounding his fist on the bar, accidentally smashing a glass under his hand. The men behind him stopped and stood there. I was so scared and wanted to run home to get Mom. I had never seen my father like that.

Dad's fist was bleeding from the glass he broke. What made me even more fearful, was that he was still pounding his fist in the broken glass on the bar. The men behind him stood there staring. I'm sure they realized what I saw. My thoughts were fixated. Didn't my father feel the broken glass under his hand?

Suddenly the words came out. "Dad, I'm not hungry, I just wanted to come see you." He stopped and turned looking at me in the doorway. "Ronnie, I'll get you something to eat. Don't you worry, boy." I said it again not knowing if I was scared or no longer hungry because of my fear. "No Dad really, I just wanted to see you." The man at the bar looked at my father, "See, he's not even hungry." My father stopped, took a long look at this tall, white, thin, scraggly, old-looking person. He just stared at him for a good while.

My father turned his head and looked at the men standing behind him, then back at the owner. Suddenly dad swiped his hand across the bar smashing all the glasses stacked up on the bar into the wall and on the floor. With blood dripping heavily from his hand, he walked over to me, "Tell me the truth boy, you hungry?" "No Dad, I just wanted to see you, really." My parents had a thing about telling the truth, so he knew I wouldn't lie to him. That day I wasn't sure if I was telling him the truth or not. I was a scared seven-year-old who wanted my dad away from that place.

## My Early Years

He stepped through the doorway turning towards home. Looking back down at me, he said, "Come on Boy, let's go home." Dad usually talked to me when we walked together, but that day he was silent. His hand still dripping with blood, I reached from behind him to get a large piece of glass out of his hand. He pulled his hand away, "Don't touch it, Ronnie." After that, he didn't say anything else. I didn't know if he was worried I might get cut or so upset he didn't care. Maybe it was a little of both.

When we got home Mom was smiling as we came in. God, she looked so happy. Dad walked right past her and into the bedroom. Confused, she looked at me, and then saw the drops of blood on the floor. "Willie, Willie, what's wrong?" She asked me, "Ronnie, what happened to Willie?" She looked back at the trail of blood. "Go in the living room and watch TV, Ronnie." She rushed into the bedroom to see what was wrong with Dad.

Still confused, I lingered by the door to the kitchen. I heard Mom talking, so I stood quietly by the bedroom doorway. I peaked in and could see her taking glass out of Dad's hand with a dishtowel. He had both his hands on his forehead propping his head up. All the while I was thinking I must have done something. One thing was for sure, the owner of that bar didn't like us, especially me.

As I looked at my father sitting on the edge of the bed, to this day, I don't know if he was crying or just holding his head up thinking about what had happened. I can't imagine the hurt my father must have felt having his only child denied a sandwich because it wasn't a day to feed blacks. I remember my mother's words as she was pulling glass out of his hand. "Willie, it'll be alright, Willie, someday it'll be alright."

After that day, my father became a target of sorts. It was a sin for a black man to fight with anyone white back then. That was unthinkable in the '50s. For instance, when we walked downtown to shop for food we couldn't get a cab home. The Red Cab Company was refusing to pick my father up because of what happened at that bar. Some cab drivers felt bad for us. I remember a few times some of them would drive by us and signal to Dad. We would walk down a side street so the cab driver could pick us up out of sight of others. I remember we sat low with our heads held down to not let anyone see us. Still others would stop for us and pull away suddenly just as we got to the car door. That was life in the '50s.

Sadly, a few years later, my father passed away. He never got that second chance to take me out to eat. After the death of my father, Mom didn't want to stay in Coatesville any longer. She thought we could do better in Bridgeport, Connecticut, where her sisters lived. I think she was afraid. The racism in Coatesville was too much for her. With the way whites treated us after my father stood up to that owner, and then with him gone, we needed to get away from there.

I remember the pastor's sermon on a Sunday and our last day at First Baptist Church on Gibbons Street. The church was old looking and modest, but huge in faith. The pastor's voice became strained and very loud. He wasn't talking about God that Sunday. He was talking about my Dad, his widow and son. I didn't understand it all, but you could tell members of the church were upset. They all remembered what my father stood for and had tolerated. Our last service in that church had my mother's name resonating. "Lucy Bailey, you and your son have our prayers. We say bless you and your husband for what was done here in Coatesville. Your husband stood up not only for his family, but for others. We thank you." After that we moved with the hopes of a better life.

## *Bridgeport, Connecticut*

I was 10 years old when we arrived in Bridgeport, Connecticut. The city was known as the "Project City." The major housing projects were Charles Greens Homes, Evergreens Apartments, Marina Village, Marina Apartments, P.T. Barnum Housing, Trumbull Gardens, Pequonnock

## My Early Years

Apartments, and the infamous Father Panik Village. There was plenty of low-income housing surrounding those projects as well. It was a flawed design straight out of hell, for low-income people. With such a concentration of poor minorities, it was certain those communities would only become worse with time.

Once we moved in, it seemed for the first time in a while, my mother was happy. She was so excited to be with her sisters again. I could sense she felt a little safer away from Coatesville. I remember Aunt Pearl telling Mom, "Don't worry, that's all behind you now." Aunt Pearl turned and looked down at me, "Look at you boy, and how you've grown." She touched my head then smiled at me with those years of wisdom black women have etched in their faces. She was my mother's eldest sister.

We moved into an apartment on Spruce Street just around the block from the P.T. Barnum Housing Project. P.T. was named after the "Greatest Showman on Earth, Phineas Taylor Barnum." Imagine a housing project notorious for drugs and shootings named after someone proudly etched in American history. Mr. Barnum must have been turning over in his grave behind such a legacy. It was said P.T. was at one time a great place to live. From what I saw one block away it didn't look so.

It's funny how my future would be linked to P.T. and other projects in Bridgeport. I played one block from P.T., who knew? A small child from Coatesville who couldn't get a sandwich from a white store owner someday would be telling the FBI and DEA where the drugs were, and what to do. But that was something destined for my future 20 years later.

After we moved to Bridgeport, Mom had problems keeping up with the bills. We had a nice apartment but couldn't keep the lights or heat on. It was always one or the other we had to do without. Desperate to make ends meet, we were forced to move into the projects. She sat me down and told me we were moving. "Ronnie, we got to move into the pro-

## No Black Heroes

jects. It's not a safe place but we can't afford anything else right now. I'm sorry baby, I'm so sorry." Our new home would be Father Panik Village that many called "The Panic." That name said it all.

The Panic was not a place for an older black woman and her child from a small town in Pennsylvania. I was scared about moving to a place Mom swore we would never live in. There were nightly shootings, people screaming and fighting. I was never allowed near the windows and had to remain inside. Sarcastically speaking, this project was named after a priest, Father Panik? Few knew the "Panic" was considered the third worst project in the nation. Watts of L.A. and Cabrini Green of Chicago were the only two projects with a worse reputation than the Panic.

Forty-seven buildings of crime, drugs and shootings; Mom was incensed when we got there. We couldn't leave the apartment for fear of being shot. She cried daily and risked going to the office every week crying so hard the manager finally couldn't take it anymore. "Miz Bailey, we will find a place for you and your son. You have my word." Mom was all I had and she lived for me.

A short time later, we moved to a smaller housing project, Charles "Greens" Homes. Greens was five high-rise buildings, eight floors high. It was a project originally built for the elderly only. Families with children could live on the first three floors; anyone from the fourth floor up had to be elderly or disabled, no kids. Mom was partially disabled. Housing decided to let us have an apartment above the third floor designated for only the elderly. I was the first young person allowed in one of the top floors of Greens, building 3, apartment 602. Mom felt so lucky for getting that apartment she wanted to play those numbers.

The first day we moved in, she was crying again. At first I thought they were tears of joy. I walked through the door with boxes in my hands, "Mom, what's wrong?" She showed me a letter that had been left in our mailbox. She couldn't read but recognized the one word she knew only too well. It

## My Early Years

said "We don't need any Niggers in this building. Move back to where you came from." I was furious. Mom never did anything to anyone. She was about church and God. We left Coatesville for this?

Surprisingly, she showed me the letter. She must have figured the time had come for me to know what was going on in the real world. At 15 years of age, an old southern black woman of peace was schooling me on how things really were. She told me how my father wanted me to know about that day in Coatesville. I did remember the man who wanted us out of his place not wanting to serve us. I always thought it had something to do with me. She said Dad never got over how we were treated.

"Your father loved you more than life, Ronnie. He never wanted you to grow up hating others. That's why I'm telling you about that day in Coatesville, he wanted you to know when you could understand. He said he expected you to be a fine man someday. His exact words were, 'Make sure my son sees to it folks respect him.'" "Okay Mom, thanks for that." It was like Dad was back if only for a moment. I missed him so.

After our talk, I finished moving our things in the apartment. Mom was still shaken by that letter, so I joked with her, "Hey Mom, how could these people know I was black? Remember what you said to me when I was little? I didn't get enough color because I didn't stay in the oven long enough." I got a hint of a smile. Mom joked a bit. "You know your father wondered about me after you arrived. When he first saw you, he looked confused. I knew what he was thinking. I told him, "Willie, you are the only man who has been in my life, ain't no one else been here but you. Ronnie's fair skinned, but he's yours." She told me I had American Indian blood which was the reason I was so fair skinned.

What was the big deal about someone's color? It just didn't make sense. It was during those times I began to think and understand things that never crossed my mind

## No Black Heroes

before. What 15-year-old thinks about race? I guess we had been through so much. I remember a few months later Dr. Martin Luther King was shot and killed. Mom pulled me in the house and wouldn't let me out for weeks. My older cousin had to walk with me to school every day. People were crying, upset, scared. The news reported black people were being killed across America. Riots, police killings, it was a crazy time. Mom wanted to make sure it all made sense. "Son, people aren't being killed because they're black, they're being killed for what they believe in, what's right."

My first year in high school was just as confusing. The slick process hair style was on its way out. The Afro was the hairstyle for blacks. There seemed to be a presence of revolution going on. James Brown was making hit after hit, and the number-one song was *I'm Black and I'm Proud*. One thing was certain; I was not going to escape the issues of race.

Race even spilled over into my school. I was in the cafeteria when it started. They said it began because whites were being treated better than blacks in school. It could have been, but the fistfight I saw started when two students bumped each other. The black student wanted an apology and the white one told him where to go get his apology. Next thing I knew the white student was on the floor holding his face. From there, everybody was throwing hands. Maybe it was about race, but it started with a simple bump. For some reason I was so hungry, while everyone was fighting, I was eating. I went back for seconds, thirds. The lady at the register said "You might as well eat up because it will all get thrown out today. No charge." She was laughing while I calmly ate my food. The whole cafeteria was tossing chairs and tables. At my house we could only afford so much, so I ate up.

Later that year, race raised its ugly head again in school. I had been playing drums for a group called The Special Occasions Band. Although we were self-taught in music, we were popular in the city, performing the top

## My Early Years

tunes. While in class one day, speaking to a girl about performing at her party, Mario bumped into me. I thought nothing of it and gave the girl my number before taking my seat. Mario looked at me, "Oh, you talking to white girls now?" I looked at him and the words just came out, "Mind your business, you pimple-faced son of a bitch." The other students were laughing so hard. Mario was clearly embarrassed.

He got up out his seat and stood over my desk. "What did you say?" "I called you a pimple-faced bitch." He took a swing at me before I could get up from my seat. I pulled my head back and he missed. I jumped up and we struggled until two teachers came and pulled us apart. I held on to his sport jacket while they pulled. Rip, rip, rip! By the time we were separated his jacket was split almost in two.

In the principal's office, Mr. Exosey called us in. We told him what happened. I told the truth, but Mario said I started the fight. Mr. Exosey took his side. "Mr. Bailey, I would like to suspend you only. I don't believe your story for a moment. You lie like the rug that lies on the floor." I looked at Mario who was smiling, and then back to "Mr. Exosey, "Sir, don't ever call me a liar again. That pimple-faced son of a bitch is the one lying." He told me to go home and threw me out of his office.

At home I told Mom what happened. I figured I was going to get it good. I guess she overlooked the swearing I had picked up. She didn't say anything other than asking me to repeat what Mr. Exosey had called me, a liar. The next morning, she got up and told me to get dressed. This huge, almost completely disabled woman, who could barely walk, called for a cab. I had no idea where we were going. The cab arrived, "Central High School, please." I wanted to ask why we were going there but decided to be quiet.

She struggled out of the cab. Mom was a large woman, beautiful brown skin yet slightly bent over from age and using a cane someone in Greens let her have. We entered with students staring at Mom and her fair-skinned son. You

## No Black Heroes

could see the confused looks in their eyes. I guess Mom should have been thin and white to match the stereotypes, according to looks we got. In the office she calmly asked to speak to Mr. Exosey. I could hear Mom who had never raised her voice before. Thinking about my father who had never raised his voice either brought an eerie sense of fear to me. "Don't you ever call my son a liar. I didn't raise him that way. His father sure enough didn't. You hear me?" "Yes Mrs. Bailey, I understand." "Good day, sir."

She came out of that office barely able to walk. I felt so bad and yet so proud. She looked at me, "Ronnie, what you did was wrong. I don't agree with fighting but I understand." She took a deep breath. "Your father Willie is smiling on you today, son." Out of breath with a hint of fear in her eyes, she had come through a time afraid to speak to what she called "white folks." That day she was defending her son. I would forever have to live up to that standard she and Dad set.

Chapter 2

*Hey kid, it's different from what you were told out here.*
—Officer Tony Brown

## POLICE RECRUIT BAILEY

So many questions were in my mind. It was July 20, 1983, and I was a police recruit on my first day of training. We were being trained at Central High School. It was the only place large enough to handle 80 recruits. The class was that big, due to all the delays in hiring while the discrimination case was held up in court. A photographer came and took my picture. Why me? Later that very picture would end up in a book written by Lennie Grimaldi; *Only In Bridgeport*. I guess it was a hint of things to come.

How did I get there? Especially after all I had been through living in the projects? I was totally beside myself at how ten years after leaving Central High I had returned there for my police training! It was not one of the places I thought fondly of. Central High had its history of racial memories for me. All I could think was, *What in the world am I doing?* I hated the police. For the next four months, I had to train with the very people I had no respect for. I didn't know if I could ever accept them, even if I became one of them. The question others would ask is why I felt that way. Let me enlighten you.

Thinking back, the first police officer I ever met was Officer John McKegan. I was still living in Greens and playing in the band. I had just turned 16. The Greens was two blocks away from the police department. On my way downtown I took my usual shortcut through the rear of the police department parking lot. I was on my way to a pawnshop for a new drum pedal.

I walked down the steep stairway behind the department and there he was, Officer McKegan. As I was about to walk through the parking lot, I said hello to him. Large groups of cops were coming in and out of the building. I didn't know it then, but I had walked into the shift change. McKegan was a husky man who looked every bit like someone who had worked overnight into the midday. His uniform was amiss and he was unshaven. "Where do you think you're going?" Officer McKegan was known in the projects and had a bad reputation. We were all warned by the older kids to stay away from him. Just my luck, there he was.

"I'm going downtown to get a pedal for my drum set, officer." McKegan pointed back up the stairs, "You're not going this way. This is for police officers only." "Okay officer." I turned to go up the stairs when he grabbed me by my collar and dragged me back towards him. He lifted me up, then pushed me face first through a nearby door. McKegan didn't say a word and I was too scared to speak. We walked through a second set of doors leading to the Youth Bureau.

I had done nothing wrong. Why was he doing this to me? Once in Youth Bureau, McKegan dropped me off, "Here!" "What's the charge?" "Trespassing." He left me there. The officer at the desk asked how old I was. "Sixteen." He seemed surprised by my answer. I guessed I didn't look my age. Officer McKegan was called back because I was considered an adult by court standards. He had to stay over and book me.

## Police Recruit Bailey

He returned visibly upset and walked me out of the office. Then he started pushing and shoving me all the way up the stairs to booking. "Put your stuff on the table." Confused and trying to figure out what I did wrong, I did as he asked. Meanwhile Officer McKegan took off his rings. Veteran officers all knew McKegan and what it meant when he did that.

McKegan looked at me, "You think you're so damned smart." He grabbed me around the throat and choked me until I passed out. I tried to breathe without fighting, but couldn't get air. When I woke up I was on the floor. You could hear the booking officer say, "What are you doing? Not here." McKegan kicked me a few times to see if I would move. While I was still dazed, he dragged me to Cell 1 and left me on the floor. I got up after he had gone and sat there not sure what to do. Suddenly the words of a song came out. The entire time there I sang in defiance, "We shall overcome." I was afraid of what could happen next, even after being told to be quiet. But I refused.

Hours later my mother came to get me. Her face said it all. She was so scared but relieved. I wasn't the kind of kid who got into trouble and she knew that. When I told her what had happened in front of the Sergeant, he looked calmly at the papers he was filling out for my release. He never questioned what I said. All he kept saying was, "You can take your son home now, Ms. Bailey." He repeated it over and over again, in the hopes we would just leave. I guess that was cop talk for "Yeah, we probably did it, so let me do you a favor by telling you your son is free to go."

You could see the look in the Sergeant's eyes. He knew what had happened, but he wasn't going to push it. Why should he have? I was just another project kid who got what I had coming to me. I got a beating for taking a shortcut and thinking the police were people we could be friends with. What was I thinking?

Mom called our previous landlord from Spruce St., Samuel Liskoff. He was an attorney and state representa-

## No Black Heroes

tive for Connecticut. Mr. Liskoff knew I was a good kid who never got into trouble. He was telling my mother how his son was going to law school with the notion of becoming the head of the Public Defender's Office in Bridgeport. He told my Mom he would take care of my case and not to worry.

We arrived at court, the Underwood Building. The judge seemed impressed with Mr. Liskoff's presence. They seemed to know each other, or at least that Mr. Liskoff was a state rep. I was guessing people in court were wondering how a kid from the projects could afford a state representative. My case was called first, out of order. I was feeling important for a minute.

The judge even asked Mr. Liskoff to speak about Connecticut politics before they would discuss my case. I had no idea what they were talking about, but the judge seemed mesmerized enough. Once he was finished, without another comment, "Case dismissed." "Now stay away from those cops Ronnie. Not all of them are good guys, I guess." "Yes sir, Mr. Liskoff." He was such a kind man. He didn't even charge us. Officer McKegan lit the fuse that caused me to hate cops with a passion.

Now the crazy part of this story is how I ended up taking the test to be a police officer. It was on a stupid dare, if you can believe that. Officer Ted Meekins was the Guardians president and approached me at the Hi-Ho Mall in downtown Bridgeport. The Guardians was a group of black and Hispanic officers formed to work with the community. Ted was one of the founding members and was at that time involved in a recruitment drive. He walked up to me as I was trying to move away unnoticed. When cops moved in my direction after McKegan, I did my best to avoid them. A big well-built man, clean, well-pressed with shiny shoes, he asked me, "Young brother, would you like to take a test to be a police officer? We need more Hispanic brothers like yourself to help your people."

I was still a little scared but spoke to him politely, "Officer, I'm sorry but I'm not Hispanic, I'm black." Without

## Police Recruit Bailey

hesitation Ted responded with a huge smile, "Oh my brother, that's even better. We definitely need more brothers like yourself to help our people with the struggle." I didn't want to be a police officer but Ted wouldn't give up. "Take the test and see how you do. You can always change your mind if you don't want the job. It doesn't cost anything to take a test."

I was still trying to get away from him politely. Finally he blurted out, "If you don't think you can pass the test I understand, and you should just say so." What a

Ted Meekins. It's all his fault!.
Picture courtesy Ted Meekins.

gullible fool I was. I took the bait. Without thinking, I filled out the application accepting his challenge. Months later I got the notification that I passed but scored low. It didn't matter at the time, because I was an assembler working at Avco Lycoming in Stratford on the Abrams tank engine. As long as I passed I was good with that.

The Guardians looked at the results of the test and took it to federal court. The city of Bridgeport staged what would be a longstanding legal battle with the Guardians. No police officers could be hired until the case could be settled. The Guardians cited in court there were only a few black officers and just one Hispanic officer on the job. They informed the court of widespread discrimination towards black officers at the hands of white officers. It was a very troubling time in the history of the Bridgeport Police.

They even cited some of the questions had been geared for whites. Attorney Beverly Hodges, who represented the Guardians, said it best. "If you ask an African American a multiple choice question about Pope Paul, most likely they

## No Black Heroes

will not have the answer. The question isn't neutral compared to a question such as where does the sun rise; east, north, south, or west. Everyone should know that equally." It did make sense.

Judge Gilroy Daly heard the case and in the end agreed with the Guardians. Once the test was revised, every black candidate moved up on that list, including me. White officers were enraged when the verdict was read. To make matters worse, white officers who had family and friends on the list were now passed over for black recruits. It wasn't a good time to become a police officer of color in Bridgeport.

There had been several years of court litigation before I received the call. Coincidently, I had just been laid off from Avco. "Mr. Bailey, the police test you took had been tied up in court for some time. The Guardians have prevailed in court, and you are in line to become a police officer. Congratulations." My thoughts were to take the training and get paid. Once Avco called me, I would go back. As it turned out, I had four months of training but never got the call. I was not looking forward to working with the very people I had no use for, police officers.

No one in my family had ever been in law enforcement. The closest I came to a uniform was as a kid in Coatesville pretending to be a superhero in my room. I pretended fighting the bad guys because it was something to do. Anyway, I finished my four months of training and was ready to hit the streets. I graduated, and was about to become the very thing I didn't think much of, a Bridgeport police officer.

Fresh out of the academy, I had some unfinished business to take care of. Several veteran officers came to speak to us about the profession. A few shut the door when the training staff left to give us the real deal. They all had the same mentality. If you had a problem with a cop you took it to the locker room. I had planned on that locker room visit my first day after graduating from the academy.

## Police Recruit Bailey

No one at the department knew that while training to be an officer I was also working out at East Coast Tae Kwon Do martial arts school. I joined the school years before the call to become a police officer. In training for my third national championship, I fought, earning the number-two ranking in the nation. My sparring partner was Billy Petrone, the middleweight champion and Olympic Team member for the United States. His competitiveness and talents elevated my fighting abilities to new heights.

Class of '83. Little did I know what was in store for me.

After my final class, I headed straight to the front desk of the police department. Officer Terry Bradshaw was there taking calls. He looked down at me from the elevated desk, "What's up, Rook?" "Is Officer McKegan around? Do you know when he's working?" "Sorry kid, John got into a motorcycle accident years ago. He got hurt really bad and retired." I looked up at Officer Bradshaw, "Too bad, I wanted to see him in the locker room." "Hey Rook, you need to watch yourself. Officer McKegan was no pushover." "Sorry,

## No Black Heroes

Officer Bradshaw. All I can say is it's a good thing he retired. If you ever see him, tell him I said hello and that I'm looking for him. He and I have a debt to settle." Bradshaw watched me walk away, "Damn, a new cop with an attitude. You sure you want to come here with that shit?" "It's a new day and I have nothing to fear from anyone in this place." Officer Bradshaw shook his head and smiled.

Chapter 3

## FATHER PANIK EARLY DAYS

Fresh out of the academy, it was immediately obvious something was wrong. There was a clear divide between the races. What I first noticed was their facial expressions when we were around. It was meant to send us a message. They were not happy the court forced the city to hire us. There were the subtle reminders that we were on the job because of the court orders, "Get your paperwork right, the court qualified you," were the comments we endured. Some were even more blatant in saying things about how their kids were on the list but thanks to the Guardians they couldn't work at the BPD. I was thinking I made a mistake. I felt safer in the projects than with Bridgeport's so called finest.

My first assignment was the East Side of Bridgeport, the infamous Father Panik Village. Father Panik was hell sitting on 40 acres, but no mule. It was home to over 1000 families stuck in 47 buildings. I can't emphasize it enough this was the third worst project in the nation. In the Panic, someone always got shot, murdered or died of a drug overdose. It

## No Black Heroes

was sad to have so many die that way. Imagine a rookie in the Panic alone. But I wanted it. Not even a few months on the job and my assignment was a solo car. I figured word had gotten around I was a little too cocky. I could only assume the solo assignment was meant to match my big mouth and take me down a peg or two.

Father Panik Village, built 1939, demolished 1994. Affordable housing turned "Gangster Paradise." Picture courtesy of the Bridgeport History Center, Bridgeport Public Library.

The surrounding cover cars for the Panic were manned by Officer Tony Brown, Officer Mike Rodriguez, and Officer Frank Jimmie. Tony was a huge, quiet black officer no one dared talk back to. He knew the kids, their parents and entire families. If Tony caught a kid misbehaving, he would give him a slap and send them home. What impressed me was when those kids went home and told their parents, the parents gave them a whipping! Then the parents came back and thanked Tony. He was just that well respected in the community.

## Father Panik Early Days

Officer Mike Rodriguez, on the other hand, was a huge Mexican and part-time bricklayer. Mess with him and you could end up under a car he lifted and put you under. No one knew it, but Mike was such a kind, gentle man. He would give you the shirt off his back. It was all a front with the tough-guy persona in case he really needed it, which was rare. Officer Frank Jimmie was Tony's partner and the icing on the cake. He was a cool, sharply dressed Italian who could punch you out before you had time to think about it. Jimmy was the man. His favorite saying was "Let's shuck and jive the Panic."

These guys were legends on the streets, and they took me under their wings. They taught me everything. More importantly, they trusted me, unlike veteran cops who had been there way longer than me. It gave me confidence. Tony, Mike and Frank kept to themselves. They wanted nothing to do with crooked cops or guys on the job who weren't real cops. Real cops knew the streets, were battle tested and not afraid.

Tony was the most influential of them all for me, for my street training. He knew everything there was to know about the streets, especially about drugs. That's how it all started for me and my interest in drug enforcement. When I first hit the streets, the drug of choice was heroin. Tony guided me through dozens of arrests taking in small bags of dope. Heroin users had their small piece of wire and spoon they used to heat up their heroin cocktail. Occasionally, we could see them shooting up in the hallways as we drove by. They were so zoned out they didn't even see us, as they filled their needles with the liquid they had just cooked up.

Tony warned me about the sores and scabbing on their arms that were swollen twice their normal size. He said it was dangerous to walk up on them. Startling an addict could cause an overdose. "Better to leave them alone, kid. One sudden move by us could cause them to accidentally kill themselves while shooting." Many of them were sick due to sharing needles. It was my early years, and AIDS was still somewhat of a mystery to me.

## No Black Heroes

Occasionally, if we had time, we would stop and watch them on the bottom stoop outside after they shot up. They would sit there leaning forward, then suddenly snap back upright. We watched them to see if one would nod out and hit the ground. Tony made a lot of money off me from those bets. Not one ever fell all the way over while nodding out. Makes you wonder why they call it nodding out.

The cocaine we took in from the Panic was junk. There was so much baking soda cut in it you could have cleaned your entire floor with it! Who could afford good cocaine in the projects, unless it was cut, anyway? That's why it was ten dollars instead of 25, it was crap. Word on the street was someone on the west end was selling the best cocaine in the state. He was somebody called Mariano Sanchez. No one from the Panic could afford the good stuff; never mind walking to the West End. An addict couldn't wait that long to get high and wasn't about to walk anywhere that wasn't close. So it was heroin, or a baking soda/cocaine mix.

I was enjoying my new career but disappointed at the way the police department was as a whole. The apparent separate set of rules for police in the department was stifling. Over and over, white officers violated the rules and weren't being penalized. I watched a white officer talk back to a commanding officer. He was told not to do it again, and that was that. I saw a black officer say something to a commander in response to a question, and he was sent home. He wasn't given an explanation or allowed to discuss the matter. It was this type of treatment that had Guardians riled. It was early in my career, so I tried to stay clear of the nonsense and work the Panic.

I was looking to do some good things on the streets. It helped knowing people in the projects from my days performing in the band. I had been out of that circuit for some time but still had a few friends. Many from my band days were shocked to hear I was a cop. Band mate Eddie "Leak" Frazier lived in the Panic and saw me in passing. He told me the guys on the streets thought I should return to play-

## Father Panik Early Days

ing in the band. I guess they weren't pleased about the arrests I made in the Panic with Tony and crew.

Eventually, Tony and the others were reassigned to a different part of town, which left me kind of out there on my own. I still had to deal with the Panic and thought getting out of the car and walking was the way to start. It wasn't the norm in the projects. But hey, I used to live there, knew the projects, so why not? I could hear from the hallways as I walked by, "Who's this Puerto Rican cop walking?" Those who knew of me would say, "What's Bailey doing?"

The Panic shootings were up and people were complaining. So the department assigned me a partner on occasion, Officer James Sheffield. We were parked on Martin Luther King Drive and out of the car talking with the local drug dealers. It was our way of stopping sales while being friendly. They knew it but what could they do? A call came over the air, "A stolen car leading police on a wild chase throughout the East Side." Suddenly the car chase drove right by us.

We both got back in the car and took off. I could see the guys on the block exchanging money as we peeled out. One of them yelled, "Hey Bailey, I got $25 on you." Sheffield and I were now on Pembroke Street. I floored the gas pedal and took over the lead. I was right behind the stolen car. You could see several heads bobbing about as the car bounced up and down the rocky streets. On Burroughs Street it crashed into a fence. Two guys jumped out and started running. I jumped out of the car while it was still sliding to a stop. One of the guys was about to jump the fence but gave up. I was right behind him before he could mount. I gave him that look, so he stayed put until Sheffield got hold of him.

The other jumped the fence and was running full speed. I vaulted the fence, catching him from behind. We both hit the ground hard. "Where do you think you're going?" Handcuffed, we walked back. I had Miguel Melendez and Sheffield was holding Manual Vega. It was apparent these guys

**No Black Heroes**

had never seen such an assault on car thieves before. They were from New Haven.

"Hey Officers, what's the big deal? It's just a stolen car." From their reaction, it was fair to say car chases in New Haven were not something that took place often. In Bridgeport, Chief Walsh was in charge, and we felt he didn't care about it. We could chase anyone, period. I walked over to Sheffield who was smiling. He had the nerve to ask, "What took you so long? I had a bet on you with our fellow officers here. You fast, man." "Sheffield, what am I, a race horse? And you guys were standing here waiting?"

We finished booking Vega and Melendez and returned to the Panic. The boys in the 'hood were waiting on the corner. "Did you get 'em?" Sheffield smiled and started counting the money he just won. They all started laughing. "Bailey catch 'em?" Sheffield nodded his head. "Yep." All I could hear was "Pay up motherfuckers, pay up. I told you Bailey could run. I had a feeling 'bout him."

In the Panic solo, I occasionally took the car off the street and onto the sidewalks to steer around the buildings and courtyard. It wasn't what most officers did, but this was my way of patrolling and keeping the Panic in check. Driving right alongside the buildings scared the mess out of drug dealers, seeing a police car up so close. The design of the buildings was an obstacle for law enforcement, but it was also hard for anyone to see me when I took that route.

I was driving around the corner of the last building, off street, and decided to get out and walk. Who did I see at Martin Luther King Drive? It was Eugene Walker. He was selling crack cocaine to Dwayne Jones. Crack was still somewhat new but making national news. It was a cheap replacement for heroin and the second drug of choice. I walk up behind Eugene without him noticing. People were looking out their windows and not saying a thing. I guess they wanted to see how it would turn out.

## Father Panik Early Days

Everyone stood by chuckling, watching Eugene make his sale. He was so focused on the sale; he didn't know I was standing right behind him. Dwayne, on the other hand, saw me and was so wide-eyed fearful, he just stood there. To my amazement, he took the drugs from Eugene with me standing there! I guess he was in shock. He stared into Eugene's eyes with a strange smile, afraid to look at me.

Eugene then spoke to Dwayne, "Hey man, wake up, you got your shit. Get going." I whispered in a soft voice, "Where do you think he's going, with me right behind you?" Eugene didn't turn around, dropping his head. He let the bag fall to the ground and put his hands behind his back. Dwayne stepped over and handed me four vials he bought, while hunching his shoulders, as if to say, You got me.

I put Eugene and Dwayne in the car. Everyone looking from the windows was laughing and shaking their heads. Eugene tried to get a little smart to maintain some pride. "Aren't you gonna pick up the bag?" "Hey, I'm only one person here, Gene." I locked the car to keep him from attempting an escape and picked up 58 vials of crack. I was on the radio, "Bailey to booking with two from the Panic." That term "Bailey to booking" was becoming an expected event radio was accustomed to.

I had been working the streets on my own for some time. Anyone doing drugs in the Panic by now had heard my name. Jason Rucker was no exception. He was 17 years old, and whose parents I knew well. It was a sunny day and Jason was driving a rented car on Hamilton St. near the Panic. He had a few of his friends in the car. I couldn't help but notice he kept looking back at me in my patrol car, so I pulled him over.

I walked to the passenger side of his car, as Sheffield arrived from a nearby post to cover me. To me, Jason was one of those kids I just knew wouldn't try anything. It was a mistake I would never make again. "Jason, why are you so nervous?" "Hey, Bailey, you done busted me too many times. I don't need anymore." Sheffield was checking the

## No Black Heroes

others in the car. The two kids in the back were clean, so Sheffield let them out to stand on the sidewalk. Jason was fidgety and nervous. I took the passenger out of the front seat, patted him down and handed him to Sheffield.

I got into the front seat and started to speak with Jason. He was leaning on the center console. I asked him to get off of it. Suddenly, Jason started to speak erratically while putting his hand near the console. "Jason, what's wrong with you?" I was smiling and halfway kidding. I had known Jason for almost all his young life and just knew he wouldn't try anything. Sheffield was giving me an intense look I'd never seen from him before. "Bailey, watch him. Don't let him put his hands anywhere." I figured he had a bag of dope in the console. "Jason, don't put your hand between the seats. You're making Sheffield nervous."

I continued to smile, "Jason, if it's a bag of dope, I don't think you can throw it away with us watching you. Pull your hand out." Sheffield was now upset, "Bailey, get his hands. I'm telling you to get hold of his hands." I looked at Jason, "Jason, give me your hands. Sheffield's going for his gun. What's wrong with you?" Suddenly Jason started having an asthma attack and pulled his hand away from the console.

Sheffield pulled Jason from the car. I looked in the console, but it was empty. In between the seats was not what I expected. It was a silver Colt .38 revolver. "Jason, I've known you most all your life, and your parents. How could you even think to try something like that?" Sheffield didn't say a thing but I got it. If you want to live long on these streets, don't drop your guard for anyone. It was a mistake I would not repeat.

Not two weeks had gone by when Jason got into a shootout with a rival drug dealer in the Panic. A small seven-year-old girl was shot in the mouth by accident. Jason somehow was out of jail with three arrests pending, including a gun charge. I had to wonder if the criminal justice system was working at all. He was out and a child had been

## Father Panik Early Days

shot in the mouth! Even though it happened on my day off, I felt like I hadn't done enough in the Panic. The next day, I visited the little girl in the hospital. They said she would never eat solid food again. I paid my respects and apologized to the mother for what had happened. The father, for some reason, kept staring at me but didn't speak.

The following day, Sergeant Richard Petite called me in the office. "What were you doing at the hospital last night, Bailey?" "I was visiting the little girl that got shot, Sarge." It caught me off guard when Sergeant Petite told me not to go there again. "The father filed a complaint against you for visiting his daughter. I know you meant well, but he doesn't want you there." "Okay, Sarge."

Some of the officers heard about the complaint. They thought it was funny and laughed about it. Officer James Halen had his sarcastic grin, "So much for your people showing you support, eh Bailey? See, they don't care about us, black or white. They don't give two cents about you, so why give a shit about them?" To say the least, it was an embarrassing day for me. Other white officers had that same "Who's the fool now?" look on them.

Shortly thereafter came a sad twist of fate. Jason was out on bond again. He just shot a kid and he's out? But soon after, Jason died in another shootout. I went to Jason's father and told him how sorry I was for his loss. He said it best, "My son lived in violence and died that way. The 'Panic' is no place to raise a child, but where else can we go? Thanks Bailey for your kindness." I left his home amazed at how well he took the loss of his son. It was like he expected it.

My thoughts were muddled after the death of Jason. I had been married only a few years before taking the job of a police officer. My newborn son William Ronnie Jr. was now deep in my thoughts. Would he turn out to be someone to make a difference in this life, or could he end up like Jason? I was unnerved by Jason's death and my thoughts turned to my own son. Thoughts of whether or not I would

## No Black Heroes

be home enough for him were troubling me. Cops' children were known for turning out really well, or really bad. I hastily convinced myself that my son would be alright. Working the 'hood, I needed to stay focused.

It was a quiet Sunday and Sheffield and I were in the Panic together. The so-called fastest man in the Panic was making a drug sale, Shawn Mathis. He was slick about his drug business. He always seemed to know when we were in the area. That time he made a mistake. We drove up from the blind side of building five, so he missed seeing us. Shawn was handing crack to this old white guy in a small beat-up car. The guy saw us coming on foot and pulled away without looking back. Shawn was standing there laughing. "Hey stupid, you forgot your change." Still laughing, Shawn turned and saw us coming.

He was surprised but didn't hesitate for a moment. He turned his back to me and put a handful of vials in his mouth. I walked up to Shawn and put my hand on his shoulder. "Shawn, what's up, Buddy? How's everything?" He looked up at me with his mouth shut tight. "Shawn, what's up?" He was bending slightly over, looking down at the ground and refusing to stand straight up. Shawn knew he had to say something or get busted.

He finally held his head up, looked at me, about ready to choke, and spoke. "Woot's gooen oonn?" I turned to Sheffield, "Did he just say What's going on?" Sheffield was laughing so hard he could hardly stand. Shawn's friends were in the courtyard shaking their heads and laughing too. I had to see how far Shawn would go with it. "Shawn, Shawn, talk to me. What was that I just saw ya do?" Shawn couldn't talk and had nowhere to run. He looked at the other drug boys, hoping someone could help him out. With nowhere to go he took a deep breath through his nose and forced a huge gulp down his throat.

He was bending over with his hands under his neck, gasping for air. He had just swallowed six to eight vials of crack. "Shawn, are you alright?" Shawn was on one knee,

## Father Panik Early Days

nodding that he was okay. His boys were standing by waiting to see if we were going to arrest him. I yelled out, "Don't just stand there, someone get this fool a glass of water before he chokes to death." All of a sudden everyone broke out laughing. A few were leaning on the building, pointing at poor Shawn. Shawn was smiling as best he could. One of Shawn's buddies brought him a small juice box. I got back in the car laughing, "Hey, Shawn. Not today, bro." Sheffield and I drove off.

It was only a few weeks later that Shawn made the same mistake selling in the courtyard. He didn't see us until it was too late and took off running. He ran right past the front of my car and almost got hit. I slammed on the brakes just before the car hit the side of the building with the slightest touch. I got out of the car, jumped up on the hood and started my run for him, right off the hood. "It's on, Shawn."

I rounded the building but lost sight of him for a moment. I ran in the direction where he may have run. I slowed down just enough to say hi to a few kids who always got excited when they saw me coming, and then picked up speed. Shawn's sidekicks were pointing a way for him to escape. They were cheering him on with huge circular motions from their arms, like it was the Indy 500 or something. He started running faster, for the hallway, thinking he lost me. He didn't know I was right behind him. In the hallway, I could hear him running to the third floor. I bumped into a kid who was running down the stairs as I was running up. I knew that was the money exchange, but I wanted Shawn.

Shawn was laughing, out of breath. As the door opened to the apartment, I yelled, "Shawn, don't go in there." He turned and looked at me in amazement. Shawn pushed the door open wider and tried to slam it shut. I reached in and grabbed for him when the door slammed on my wrist. I braced my foot at the bottom of the door, and tapped on the door holding keys from the car tight so they wouldn't jingle. It sounded like I had placed my gun barrel on the door.

**No Black Heroes**

"Guess what I'm gonna to do next?" Suddenly, the door eased, and I heard rapid footsteps moving away from the door as I entered. Everyone started yelling like it was a Sunday football game, "Bailey, I had nothing to do with this shit." You could see they were looking for the gun they thought I had used to tap on the door. It was still in my holster. They all kept saying the same thing; we had nothing to do with this, we had nothing to do with this.

I could hear the toilet flushing in the rear of the apartment. I walk over to the bathroom, "Shawn, come out." He walked out smiling, as if he had nothing to worry about. "Shawn, let me tell you how much trouble you're in. First off, I know the kid I bumped into in the hallway had the money. No problem." Sheffield was coming into the apartment with a few more officers. "Guess what, Shawn." I looked over to the kitchen table and Shawn followed the direction of my eyes. On the table were scales, cutting materials and packaging for drug sales.

"Shawn, this is a drug factory situation. You would've been better off with a sale. And let's not forget you assaulted an officer." "But Bailey ..." We took everyone in the house for operating a drug factory. That was the last time I saw Shawn. Some say he messed up the entire operation at building five and could never come back. People were supposedly looking for him. That's how the drug game was. You messed up and you were out for good. Come back and you might end up dead.

Back at the station, officers were saying they knew it was just a matter of time before I got hurt. Mathis slamming the door on my arm seemed to make several officers pleased, as if they had been looking forward to it. All I wanted was to take some drugs off the street, giving people who lived in the projects some peace. Drug dealing and shootings on a nightly basis was something I had gone through myself. Here was my chance to make a difference. Cops who had not lived in Bridgeport couldn't understand that. "Let them die. Who told them to sell drugs?" Some officers just didn't care.

**Father Panik Early Days**

Building five had been off its game since Shawn's arrest and disappearance. A few "New Jacks" were out there selling in the courtyard. Robert Hatton was on Martin Luther King Drive by building five, and he had a huge bag of crack cocaine in his hand. Wait, crack cocaine and Martin Luther King Drive? That just doesn't seem right saying it in the same sentence.

I was warned by Sheffield to take it easy that day, with post car numbers down because of training. I pulled up in my police car, catching Hatton off guard. Hatton saw me, turned and looked away. The car door was open with me standing with one foot on the ground and the other on the brake. "Don't even think about running." He kept his back to me and put the bag in his jacket while moving away. I couldn't just let him walk away. He looked back with his eyes wide open, sweating profusely, as if possessed. I wasn't sure from that distance, but Hatton looked high. I figured it was crack.

He ignored my calls and quickened his pace away from me. I drove my car towards him with my foot still hanging out when he took off. I shut the door and quickly maneuvered my car to drop off one curb, then across the street to mount the sidewalk. Hatton ran between the buildings to where a bunch of clothesline poles were. I had to stop the car there and get out. He ran past a dumpster and threw his bag in it. I caught up to him, grabbing his jacket, but he pulled out of it and continued to run. We ran a little ways before I was able to jump on his back, forcing him to the ground. He put his hand in his pocket and pulled out a keychain with a knife attached. I knocked the knife from his hands as we wrestled on the ground.

While fighting with Hatton, several drug dealers stood by and watched. They weren't going to interfere, but they were not going to help either. They had never seen me on the ground before. I was just as surprised. Hatton was pushing himself from me in an attempt to get away. Then he did something I couldn't believe. He grabbed for my gun. He was super strong and I couldn't get his hand off of it. I

## No Black Heroes

punched him in the face, but he didn't seem to feel a thing. Anyone else would have been lights out!

Busy fighting with Hatton, I couldn't get my radio out to call for help. It was all I could do to keep him from getting my gun. That's when I yelled at him, "That's it; I'm gonna kill ya. I'm tired of this shit." Hatton looked at me with a crazed look, let go of my gun, got up and started to run. During the fight, Hatton's shirt was so ripped from the ground it was hanging by a few strands. He pulled what was left of it off and threw it down. I could see a few red-capped vials falling out of his shirt pocket as I ran by.

I tried to scare him into stopping. "Stop or I'll shoot." Hatton heard my threat and ran so fast I thought I had stumble upon a professional sprinter. By the time I got to the other side of the building, Hatton was nowhere to be seen. As luck would have it, a drug dealer I gave a break to weeks earlier saw me. He pointed to the hallway Hatton was in. "I owe you one." "Naw Bailey, you looked out for me, we straight." Then I remembered. He was a small part-time drug dealer who I knew had been selling drugs every now and then. He only sold drugs to feed his children. Knowing the players and what they did, how could I arrest a man for that? Besides, I had more than enough work in the Panic. When I saw him selling one day, I just kept walking. He was returning that favor.

I ran to the hallway and heard movement on the third floor. Hatton was standing on the top stair with his fists balled up tight. I looked at him and the words just came out, "Are you kidding me?" Hatton took a swing and missed. I leaned back then forward, punching him in the shoulder bone. His arm dropped and became useless. It was a technique used many times at tournaments to disable a fighter. Hit the shoulder right and that arm was done. Hatton yelled out.

Cradling his arm, Hatton jumped headfirst over the railing, falling down the stairs. Oh my God, he killed himself. Everyone is going to swear I threw him over the railing. I ran down the stairs, only to see him getting up from the concrete floor. He ran from the hallway into another building, with me right behind him. I remembered that the training academy sent out a memo warning us about crack cocaine and its effects on a person. They don't feel anything. We were also taught that when a cop gets tired, he becomes vulnerable. So then I was really concerned.

Shaking my head, I entered the hallway ready for round three. I could hear the sirens in the background. Someone must have called for me. I had pretty good idea who. I was so involved, I never got a chance to use the radio. Finally, I got on and told dispatch the building number and started my walk up the stairs. There he was on the third floor again in his fighting stance. This time his left arm was hanging so badly it could only qualify as half a stance.

"Hey, my man, you're gonna make the papers today. But not for getting away." Hatton rushed down the stairs towards me. Desperate, I jumped up and hit him on the temple with a shin kick. That kick was a technique I used to break baseball bats. The hit caused Hatton to roll down the stairs. Finally it was over. I got up, fixed myself and looked down the stairs. He was getting up to run again. Tired and out of breath, I staggered down the stairs and jumped on his back.

We both fell down the last set of stairs. Hatton's body cushioned my fall down, but I was worried as his head kept striking the concrete stairs all the way down. If he wasn't dead, I would have to have believed he wasn't human! Unbelievably, he was trying to get up again! I looked at him in total disbelief. "I've decided to shoot you so I can go home." Both his arms were limp, so he couldn't help himself up. I heard the sirens in front of the building. "Thank God." Hatton had the nerve to try to open the door, pushing at it with all he had left, his leg. I was sitting on the stairs wondering if I should shoot him for real.

Sergeant Jimmie Viadero entered the hallway and saw Hatton on the floor desperately trying to get up. Viadero

## No Black Heroes

looked at me then Hatton. "Hey Sarge, I swear it's not what it looks like." "Bailey, it must have been one hell of a fight. Make him pay the price. Someone called and said you might need help. We figured if you didn't call for backup you were in trouble." They lifted Hatton up and he had the nerve to try and resist.

I exited the building as the ambulance arrived. They stopped and insisted I sit down. I didn't know it, but I was as pale as a ghost. They pulled out some wipes and began to remove the blood from my face and hands. I could see the relief from them that it wasn't mine. They pulled out a canister of oxygen for Hatton and me. The ambulance worker said because of the heat we both needed to stay put for a few. After a few minutes, they let us go. Hatton was transported to booking.

With Hatton on the way to lock up, I returned to the dumpster. The drugs, knife and his shirt were gone. People in the projects were upset about Hatton being transported to booking a bloody mess. The complaints were, of course, about police abuse. All that was left on Hatton in booking was one red-capped vial of crack cocaine in his pants pocket. With him looking like he had been beat up, it was sheer luck I had something to show why he was under arrest.

Hatton was complaining he was in pain. He had lumps all across his face. He couldn't raise his arms and had to be taken to the hospital. The hospital staff told me he seemed immune to pain because he was high on something. All I knew was it was the first time I had to use my martial arts on the job to stop someone. A kick that breaks bats at tournaments had no effect on that guy. If it was a sign of things to come, we were in deep trouble.

The next day, the story hit the newspapers, "The Brawl in Father Panik Village." People were asking all kinds of questions after the news article. "Is Bailey all right?" and "Cops can't fight like that, can they?" Others were saying it was police abuse. The dealers had their own comments,

## Father Panik Early Days

kidding me a little, "Bailey, you let a crackhead beat you. What's up with that? We heard you were this 20th degree black belt or something." I just smiled. "My next fight I'm gonna take a hit of crack first." "Damn Bailey, you all right."

At court I ran into Judge Ford in the hallway. He stopped me, "Officer Bailey, you know, sometimes you can be honest and not have to say everything. 'I'm gonna kill you and I'm sick of this shit' on Hatton's arrest report?" "Your Honor, I was bluffing. I wanted him to let go of my gun." "Officer Bailey, you are going far in this profession. Of that I'm sure." "Thank you, Your Honor." Judge Ford walked off shaking his head, with a huge smile on his face.

The word in patrol was two officers were going to be cited for their great work in the Panic. We assumed from the rumors it was going to be Sheffield and me. We had more numbers in arrests and drug seizures than anyone assigned to the East Side. Sergeant James Honis made the official announcement. "Lineup, please congratulate Officer Robert Bigelow and Officer John Pribesh. They will be receiving awards for outstanding service in Father Panik, from the Board of Police Commissioners."

Everyone in patrol walked over and congratulated them. Sheffield and I smiled, hunching our shoulders. I walked over to John and Bob and shook their hands. They both said thanks. Sheffield was headed out the door, and I turned to follow him when Officer Bigelow spoke to me, "You guys should have got something too. It wasn't just us out there." John chimed in, "Hey, you and Sheffield did a great job out there. Keep it up and don't worry about it." You could sense the uneasiness from both of them. "Hey, you guys didn't put in for those citations, a supervisor recommended you. Don't worry 'bout it."

I walked past the patrol window where the supervisors hung out and muttered to them, "I think there's a need for more black supervisors here." I caught a glimpse of a few quick stares and red faces from the office as I walked out

## No Black Heroes

the door. On the way to my car Sheffield said not to let it bother me. "Hey Sheffield, it doesn't. Now that I see how the game is played, I can have some fun." Sheffield looked a little worried by what I had said. I was a little upset, but not for me. Sheffield had put so much effort into covering me. He worked the drug trade in the Panic even though he really didn't want to. He did it for me. I felt he should have gotten something for his efforts. It wasn't right.

Officers Bigelow and Pribesh had some good arrests, but the numbers didn't add up. I kept all my receipts for the guns, drugs and money we took in. When the department cited the numbers for Bigelow and Pribesh, our numbers were much higher. When I told Sheffield about it, he was surprised. "You kept the receipts and a count on our arrests?" "Yep, for the same time period as Pribesh and Bigelow. We were off the charts." "Let it go, Bailey."

I walked into patrol, "Hey Sergeant Honis, I did a count of the activity Sheffield and I had compared to Pribesh and Bigelow. Did you know our numbers were four times what theirs were?" Sergeant Honis looked at me, "Hey kid, I don't make the decisions here. Where did you get your numbers from?" "I got them from the activity sheets posted on the bulletin board, Sarge." The next week the activity sheets were gone. Go figure that. Guess I'll keep doing what I do best.

Over the next several months, things got busy in the Panic for me, but also the surrounding areas. At the corner of Stillman and Orchard, a 13-year-old kid came running towards my car with a rope on one of his hands. He looked so scared I could only imagine what had happened. "They tied me up. They tied me up and took stuff out our apartment!" I called Sheffield who was close by to keep the kid safe. I had descriptions of two men from the kid. Where would I go if I were them?

Driving slowly along Boston Avenue near the cemetery, not far away, I spotted them. I jumped out of the car and chased one of them. I knocked down Alex Pratt, arrested

## Father Panik Early Days

him and put him in my car. I told the cars in the area to look for the other guy back where it all started. They thought I was crazy but doubled back. It's what I would have done; throw the police off by going back to where it all started and play it off like you had nothing to do with it. A short time later, Anthony Rodriguez showed up and was arrested at the very place where it all began. "Bailey to booking with two."

A few days later, I was at Ogden Street near the Panic. All I did was look at Isidro Rosa and he panicked, throwing a leather bag under a car. He tried to run, but I tackled him before he had chance to get too far away. We walked back to the bag. "Don't move. It would be a bad career decision if you did." I reached under the car and got the bag. In it was 43 vials of crack and $340.

I was about to put Rosa in the car when his friend Luis Ramirez came over. He told me I needed to go back in the Panic, where I belonged, before something happened to me. I pushed Rosa in the car with one hand and grabbed Ramirez with the other. Rosa asked me to let his friend go as a favor. "Come on Bailey, he didn't know who you are." "He does now. Bailey to booking with two."

I continued to work the areas around the Panic. Manuel Arbelo was on Hallett Street in the middle of a sale with two guys in a car. He saw me and quickly took off running. He jumped two fences, before I caught up with him. I handcuffed him and ran with him back to the car. I was sure he wanted to know what the hurry was all about. A few blocks away, I found the car Arbelo sold to.

In the car, about to get high, were Patrick Higgins and Neil Williamson. I arrested them and took their drugs as evidence of a sale. Arbelo never carried more than what he would sell. This was the only way to catch him, by getting the buyers he sold to with the stuff. The arrests turned into a new way of dealing with drug sales. "Bailey to booking with three."

## No Black Heroes

I made so many arrests that word at City Hall was platoon two, where I was assigned, were the go-getters of the department. Mayor Leonard Paoletta came to lineup and congratulated all of us on the fine job we were doing. "So you're the guys who are taking crime down a notch. You're doing an outstanding job and I commend you. Please keep it up." After lineup, Officer Manny Cotto walked over to me. "See Bailey, you did all the work and they got the credit." He was right, but the community was what I cared about. They deserved my best efforts.

Meanwhile, the federal court was still overseeing racial concerns at the police department and ordered the rotation of all officers. It was a way to keep black officers from being stuck in an assignment because of a biased system. The court said it would not let history repeat itself. What the court was referring to was Officer Art Carter as an example. He had been assigned a high-crime car on the East Side of Bridgeport for years. Carter had developed high blood pressure and requested to be reassigned for health reasons. He even had medical documentation. Because Officer Carter was the Vice President of the Guardians, his request was not only denied, he was reassigned to an assignment far worse than the one he had.

Documents produced in court showed officers who asked to be moved were granted their requests immediately. What was worse was, they didn't need a reason for their transfers, just a request. It was apparent that Judge Daly couldn't believe what he was hearing. So to prevent the Bridgeport Police Department from reverting to its old ways, the rotations were court ordered and monitored.

Chapter 4

# RACE A PROBLEM, SO IS CRIME

After my tour of duty in the Panic, I requested a temporary assignment that was open in the Youth Bureau. I didn't think I would get it but requested it anyway. It was a chance to get some experience in investigations and have the title of Detective for a while. In the back of my mind was Officer McKegan and what he had done to me as a kid. The Youth Bureau, where he had arrested me years ago, still had a few ghosts. If I saw his, I would shoot it! A week later, to my surprise, I got the assignment, which meant no one else wanted it.

With one week left before reassignment, the department put me in the radio dispatch center. There were so many officers being moved for the court-ordered rotations, they needed someone to cover the radio room. All I could see in there were guys who had been on the job well past their time. I was the junior officer, so they put me on the radio. And the way it worked was a joke. When a call came into dispatch, the call taker wrote down the reason for the call on a piece of paper, and sent it up to the dispatcher, who at

# No Black Heroes

that time was me. It actually came on a conveyor belt! If a call came in that wasn't an emergency, I got the paper from the belt and dispatched it. If there was a call of shots fired, or some other emergency, the officer who took the call would yell out, "Hot call coming!" I would get on the radio and let the guys in the field know to be ready for an emergency call, so they could get better prepared.

One night, I was working with none other than call taker Officer Donnie Fitz. Senior black officers warned me Fitz was a confirmed racist. He hated us with a smile. Fitz was assigned to the radio room, because he had shot an unarmed man during a foot chase. Some of us heard that a knife had been dropped at the scene of the shooting to protect Fitz. Rumor was a Hispanic cop named Officer Vic was said to have planted it. With a federal indictment pending, Fitz was put inside.

A call came through and Officer Fitz decided to get cute. He yelled out, "Hot call coming, Kid." He sent the paper up on the conveyor belt. I was about to reach for it when I noticed the paper was on fire. "I told you it was a hot call coming, Rook." Everyone was laughing, but I wasn't amused by the likes of Fitz. I decided to make sure they knew I wasn't someone to mess with. "Hey Fitz, are you sure this is a good time to be kidding around with the Feds looking at you?" You could have heard a pin drop, it got so quiet. He wasn't happy with my comment, and I didn't care.

It was the last day in dispatch that surprised me. Calls were coming in, one after another. Officer Fitz seemed more intense than usual. He was yelling on the phone and slamming the receiver down on some of the callers. Suddenly came a shock I would not soon forget, Bam! Bam! I turned to see Fitz sitting there with his gun in hand. "Fitz, why'd ya shoot the fucking phone?" I just sat there quietly. Is he gonna flip out and shoot us all?

He had blown the phone off the table with two shots. Officer Blue, who was sitting next to him, dropped his cigarette from his mouth right into his lap. Blue was the nick-

# Race a Problem, So is Crime

name given to him because he was so dark, he seemed bluish-black in color. I didn't like the name or its reference, but he didn't seem to mind.

Officer Joe Worthy got up and took Fitz's gun away from him. Blue was sitting there with his lap smoking. He suddenly jumped up and let it drop from his lap to the floor. Two other officers got up and walked Fitz out of the dispatch room. No one called for the commanding officer. We just kept answering calls like nothing had happened.

At the end of the night Officer Worthy walked over to me as I was about to leave. He was an old street cop with the most time on the job, at the time. "Hey Officer Bailey, Fitz has been under a lot lately with the Feds and all. I was hoping we were not gonna talk about this, if you know what I mean." I smiled, "Hey, all he shot was a phone. But I am a little concerned about the phone being black." Worthy laughed and went back to his seat. Officer Fitz was quietly retired a short time later.

The following week, I was working the Youth Bureau in plain clothes. I was investigating child rapes, youthful offenders, and a few murders linked to children. It was a terrible assignment if you couldn't stomach investigating children being victimized. I wasn't sure how long I could take it. Sexual assaults were on the rise by mostly stepdads and babysitters. To my absolute disgust, most rapes were committed by family members. In one case it was a grandfather.

For some reason, kids could talk to me. Lieutenant DiNardo, who ran the unit, said I had a real talent. Advocacy groups on rapes sent letters to the department commending my work with children. If not for copies being sent to me I would never have known. Those letters of praise never got to the Awards Panel for a recommended citation. It was becoming clear how things worked. If you were white you were praised; if you were black, expect an attaboy and handshake from your sergeant, maybe.

## No Black Heroes

Knowing the department's unwritten policy on awards for officers of color, I asked the department clerk to put those letters of praise in my field file. The clerk was some unknown sergeant nobody knew about working for the chief. He was about to retire, from what I gathered. He didn't want to put anything in my file. "Hey Sarge, it's just a letter or two, what's the harm?" Reluctantly, and on his way out, he put them in my personnel file. I made copies and kept them at home in case someday they went missing. Ted had told me to keep copies of all my good work. "They always lose things when it comes to us, Brother Bailey. Keep copies and check your file every now and then."

Investigating child rapes was difficult, but I did have other duties I enjoyed. There was a huge backlog of Take into Custody (TIC) orders from court that had to be served. They were court papers to arrest some of the worst kids in the city; kids who sold drugs, committed burglaries, robberies, or shot people. No one in the bureau wanted to look for them, never mind chasing them.

I enjoyed the challenge of the chase. More importantly, it was an opportunity to get some of these kids in the system, which could possibly change their lives. Most people didn't look at it that way. Lieutenant DiNardo, one way or the other, was happy with the numbers being produced. He had five words for me every morning. "Bailey, you got the fort." He gave me a number where I could call if I needed him, and that would be it for the day. After he was gone, the other detectives in the unit took off as well. I was in the office alone and loving it. First thing every morning, I pulled the TIC court orders and hit the streets.

Those poor kids were easy enough to find. They weren't going to school and didn't work. I found them in hallways, hanging in the streets and abandoned houses, kicked out of Mom's house with no Dad in sight. It was a sad story of young black and Latino children left to fend for themselves. Either they were out of control or the parents just didn't care. The inner city was breeding new street-smart people

## Race a Problem, So is Crime

who were destined to be the next generation of crime. And society had no answers.

As expected, some in the community were upset that suddenly those kids were being arrested and brought in. While arresting a kid for a shooting, one woman asked me, "Don't you have something better to do besides chase after these kids, Detective?" I fired right back, "You wouldn't say that if he shot someone in your family. May I add that the only kids I'm arresting are black and Hispanic in a mostly white city?" The woman was speechless. I was doing what I had to, but she realized what I was really saying. Mostly kids of color were involved in the court system, from what I was seeing.

I started to open my eyes. Those kids were coming from troubled single-parent homes most of the time. Nine out of ten times the parents were uneducated, and many times involved in alcohol or drugs. Their families were crumbling from drugs, a lack of education, domestic violence, or incarceration. The grandparents, or other relatives were sometimes all those kids had. I had firsthand knowledge as to why we were failing. The future of our children was doomed to a system geared for incarceration rather than education.

"Bailey likes young girls. He's sleeping with kids." What? Where'd this mess come from? It was a total shock to hear rumors being circulated in the department about me. The accusations were about me abusing young girls involved in my sexual assault investigations. Someone was trying to label me a child lover, but who and why? At first I took it as a joke. The rumors persisted and were no longer funny. Detective Nick Nelson asked me if I was alright. "What do you mean, Nick?" "Bailey, those rumors started for a reason. Someone has it out for you." Before I could say anything, Nick blurted out, "Bailey, you were hated before you got here." Nick was apparently talking about the court order that forced the city to hire minorities. There were 20 African American officers in my class of 80. Fortunately, more training classes and new officers were on the way by court order. Nick was of the opinion that the rumors were linked somehow to the racial tensions we were experiencing. I needed to find out who was behind it.

Not much later, my bandmate Leak called wanting to know what was going on. The rumors of me with underage girls were now in the streets. Someone was determined to ruin my reputation. Detective Alonzo Johnson, who was a long-time Guardians member, was working next to my unit. I asked him about the rumors, hoping for some answers. He told me about a group of all-white detectives who were probably behind the dirt campaign. "Bailey, they call themselves the Ad Hoc Committee." It was said the Ad Hoc were committed to keeping blacks off the job. Most Guardians were not sure who the Ad Hoc Committee members were. It was a very clandestine group.

A very attractive girl walked into Detective Bureau to speak with her father while I was getting some paperwork together. About to leave, she turned and looked back with a smile. Her father peered my way with an expression fit to kill. I guess he didn't want cops messing with his daughter, perhaps just not me. I had seen her before in Records, but was told not to fool around in the department. It was a sure way to get fired. The next day, while in the record room getting a copy of a warrant, she called me over. "Hey, don't let my father scare you. He has issues with you for some reason." I joked, "Now there's a surprise." I sensed there was more she wanted to talk about, but the record room was not the place. "My name's Rita, what's yours?" "Everyone calls me Bailey, but please, call me Ron." "Well Ron, if you ever want to talk, this is where to reach me." "Thanks Rita, I will."

Over time we became good friends and met occasionally for late lunches. It had to be in the evening, away from the department. We couldn't chance her father finding out we were talking. She confided in me that her father had a thing about African American cops. Rita trusted me and asked that I not let anyone know what she was about to say. "I hate these fucking nigger cops, especially that light-skinned

## Race a Problem, So is Crime

nigger Bailey." I looked at her as if she had lost her mind. She then explained, her father had said it at home to her mother while talking about his day at work. I could tell Rita hated her father's racist rants. We were standing by her car when she started to cry. I held her, hoping she would stop. "Hey, you want to make your father really mad? Let him see us like this." She looked up with tears rolling down her cheeks, halfway smiling. "Ron, from now on anything I hear I'll pass to you. Dad talks loud at home when he's upset." It felt like Rita wanted to pay her father back for something, but what? Maybe it was just his one-sided views she wanted no part of.

I couldn't dwell too much on Rita's father or the Ad Hoc Committee because the department was pushing hard to find some young teenaged kid named Alex Palmieri. He was missing. Not that I didn't want to find him, but what about all the black and Latino kids missing? Now suddenly the flags were out to find this one kid. I did the usual checking with his teachers at school, his family and friends. No one knew where Palmieri was. The newspapers called the office requesting a comment. They were all over this missing kid's case. All I could say was it was under investigation. When I hung up, I happened to look at three missing kids posted on the board, all black. Not one question in weeks about them. Don't these children matter too? The system was upsetting, to say the least.

Then the news broke months later, a foot washed up on Pleasure Beach in Bridgeport. Eventually, it was reported to be all that could be found of Alex. The case was solved with the help of the FBI. Thomas Marra, who was linked to organized crime, was charged with Alex's murder. Court documents reported Palmieri had been arrested several times and Marra had become concerned. He didn't trust Palmieri, thinking he might turn on him to get rid of his own court cases. Marra bought him a ticket to leave the country, but Palmieri refused to go. Reportedly, he was bludgeoned to death with a baseball bat and stuffed in a refrigerator. The rest of Palmieri's body was perhaps somewhere buried in the sea sediment, never to be found.

## No Black Heroes

I was overwhelmed with all the cases that needed investigating. Seemed like children missing, kids with guns and selling dope were on the rise. The child rapes were still the worst to me. Those poor kids were coming into my office telling me about their family members taking advantage of them in the worst ways. Children had to be befriended before they could open up about such things. In many cases it took several visits before they would even think to talk about what had happened. I originally thought that was the reason the rumors started, but Detective Johnson had my vote on his assessment. I believed the Ad Hoc Committee was behind it, and I now knew who one of them was, Rita's father.

Working conditions were bad and getting worse. The department was in chaos. Chief Joseph Walsh was at war with the newly elected mayor, Leonard Paoletta. The mayor wanted Chief Walsh out and eventually had him removed. He then gave authority to the Board of Police Commissioners to run the department. Walsh's ouster, of course, made national news. He showed up for work as always, only to be turned back by two officers blocking the elevator door. The place was off the charts.

Curiously, Chief Walsh had made national news just a few years earlier. That was when the same name linked to the Alex Palmieri murder popped up, Thomas Marra. News accounts said Marra tried to set Walsh up with the aid of the FBI in taking a bribe. I couldn't help but wonder if it was all somehow linked in some kind of crazy conspiracy. Marra tried to set up Walsh, later Marra is convicted of Palmieri's murder. Walsh had been forced out of a job and Marra was in jail. Some rumored Mayor Paoletta had something to do with the failed bribe attempt on Walsh using Marra. Who knew what this whole mess was really all about?

The police department was not only facing a racial divide, an underground hate group, a power struggle and the FBI lurking about; there was also a spike in crime. A new group of drug gangs were taking over the projects. Someone

## Race a Problem, So is Crime

was in control and had organized the drug trade. We were about to get hit with a crime spree the city had never seen before. It couldn't have happened at a worse time.

Chief Walsh fought and eventually won his court battle to be returned to work. Mayor Paoletta complied with the court order, sort of. The chief returned, but his authority was limited. The mayor assigned him to a small office, instructing him to write policy. Many figured only an election and new mayor could restore Chief Walsh back to full power. At the Guardians meetings it was said, "Better they fight with each other than coming after us."

I had been in Youth Bureau too long and realized it was time to get out. The rumors of me dating young girls were not going away. It had come to the point where I was supposedly giving drugs to girls for sex. With the Ad Hoc lurking about, it was time to go. The Board of Police Commissioners granted my request. Chief Walsh heard about the transfer and pulled me to the side, "Bailey, in a few months Tom Bucci will be the new mayor and I'll be back in charge. If they are forcing you out, I'll have you put back when Bucci gets elected." I looked at Chief Walsh, "Thanks Chief, but I asked to be reassigned."

I appreciated Chief Walsh's offer, but it wasn't about me. He wanted to show the Police Commissioners who was in charge when he got his power back. As expected, Mayor Paoletta lost his bid for re-election. Mayor Tom Bucci was successful, and Chief Walsh was ordered back in charge of the department. That's when he went after anyone who had taken Mayor Paoletta's side. Officers DiNapoli and Deltoro, who had blocked the elevator door keeping Walsh out, were the first targets of his wrath. It was payback time and he was relentless. They both eventually retired. Although it was well known Ted had supported Paoletta, Walsh didn't dare come after him. With the court still watching the department, we all surmised Ted was not an option for Chief Walsh.

## No Black Heroes

As for me, before I was removed from the Youth Bureau, I racked up a lot of overtime. I had been working a witness protection program to guard a local prostitute named Annie. She had turned informant for the FBI, involving organized crime in Bridgeport. Although it was a hunch, the Guardians believed that the majority of the Ad Hoc were the older detectives in the bureau. It was my belief that they didn't want to work the Witness Protection Program, thinking it was a setup to discover more about their underground organization. That left me with all the overtime I could handle. Armed with a shotgun, I was assigned to Annie for weeks and getting paid.

With so much money banked, it was time for a new car, a Corvette. It turned out to be somewhat of a mistake. The rumors had now gone from child molester to cop on the take. It was actually a more believable rumor with me driving a car that seemed to symbolize wealth, or corruption. Someone was really out to get me, and I gave them more ammunition with my new car.

Even my good friend Officer Manny Cotto warned me, "Hey Bailey, you can't let these guys see you with a flashy car and women. They frown on that kind of lifestyle." I had to ask, "Manny, is that a police thing, or something they don't want me to do? I mean do they expect all cops to be virgins or something? It's just a car." Manny said the unwritten rule was police don't hang out or drive fancy cars. It was an old way of thinking if you asked me.

I was at Seaside Park polishing my car when correction Officer Willie Velazquez rolled up. He had a "badass" Datsun 240ZX. We parked close to each other and just hung out. Women kept coming by, not sure which car they wanted to get in. While at the park, a few of Bridgeport's finest came by. They were the older guys and didn't seem to like what they saw. Willie wanted to know what their problem was. "Changing times I guess, Will."

Then came a few more girls. "When are you going to take me for a ride, Bailey?" They always put emphasis on the

### Race a Problem, So is Crime

word ride, to make me think. Suddenly, Willie tapped on my car to get my attention. The two cops who had just come by returned. I stopped talking and looked over to them. "What's up, guys?" One of them asked a stupid question, "Seen any cute kids lately, Bailey?" Then they drove off smiling. Willie looked confused.

"What did they mean, kids?" "Will, I've made a few enemies at the police department. Someone started a rumor I was messing with kids. Maybe if I hold my hat in my hand like a good Negro, all will be forgiven?" Willie could see I was getting upset, "Hey Ron, fuck them. Live your life, bro."

A second police car drove by with different officers and more of the same hard looks. I guess they were talking to each other on channel two, our private channel. It was time to let them know I didn't need to see them. "Hey guys, is that what the city pays you for, to ride around the park and watch my chocolate ass?" That was the last police car to come by that day. Willie seemed concerned after my comment. "Hey Ron, maybe you need to chill a little with that attitude. You know those guys can make life miserable for ya." "In the words of my brother from another mother, f 'em." These guys needed to know I was someone unafraid to speak up.

Monday, I reported to patrol to the reception of hard, cold stares. I guess word got around about me telling veteran officers to kiss my chocolate you-know-what. I ignored the looks and asked about my assignment. Now here was a surprise, I was a floater with no assigned car. Punishment for speaking out, I guess. No matter, I could handle anything they had to throw at me.

My supervisor was Sergeant Robert Mangano. Talk about a stroke of luck. Sergeant Mangano was a good cop who knew his stuff. He had no problems working with anyone, and everyone liked him. He saw me looking at the assignment and came over. "Officer Bailey, please don't repeat this or get offended. You're an African American officer, right?" I guess my fair skin still had some confused. "Yes

**No Black Heroes**

Sergeant, I'm black." He continued with a slight smile. "I just want to tip your hat, if I may. You're a black officer with a white Corvette linked to women, clubs and rumors floating that concern me. From what I've been told, you made some unwanted comments to veteran officers who can make life difficult for you. Don't you think you should tone it down a bit?" I really appreciated Sergeant Mangano being up front with me. Most there didn't care about anything when it came to us. "Sarge, I haven't done anything wrong. I have a feeling the older, and please excuse my words, the older white cops have a problem with me standing up for myself."

Sergeant Mangano gave a subdued smile. "Hey kid, that may be true. I don't know. I can tell you this. Guys here, and especially the brass on the third floor, don't like officers to stand out. A white Corvette and those remarks you made?" He hunched his shoulders. "Hey Sarge, thanks for looking out. I really appreciate it." Before he left I had to ask him a question as a joke. "Sergeant Mangano, if I told these guys I was only half black, do ya think they might cut me some slack?" Sergeant Mangano walked down the hall with a broad grin while shaking his head.

It was my first day back and I was returned to the Panic. On my way to the car I saw my mentor, Tony Brown. "Tony, what's up?" Tony spoke to me in a low tone. "Hey kid, these guys are upset with you. They say you need to shut your mouth. Just so you know, the Ad Hoc may be looking to get you off the job." "Tony, how do you know that?" "Bailey, I got a few friends here. You need to tone it down and be careful, kid." "Thanks Tony. I can handle myself." "I know. I'm just looking out for ya."

With a city loaded with projects and a whole slew of poor people facing a crime epidemic, I had better things to do than worry about those fools. The new organized drug crews were ruthless in the projects. The name we kept hearing was Sanchez from the Number One Family on the west.

## Race a Problem, So is Crime

Bridgeport was national news again. The guys were talking about the New York Post printing an article saying Bridgeport had more crime per capita than New York City. Our crime rate for the amount of people we had was three times higher than a major metropolitan city! Some officers were actually proud because we were the ones out there dealing with it. The shootings were so frequent, vendors in Bridgeport were selling t-shirts with a happy face on them. On the happy face was a bullet hole with a trickle of blood in the forehead. The words, "Bang, You're Dead, Welcome to Bridgeport" were on them. With 69 murders that year (two to three bodies due to overdoses, weekly), the t-shirts had it right.

It didn't help the city's image that we also had a serial rapist lurking about. Bridgeport's infamous reputation was growing with the "Bumper Rapist." He got that name from the way he operated. Women who drove alone at night would have their cars bumped into by a lone driver in another car. When they stopped to get out and check for damage, a man wearing a ski mask would kidnap and rape them.

In response to the Bumper Rapist, an undercover sting using a female officer was set up. In the rear of the car was a second officer in hiding. As with most major cases, many times it's about luck. A man wearing a ski mask bumped into the undercover car the first week of the sting. When the officer got out checking for damages a man wearing a ski mask tried to take the officer at gunpoint. A shootout took place, but he escaped.

As luck would have it, Edwin Palmer was arrested three months later on a burglary charge. The rounds fired at the police months earlier matched the gun Palmer had in his possession. The court convicted him on the ballistics of the case and the crime spree ended. It was one of the many reasons Bridgeport was being publicized as the crime capital of America.

## No Black Heroes

Back on the streets, another bandmate of mine, James Barksdale stopped to speak with me. "Hey Ron, what's with these rumors you're sleeping with kids, keeping drugs and money you take off the streets?" "James, that's all stuff rumored by some cops there because I speak up, and they don't like it." "I kind of thought it was nonsense. The Ron Bailey I performed with wasn't about drugs. You know I got juice in the Panic. If you need me, say the word. I got ya back." I thanked James who then told me the boys in the Panic had my back too. It was no secret the dealers had no use for the police, period. It was definitely a badge of honor, the streets would even think to look out for me. I was from the projects, and I guess they respected that.

Rumors abounded that Walter Jefferson owned a main part of the Panic drug trade. We had never met before, other than in passing. Confused by what he was hearing, he walked up to me. "Hey Bailey, I'm Walt. I got to ask, what's up with your boys? These so-called black-ass cops don't like you?" That really threw me off my game. "Aren't they supposed to be your coworkers?" I'm thinking, what in the world was he talking about? "Walt, what's up?" "Your so-called cop buddies, that's what up. Did you know they're saying things like 'Who does Bailey think he is? He must think he's some kind of super cop' and shit like that." "Hey Walt, some people are haters." I didn't want to say anything for the streets to latch onto. Truth be told, word was getting around I was talking back to any cop who tried to provoke me. I guess the bitterness was stewing on both sides of the fence. I played it off. "Hey Walt, I just work there. They can say what they want. I'm gettin' paid." Walt smiled. "I know that's right, Bailey. Keep the faith, my brother." I didn't even bother to ask who or how he had heard about officers badmouthing me. Whatever their reason, I was capable of taking care of myself.

With so much bitterness at the police department, I needed to be ready to go it alone if need be. I got a backup gun, packed three sets of handcuffs on my belt, and came to work prepared. I even trained by running with all my gear, so I wouldn't get tired. At the martial arts school I

## Race a Problem, So is Crime

fought heavyweight black belts to increase my stamina. I was adapting to a mindset of being on my own.

On the streets, I think the extra police gear had a negative effect. The boyz in the Panic noticed I was carrying extra handcuffs. Many of them saw the backup gun on my ankle when I got out of the car. My street friends were not stopping to speak with me like before, opting to wave and keep it moving. I needed to think of something quick before alienating the only friends I had. It then dawned on me, having lived in the projects all those years. How could I have overlooked the one thing we all had in common? I started playing music in the police car, loud enough so everyone could hear. That was the bridge we could all relate to.

I was pumping out songs on the radio the 'hood always played. I lucked out on the radio with the first song being the hit rap tune by Public Enemy, *Fight the Power*. The song became famous by Spike Lee's movie, *Do the Right Thing*. It was a complete about-face in the 'hood. I was playing a song made famous by a movie that focused on racism and the murder of a young black kid at the hands of the police. The boyz in the Panic were yelling, "Oh shit, Bailey, it's like that? Cool, motherfucker." Spike Lee's movie had depicted the struggles and frustrations due to white cops' hatred towards blacks. The isolation I felt had me feeling just that way.

The next day, I got in my car and the radio wasn't working. I took it to the garage and was told the radio somehow had been damaged. Somehow? Someone at the department knew I was playing music in the projects and was messing with me. I went to Bradlees department store and bought a large boom box with several tapes that were sure to raise some eyebrows on the job.

After lineup, I got into my car with my box and blasted the song *Fuck the Police* by N.W.A. in the police parking lot. I turned it down immediately and looked up. "Sorry guys." It was a sarcastic apology and they knew it. You could see an ocean of white faces with cold stares they gave me.

## No Black Heroes

Black officers were hurrying to their cars and driving out of the lot without delay. A few blocks away, I received a call over the radio to return to patrol.

It was Sergeant Howard who called me in. He said officers had complained about my having a boom box in the car and playing a song insulting to them. I calmly looked at Sergeant Howard, "If any one of those guys complaining would like to tell me who broke my car radio, I'll be glad to put the boom box away. Then we can go to the locker room and settled it cop style." Sergeant Howard looked surprised by what I said. "Sergeant, if there's nothing further, I'd like to get back out in the streets where I belong." His look was one of astonishment. "Okay Bailey, I'll relay your message. Be safe out there."

I was in the Panic playing music when my attention was drawn to Eugene Rodgers. He was sitting on the passenger side of a car looking all about in a frenzy. I put my lights on and made the stop right on Martin Luther King Drive. Just before the stop, I could see him bend forward and put something under the seat. The driver was getting out of the car looking back at me. I called for backup.

"What the fuck you stop me for?" A crowd was gathering. Alone, I had to play the bad cop out of control thing. "Get the fuck back in the car and don't move!" "What did you say?" "You heard me. Back in the car or take your chances getting fucked up." A few curse words and people think this is a dangerous man, and it worked. He got back in the car and didn't say anything else.

Rodgers was perfectly still. I yelled out, "Eugene, put your hands on the dash and don't move." The driver looked upset but remained still. I walked over to the passenger side of the car and pulled Eugene out. No backup cars had come yet. I cuffed him to be safe. Under his seat was the handle of the largest handgun I had ever seen. The driver was now scared as I pulled out the gun. He figured he was going too, because that's what most cops did, take everyone.

### Race a Problem, So is Crime

My thoughts were about Eugene who was 6'1" and well built. If he started to fight with me, there would have been a shooting for sure. With a gun in the car and me out there alone, it could have turned bad quick. Where was my backup? Fortunately, the bad cop thing worked. The driver nervously asks, "What did he do?" "Come on man, you saw that Dirty Harry special." "Am I under arrest too?" "Sir, I'm sorry I had to talk to you like that, but I couldn't take a chance out here alone. You're free to go." It wasn't his gun, it was Rodgers'. He leaned over in his car and spoke. "I'm glad someone out here knows what they're doing. Thanks, Officer."

Instead of arresting everyone, this was the way to go. It made people trust in what you were doing. I earned the respect of quite a few out there that night. I arrested the right person and apologized, something cops just didn't do. Eugene was already facing felony charges from a previous arrest. With the gun charge, the FBI took my case from state court and made it federal. The Rodgers family was running a large part of the Panic drug trade. The FBI was sure to ask Eugene if he wanted to make a deal.

## *I'm Alone; Guardians Challenged*

It was a bad day for me. One of the kids in the Panic got away from Officer Joseph Pitch. He was on a personal mission to find that kid, which meant trouble. People in the street called him Officer Punch. Word was, if he arrested you, there was an automatic "punch" in the face for extra measure, hence the nickname. I got the call he needed cover at Building 13. I got there just in time to see the tail end of him slapping a kid in the face. I could just about hear him, "Don't you ever run from me again." I hurried over to Pitch and pushed him before he had chance to hit him again. "Hey Pitch, this kid's in handcuffs. Have you lost your mind?"

Pitch looked at me, "What do you think you're doing, Bailey?" At that very moment the father, mother and two of this kid's brothers were running our way. They were upset

**No Black Heroes**

Pitch had hit their kid in cuffs. The mother took a broom she was holding and swung it at Pitch. She just missed him. The father had his belt in hand and actually tried to whip Pitch with it. Pitch was moving around in a circle while calling for backup over the radio. Dad was old but giving it to him good. I was trying to keep the family back but couldn't stop laughing at the father's attempts to discipline Pitch.

The backup cars came and pushed the family back. The parents were upset having seen their kid slapped like that. The father spoke, "Bailey, you know that wasn't right. Do something." Sergeant Howard pulled me to the side and asked what happened. I told him straight out, "Sergeant, Pitch slapped that kid in handcuffs. That's when all hell broke loose. The mother tried to hit Pitch with the broom. The father whipped him with his belt." Sergeant Howard stood silent. He asked me if I knew the family. I took that to mean is there a way to smooth this over. "Hey Sarge, I can ask the parents what they want to do." I walked over and spoke with them. The mother's response was so sweet, "Bailey, just don't let them hurt our son. We know he has a warrant, but don't let that Officer "Punch" touch him again." Wow, even the mother knew Officer Pitch's street name.

They were good people who only asked that we not beat on their son. "You have my word. He won't touch him." "Thank you, Officer Bailey." I walked back to Sergeant Howard and told him it was all set. "Sarge, Pitch can't touch that kid. I'll take him in." Sergeant Howard said something to Pitch before they both got in their cars. I took the kid to booking.

While in lockup, the commanding officer walked in and asked me to come downstairs to patrol. He was very blunt. "Bailey, a lot of cops here don't trust you. Officer Pitch told me you let people in the Panic attack him and did nothing." "Commander, if this is about Officer Pitch, he—" Before I could finish what I was going to say, the commander stopped me. "I don't want to hear about Officer Pitch. I just

58

## Race a Problem, So is Crime

wanted you to know you're making enemies here." I could see where this was going. So I kept it short, "Commander, I didn't let Pitch get beat by a crowd. He was disciplined by an elderly man. As for me, I'll be fine out there with or without these guys." It wasn't what he wanted to hear, I'm sure. He didn't say anything, got up and walked away. I made sure no one else touched that kid as promised and went back out.

After the episode in the Panic, guys in patrol distanced themselves from me like the plague. They gave new meaning to the phrase "Smile in your face" as they walked by. I did what no cop should ever do, tell on another. I had crossed that blue wall of silence. People in the community just don't understand how that works. I was now someone cops couldn't trust. It wasn't enough I'd talked trash to them, I broke the unwritten code. I could count on having to do things on my own from then on. Cops don't like to be ratted out, even if they are wrong.

At the Guardians meetings we were in discussion about the department's resistance to black officers. My name came up a lot, as one would imagine. There was discussion about the court. As more time passed, the city of Bridgeport became desperate to get the federal court oversight out of the police department. They were tired of the federal court reviewing any decisions the department made. Judge Gilroy Daly was dead set on having the department follow his orders. He assigned a Special Master to review any issues of unequal treatment, race and discrimination at the department; Judge William Clendenen.

It was a constant struggle to keep the city from removing the court and Judge Clendenen. They were filing motions weekly, even going to the Second Court of Appeals in their attempts to have the process removed. Yet we were seeing the writing on the bathroom walls, "Niggers go home." Cartoons were on flyers placed on the desks in patrol depicting gorillas in uniform, holding bananas. Nothing had changed, so the court remained.

## No Black Heroes

Ted, who was stepping down as the Guardians president, asked the supervisors in patrol if they knew where the flyers came from. Their response was cautious and a tad belligerent. "We can't say, Officer Meekins." Ted had a stern response, "You can't say sounds like you won't say." They were upset with him but kept quiet. Ted was not afraid of them, and that was for sure. I personally admired how he stood up to anyone who was not right in how they conducted themselves. He commanded respect, the very same values my parents instilled in me.

With all that was going on, the city was still determined to find new ways to remove the federal court from the department. Unsuccessful in their previous attempts, they authorized a study to see what changes could be made to improve conditions at the police department. The Guardians knew the study was a front and another attempt by the city to show the court there was no need for any further court intervention. Why couldn't the city just go along with the court to improve things for everyone? The constant fighting made no sense.

The city hired a firm called PEI. They were to conduct an evaluation and make recommendations to improve the police department. Once completed, what they recommended wasn't a surprise. They endorsed one-man cars instead of two. There went the racial balance in having us work together, both black and white officers! They called for community policing, which meant no more rotations of officers. That would have been a good thing, but none of those guys or command cared about community policing. It was just a feeble attempt to end the court-ordered rotations. If that was approved, I could see myself stationed at the city dump forever.

The recommendations were lengthy and what supervision and the city wanted. The Guardians had the ultimate say in any changes the court might consider. The court had banned the practice of white officers riding exclusively with white officers. Assignments had to be racially balanced and approved. The court approved the one-man car assign-

## Race a Problem, So is Crime

ments. Hardcore anti-Guardians got those assignments. It did allow for some racial tensions to go down. The PEI recommendation to end rotations was soundly rejected. If there were to be a true community policing effort, it would have to be done during rotations.

What really hurt was the divide that crept in. As the years moved on, Hispanic officers were up in numbers. They no longer wanted to be a part of our organization. They felt we were not representing them as we did black officers. Enter the Hispanic Society. Ted felt betrayed. He fought hard to bring black and Hispanics on the job. Now with their numbers up, we were no longer needed. Some of us tried to join them as well, to be more united. We were told you had to be Latino to be a Hispanic Society member. I asked Manny, "Does Latino by injection count?" I was talking about my dating Latino women. He just said "Bailey, please," with a smile.

In federal court, the Guardians were still considered the organization recognized in the efforts to end racism. What took us all by surprise was that the Police Union filed papers and requested to enter the federal court process as friends of the court. Friends? What were they up to? I saw it as an agenda to oppose everything we asked for. They told the court it was about fairness, and they supported equal treatment of all officers. To my disappointment, the federal court allowed them in. It was something the Guardians would regret, of that I was sure.

Chapter 5

# NEW ASSIGNMENT

Rotations had come again and I was no longer a floater. I was assigned my own car, West Side Blue 13. I still had to depend on myself. Most cops were troubled with my stopping Pitch from hitting that kid in cuffs. They were still brooding about it. I had survived the Panic, so I'd make it on the West Side too.

The name that kept coming up was Sanchez, and his family. Word was he had taken over several city blocks on the West Side but sold mainly on Clinton Avenue. The Number One Family was considered a ruthless gang of dealers with tons of cash, beautiful girls, dope and guns. What had me worried was I found out my nephew Benjamin Grant was working for him.

Sanchez could have run IBM, or any other big business in America. He set up an organization that would have made any corporate empire jealous. He paid his people well and handed out gifts such as motorcycles, gold, jewelry, and expensive trips to the casinos. There was a genius to

## No Black Heroes

his madness. He commanded loyalty in return for big-time cash, and he got it. His organization was like the military or any police department. He had captains, lieutenants and street-level commanders. Someone had to answer to someone in the chain of command. It was that command structure that made him so successful, compared to rival drug dealers. Everyone wanted to work for him, and his product was considered the best in the state.

Sanchez had worked on the 'good guy' routine. On the Fourth of July, he provided fireworks displays for the neighborhood and gave families on his block money for their bills. Sanchez was a Robin Hood of modern times and worked that angle well. The police department's Anti-Crime Unit, under Mayor Paoletta, tried its best but couldn't touch him or his crew. After the elections, Chief Walsh was back in charge, and Anti-Crime was dismantled. Anything Mayor Paoletta had done was undone. With no real drug unit in place, drug gangs were on the rise, and especially the Number One Family.

Working the West Side was not as easy as the Panic. In the projects you could go in anytime and catch someone out there selling. On the West Side it was low-key. Anyone who sold drugs on Clinton did so from the back of a house, in an apartment, or from a car. Sanchez had only the best-paid lookouts to protect his spots. He even separated those who sold drugs from those who held the money. If you got caught selling drugs, the money stayed on the block. The workers who brought in the cocaine did so with the strictest of countersurveillance. That was to ensure no one got busted. It was very organized, according to my informants.

I never saw my nephew Benji when I was on patrol. I decided to go out there on a day off. I had to wonder if those guys and Benji knew my schedule. As expected, he was out there. So I pulled over. At first, he was about to leave. "Benji, what's up with you? Come on kid, this ain't gonna work out, trust me. You need to leave the block." "Uncle Ron, I'm just hanging out, that's all." "Okay, but all eyes are

## New Assignment

watching ya, kid." I didn't want to push it. I said what needed to be said and drove off.

The very next day after lineup, "Bailey, I heard you got some new friends on Clinton Ave." It was Officer Angel Vic, one of the loudest Latino cops on the job. He always had something to say. Officer Vic would not be caught dead hanging around the likes of anyone black. He thought of himself as superior and stayed drunk, even on the job. Knowing the nature of the beast, "Well Officer Vic, why don't you tell your white buddies who put you up to this I work Clinton Avenue. It's called getting to know the block. But your friends wouldn't have a clue about that, would they?"

Boy, what a hornet's nest I stirred up. "You're a turncoat, Bailey; you're sleeping with the enemy. That's right; you're sleeping with the enemy." "Vic, get your punk ass away from me. I'm not white nor do I pretend to be, like some folks I know." Then came the scare tactic. "I'll have you written up for making racist remarks against white officers, Bailey." He said it loud enough to get the attention of the others breaking lineup. So I returned the favor. "Vic, if we're gonna threaten each other then let's start by looking in your locker. Vodka, right? Right? This conversation is over."

Vic stormed towards me like he was going to do something. I turned and walked to the locker room where things got settled and stood there waiting. When I turned back around he was red-faced and slowly moving back for the door. I came out of the locker room. "Plant any knives lately?" A few officers standing there had that someday you'll get yours look about them. Perhaps I did go a little over the top with my comments. Officer Vic's air of arrogance was a show for his peers, and it irked me. Thinking back, I realized it was a time in my life where my past racial wounds were creeping up on me.

The rumors changed from me being a child molester to me getting money from Sanchez to protect his drug busi-

## No Black Heroes

ness. I hadn't even met the guy! No one knew Benji was my nephew, so it did look bad being out there off duty. I made a promise to Benji's mother before she died to look out for him. So every now and then, I went on the block to speak with him. But it was no use because of the easy money. "Benji, please get off the block."

"Uncle Ron, you need to stop coming out here. Everyone's talking about you and your Corvette." I knew he was right but I had to try. The Feds had to be watching Sanchez and most likely saw me out there as well. With no choice, and unable to stop Benji, I turned to my investigative side. It was time to get to know the players on Clinton Av.

The strategy was simple. The girls on the block had heard about my car. There was also a certain attraction in hanging out with a cop, so I used it. I began by stopping on the block in my police car, and over they came. After we talked a bit, I would ask out of the blue, "So how's my man doing?" I would then look over to one of the Family members walking by. They figured I knew everyone and would say "Oh, Carlos. He's fine. Oh, Big Red Giusti, he's good. Little Lee Sanchez is okay." I was learning who those guys were, and they had no idea they were telling me.

The Number One Family was growing and getting bolder. Things were getting out of hand on Clinton. They were so brazen they had designed black and gold jackets with the logo, "The Number One Family" on them. They were telling everyone who they were and not afraid to let people know they owned the block. I could not think of any drug gang with cojones like that.

A new officer, who previously worked at a smaller department, transferred to the Bridgeport PD. Officer Billy "Chase" was a tall, thin black officer with a talent for talking. When I heard him speak, he reminded me of a preacher. Anything he said you believed. He had to be good, because he convinced the police department to take him out of training and put him in the Narcotics Unit. Nobody had ever done that before! Chase was working with the DEA

## New Assignment

and FBI. He was the first African American sent on special assignment to the task force. I was amazed.

Back on Clinton, looking to see what was going on, oddly none of Sanchez' people were on the block. Suddenly, this 15-year-old Hispanic kid ran out of his house and flagged me down. He was telling me something in a heavy Hispanic accent, "Bailee, dares dis guy in da yard wit a goon." "A gun?" "Jest." Hee say he going to choot me." I got out of the car, ran to where the kid was pointing, and called dispatch to let them know where I was going. An uneasy feeling came over me knowing this kid was so calm while someone was threatening to shoot him. And he knew my name? He didn't say why the guy was going to shoot him, wasn't upset, just reporting it like he had been coached on what to say. Something wasn't right.

Running to the rear corner of a house was a Hispanic-looking guy carrying a briefcase and rifle carry case. He saw me coming and took off. I radioed where I was running and that the guy had a gun. Not sure if anyone was going to cover me, I prepared to take the guy out on my own. We ended up in a shack of a house that looked abandoned. "I'm at 93 Colorado Ave., radio. I'm going in."

The door slammed before I got to it. A turnaround back kick almost took the entire door off the frame. I pulled out my gun. In the living room was an older Hispanic couple with several children hiding behind them. The older guy asked me in a heavy accent, "Weird chor Warlent?" "What is this, heavy accent week? Here's my warrant right here." He looked at my gun and stepped back, not saying another word. For Christ's sake, I'm chasing a guy with gun.

I took my time looking through the apartment and noticed the basement door was open. Radio was alerted that I was going into the basement. My descent was long on those rickety stairs to the basement, when a knock on the door could be faintly heard. Officer Kevin Zwierline and Officer Tony Armeno had come to back me up. Sergeant Walsh was with them and yelling, "Bailey, what do you have?" "I got a

## No Black Heroes

guy with a gun, Sarge." Sergeant Walsh yelled back, "Hey Kid, do you know what the hell you're doing? You shouldn't be in here without a warrant."

I was making my way through the basement wondering what took them so long. Several calls for backup, well over 10 minutes ago, and they were just showing up? The nearest post car was three minutes away, at best. Now they want me to hurry up! "Hey Sarge, can you give me a minute? There's a guy down here with a gun!" Funny, I was looking for a man with a gun and they're upstairs. Rushing me, the Sarge said, "Time's up, Kid, let's go. We have some things to talk about on this one." Still determined, I searched in the dark alone. The sound of movement was heard to my right. I pointed my gun in the direction of the sound. "Hope you speak English, motherfucker. The next sound you hear'll be a bang." I cocked the trigger back, knowing he would hear the sound of the trigger click in place.

"Okay, okay, I'm coming out. Don't shoot." Out of the darkness came Guillermo Rivera. I handcuffed him and brought him upstairs. After asking Officer Armeno if he could hold onto him for me, Sergeant Walsh asked me where the gun was. I went back downstairs and fumbled around until I found a light switch. "Hey Sarge, you better come down here." On a small dirty bed was the briefcase. I opened it and found 12 ounces of uncut brown cocaine. A quick check under the bed revealed a 12-gauge shotgun too. Sergeant Walsh gave me a smile, when I went back upstairs with the briefcase and shotgun. "Okay, clean this up and make your way to booking with your prisoner, Bailey."

At booking, Rivera told me Sanchez set him up. It made sense. The small kid who pointed him out was nowhere to be found. Later, the detectives from the Special Service Drug Unit (SSDU) came to booking with the FBI in tow. I was sure they were going to ask Rivera to help with Sanchez. Sergeant Roger Falcone, who ran the SSDU, walked over to me, "Good job, Bailey. Write a good file." "Okay Sarge."

## New Assignment

The next day after lineup, as I was on my way to the car, I overhead a supervisor at the patrol door. He was congratulating Officers Armeno and Zwierline for a job well done. Some things never change. The newspaper article credited all three of us with Rivera's arrest. Someone from the department must have reported it that way. I knew black officers were not being credited with good work, but this was ridiculous. How do you give praise to someone else for my work?

It was a difficult situation. It would have been embarrassing to ask for what I had earned and was entitled to, recognition. And it would have looked self-serving. If we remained quiet, no one would have known we worked just as hard as anyone else. It was also a well-known fact that any officer seeking a special assignment had a better chance of getting it if they could show their citations and solid work in the field. Talk about a Catch-22, we were destined to look like do-nothings. The department was not going to acknowledge us.

At the next Guardians meeting we discussed what was going on. "No matter what we do, they flat-out refuse to acknowledge our work. It's as if we don't exist." Officer Carwin Spearmin was the new Guardians president and had an idea. "Why do we need them to recognize us? White officers are gonna have their files loaded with the things they do. We, on the other hand, look like we don't do a damn thing." Carwin had a brilliant idea. "The Guardians can have an awards banquet and recognize our own officers yearly." Ted chimed in. "Carwin, that's a great idea. You guys are going to change the face of the Bridgeport PD. We can have our own affair and demand the department place those citations in our folders." Ted made one last comment. "Make sure you guys keep track of any good work you do, including our members who make an outstanding difference in the community." "Meeting adjourned."

I was back on the streets looking forward to our guys being recognized. I was a little off post by George Street in the Hollow area. There had been a great deal of holdups

69

## No Black Heroes

there, so I was just being seen. Officer Brooks was close by and called out a man with a gun who took off on him. This Hispanic-looking kid was driving my way at top speed, almost striking my car. I turned around and went two blocks over, cutting him off. I saw the car coming my way but the street was blocked. It looked like he wouldn't stop and we were about to have a head-on collision. What was I thinking?

Suddenly, his car slid to a stop inches away from mine. He jumped out running, with me right behind him. Then he turned to push me away. Not knowing where the gun was, I ran at and hit him with a roundhouse kick to his rib cage, knocking him down. It was Anthony Martinez who was said to be a stickup kid. He was struggling to get free, thrashing around on the ground. I had my hands full keeping hold of his arms and hands. Officer Valerie Day showed up and helped me cuff him. Once we had him under control, I pulled deep out of his waistband a 9mm handgun with cop killer bullets. That ammo in Martinez' gun was made to penetrate a bulletproof vest. They were the same type of bullets Officer Keith Bryant was shot with during a holdup attempt a few weeks before. Martinez was taken to the Detective Bureau for questioning. It was a great arrest. Of course none of the supervisors mentioned it, even though it made the papers.

After lineup, I thanked Officer Day loudly enough so the guys in patrol could hear it. I later asked the Sergeant if I could keep a copy of Martinez' arrest reports. He looked bewildered but let it go. I was not about to take any chances. Someone could complain that I took police property home against department policy. It would have been a stretch, but the atmosphere dictated I cover myself and be careful.

Chapter 6

## Girls; A Stranger

Sanchez' Number One Family was becoming more brazen by the day. They had taken over four city blocks surrounding Clinton Ave. and a small park. Chase saw me in patrol. He was in plain clothes. "Hey Bailey, can I speak with ya? I heard about all those arrests you made. If you get any arrests in or around the Sanchez family, can you give me a shout out?" "No problem Chase, you got it." He surprised me with his next comment. "Bailey, these guys here hate me. They think I should be in patrol paying my dues instead of working undercover. I asked them for any intel they might get and they laughed at me." "Hey Chase, don't let these fools get to you. They either swear we can't do the job, or they figure they're the only ones who should."

We discussed Sanchez and the players working for him. I confided that my only reason for being out on the block off duty was to get my nephew Benji away from there. He looked stunned. He had no idea, nor did the department. "By the way, some are saying I kept money from my drug

## No Black Heroes

arrests to buy a car. Others are saying I work for Sanchez. Don't believe it." Chase threw a joke back at me, "Don't worry about it. The state wants me to keep an eye on you." It was then that I knew he was investigating me. He played it just the way I would have. Throw it out there in the form of a joke, and see what reaction you get.

Chase and I became very close friends. We exchanged information regularly. By then, the FBI and DEA were working hard on drugs in Bridgeport. The drug trade in the city had morphed into divided sections. On the west Sanchez controlled Clinton. In P.T. the project was divided between a family called the Joneses and the "Million Dollar Kid" Frankie Estrada and his Terminators, and my cousins the Holmans had the rest. With all the rumors about me being involved in drugs I was not going to talk about anyone else selling drugs in my family.

Off duty and still desperate, I stopped by to see Benji, hoping to get him off the block. I rolled up in the Corvette and was quickly surrounded by girls. When they finished saying hello, Benji looked at me. "You know these girls out here got a thing for you. You should have never let them see your car." Benji was changing the subject. I didn't go out there again, because I knew he wasn't going to leave the Sanchez family.

A beautiful girl I had never seen before walked over to me. Benji excused himself and left. "So you're the cop everyone wants to get with. My name is Lily Torres. Just so you know, I don't like cops." "No problem, they don't like me either." She chuckled. "You're all right, Officer Bailey; maybe I can change my mind about you." She turned and walked away.

What was I doing? I had gotten married just before taking the job. There was no doubt that my wife and I were headed down a path of no return. I was never home, and we hardly spoke when I was. The demands of the job were taking a toll on both of us. A cop's life was a disaster on rails for any marriage, but my passion for the streets sped that

## Girls; A Stranger

train up. There was one additional weight that would end our marriage for sure; I was obsessed with my pursuit for equality at the Bridgeport Police Department.

As time went on, Lil and I got to be close. She was smarter than the other girls and never fell for my indirect questions about the family. I even tried a more direct approach with her. "So how is Big Red doing these days?" Her answers were always vague. "Red is on the block as always." I changed the subject. "Girl, you're looking hot today." "Bailey, I would be your woman in a minute but I don't date cops." I always had an answer, "I don't date cops either." She would laugh as always and walk off. That was the last time I saw her.

Lillian went missing only to be found a few days later in an abandoned van by Marina Village project. She was wrapped in an old rug. The autopsy said she died from a drug overdose. The girl I knew from Clinton didn't use drugs. Word on the street was she couldn't be trusted and was given a hot dose to make it look accidental. How do you end up dead of an overdose in an abandoned van, wrapped in a rug? Did she roll herself up in it? She was dropped there. Word on the street was that someone name Edwin had done it. Sadly it was a mystery the investigators didn't have time to solve and closed it out.

Back on Clinton Avenue it was as if no one out there cared. Benji said Lil had been close with everyone on the block. She was dead and not one person said they were sad about it. Street life was cold. That same day Sanchez' sister Suzie was on the block. She came slowly to my car. "So you're Benji's uncle. I heard about you. You're cute." She began to tell me about herself. "So you think we can go out sometime, or would your job get mad at you for dating Sanchez' little sister?" That was my chance to get some info for Chase if I played it right. I chimed in on her question. "I can go out with anyone I like. Besides, haven't you heard? I'm crooked, according to them." She smiled and gave me her number. "Call me and don't make me wait." I called and we had dinner in Fairfield. She thought I was trying to stay out of sight of the cops in Bridgeport dining in another town. I actually wanted her to feel safe so we could talk. We started seeing each other several times a week. I was getting some information but had to be careful how much I asked her.

Someone must have tipped off the department. Word had gotten back that I was dating Sanchez' sister. This time the rumor was not from within, it came from Clinton Avenue. Someone out there knew where we were meeting and how many times. No cop could know that. I was now rumored to be getting high in my car with Sanchez' sister and tipping Sanchez off on police activity. Officer Al Best was one of the very few black officers who could get information from Chief Walsh's office. He told me someone on the streets was giving information on me. Al said he didn't know who it was, but the department was convinced it was true.

I asked him if he thought the Ad Hoc was involved, but he said it definitely wasn't them. "Someone wants you bad, Bailey. Think about what you're doing. You've made a lot of enemies here. Someone hates you to the point they would be happy if something happened to you." "Thanks Al, now come to a Guardians meeting sometime, will ya?"

I wasn't even out the door when Suzie called. She was in a state of panic, "Bailey, I got to see you, someone's out to get you." Now there's a surprise! We met at Seaside Park and she jumped in my car. "Bailey, I saw this guy talking shit about you on the block with my brother Mariano. He was trying to buy drugs from him." "What happened, Suzie? Calm down." She said the guy told Sanchez I was a crooked cop, get high and not to trust me. Suzie said Sanchez didn't fall for his comments and told the guy he don't sell drugs. Sanchez told him to leave the block.

Sanchez was suspicious of this guy who came to him out of nowhere. He knew everyone from the FBI, State, and DEA were out to get him. What had me puzzled was the guy trash-talking about me, why? Who was he? Suzie was so upset she seemed terrified for me. "Bailey, I got a good look

### Girls; A Stranger

at him. He's six foot tall on the thin side. He's cocolo." "Suzie, calm down. I don't speak Spanish." "He's black and wears shades." I thought it was Chase. She told me the guy had been out there day and night wearing those shades, trying to buy off the block. I asked her why he wore shades. "My brother made him take his shades off. He has a scar across his face. It goes from one side to the other, across his eyes. One of his eyes is all white from the cut. He looks possessed." For sure it wasn't Chase. "Bailey, he looks fuckin' crazy. Please be careful."

Suzie was terrified and blurted out, "Sanchez told me to stay away from the block when this guy's out there. His name is Mark, or Markis. You need to arrest his ass, Bailey." "Suzie, I can't just arrest someone for nothing." She then asked me something under normal circumstances she would never say. "Do you want me to have my brother get someone to fuck him up, Baby?" I had to calm Suzie down. "Come on girl, you know I don't roll like that. I'll look into this Markis person and see what his claim to fame is." Someone was out to get me, and the list of possibilities was growing. I couldn't remember arresting anyone with a white eye. Maybe he got cut across the face in jail and blamed me. Could someone have sent him? Maybe Sanchez was setting me up for dating his sister. Whatever the case, the whole thing had the stench of a setup with my name on it.

Chapter 7

## THE INFORMANT

I wasn't familiar with the name Markis. Faced with so many unanswered questions, it was time to take a break. I could start fresh on the mystery guest later. My enjoyment was in working out. I was on my way to train a bit when the call came in. The school had been set on fire. The papers later said it was suspicious. "East Coast Tae Kwon Do School Severely Damaged By Fire." What in hell was going on, and did the arson have anything to do with me?

With the school being rebuilt, I needed something to keep me busy. I was wandering in the mall hanging out when I saw someone I hadn't seen for a while, Janice Rodriguez. Janice was a cop lover. She respected how we did things for others and admired us. I met her at Harding High one day while on a call. We had not been in touch since, but surprisingly she remembered me.

"Officer Bailey, I think it's safe to say you're doing some great things for this city. I read about you a lot." I walked

## No Black Heroes

over to her. "Jan, how are you, girl?" "Officer Bailey, what brings you to the mall?" "Oh, just hanging out with nothing to do." She asked if I was busy on the weekend. Jan was a connoisseur of clubs and knew of a brand-new one that just opened in Bridgeport, Club Scruples. With some time on my hands, I went there to relax.

I soon realized Jan was the go-to person who knew everyone and all the hot spots to party. It was safe to say Jan was a club-aholic. She loved hanging out and clubbing with cops. She even knew a few drug dealers who would hang out with her occasionally. She walked over to the bar to buy me a drink. I asked for a soda. She seemed stunned. "Hey, what can I say, I don't drink." She was mortified. She handed me the soda. "Here's your vodka and juice, sir." She smiled, "You must be the only cop in America who doesn't drink alcohol. Shall I order you a Virgin Mary next?" "Very funny, what's going on, girl?" "Same old stuff Ron, everybody hanging out and talking shit."

Jan was trying to convince me to dance when I noticed a tall dark-skinned man with shades at the bar. He was looking right at me. Jan turned to see what I was staring at. "Who's that? He's creepy looking and a tall motherfucker, Ron." "Jan, I think you should go dance with someone while I see what this guy's all about." "Ron, please don't start nothing in here. You could lose your job." "I promise to behave. Don't believe all those stories you read in the papers about me."

Like a scene from the movies, the guy took a sip of his drink while still staring at me. Obviously, he must have known me, but who was he? Jan looked concerned but walked away. He was a lot taller up close and blurted out something I could never forget. "You know who I am. You can't stay here." At first I thought he was on drugs. "Excuse me?" "You heard what I said, you can't be here. You have to leave." I thought about doing a roundhouse kick to this guy's face. Something just didn't add up. "You must be Markis. How do you know me, Mr. Markis?" He paused a second, "It's not Mr. Markis, its Markis Cruz Majors. You

## The Informant

don't have to try and trick me into telling you who I am. What you need to do is leave like I told you too." "Okay Mr. Majors. Why are you messing with me? Why don't you go about your business and I can go about mine?" He inched closer, and I stepped back for room. "Is that your final answer?" I guess the subtle approach didn't work. "Let me make this clear to you. Stop fucking with me or you're going to get arrested on top of an ass kicking. Have a good night, Cruz." "Hey, you don't call me Cruz. My name is—" I cut him off, "Shut the fuck up, Cruz." I turned my back and walked away. The mirrors on the wall provided me a good view in case he tried anything. He looked pissed. How was I gonna get a kick off to this guy's head with so many things in the way? He followed right behind me. "Are you going to leave or not?" I turned, only to see my reflection in his shades. "Look, let's go outside and settle your problem." He headed for the door with me right behind him.

Outside the club he was waiting but with his hands at his sides. Either this guy could fight or it was a setup. I wasn't falling for it. At the door I turned and showed the bouncer my badge. "This guy is done for the night." I turned and went back in the club. I could hear the bouncer say to Cruz he had to leave. The bouncer was standing in front of the door with his arms folded. Cruz made one more comment. "I'll see you later, Bailey." He asked the bouncer, "Do you know who I am?" "Hey man, the cop says you're out. So you're out." I caught a final glimpse of Cruz walking towards the parked cars. He was yelling, "I got something for that cop, I'll be back." He got into an older model BMW and drove off. Not sure if the guy was talking trash or not, I went to my car. If Cruz returned with a gun, he'd wish he hadn't. I got my backup 9mm and stuffed it in the small of my back.

Back in the club I was surrounded by Jan and three of her friends. "They all wanted to meet you Ron, what can I say?" We were having a great time when Jan looked back towards the end of the bar. "Ah Ron, isn't that your friend from earlier?" Cruz had gotten back in the club and was sitting at the bar watching my every move. "Ron, did you see

## No Black Heroes

him come in?" "Yeah, I saw him in the mirrors. I didn't want to say anything to you." "What are ya gonna do?" I walked past Jan. She tried to stop me. "Ron, don't."

"Hey Cruz, you're starting to piss me off. You're scaring the young lady over there. Let me be clear. I'm not going anywhere. Got it?" I took a quick look but didn't see a gun. He had the nerve to ask me if that was my final answer. "Try something and see what my final answer is." His facial expression was priceless. I turned and could see him in a mirror get up, but he stopped short and plopped back down in his chair. Good choice, my man.

The girls and I had moved to a different part of the club. We were out of Cruz' sight. Jan was keeping an eye out for him. "Ron, who is this guy? Have you arrested him before?" Cruz was so focused on finding me he didn't see Jan watching him. He got up from the bar and walked over to where he thought I might be. When he turned, I was standing right there in his face. I pretended to trip and bumped him in his chest with my shoulder.

I was sure the shoulder hit hurt him. He was holding his chest. I apologized for tripping into him, but with a sarcastic smile. I turned to Jan and lip-synced to her, "I'm leaving." I walked past Cruz, ignoring him as he tried to speak to me. From the mirror I could see him moving fast towards the door behind me. Once outside, I moved quickly to my car but with my gun in my hand at my side. No one saw it. Cruz came walking my way. He had parked near my car and obviously knew it. Something was very wrong.

He walked towards me but stopped short at his car across the street from mine. Cruz had a friend sitting in the driver's seat who had been waiting for him. He was a well-built Hispanic-looking guy. No matter, I'd kick his ass too. Cruz smiled and placed his hands on the roof of the car. He made a gesture like he had a gun and was pulling the trigger. Not to be outdone, I put my gun on the roof of my car, carefully pointing it in his direction. Where's an accidental discharge when ya need one? Damn! Cruz stopped smiling

# The Informant

and got in the car. My expression was nonexistent. I put my gun back in hand, got in and drove off.

The next morning I filed a report and asked Sergeant Mangano if he could forward it through the chain of command to the third floor. One of the detectives was in the office and heard my request. He was rumored to be an Ad Hoc Committee member. "Hey Bailey, maybe you should stop hanging in the clubs." I looked over at him, "I guess no one takes this seriously. Maybe I should join the Ad Hoc so someone will." He slammed some papers on the desk and stormed out of the office.

Sergeant Mangano looked at me with disappointment. "Hey Sergeant, I don't want any trouble. This guy Cruz is threatening a police officer and knows my car. Something isn't right here." "Officer Bailey, antagonizing the guys you work with is not the answer. Stick with your issues." "I'm sorry. I'm just tired of the nonsense. Just so you know, Cruz is spreading rumors on the streets that I'm a crooked cop." "How do you know that?" "Let's just say I have a few friends who are watching my back, Sarge." "Bailey, I suggest you stay away from this guy, but keep filing your reports."

If I were white asking for help they would have called in the National Guard. Anyone who says otherwise would be kidding themselves. The reaction from that detective made that apparent. His comment wasn't about someone threatening a cop; it was about me hanging out. Sergeant Mangano was doing all he could, but I had doubts about the police department. Needless to say, I heard nothing from the third floor.

The department was not taking the Cruz thing seriously. My guess was they were ignoring it on purpose. Did they know the guy, or was someone in the department telling Cruz what to do? Was he an informant, maybe even an undercover cop from another district? Why was he after me? I needed answers. I returned to Scruples to speak with the owner of the club, Capozzoli. He was supposedly linked to a

## No Black Heroes

lot of things in Bridgeport, but that wasn't my area of concern. I worked the streets.

After describing Cruz to him, he was nice enough to tell me, "Officer, that guy works part-time at the Yellow Cab Company in Bridgeport." My next stop, Yellow Cab. Leak worked dispatch there, so I was in luck. "Hey Leak, are you still playing keyboards, brother?" "Ron, what's up man, any more rumors about you since we last talked?" "Hey Leak, I need your help, what do you know about Markis Majors?" Leak's expression turned serious. "How did you get mixed up with him? He's bad news, Ron. Stay away from him. He's connected and dangerous." "What do you mean, connected, Leak?" "He works for the State Police." "You got to be kidding me. Cruz is State PD? What as, an idiot?" "Ron, I know you're not about to back down, but listen. Cruz is as dirty as they come. I don't think he's a state trooper; my guess is he's a snitch and someone put him up to messing with you. Your boy lives somewhere in Fairfield if that helps." "Thanks Leak, I owe ya."

Fairfield, Connecticut, is a small town for mostly the well off. What was a guy like Cruz doing living there? Leak told me Cruz had bragged about how no one could arrest him. That smelled of an informant. I called the Fairfield police to see what they could tell me. The officer who answered the phone wasn't surprised when I told him I was a Bridgeport badge having problems with Markis Cruz Majors. "Officer Bailey, stay away from this guy, he's connected." "I've heard that before." The officer told me Cruz worked for Inspector Bill Spencer of the State's Attorney's Office in Bridgeport. That meant the state was somehow involved in him coming after me. The officer talked about Cruz like he was a state-owned pet or something. "We know about Cruz because every time we arrest him, it's always dismissed." "Thanks, Officer."

Over the next few weeks, Cruz made a habit of being wherever I was. He was at the stores where I shopped, downtown waiting when I went to get my paper. He even knew where I was working on overtime. Someone at the de-

## The Informant

partment was feeding the guy information on me. I needed to talk with Rita and see if her father was saying anything about Cruz being linked to the Ad Hoc Committee.

"Rita, I'm up against a wall. I hate to ask, but have you heard anything about the Ad Hoc? And if so, do you know if they have someone coming after me?" "Ron, my dad was at the table the other day laughing. He said someone is going to take you down soon. But he hinted something about the state coming after you. What's this all about?" "I'm not sure, Rita, but I'm working on it." "My dad said you were taking care of yourself by way of some guy named Sanchez." "Thanks Rita. I'll be in touch." Jesus, more rumors, but from where?

I began to write reports every time Cruz came near me. Details of stalking for months, making gestures he was going to shoot me. The entire police department knew about Cruz and his crazy behavior, and they did nothing. Officer Rob Novice caught me in the locker room and pulled me to the side. Rob was a rough rider of sorts. He said, "Just shoot the son of a bitch and drop a knife by him." Smiling, I didn't say anything. Wow, he actually meant it.

I decided to take the Cruz thing up a notch. I took my reports to Lieutenant Mike DeCarlo in Detective Bureau. "Hey Lieutenant, I'm sure you know about Cruz. I just had a run-in with him again. Is DB going to do something on this?" "Bailey, we got nothing on this guy. Maybe you should start going to another club." "Are you kidding me? If I was a little lighter you wouldn't be saying that." Lieutenant DeCarlo looked my way, "I'm sorry Bailey, but we can't do anything with what you've given us so far." It then dawned on me from Lieutenant DeCarlo's response that they knew about the club and problems Cruz was causing. It smelled of my own department somehow behind Cruz coming after me. It was important to think carefully about what my next move would be.

There is a God and revenge is sweet. I was assigned to East Main Street and got a call to report for a DOA, dead on

## No Black Heroes

arrival. I could smell the body as soon as I entered the hallway. It was a few days old and it was 90 degrees out. The deceased, needless to say, was ripe. When I broke into the apartment, there was an older guy on the floor, half naked. It looked like he had collapsed. Detective Bureau showed up. It was Lieutenant DeCarlo and a few investigators.

The body's eyes had been eaten out by maggots. They were coming out of his mouth as well. His skin had bite marks and flesh missing, from the rats. It was a gruesome sight, not for the faint. The investigation was taking a while. Near the body, on the table, was a large dish of candy bars. Hershey's with almonds. Flies were everywhere. I asked Lieutenant DeCarlo if I could go to the car. He said go ahead, they were almost done.

I ran to the corner store and bought a few Hershey bars and returned just in time. Lieutenant DeCarlo was coming downstairs. I leaned into my car pretending to grab a few and offered him one. He took it. After a few bites I asked him, "Hey Lieutenant, not bad for free, right?" At that very moment the body was being brought out in a body bag. "Bailey, what are you talking about?" He looked confused. "Lieutenant, remember that candy dish upstairs next to the dead guy? Well, there you go. I'm sure the flies didn't get on these, they were on the bottom." DeCarlo must have turned several shades of gray before throwing his candy bar down. I had never seen so much fluid coming out of someone before. "Hey Lieutenant, I was just kidding. I bought them at the store." "Bailey, you asshole!" He was trying to yell while choking at the same time. It was a little prank to get even with him for ignoring the Cruz mess. Score one for the home team.

I still needed answers on Cruz and the Ad Hoc Committee. Did they have anything to do with Cruz was the million-dollar question. With no way to look closer at the Ad Hoc, I turned my attention back to the Fairfield PD. "Hi, this is Officer Bailey from Bridgeport. Can you tell me if Markis Cruz Majors has a gun permit?" "Yep, he does offi-

## The Informant

cer. Good luck trying to take it." I guess Cruz making threats he was going to shoot me made no difference to the state or my department. They were sent my reports. He had his permit and no one was going to revoke it. The officer had one more thing to say, "Officer, you're a cop so you know what you might have to do. Protect yourself."

I had a theory that needed testing. Every time I went to club Scruples Cruz showed up. Jan said he was only there when I was. I didn't go every week, so how did he know? Then it dawned on me, I made a habit of telling a few in patrol where I was going just to gage their reaction. It was a long shot, but I had to find out if Cruz was being told of my whereabouts by someone in the department.

As always, I mentioned where I was going. But this time I told just a few where I was going, Gumby's in Fairfield. To make sure my plan had a chance of working, I spoke about Gumby's at the patrol office window where only the supervisors could overhear me. I needed to narrow down the possibilities. I had a feeling it was a supervisor passing information on me upstairs.

I had never been to this club before. If Cruz showed up at Gumby's chances were a police supervisor was involved, or knew who was. That night I went to Gumby's to meet up with Jan. "Jan, I'm not staying. I'm looking for my friend Cruz to show up." She looked confused. "You're expecting him?" No sooner than she said it, he came in with someone I'd never seen before. I gave Jan a kiss on the cheek and carefully slipped past Cruz and his mystery guest.

Someone in the department was feeding Cruz information. Knowing what my department was doing would be an ace in the hole. I could turn the tables on them if I played it right. Was a patrol supervisor connected to Cruz, or did a supervisor make a call upstairs to the one controlling him? Jan called later to tell me Cruz was all over the club looking for me.

85

Chapter 8

# First Shooting; Black Officers Denied

Just when I thought things couldn't get worse, they did. It was a sunny September day. The call came over the radio, "Blue-13, there's a man with a gun at the corner of Columbia and South Avenue. Proceed with caution. You can use lights and sirens to get there." Radio described a tall, fair-skinned man with a gun on the corner. "Radio, I'm here at Columbia and South. No one's here." All cars were called off. No one came to cover me anyway.

About 15 minutes later, the same call came in but at a different location. "Officers are advised that we have several calls of a man at South and Lafayette Street pointing a gun at cars passing by. Use extreme caution." "Radio, I'm responding and almost there." It was Officer Pete LaLuz' post, and he was the first to arrive. "He's here guys, pointing the gun at me. I'm backing the car up." South and Lafayette Street was home to Pequonnock Apartments, a high-rise complex. "Pete, I'm out of the car and making my way under the buildings through the parking lot to you. I'll let you know when I'm in position."

87

## No Black Heroes

I peered out from the corner of the building by the underground parking lot, and there he was. Eric Williamson was pointing a black semi-auto handgun at Pete's car. Pete couldn't move forward without getting shot. I edged out slightly from the corner of the building with gun in hand. Officer LaLuz responded over the radio, "I see you Bailey, watch it, you're too close." I edged a little more out, "Drop the gun." Without hesitation, he turned and fired several shots at me. "Shit!" I leaned back as quickly as I could, only to feel one of the rounds whiz by the right side of my forehead. Boy, was that close!

Williamson started running away from me, but still shooting in my dirction. Going down Lafayette Street he fired several more shots from under his arm. "Oh, you want to play cowboys and Indians, let's do it." I shot back at Williamson, striking the metal fence pole right by him. Either he heard what I said, or the bullet striking the pole was all it took. Williamson was in high gear, running his behind off.

He shot a few more rounds at me again but from under his arm. The boy had been watching too many cowboy movies with that under-the-arm stuff. Aiming, I pulled the trigger back slowly. At the very last second, I jerked the gun back and up in the sky, letting it fire away from my target. Officer LaLuz saw me and asked over the radio, "Bailey, what are you doing?" I didn't have time to talk. Just before I was about to shoot, a car was passing by with kids in it. I had to pull my shot or risk shooting one of those kids.

People were now running all over the place. Williamson pointed his gun and fired at me one more time. I fired back, striking another metal pole. Talk about lucky. I had to stop him before he killed someone. Looking back at me, Williamson ran into an old lady, knocking her to the ground. He got up and ran out of my sight. I could hear the police sirens and more shots being fired. Williamson was shooting at Officers Bernard Belcher and Danny Holland. They almost crashed the car, ducking to avoid being shot. Talk about black on black crime.

## First Shooting; Black Officers Denied

Williamson was headed for the underground parking lot, so I turned and ran through the building to cut him off. He was running my way and fired a few more rounds before ducking into the next building's hallway. I fired back, striking the metal door with a round, and then suddenly, I heard a click. I was out of ammunition. If he came back, I would be done. My thought was to rush him, in the hopes of knocking him down if he returned. I tried to reload, but it was difficult while looking to see if he would come back out shooting.

I finally reloaded my gun while running towards the door. At that moment, close to a nearby doorway, someone yelled at me. "Stop shooting at my brother, you better not hurt him. Run, Eric." The guy yelling was Troy Williamson, Eric's brother. Troy ran up the stairs of the hallway. I needed to remain calm. Who built this place? It's meant for people who want the bad guys to get away? I stopped at the stairs, and radio reported, "Officers on scene, someone called and said the guy shooting is Eric Williamson. He lives on the second floor, apartment 215."

Officers Belcher and Holland were running towards me with their guns pointed in my direction. Holland was out of breath, "Where is he, Bailey?" Belcher was sweating like crazy. They both looked so intense, I tried to break the mood, "Hey guys, you know this is black unity, right? You, me, the bad guys?" Belcher looked at me, "Not now Bailey, please, not now."

We were about to go up the stairs when an adjacent door suddenly opened up. Belcher pointed his gun and was about to shoot. "Bernard, wait!" It was Winifred Timberlake, president of the Tenants Association. "Don't shoot Bernard, it's not him!" Mr. Timberlake stumbled from the opening of the door almost falling forward, with Belcher pointing his gun at him." Sir, please go back inside until we find this guy," "Okay officer. Go get him." It all happened in just a few moments. If only people realized what could happen at the drop of a hat.

89

## No Black Heroes

We all started the long climb up the stairs. Not knowing where Williamson was made the trip seem a lot longer. I could hear more sirens and cars finally arriving. On the second floor there was a long hallway to apartment 215. We had no way to protect ourselves if Williamson came out of that apartment.

"Bailey, it's your call, so you can go first." "Thanks, I thought you said no joking." "Who's joking?" Belcher and Holland were smiling for a moment. It was a long, uneasy walk down that hallway. I listened for movement at the door. Not a sound. I knocked. "Open up, it's the police." Belcher and Holland leaned into a doorway two apartments back. "Hey guys, get ready. If he comes out shooting, please shoot that son of a bitch, okay?" Belcher nodded yes with a slightly nervous smile.

Just as I was about to knock again, a small boy opened the door slowly. Did dispatch give us the right apartment? "Hey kid, anyone home?" Before the little boy could answer, Troy came to the door. "What do you want?" I was thinking this kid wasn't supposed to open the door. "You're the guy that was yelling at me downstairs. Where's your brother?" "I don't have to tell you anything." Before I could say another word Troy got pushed aside.

A young woman came out. "You got a warrant?" "Miss, who are you?" "Don't worry about who I am. If you don't have a warrant, say goodbye." She pushed me back with her hand to close the door. I grabbed her by the arm, pulling her out of the doorway. "Keep your fucking hands off me, cop!" She pulled away then slapped me in my face. "You're under arrest." She raised her hand to hit me again. I punched her in the jaw, and with a wobble, down she went.

Troy yelled out to me, "Are you crazy?" "No, and she should've kept her hands to herself. And I'm not leaving here without Eric. What's her name?" "Audrey Sharpe officer, please don't hurt her." "Miss Sharpe, you're under arrest." I handcuffed her and then Troy. Belcher, who was

## First Shooting; Black Officers Denied

smiling nervously, joked, "Bailey, you hit a woman." He had a big sarcastic, smirk on his face. "She hit me first." Sharpe leaned against the wall, still groggy. "You hit me. You can't hit a woman." "Wrong. You've been watching too much TV."

Belcher touched me on the shoulder, "Bailey, calm down." "I am calm. By the way, the next person who gets in my face is going out the window." I asked Troy one more time. "Troy, you want to tell me where your brother is or what?" "He jumped out the window when you knocked on the door." I called dispatch about the arrests and Williamson, who may have escaped out the window.

We checked the apartment but he was gone. The gun Eric used was on the window sill, still hot. I handed it to Belcher. The little boy was taken next door to a neighbor, until his parents could come. Troy and Audrey were escorted away once the apartment was secured. Patrol arrived and did a floor-to-floor search. I guess in a gunfight even those who couldn't stand me wanted a piece of the action. Then the news over the radio, "We got him, we got him."

Eric Williamson was hiding on the seventh floor under some construction material. By the time we got to booking, they were bringing him in. He was sweating and had that same look Hatton had in the Panic brawl. There was no doubt he was high on something. Then he yelled out, "People are mannequins, and mannequins are people. That's why I shot at him. I couldn't tell the difference." Welcome to the crack cocaine era.

Belcher and Holland took Troy and Audrey inside booking. With the press standing close by, Sergeant Connelly says, "Bailey, you'll get a department citation for this, great work." I got to booking only to see Belcher covering his face, hiding his laughter. "You're some kind of class act, Bailey. I ain't ever seen anyone hit a woman like that before." "Oh well, she should've worked on her boxing skills."

The newspaper article was front-page news. "Bridgeport Officers Are Outgunned." My report on running out of

## No Black Heroes

ammo got the attention of Chief Walsh. He made a formal announcement. "The Bridgeport Police are going to get semi-automatic handguns. One of my officers ran out of ammunition. That could have cost him his life." A few months later, a second article appeared in the papers. "Officer's Shootout Brings More Firepower." We were in training to carry the Beretta 9mm semi-auto handgun. All eyes were on me, and I was the flavor of the month.

With so much attention on the shooting and the department about to get new weapons, the rumors about me quieted down. Cruz was nowhere to be found. The shooting and how it was handled brought so much attention, I guess it wasn't a good time for the department to keep coming after me. One word about how the department was treating one of its own would've caused a public-relations nightmare. There was nothing but praise from community leaders about the handling of Williamson. He was captured and no innocent bystanders were hurt. The community was pleased that a police officer didn't have to take another life. I was glad it turned out the way it did.

It had been several months since the shoot-out. There'd been no mention of the Bridgeport Police Department having an awards ceremony for the Williamson shooting. Ted had his take on it. "Brother Bailey, you didn't think that you, Belcher and Holland were going to get anything from the police department? There's no way three black officers will receive something from Chief Walsh, or this department." Ted had a smile like the Cheshire Cat. I couldn't understand why. I had completely forgotten the Guardians' discussion on having our own awards ceremony. "Just so you know Brother Bailey, we are having our first awards banquet in a few months. You, Belcher and Holland are going to be honored by the Guardians." I was certain it would be a curious turn of events. I couldn't wait to see how the department was going to react.

"Wait until Chief Walsh hears about this. He'll hit the ceiling." Ted was smiling so hard, he looked like he was in a toothpaste commercial. "We are going to force the police de-

## First Shooting; Black Officers Denied

partment to place those awards in your files. If they refuse, we'll take them to court for leaving us out of their awards ceremonies." "Looks like I'm going to be not so popular on the third floor, not that I am anyway." "Brother Bailey, you're going to be just fine."

Being outspoken wasn't enough. Now I would have the distinction of being the first to force the department to recognize an award from the Guardians. They were really going to love me now! Nonetheless, being the first officers to receive awards from the Guardians was an honor for us. You could bet everyone in that department would hold me responsible. I could picture the gossip, "The Guardians honoring their own. Bailey this and Bailey that."

Ted was in his glory that night, "Welcome to our first awards banquet to honor the officers of the Bridgeport Police Department." Ted took to the podium and explained the history of the Guardians and the selection process to honor our members. "For bravery, courage, and heroism under fire, the Guardians honor Officers Ron Bailey, Bernard Belcher and Danny Holland." Everyone stood up for a standing ovation. I had to admit, it felt good to see people appreciative about something we did.

Our new elected President Carwin Spearmin believed we should honor community members whose ideals mirrored what Guardians stood for, the people of Bridgeport. We also honored Mayor Tom Bucci, State Senator Margaret Morton and Bishop Walter Plummer. To put the icing on the cake, the Guardians Award Committee invited the Connecticut Post. It should have been an enormous news event. Sadly, the article about the banquet was so small you had to search for it. You would have thought that if a mayor and state senator received citations from a fraternal organization, it would have been bigger news.

Rita called to congratulate me. She knew why the news on the banquet was squashed. It was the Ad Hoc Committee. Rita said her dad was home laughing about it. One of their members called the news and threatened to withhold

## No Black Heroes

future information related to major cases the Detective Bureau had, opting to give it to rival newspapers. Our banquet was scaled back in the news to appease the Ad Hoc and their threats. "Well that explains a lot. Thanks, Rita."

That Monday no one from the police department said anything about the Guardians banquet. Not one supervisor at lineup acknowledged it. You could sense they were all upset about it. Then came Officer Vic. "Just so you know, Bailey, if it's not a Bridgeport Police award, it doesn't count." "I notice you have something to say, but you're still walking. At least you know to keep moving when you talk to me." If only I could catch him in that locker room. That would shut him up for good, the little weasel.

On the way out the door, you could hear someone talking in the patrol office. I wasn't stupid. They were speaking loud enough so I could hear them. "The Guardians can have all the awards banquets they want. We don't recognize them or their dumb-ass awards. Who do they think they are? They forced their way on the job, now they want awards?" I could hear one of them crumpling a newspaper.

It sounded like a challenge to me. I went to my car and got a copy of my award. Sheffield was on his way to the car when he saw what I had in my hand. He shook his head. "Bailey, don't do it. Just keep it at home. Belcher and Holland didn't bring their awards in. Ted means well, but you're gonna rile things up if you try and force them to take that." "Hey, Sheffield, all they can do is say no." "Bailey, let me get to my car before you go in there." "Sheffield, cut it out, will ya?"

Sheffield headed straight for his car. I walked into the patrol office and asked the small group of supervisors if I could go upstairs to see the department clerk. The Sergeants glanced my way like I wasn't there but said to go ahead. They knew why I was going to the third floor. At the clerk's office I placed my award on his desk. "Officer Bayyyleee, what do you want? I was expecting you." Guess someone from patrol called ahead. "First of all, it's not Bay-

## First Shooting; Black Officers Denied

yyleee, its Bailey." He turned and gave me a look of displeasure. He was another Sergeant I had never seen before assigned to the clerk's office. "Sergeant, I have an award here from the Guardians. I want it placed in my personnel file." "Officer Bailey, the department doesn't place anything in an officer's file but police-generated documents." "Sergeant, let me just say this. This award came from the Guardians, and therefore it is police-generated. I'm requesting that it be placed in my file. I'll be back in a few weeks to check and see if it's there. If not, I'll simply take the matter up in court. Thank you for your time, Sergeant." I left the citation on his desk and walked out. I didn't want to hear his response, even if he had one. If looks could kill, his would have burned me at the stake!

I returned a few weeks later and checked my personnel file. It was there. At the next meeting, I told the Guardians what I had done. My good friend Officer Keith Bryant said I was now Public Enemy Number One, but only after Ted. He still had the honor of being the most hated black officer in the department.

It was my day off and I still wasn't comfortable working overtime jobs, not knowing where Cruz was. I went for a drive, ending up on Arctic Street. In passing, I saw a 60-year-old woman getting punched in the face and being robbed. Debra Newby hit the woman, grabbed her purse and jumped into a getaway car. I pulled my Corvette right in front of them. They stopped, and Newby quickly jumped out and ran down the street with the woman's purse. The driver didn't even have time to react. All he saw was my gun pointed at him, so he stayed still.

I flashed my badge and arrested Ray Newby and Joe Bass for the purse snatch. An ambulance took the older woman to the hospital, while I drove Newby and Bass to booking. Imagine taking two guys to the police department in a two-seater Corvette. It was tight. "Guys, you get one chance at this. Where's Debra, and how can I get in touch with her? The wrong answer could get you 20 years." Ray gave me a number to call, so while both of them were

## No Black Heroes

locked up at booking, I called Debra. "Debbie, its Ron Bailey. I can give you 30 minutes to come in. After that, I'll be coming to find you." Debra arrived at the front desk a short time later.

I went downstairs to get Newby when a gentleman called to me. "You must be Bailey, but where's your uniform?" "Excuse me, sir. Debra, go upstairs with the booking officer. I'll be up shortly." Debra blurted out, "I thought you were darker. I heard you were black." I turned to the older gentleman. "I'm sorry, but I didn't have a chance to put it on, sir. This was an off-duty thing. How can I help you?" "I heard the officer call your name to come downstairs. I'm Police Commissioner Larry Harris, but retired." "I had no idea there were black police commissioners, sir." "Oh, there are a few of us." I was curious about what he wanted. "Officer Bailey, I just wanted to ask, did this department cite you for the shoot-out in Pequonnock?" "Commissioner, I got something from the Guardians, but not the police department. Truthfully, I don't think I ever will." Commissioner Harris looked at me with a reassuring glare, "We'll see about that." He gave me his address and asked me to mail everything about the shooting to him.

I mailed all my paperwork, and a month later, Commissioner Harris sent me an invitation. "The Police Commissioners Association of Connecticut cordially invites you to their annual banquet, in honor of your outstanding achievement." It was the highest award an officer could receive in the state of Connecticut. Belcher and Holland also received their invitations and were stunned about the event. We showed up, still reeling about how the State Police Commissioners were honoring us, despite our own department ignoring it. An even greater surprised was Chief Walsh; who was there and presented us with the awards.

This time, the Connecticut Post came, took pictures and interviewed guests. Clearly, it was a black eye to the police department, if you asked me. Another organization honored us, but they had not. After dinner, Officers Belcher, Holland and I were requested to speak. They both declined, looking

## First Shooting; Black Officers Denied

to me. I shook my head but got up. I thanked everyone in attendance, especially Commissioner Larry Harris, for his efforts and the honor. The entire assembly of Commissioners stood up and applauded us. Commissioner Harris looked my way and gave me his wink of approval.

Curiously, not one Bridgeport officer showed up to the event. Even the police union that always attended to show support for an officer was a missing entity. That picture of how things really worked at a police department was very clear. African American officers were not worthy of departmental citations, and the police union was something we, as black officers, needed to look at. Before the event, Bernard told me that the banquet was discussed at the Guardians meeting. Since the Guardians' banquet was buried by the press, it was decided that the organization would stay out of it. The Guardians felt a better news story would appear, and it did. The newspapers printed a huge article with our pictures and awards. I guess the Ad Hoc couldn't stop that news article from going forward.

When I showed up to the clerk's office with a second award, the clerk again refused to take it. "Why not?" He had a smirk on his face. "The Bridgeport Police Department doesn't recognize awards from any organization except ours." "They are the POLICE Commissioners. Hello!" I then made my point, "Sergeant, let's have a heart-to-heart, shall we? If the police department won't recognize black officers' good work then how else can we get recognized?" He became infuriated and loud. "It has nothing to do with color, otherwise I'd be right there with you in federal court." "Okay. I think you need to know I'm not going to have this discussion every time I come here. If that citation isn't in my file today, tomorrow you will get papers. Then you'll have your chance to stand next to me in court." He snatched it off his desk. "I have copies if you need an extra. By the way, thank you for your support." I have to say, he was a nervy little bastard. He gave me the finger, and I kind of respected him for that.

Chapter 9

# Informant Out of Control

It was Sunday, and I was shopping at Bradlees Department Store. A woman approached me. "Are you a police officer?" "Yes, I am. How can I help you?" My first thought was, how she knew I was an officer. She spoke to me with fear in her voice, "I've been having problems with this guy. He won't leave me alone." She told me about her beatings and abuse. In the middle of me telling her how she could protect herself, a guy suddenly walked into the store. I glanced over and realized it was Cruz.

He looked around like he had lost someone. Our eyes locked and he stood there with the most intense stare I'd seen from him, ever. The girl panicked. "It's him, it's him." She walked away quickly without saying another word. "Hey, don't be afraid. He's not gonna do anything while I'm here. When I turned back, Cruz was gone. Can someone say "setup?"

The woman returned looking all around for Cruz. "Officer, that's the guy I was telling you about, Markis. He works for the state. We're both dead." "Miss, I know his name. Cruz is not gonna do anything to you or me." Before I could get her name, she rushed out of the store. I ventured outside to see her run across the lot and out of sight. It looked like she didn't have a car. Maybe Cruz was waiting around the corner for her. The plot thickened! I wasn't taking any chances and would file another report later.

Still faced with a multitude of unanswered questions, I sensed something was about to happen soon. With my life challenged to no end, I was outside Bradlees speaking to myself ever so faintly, "What in the world is going on? My department can't stand me. People out to get me. Am I gonna get killed for standing up for what I believe in?" An older black woman was moving slowly towards me; could she have heard what I had said? She stopped and looked right in my eyes, as if she knew me well. "Son, God hears you, and you will not be harmed. He told me to tell you that." I looked at this woman who had an aura of peace and wisdom about her. She had me so at ease, as if she were sent to calm me. "I'm sorry, Miss. I'm not crazy. Just beside myself, talking to myself, I guess." "No, son; God hears you." She smiled and walked away slowly, leaving a distinct certainty in her comments. Years later, as I reflected on our encounter, I knew in my heart that she had been sent to bring me a much-needed peace. I completely forgot about my worries and remembered Mom's teachings about God.

That night, I called Mom to tell her how much I appreciated her raising me. When I told her about the old woman, she responded, "Don't doubt God spoke to you, son. He did through someone you may never see again, but God did speak to you. I can rest now because no harm can come to you." I knew what was coming next. "I know you're not going to tell me what's wrong, but you need to go to church and thank him." "Mom. "You hear me, boy?" "Yes, mother."

The next Sunday, I was at church. The pastor's words seemed meant for me. "When God speaks to you, listen to him. He'll never let you down. You can walk through that valley of death and no harm can come to you. Victory is yours." This couldn't be a coincidence. What the old woman told me, and now the pastor!

I started to formulate the game changer to end the thing with Cruz. I asked a woman I'd met some time ago out on a date, Carmen Colon. She was excited to come out with me. I dropped rumors at the department about where I was going, club Gumby's. It had been weeks since I'd been there. Jan said she had not seen Cruz since the last time I was there. I wondered if this would work. We got to the club and Carmen wanted me to show her around. She didn't know it but she was about to become a witness.

Not ten minutes after I got there, he showed up. Cruz walked through the door with his usually brashness and the same guy who was with him the last time. His face looked so familiar, I knew I'd seen him before. I then realized it was Terry Griffin, brother to Bret and Rodney. The Griffin brothers were on the run for murder, including allegedly killing a witness. Their case made national news and added to Bridgeport's already notorious legacy. I surmised Cruz was working on Terry for the state police.

Again with the cold stare routine. Let's see if he'd go for the bait. Carmen and I took a walk to the car for a bit of fresh air. My plan was simple, to get Cruz outside. We walked toward the car and I glanced back. Griffin and Cruz were coming up behind me fast. "Carmen, get ready to move away from me." She looked confused, not sure what was going on. I turned, ready. "Bailey, what's up, you all right?" It was Officer George Vivo with a few more off-duty cop friends of his. They were standing just behind Cruz and Griffin who hadn't even seen them.

"George, I didn't know you were here. I thought the only police officer that goes to clubs was me." "We heard about Gumby's and figured why not. The department can't mess with all of us because we want to hang out. We're the new and improved." Cruz and Griffin turned and walked away quickly. "George, you guys just saved them from a serious ass-whipping." "Hey man, don't let us stop you. I heard

## No Black Heroes

about you and that Korean shit. Show us some moves. We won't say a word." I smiled at George. "Man, I'm out. Thanks for the cover." It would have been nice to read in the papers, "Cop Knocks Out Informant." The exposure would have forced him underground and away from me. Cruz didn't know how lucky he was. I was going to hurt him and Griffin really bad. I figured the more the damage, the bigger the news.

It was time to follow up on the rumor that Cruz worked for the State's Attorney's Office. I called and spoke with Inspector Spencer. "Inspector Spencer, hi, my name is Bailey. I was told Markis Cruz Majors works for you. Is he your informant?" Inspector Spencer hesitated, cleared his throat and asked who told me that. "Inspector, your guy is out of control, constantly threatening me. I'm not going to tolerate his nonsense much longer. If you want him to stay safe, I suggest you keep him away from me."

Inspector Spencer asked me to hold on. Guess he thought I was born yesterday. He was rigging the phone to record my conversation. He came back on and apologized for the interruption. He asked me again about who said Cruz was an informant." "Inspector, I called the Fairfield PD. They know about him. Do I have to blow this guy up to get him off me?" "Officer, did you say you were going to blow Mr. Majors up? I don't have anyone by that name working for me." "In that case, I apologize. If Cruz doesn't work for you then blowing him up won't be a problem."

Spencer didn't understand what the words "blow him up" meant. How could you be a cop and not know street language? I explained "blowing him up" meant exposing him as a snitch on the streets. "Officer Bailey, I advise you to let Chief Walsh know before you do something like that." "Inspector, Chief Walsh's life isn't in danger, mine is. If Cruz won't leave me alone I'll deal with it my way. The boyz in the 'hood will love to know about him." I thanked him and hung up. I stood there knowing Inspector Spencer took the bait.

## Informant Out of Control

I figured the phones would be ringing off the hook. There was no doubt Chief Walsh got a call from Inspector Spencer right after I hung up. Stacks and stacks of reports on Cruz and nothing. Let's see if they're paying attention now. It was time for a little trip to the record room to see if there were any interesting police reports on Cruz. Sure enough, he'd been arrested more times than anyone I'd ever seen, and all were dismissed. Time for some fun.

The list of drug arrests I made was long, but I remembered most of their names. I pulled out their arrest cards and jotted down their addresses. Grabbing the phone book I wrote down the locations of a few strip joints as well. Rita was watching me and wondered what I was up to .She was confused because I always had a smile, but not that time. After taking down a few more addresses, I started slamming things around. I even kicked the table for added attention.

Rita wanted to know, "Officer Bailey, what's wrong?" "Nothing, I have to get someone off my back. This place won't do it, so I will, my way." The workers in Records had never seen me like that before. They were very concerned. I had hoped word would spread that I was out of control in Records. I was hoping someone in the department would check and see what I had been doing there.

Rita called after I left. "Bailey, you scared the mess out of me. What's wrong?" "Sorry Rita, I'm working on something." She didn't understand but left it alone. The other workers in the record room did what I had hoped for. They were all talking about my losing it and slamming things around. It was my hope that some of the officers would get wind of it as well. Sure enough, word got around that I was out of control and taking down information from arrest cards. You didn't have to be a rocket scientist to know what it looked like, that I was about to send information on Cruz to local drug dealers and the strip joints where the most infamous bad boys hung out.

A few days passed, and without warning, Detective Mike Supple pulled me to the side. He was one of the few cops

## No Black Heroes

who really cared about other cops. "Bailey, the third floor knows you're about to expose some snitch. I thought you should know Sergeant Scanlon and Inspector Spencer are working with Cruz." I was curious. "Mike, how do you know that?" "I overheard Scanlon talking to Spencer on the phone. When he got off the phone, he spoke to the commander. The commander said you could be brought up on charges and maybe fired for exposing an informant." Mike had a serious look on his face. "Bailey, they know you were in the record room getting addresses. They know what you're up to." My little ruse worked. "If they're so concerned about Cruz, then they should pull him." Mike said he had a present for me and asked that I hold off on exposing the snitch for a week or two. I was totally confused by the "present" thing Mike was talking about but would wait and see. "Thanks Mike, I'm glad someone here knows this ain't right, what they're doing."

It had been two weeks and Cruz was nowhere to be found. My guess was the state pulled him, unsure of what I was up to. It was a real-life chess match. Then a letter came to my home with no return address. It was a picture of Cruz with the negative. On the back were the words, "State Informant Markis Cruz Majors." There was a note attached that said, "Make copies and send them out." Knowing the 'hood the way I did, I knew if those pictures got out, Cruz would be on the eleven o'clock news.

It was an ongoing turn of events. The new word on the streets was some guy telling people he was an undercover cop. What cop in his right mind would do that, expose himself? That didn't make any sense. "Describe him to me." "Bailey, he's tall, wears shades, and ..." "Stop right there. Cruz." Nice try. Cruz must have thought he could counter the claims he was a snitch by telling people he was an undercover. Undercover or not, no one was going to sell or deal with him. He was doing what I thought he would, making stupid moves.

Officer Best caught me in the hallway again. He looked a little encouraged. "Officer Bailey, can I talk to you, in confi-

## Informant Out of Control

dence of course? I got it from the third floor, unofficially, this Cruz thing would go away if you just tone it down." My only question was, "Tone down what?" I didn't understand. "Bailey, it's your comments, the combativeness, the supposedly white privilege you keep spouting. They would like the black and white rhetoric to stop. You're causing problems."

I had to assume some high-ranking official from the third floor figured there was no happy ending with what they thought I was up to. Why would they want to help me now, and how did Cruz get linked to the racial problems we were having? It sounded like they wanted me to back off, buying more time for Cruz. This didn't make sense. They must have known by then that the rumors about me weren't true. Something else was behind this and I wasn't buying it.

Al must have had some good connections on the third floor. Was it Chief Walsh, Assistant Chief Dominic Fugazzi, perhaps Deputy Chief John Bracy? Who was asking him to try to reason with me? No way was Cruz getting more time to do whatever they had assigned him. The peace offering was a stall. Two could play that game. "Al, let me think about it." "Bailey, these guys don't play. By the way, we didn't have this conversation."

The mystery of their fake peace offering had me reliving the nightmare my father had gone through. Decades had past, but racism still hounded me. Al's words were ringing in my ears. They wanted me to tone it down on the racial issues? Tired and deep in thought, I went home.

At the door was the greatest surprise of my life. Mom had come for a visit from Santee, South Carolina. "Mom, why didn't you tell me you were coming?" "I just wanted to see my only child and of course my grandbaby Little Ronnie." "I wish you had told me you were coming. Is everything alright?" "Boy, don't you worry none 'bout me, I'm just fine." I couldn't recall her ever showing up unannounced. It was odd.

**No Black Heroes**

"Where's Little Ronnie and your wife? Are they out shopping?" It was time to let her know, "Mom, Little Ron's mother and I aren't getting along. She stays at her mom's house. It's been an on and off relationship for some time now. I do have some good news. We're going to have a baby girl, but we both agreed, it's over. Thought you should know we're naming the baby after you, Ashley Lizbeth." She didn't say anything and just smiled. I guess it was too much for her to digest so suddenly. "I'll call so she can bring Little Ronnie over, Mom." She asked me one question, "Ronnie, you all right?" I couldn't tell her what was going on at the police department. I honestly didn't understand it myself. While talking about things; in popped Little Ronnie with his mother. "Little Ron's here."

Mom struggled but stood up from the chair with that big smile for her grandson. The phone rang. It was the police department offering me an overtime job. Mom looked at me like the mind reader she was. "Go to work boy, and make that money. I'll be just fine." "Are you sure?" "Get going, boy." I told the duty sergeant I'd take the job and come in. This was a last-minute opening, which meant Cruz would most likely not know I was working or where. It seemed strange that Mom wanted me out of the house, but I figured she just wanted to relax with Little Ron.

What should have been an eight-hour job turned into 12. Radio called, "Officer Bailey, report to patrol, now." "10-4." Now what? Taped to a door at patrol was an envelope with my name on it. I opened it cautiously, "There was a call of an emergency at home. Radio has been told you're off for the night." I called home, and my ex-wife-to-be told me Mom wasn't feeling well. "I'm on my way." Damn, the guys in patrol hate me so much they couldn't even tell me I had an emergency at home?

Something felt wrong. I took off my gear and stored it. By the time I got home, an ambulance was there. "Officer Bailey, we don't think there is anything serious to worry about, but we are taking Mrs. Bailey to the hospital as a precaution." They took her out of the house wearing an

# Informant Out of Control

oxygen mask. It was strange how she wasn't afraid. What was she hiding behind that look of strength that she didn't want me to see? Mom, I'm sure everything will be fine. I'll be right there, okay?" She reached out with her hand, but there was no strength in it. We just kind of touched each other.

I told myself everything would be fine. Having convinced myself, I went in the house to change my clothes. I was just about out the door when the phone rang. It was at that point I felt a distinct feeling of loss. I should've gone straight to the hospital when I first came home. I picked up the phone. "Mr. Bailey, we need you to come to the hospital, sir." "What's wrong, what happened?" They wouldn't tell me anything, other than I needed to come.

The drive to the hospital was calm, without urgency. I had been a cop too long and knew what that call was about. When I arrived, a nurse was standing there waiting, "Are you Mr. Bailey?" "Where is she?" "Mr. Bailey, we need to speak with you in private." "Nurse, no offense but I've been a cop for years. I'm alright. Where is my mother, please?" "The nurse then knew she couldn't soften the blow and walked me into the room. "Do you need anything, Officer?" "I'll be fine, thanks." She walked out of the room and pulled the curtains. Mom looked so at peace, like she was taking a nap.

I looked at her. "You always knew how to keep me from things that could hurt me. You knew you were leaving. Why didn't you tell me?" I looked up, "God, who do I talk to now?" With one last look, I leaned over and gently kissed her on the cheek. Back home I hugged Little Ronnie. He wanted to know where his Grandma was. I had no words for him.

Doctor Joseph Williams called me a few days later. "Officer Bailey, your Mom had heart problems. She wanted to see you and wouldn't listen. I asked her not to take that trip, but she said you were all that mattered, and her grandbaby." "Thanks, Doc, I guess she outsmarted me

## No Black Heroes

again." The funeral home prepared her for the trip back south. I had her flown back and drove with my cousin Bill and Little Ron.

On our way to bury her, Bill wanted to drive and give me a break. We got stopped by a North Carolina state trooper. Bill was only doing five miles above the speed limit. When the trooper came over, I introduced myself. "Trooper, I'm an officer from Connecticut, I'm on my way to bury my mother. If you could give him a break I would really appreciate it." I gave the trooper my badge and identification. He went to his car, and then returned. He handed me my badge and papers. "Sorry about your mother, Mr. Bailey. Here's your ticket, Mr. Lary." He looked at me one more time, "By the way, y'all have a nice car. Have a nice day." His comment about my car was his nasty way of saying he didn't care if I was a cop or not. Bill looked at me, "I know you have a lot of anger in you, but don't let this get to you."

"Bill, did you understand the meaning of his calling me Mister Bailey? In other words I'm not a police officer to him. And the "nice car" comment? I'm burying my mother and that was his final comment to me?" "Cuz, I know what he said was messed up, but this is not the time." It was the worst time in my life, and my so-called brother officer couldn't have cared less. The stuff they taught us at the academy was bull. Brother officers? A brother would never treat his kin like that. That's a bullshit term for them to use when they need us.

We buried Mom on a sunny Thursday morning at the Old Oak Grove Cemetery in Santee. Little Ronnie was so young, like me when my Dad passed. He didn't understand everything but knew his Grandma was lying still, in a gorgeous dress. Thank God for Aunt Pearl, who dressed her. Mom looked beautiful.

I returned home thinking hard on Mom's advice during my younger days. She wanted me to always be honest and stand up for what I believed in. Reality was setting in, and her words were what I'd continue to use to take on anyone

### Informant Out of Control

who tried to hold me back, or treat me different, with God as my witness.

Back home, there were cards and a fruit basket from the Guardians. Curiously, the police union didn't send a thing. Not ready to be around anyone, I stayed to myself for a few weeks. Willie called to let me know he had a friend he wanted me to meet. It was a surprise, and it had been a while, so I figured I'd give it a shot. When I got to Gumby's, Carmen was there hanging out with Willie and another woman, Maggie Sanchez. Both somehow knew about my mother, and they told me how sorry they were. I leaned over to Willie, "Maggie Sanchez?" He smiled, "I thought the name would get your attention."

Maggie was the cousin of Mariano Sanchez. Before I could get a chance to talk to Maggie, Carmen asked me to dance. After my dance with Carmen I returned to the bar with Willie. While Carmen was in the bathroom, Maggie slipped me her number. "Call me when you have time. We have a lot to talk about." "I will." With all the fun I was having, it dawned on me, Cruz wasn't anywhere to be found. I guess the powers that be didn't know I had returned from South Carolina.

Both girls were feeling their drinks. "Bailey, if you're a good boy I'll buy you some chocolate milk." I had to smile at that one. Maggie chimed in, "Yeah Bailey, if you're real good we can both give you some chocolate milk." Did I just get an invitation from two women? It was time to go home.

A few days later, I returned to work. A call came over the radio, "Officer Bailey, meet the complainant at Kossuth by Kolbe Cathedral High School." "10-4." I drove to Kolbe and saw my girl Margie. She had been on drugs for years and that was her spot. I had always been respectful to her, and even kidded with her that if only I had enough money to take her out. She would tell me I couldn't afford her. I couldn't imagine why she wanted to meet with me.

**No Black Heroes**

"Hey Bailey, I know your son goes to the school across from Kolbe. I see you dropping him off every day. I called you because that guy Cruz has been watching your son when he's on the playground." "What?" "I just wanted you to know. You've always been good to us girls out here." "How do you know Cruz?" "He's been having sex with a few of us girls and tells us it's on the house because he's a cop. He's been asking about you, and we know he doesn't like you. We hate him but what can we do?" "Marge, thanks for looking out. By the way, Cruz ain't no cop. He's a paid snitch." "For real? That motherfucker! Bailey, I know you're pissed but don't do anything that could get you in trouble. You're the only friend we got out here." I turned and walked away, but she called to me one last time, "Bailey, babe. Shit." She knew I was furious. I wasn't filing a report this time. Cruz had crossed the line. No one would convict me; he's messing with my kid. I dropped rumor at the department that I'd be hanging out at Gumby's. I hoped Cruz would take the bait.

When I got there, Willie was at the bar laughing at some of Jan's jokes. Carmen and Maggie snuck up behind me. They both had a glass of chocolate milk for me. Now that I think about it, where did they get it from? Carmen asked, "Which one of us are you going to take the milk from first?" Oh my God. Willie was sipping on a juice when he started choking and spit some out. My mouth was wide open, not knowing what to say. I was waiting on Cruz to come, but he never showed. Where was that fool? Figures, the one time I was ready for him he didn't show. The Almighty was protecting one of us!

Chapter 10

## THE FIRST TACTICAL NARCOTICS TEAM

I was at home trying to get my thoughts together. My mother's death was still on my mind. The front-page news was a shocker. "Church Broken Into, Drugs Left Behind." That was crazy. Someone broke into a church and placed cocaine in the bathroom. Reportedly, scrawled on the bathroom wall was, "It's on us." A pastor of the church on Colorado Avenue said the local drug dealers from Clinton Avenue did it. He had asked them to not sell drugs by his church. Sanchez and his Number One Family crossed the line.

The public was outraged and demanded action. There was so much press Chief Walsh was forced to form an emergency unit to deal with the drug problems in Bridgeport. It would be the first Tactical Narcotics Team (TNT). Sergeant Joe Convintito was chosen to man the unit and oversee the selection process. The word was no one was going into that unit unless you were willing to do whatever it took to shut down the drug trade.

## No Black Heroes

Sergeant Convintito also made it clear that no one was going in the unit by seniority. With the recent public outcry for action, not even the union had a say in the process. The FBI and DEA were all over the city looking to take Sanchez out. The Statewide Narcotics Task Force had tried to put a dent in Sanchez' empire using Chase, but so far nothing was working.

I didn't put in for TNT thinking they would turn me down anyway. After all, I was giving the department a hard time. Why would they select me? Imagine my surprise when Sergeant Convintito called me at home. "Officer Bailey, I have an opening for you in the new Tactical Unit. You interested?" "Yes I am, Sergeant. But you may want to think about this. I'm not very popular." "Bailey, come see me tomorrow."

At his office he said I was needed on the team. "Bailey, I heard all the things going on with you. Guess what, I could give a shit. Chief Walsh wants this Sanchez thing shut down and he doesn't care how. He just wants results." "Sarge, if you want me, I'm in." "Just one thing Officer Bailey, there's no black and white here. If anyone gives you a problem let me know and they're out." "Fair enough, Sarge."

The élite.

It was our first lineup. "Gentlemen, the first few days you're going to walk parts of the city so people can see us." With the all-new black tactical uniforms, we needed to be seen first. That way no one could say we were not identifiable police officers. A few days later, Sergeant Convintito called the news to let them know we were about to officially start. He then introduced the team to Sergeant Leonard Samatulski who was

## The First Tactical Narcotics Team

assigned an alternate schedule when Sergeant Convintito would be off duty.

At our private lineup, we were given information on several drug gangs reported to the department. The list was long; the Terminators, the Jones Family, Holmans, Jeffersons, Rodgers, the Bush Mob, and Mariano Sanchez and his Number One Family. There were others, but we were to focus on them. "Guys, you have more work out there than you can imagine. We will get to as many of these guys as we can. Go out and get 'em."

We came out of lineup and were met with a group of journalists and photographers. Sergeant Convintito named the target. "Gentlemen, our first hit for this unit will be the Panic. We're going to do a Rambo and see what shakes." One of the news guys asked what a Rambo was. "A roll-up." One of our team members devised the Rambo as a scare tactic. When you rolled up on someone holding, they would throw down the drugs and run. After the throw, all you had to do was catch them. We saddled up and headed out.

We hit building 25. All cars had four officers each. We drove in fast, with tires screeching for effect. Before we were out someone yelled, "Five-O, Narcs, Five-O." He was looking left, right and behind him. Trying to warn the drug dealers, he yelled again, "Five-O over here, Five-O over there, Five-O everywhere!" I had to laugh at his we were everywhere shout.

Everyone standing in the courtyard looked like deer in headlights. They were frozen for a moment, then their senses kicked in, and they took off running. I looked to my left and saw Reggie Upchurch heading towards Crescent Street. Reggie was the new legend in the Panic no one could catch.

It was a madhouse with cops and dealers running all over the place. Reggie saw me and picked up his pace. Man, was he fast. He ran the length of three buildings and looked back with me closing in. Still running, he ducked into a

## No Black Heroes

hallway and into an apartment. I could see the last bit of light from the slight opening of the door before it closed. That was when a woman screamed. "Get out, who are you? Get out of my apartment!" I pushed the door open. The woman was pointing to the bathroom. I kicked the door open. Reggie was standing there out of breath, flushing the toilet. He had the nerve to be fixing his pants like he had just gotten up from the toilet. "That had to be the fastest dump ever, Reg." He smiled nervously. "Come on Bailey, when you gotta go, ya gotta go."

"Reggie, are you out of your mind? This is a burglary." I put Reggie up against the wall, cuffed him and looked into the toilet. Still floating were six packets of cocaine. "Reggie, I got bad news, bro. Not all your stuff made it out. You're under arrest for burglary, possession of narcotics with intent to sell, and tampering with evidence." "Bailey, come on, man." On the way out of the house the woman yelled at Reggie, "Stay out of my house! From now on I'm keeping my door locked." Ya think?

Sergeant Convintito was frantic. Everyone had reported back to their cars. I was missing and hadn't answered the radio. "Sergeant Convintito, I'm on the way back with one." Back at the drop-off, the cameras and crews were waiting. I explained to Sergeant Convintito what happened. "Outstanding arrest, Bailey." It was a bit of a let-down to the news with just one arrest, but they printed it. They were looking for more. The other team members came up empty that night. Reggie Upchurch had the honor of being TNT's first drug arrest.

After that, the news backed off. They had their story. We needed to get busy with the drug trade. Bridgeport was drug-infested with over 150,000 people looking for relief. The complexion of the city was now turning more minority-based on its racial makeup. Drugs and shootings were in every section of town except Black Rock, the home of the wealthy. TNT was averaging about five arrests a night. The third floor was pleased with our efforts but was asking for more.

## The First Tactical Narcotics Team

The Rambo roll-ups were becoming stale. Street dealers were getting wise to that routine. They were now stashing the drugs instead of holding onto them. Sergeant Convintito, looking for new ideas, asked, "Officer Tony Brown, you did this kind of work before when you were a housing officer. What do you think?" "Hey Sarge, have one of these guys go out and do a surveillance. Set up on a drug spot and watch until we get something." It was a great idea, but easier said than done. Surveillance in the projects meant one of us had to sneak into a spot, set up and stay there without being seen. No matter how you sliced it, no one white was going to sneak into a drug spot in Bridgeport. That was not an option. Drugs were run in the streets by blacks and Latinos. Anyone white came from the suburbs to buy and get out. That's just how it was.

Most of the team was new, except for a few seasoned cops who enjoyed that kind of work. The older guys wanted nothing to do with sneaking into anything. Sergeant Convintito asked for volunteers while looking at Carwin and me. We could definitely sneak in, if done right. We looked at each other, nodded, and agreed to do it.

Word was getting around in the 'hood that TNT was no joke. At lineups Sergeant Convintito had a list of drug spots he got from our tip line. It was going to be hard to sneak two officers into a surveillance spot. People tend to look at who doesn't belong in the project, especially two walking in together. The Sergeant wasn't taking any chances on a one-man surveillance though. Carwin devised a plan to take another route, but in order to make it work, we needed unmarked cars.

Jim's Auto was the exclusive towing company for the police department. We went to him asking for his help, and he thought we had lost our minds. "Jim, the stolen cars you take in, can we use them until the owners comes for them?" He paused for a long moment, "Sure, but if you get into an accident, it's your ass. I don't want to know nothing." We didn't have undercover cars, so we had to improvise. It was my idea and Carwin loved it.

## No Black Heroes

We set up our surveillance spot close to the dealers. In a stolen car, it looked natural to be there. I never knew how but everybody in the streets knew the stolen cars. If they spotted one, it meant nothing to them. Our takedown cars were hidden on the border of our surveillance spots, and Carwin did the driving while I conducted the surveillance. It was easy at first. "TNT, we got a black male at the corner of building seven in the Panic, wearing blue jeans, a black pullover shirt and white sneakers. His stash is in a brown paper bag by the clothesline pole."

Once we saw where the stash was hidden, we called the chase units in. They came in from every direction you could run, so no one got away. Every site we surveyed was mapped out before we set up. A few of the dealers tried to play it off when we came in, by walking away slowly. They didn't run because the drugs weren't on them, but we knew where they were.

It was a nightly event. "Bailey on, we got a paper bag with about 40 vials, we got a potato chip bag with about 25 vials, and it looks like we got 15 bags of marijuana stuffed in an old sock." "Bailey on, we have several bundles of coke stashed under a milk crate." Then after the arrests, "Tac unit to base with one." We were making great arrests, but the numbers still weren't hurting the drug trade.

I decided to try something new. I went to look at surveillance equipment. The police department didn't have what we needed, so I bought my own. Carwin was in the car when I pulled out a 50 x 100 spotting scope. The military used them for spotting gunshot hits on the range. I was going to use it to spot drug sales. "Where did you get that thing?" "From the military surplus, and you can see what's in a person's hand from three blocks. I tested it today, just to make sure."

Before lineup, I went to see both Sergeants. "Hey Sarge, instead of one dealer, can we try taking out a whole crew?" "What do you mean, Bailey?" "We can take out a few buyers, then the dealers. If we see who's holding the money, we

## The First Tactical Narcotics Team

can take them too." They weren't too sure what I was talking about, so I laid it out. "If we arrest one buyer with drugs, we have the dealer on a sale. So he's done. Then we can take our time looking at the whole operation. We wait and see where the drugs are, who takes the money and maybe get a gun or two. We can take down whole operations on the charge of conspiracy. If two or more are working together, it's a criminal enterprise, they all go." Both Sergeants liked the idea. "Sounds like a plan, Bailey. Let's go with it."

At lineup we told the team about our plan. "The key is you guys need to stay hidden. When we call out a buyer, try to take them down out of the area. That's a sale." Officer Ray asked why we would mess with nasty drug users. "I need time to take out the whole set. The buyer will make my case, so we can shut the whole thing down." Some of the guys looked confused, but I was sure it would work.

The TNT motto: To Protect, Serve, and Shut 'Em Down!

On the first couple of surveillances, I took it slow. We took out a few buyers, and then arrested the dealer and money man. The conspiracy charges had the court prosecutor in heaven. The cases were always pleaded out instead of going to trial. With five or six counts of sale on you, what choice did you have?

Once the team got accustomed to the new system, we started making more arrests than the court could handle. Cases increased from one dealer to about 15 arrests each. The court began having special sessions on weekends to keep up. Sometimes we were so backed up on arrests the Sergeant would call over the air, "Hey Bailey, that's enough. We have no more room in here." "Okay Sarge, we're coming in. Any of you guys free? We have the dealer in sight."

Chapter 11

# Mariano Sanchez and More

In five months, we made over 1,100 arrests. It was an amazing record, even by larger city standards. New York contacted us on our success and sent two police officers for a ride-along, to see how we did business. And they were impressed. TNT was knee-deep in street arrests, but we still hadn't taken steps to go after the Number One Family and Sanchez.

Sanchez was so far ahead of the game, he was becoming untouchable. Billy Chase was still on assignment but couldn't get close enough to Sanchez. Statewide had a few informants buy and bring back Sanchez' product, and Chase said it tested better than anywhere in the state. Most cocaine tests resulted in a pale blue color; Sanchez' were so dark blue, they looked purple. We had never seen cocaine test at that level before. He must have had one of the best cooks in the business mixing his stuff. No wonder everyone was going crazy for his coke.

## No Black Heroes

My nephew Benji saw me downtown and waved to me. He seemed afraid. "Uncle Ronnie, this guy was on the block saying you're a crooked cop. He started asking Big Red a lot of questions about you, and said the Family shouldn't trust you." "What did Red say?" "Nothing. Sanchez told us to stay away from the guy. He hasn't been out there for some time, but now he's back. He's dark skinned, tall and always has on these shades." "Cruz. Cruz is back." "Who's that, Unk?" "Benji, stay away from that guy. He's dangerous."

Word travels in the streets fast. I hadn't heard from Suzie or her cousin Maggie in a while. Both called and had the same thing to say, "Hey Bailey, that guy Markis Cruz is on the block badmouthing you. He swears you work for Sanchez." I was thinking Sanchez was smart and must have known Cruz was a snitch. Keep your enemies close, I guess. I thanked both girls and asked them to please keep me up on that fool. They both wanted to know when we could hang out again.

It was becoming clear that Cruz was trying to link me to the Sanchez family. If Cruz could manage even a few people to buy into it, true or not, he could make good on his setup attempts. That was what it seemed to be about for him; he wanted me to appear crooked, so the department could finish me off. At least I had a better idea about what the police department was up to, but why was the state so obsessed with me?

I called Chase. "My brother, you need to tell the state to pull Cruz. He's making things worse out on the block. They're not gonna sell him shit." Chase pretended he didn't have a clue what I was talking about. "Chase, this department needs to stop the nonsense. I don't sell drugs. Cruz is a liar. If I were a drug dealer, wouldn't I have money and could just leave this place?" Chase laughed, "Yeah, that does make sense."

Just for the heck of it I told Chase I knew he was investigating me. I asked if I could help end this by cooperating with him. He was good; I'll say that much for him. "Wait a

## Mario Sanchez and More

minute, Bailey. I don't do cops. That's not my job." "Chase, before you try to defend yourself—look, if anyone is going to investigate me, I'm glad it's you. That way I know it'll be someone telling the truth." He didn't say anything, so I told him to do his thing.

On the streets, drug dealers were saying my name with a passion. "Hey man, this Narc Bailey is out here. He ain't no joke." Most of the dealers in the Panic knew me. The rest of the city hadn't seen me, except for the Sanchez family. The question from most on the streets was, "Who is this Narc Bailey?" I answered by having my people spread more rumors on the streets. "Bailey is this big tall black cop. The brother is huge." It bought me some time for what I was planning for the streets next.

Carwin got injured and was out of work, so Sergeant Convintito had a new team doing surveillance; Officer Tom Brophy and Officer Ray Muñiz were trying their hands at surveillance. It was extremely hard for them to sneak into the projects. They just stood out! Only one white family lived in all the projects combined, and it wasn't them.

I asked Sergeant Convintito if I could go it alone, and he was not happy with my request. "Sarge, I can handle myself. I have a few targets I'm looking at." "Okay Bailey, but for God's sake, be careful." The cardinal rule had always been no one-man surveillance. It was risky, but I was sure I could do it.

My first target going it alone was Bernard "Sasquatch" Johnson. Sasquatch was the biggest guy on the block in Pequonnock apartments, maybe even the city. He was as sneaky as they came. We were not going to catch him outside selling. I took a shopping cart from a nearby lot, put some old loose papers in it, tightened my hoodie down, and walked into the project. I was able to sneak in with no one suspecting. If Sergeant Convintito found out I was in the buildings alone, there would've been hell to pay.

## No Black Heroes

Once in, I positioned the carriage up against a wall and walked up the stairs, listening for voices as I went up. Someone was on the sixth floor making a sale, so I slowly peeked around the corner. It was Sasquatch with some black kid. He was taking the kid's money and giving back several vials. I snuck back to the stairwell and called out the description of the kid he sold to. Looks like the buyers were getting younger and younger. I had to quickly run down to the floor below, to see what car the buyer got into. By the end of the night, we had several sales on Sasquatch, but my legs were done from all the running.

As Sasquatch headed to the elevator, I called the team, but they were on arrests. I ran down the stairs and watched him get off the elevator. I had hoped he would hang around downstairs, but he was walking for Marina Apartments, just one block away. I figured he was on his way to sell, or maybe to pick up more stuff. Either way, we needed to arrest him before he got away. I called one more time over the air to let the team know I was out following the target, Sasquatch. "Guys, I'm out on Broad Street following Sasquatch."

Walking behind him with the all-black uniform, even with a hoodie, didn't fool Sasquatch. He looked back several times then took off. There was no time to call for help. I caught up to him in Marina near the kid's playground. He took a swing at me, missing my chin. I leaned back away from his punch, while simultaneously kicking him to the back of his left leg. He wobbled while trying to punch me again. I hit him in the same spot with another kick, and his leg gave way. Down he went.

I jumped on top of him in an effort to keep him from getting back up. He pushed himself up off the ground with me on his back, like I was nothing but a light nuisance. Man, Sasquatch was strong! With a twisting motion, he threw me off his back. I recovered, got back up, and punched him in his temple with a knuckle punch. Down in the sand by the swings he went. "Bailey, I'm sorry. I just don't want to go back to jail." "How da hell you know me?" "I don't, but eve-

## Mario Sanchez and More

rybody out here heard about you and that jiu-jitsu karate shit. I thought you were darker." "Yeah, I get that a lot."

Sergeant Convintito was not pleased to hear I got out of the car. He was surprised to see how Sasquatch looked after our fight. He joked a little, "Mr. Johnson, did you run into a wall?" Sasquatch didn't say anything. "Officer Bailey, in my office, please." Sergeant Convintito was a little upset. "Bailey, you're my best officer, but please don't do that again. What if you got hurt or we couldn't find you?" "I know, Sarge. I just didn't want him to get away." He was right; I had to be more careful out there alone.

The next day, Bernard "Sasquatch" Johnson's arrest was in the papers. As I came into work, I saw Officer Vic. "Bailey, why are you hanging with drug dealers? You're sleeping with the enemy." "Didn't we have this conversation?" I countered? "But just to be clear, if I had to choose, I'd hang out with them over someone like you, anytime. I can trust them, unlike some cops I know." "You're an asshole, Bailey." "Yeah Vic, and some people will do anything to belong. You get your Klan card yet? Ya little shit."

Officer Vic stormed off, just as a good-looking woman came in asking for me. She said her name was Melody McKay and she could help me with the drug trade. I took her to the back office. After speaking with her, it was obvious she had connections all throughout Bridgeport. She provided me with details about people she knew, where they sold, their girlfriends, and even where some kept their stuff. It was astounding to me that she knew every drug dealer's address and what they sold.

I wanted to sign her up so she could get paid, but she refused and said she had her reasons. Melody didn't trust anyone but felt her identity would be safe with me. I told her from that point on she would be referred to as M&M. She laughed at her new name and we exchanged numbers. It was odd that she didn't want to get paid like all the other informants. Maybe she just wanted to help Bridgeport get its act together, so people could be safe. I was certain her reasons for wanting to work for me would be revealed later. I kept M&M a secret from the department. Since she wasn't a paid informant, no one could force me to expose who she really was. From the names she threw at me, she was clearly going to make a huge difference in my work.

I started working her on a few small cases, so the court could get used to hearing the name M&M. That was how to transform a new informant into a reliable source, through a history of accurate information on cases. Time after time, she was right on target. Her only concern was that if anyone found out what she was doing, she could end up dead. No one knew who she was, and I promised her no one would ever know.

M&M called and asked me to meet with her. I went to P.T. in one of those stolen cars Jim had. She looked out the window of a friend's apartment and signaled with a nod. We met at the nun's convent a block over from the project. Why would someone build a convent by a housing project? M&M told me a few things, and then explained how she knew all the drug dealers in Bridgeport. She had a business that catered to them. When she told me what it was, it all made since. She said she was tired of the shootings, drugs, and kids being killed. It was then evident why she was helping me; she cared about the community.

M&M changed the subject and told me something that surprised me. "Bailey, I called you because there's a tall man with shades that comes out here asking about you. He's been in P.T. several times. Yesterday he told one of the guys from the Terminators you take money off the streets and keep it." My thoughts immediately went to how the department had used their stall tactics for Cruz. Bailey, if you tone it down on the race issues, we will make sure that Cruz becomes a memory. There he was back to his old tricks again. "Do me a favor and spread the word. That guy's a snitch." "Are you sure?" "Bae, it's time to let the dogs loose." She called a few days later to tell me the boys shot at him. "Good."

## Mario Sanchez and More

I sent a written request to Chief Walsh's office asking for protection for my family. I let them know I was forced to take my son Ronnie out of school because Cruz had been watching him a while back. After the reports were sent upstairs, Detective Bureau called me in. Finally! Chief Walsh ordered Lieutenant DeCarlo to contact Cruz and the State Police. After Lieutenant DeCarlo cussed me out over the candy bar thing, he said he had spoken with Cruz and his attorney. "Bailey, they're saying you have problems with drugs." "Then why don't they come get me and stop the nonsense? Someone is gonna get hurt."

Lieutenant DeCarlo asked me to sit down. Cruz made a formal statement that I sold drugs and was sleeping with kids." "Lieutenant, I couldn't care less what that man says. The state would've arrested me by now if that were true. I need protection, and someone needs to stop running interference for this guy." "Who saw Cruz by your son's school?" "I'm not telling anyone about people looking out for me, so Cruz can go after them. The street is the only place that has my back." Lieutenant DeCarlo told me he couldn't do anything because Cruz hadn't broken any laws. "You guys should just shake hands and leave each other alone." I responded with a sharp one-liner, "Yeah, I got something he can shake."

Before leaving the Bureau, I left them with something to think about. "Because this place has refused to protect my family, if anything happens, I will hold the department and state responsible. This guy has been by my house, my son's school, and is following me around. It's documented." Lieutenant DeCarlo asked me, "Who saw him at your home?" "My next-door neighbor, retired Officer Sam Palmer. Remember him? He's a legend." The Lieutenant was surprised but had his same old line, "Just stay away from him, Bailey. Just stay away."

It was time to send a message. "Hey Lieutenant, do me a favor. Could you pass word to Cruz, he needs to stay out of P.T.? They're looking for him." "What are you talking about, Bailey?" "If you get word to Cruz, he'll know what I'm talk-

## No Black Heroes

ing about. Oh, if you could add this phrase, 'Fame can kill ya'." I was sure they would tell him what I said. That meant Cruz would be pissed, and blame me for his being shot at in P.T. He would come after me, and I was counting on it.

I was sneaking around Bridgeport in an unmarked looking for drug activity, when there he was. Cruz was with some guy in his car, probably another drug boy he was trying to get info from. I called for a patrol car and had him pulled over. I knew Cruz didn't have a license, so I wanted to push him a bit. Once the patrol car stopped him, I parked where no one could see me and walked over. "Mr. Cruz, where's your license?" He didn't answer, as I wrote and gave him a ticket for driving under suspension. The bulging vein on his forehead said it all, when I handed him his ticket.

"The great Officer Bailey. I'll have this taken care of just like all the others, you asshole." "Mr. Cruz, if your friend has a license, he can drive the car." "Hey, Bailey, I told you my name, it's Markis." Cruz switched sides with his passenger. "Have a great day, and please get your license." Cruz then yelled to some people nearby that he was being harassed. I laughed as I walked back to my car and disappeared.

Cruz didn't waste any time in filing his complaint with the Office of Internal Affairs (OIA). I received a notification from OIA informing me about his complaint. I was ordered to stay away from Markis Cruz Majors. I called them immediately. "Let me get this right, you want me to let Cruz drive without a license?" Detective Tony Paul was on the phone and had no answer to my question. "I didn't think so." I hung up abruptly. Anyone who went to bat for Cruz was no friend of mine.

Leak called me from his job at the cab company. "Hey man, Cruz is in the office telling everyone he's going to get you. What are you doing about this guy? I told you he's dangerous." "Leak, I got this, trust me." I hung up but called back. I asked to speak with the owner of the cab

## Mario Sanchez and More

company. I told him Cruz didn't have a license to drive. "If you continue to let Cruz drive, I'll have no choice but to call the Department of Motor Vehicles. They will shut you down." Leak called me back and said Cruz just got let go. He said the owner told Cruz it was because of me that he had to let him go. "Good, things are heating up for 'Mr. Untouchable' Cruz."

I went about my regular routine knowing Cruz would be looking for me. I was downtown getting my morning paper, and there he came, but his friend was driving for him. I smiled, turned, and started talking to some of the guys on the corner. Cruz had his friend pull over to the curb. "You're a fucking asshole, Baileeee; I'm going to get you." I turned around and spoke loudly enough for everyone to hear. "How's a lowlife paid snitch like you going to get me? You're a joke." With nothing left for him to say, I lifted my hand where I had hidden a small camera and snapped his picture before he had time to cover up. The guys on the corner all started to stare closely at Cruz. The driver had to hold Cruz back so he couldn't get out. "Hey, you can let him out. It's a Kodak moment." I went home to wait for the call.

The phone was ringing before I could get in. It was Detective Paul again. "Officer Bailey, you have to bring in the—" I hung up on him. He called back. "Did you hang up on me?" "What do you want? I don't want to talk to you." "Did you take Markis Majors' picture? You have to turn in the picture and negative." "There's no law that says someone can't take pictures in a public place. Don't call here again unless you're interested in going to federal court with me. Harassment of an African American officer is something I'm sure the court would want to hear." I hung up again. The department's next move was not completely unexpected. The commander of the Detective Bureau called me in, and I was ordered to meet with Agent Graham of the FBI.

When I got there, not one Ad Hoc Committee member was in sight. Nothing like watching crooked cops hide. That

## No Black Heroes

made my day. Agent Graham greeted me and got right to the point. He wanted me to tell him everything I knew about my nephew Benji, Sanchez, and the Number One Family. I figured word would get around eventually that Benji was family. The FBI was asking about him. There was no doubt in my mind it was all tied in to Cruz' accusations of me being crooked. I told Agent Graham all I knew, but it wasn't much. Suzie and Maggie Sanchez didn't know a hell of a lot. I sensed he didn't know about Maggie, so there was no need to expose her. Benji, on the other hand, never told me anything about Sanchez. He refused to admit he was a part of his drug family. Agent Graham asked me about my relationship with Suzie. "So far she's not telling me much. She did slip and tell me Sanchez has investments in Puerto Rico, something about a small mall he owns."

"Officer Bailey, you should be careful who you date and hang out with. Why are you out on Clinton when you're not working?" "Agent Graham, I'm trying to get my nephew Benji off the block. He's family, you know that. As for the girls, you do know they can be a great source of information. But that takes time. If you push it, they back off." I told him what I could, careful not to mention everyone who gave me information out there. They were people who trusted me, and I was determined to protect them. I was later told that Agent Graham didn't believe I told him everything.

What the FBI didn't know was that Sanchez had another sister, Maria Sanchez. Maria and I met while cashing my checks at the bank where she was a teller. I noticed her last name and joked that she must be related to Mariano. She said yes, I'm his sister. Without hesitation, I invited her to lunch. Maria didn't have any real connections to the Sanchez organization. He was her brother and that was it. She did say that once she held something in her house for him. It was the one time, because Sanchez was desperate for her help, but never again. I believed her. It was scary enough telling the FBI I was tight with Suzie Sanchez, no way was I going to tell them about another Sanchez sister and their

## Mario Sanchez and More

cousin Maggie. They would have thought I was some kind of a pimp or something!

It had been several weeks since my meeting with Agent Graham, and Cruz had not been seen for a while. With him off my back, I could try to do some damage to Sanchez' Number One Family. I just hoped Benji wouldn't be out there. I wasn't looking forward to arresting him. I kept reminding myself that, before her death, I promised his mother I would watch over him. I'm sure my arresting him was not what she had in mind.

I used one of Jim's stolen cars and drove out to Clinton. The Number One Family was getting bolder. They were selling drugs in the middle of the street, and the lookouts were sitting on a stoop smoking joints. Everyone in law enforcement was obsessed with getting Sanchez, but no one had arrested any of his people to date. TNT had been told to stand down, and I suspected it had something to do with Cruz and the rumors. I convinced Sergeant Samatulski to let me take a shot at getting some of Sanchez' people.

Mariano Sanchez' home turf.

Sergeant Samatulski was hesitant but decided to take a chance. "How do you know they're selling out there?" "Sarge, I just went by in an unmarked and saw for myself." "Alright Bailey, but if you mess this up, it's my ass." Carwin was still out injured, so he assigned Officer Judy Tesla to go out with me. Sergeant Samatulski looked worried. "Hey Sarge, I'll make you a household name, trust me." "That's what I'm afraid of, Bailey." He laughed and told me to get my ass out there.

Before leaving, I showed him a map I drew of Clinton Avenue and the surrounding streets. Sanchez' people had scanners and were monitoring our channel, so they always

## No Black Heroes

knew where we were. "Sarge, when I go on the air, I'll tell the team I'm in P.T. housing projects. The Family will think we're there, instead of watching Clinton Avenue. I also changed the street names to numbers, which would confuse them. They would keep hearing P.T. thinking that's where we were. "Looks like you have this all planned out, Bailey." I asked Sergeant Samatulski to hand out the maps and give the team the plan, before heading out.

On Clinton, there were way too many lookouts to watch them from a car. I needed to be out there awhile, watching the entire block and side streets. We went to the Rent-a-Space storage center. It was across the elevated railroad tracks, one block from Clinton Avenue. Judy looked confused. "How did you know about this place?" "I've been here several times, watching these guys getting ready for this day. I didn't tell anyone because word has a way of getting out."

I set my scope up on the window sill and started smiling. Judy looked at me, "What?" "Guess who's out here and never sells, William "Big Red" Giusti." "Bailey, you're kidding." "Tell the cars to go to their spots. I'll be calling out sales soon." We got comfortable. "TNT, I'm out in P.T. and will let you know when I see something."

Sanchez' people spent a lot of money on countersurveillance. They had radios, binoculars, pagers, hand signals, and even had people on the block with one purpose, to yell "Narcs" if we rolled up. Their lookouts were good at what they did. The first buyer came and went right to Big Red. He gave the guy several folds and took his money. I promptly called the chase units. "We got a white male in a tan car going down street one. He took a right." Big Red looked over to the lookouts and one yelled out, "They're over in P.T." Everybody smiled and kept selling. Big Red was showing off for his crew and shouted, "This is how we do it, Number One Family for life!" Frank called over the air, "We got it, Bailey." It was the first drug arrest linked to the Sanchez operation. Frank repeated it over the air, "We got drugs, Bailey, several folds." "Thanks, Frank." The lookouts

## Mario Sanchez and More

yelled to Red that we made an arrest in P.T. He and his boys were laughing it up. Red hollered out, "That won't happen to us." Judy was laughing. "Bailey, I can't believe they're falling for this."

The surveillance continued until we had nine buys into Big Red and his boys. Frank called to me over the radio, "Bailey, we got drugs on this woman, but there's something strange here. We got to call the State Police now." I wasn't sure what Frank had, but he sounded serious. Big Red was about to make another deal when I called the team in. Red and his crew were all standing there in disbelief. We took Big Red and five of his workers. The money guy tried to walk off. Good luck with that. He was under arrest, too. Sanchez' little brother Lee was on the last sale, so he was arrested as well.

After everyone was cuffed, I asked Tony to look in a hole in the ground where Big Red was keeping his stash. It was hard to find at first. "Tony, it's in a hole and probably covered up. Look for some loose ground." "Got it!" Most of the lookouts walked off while the team was making arrests, except for one. Frank called to me over the radio to be sure, because the kid said he had done nothing. "Frank, tell him the headphones he has are connected to a scanner. He was listening to us to make sure we weren't on Clinton. That's conspiracy." Not sure what conspiracy meant, the kid responded, "Hey man, I ain't conned no one." Frank was laughing so hard, he almost choked.

While I was shutting down the surveillance, M&M called. "Bailey, are you out here? Everyone is running yelling Bailey's raiding, Bailey's raiding P.T." "No Babe, they got scanners in P.T. We were just having some fun with them." "Well just so you know, the Terminators said they were done for the night." "Thanks, Bae."

Inside the office we had Big Red, Carlos, Lee, Limpy, a 16-year-old with headphones, and a whole bunch of buyers. Big Red was a Lieutenant in Sanchez' organization. This was a major series of arrests in the Number One Family. I

131

## No Black Heroes

was thinking this had to end the rumor that I worked for Sanchez. Then Big Red started talking trash. "Bailey, we know you planted that shit out there. Everyone knows you're a crooked cop." I walk past him and smiled. Sergeant Samatulski pulled out a tester and sampled some coke in front of Big Red, "Whoa, whoa, now this is some good shit." Red looked angry and told me he'd see me in court. Of course, I wrote everything he said in my report. Sergeant Samatulski pulled me in the office. "Bailey, this is a major breakthrough. Excellent work. Take your time on this one. The Feds will be looking at this for sure. You did it, kid." "Thanks for trusting me, Sarge."

Officer Frank Jimmie called me into another room to show me something. The girl he was concerned about said she wanted to cooperate. "Bailey, this girl has pictures of dead kids in her purse. I don't know what to make of it." "No way, why would she? Wait a minute, wasn't there a baby boy found at Lake Mohegan in Fairfield not too long ago?" I remembered something about a ritual and the child being mutilated.

The thing with the pictures was way above my pay grade. We called the State Police, which had more resources to take on that type of an investigation. They came and took her away, and we never heard a thing about it after that. It wasn't enough that we had drug problems in Bridgeport, now dead kids? We logged her arrest and referred it to the state.

It was the first major arrest of the Family, but Sanchez was nowhere to be found. He knew he had to take a low-keyed approach and make some adjustments. Days later, Clinton Avenue had new people out selling, with no ties to Sanchez. His main people drove by occasionally to check the block, but that was it. It was a shrewd move on his part. For him though, the adjustments kept him from making money like before. His main people were now being paid to watch an operation they'd once worked. It had to cost big-time.

## Mario Sanchez and More

With Sanchez' main people off the block and business hurting, Benji was nowhere to be found either. I hoped he was done with drugs. TNT kept making arrests no matter who was out there. Word got around that Clinton was way too hot to buy cocaine without getting arrested. Only Sanchez' die-hard followers would come to the block. I used the same surveillance spot over and over again! They would have killed to find out where I was.

After months and months of keeping Clinton Avenue down, desperate times caused Sanchez to make some risky moves. With profits taking a hit, he took a chance and sold to Chase. Not long after, the FBI, DEA, and Statewide came in for the roundup. Anyone connected to the Number One Family went down. I had hoped not Benji, but they picked him up too.

The papers said Benji was making double his money running crack in the Panic and working for Sanchez on the side. All the credit for Sanchez' downfall went to the FBI. There was no word about Chase buying from Sanchez, but there was no doubt it was that first major arrest that got the ball rolling in Sanchez' downfall. TNT was never mentioned, and there was no way in hell they were going to give any credit to me. It was of no consequence to me, people in the 'hood knew.

I was at Seaside Park enjoying the day when Big Red drove up in a blue Porsche. "Bailey, if I go to jail you better watch out for your son." I was about to shoot up his car, but caught myself. Red was all mouth, so I chose my words carefully. "Red, if you know what I know, you'll never say that again. I'm not someone you wanna fuck with!" He tried to play it off but sensed he had crossed the line. His new wife Zennie got out of the car. She was clearly upset at what he said. While Red was parking, Zennie came over. "Bailey, don't listen to him. He's upset 'cause he might go to jail." "Zennie, if I thought Red was serious you would be calling an ambulance. Let's hope he doesn't say that again." "Thanks, Bailey. That was a terrible thing for him to say."

**No Black Heroes**

Big Red looked my way, "Zennie, stop talking to that Narc." He said it loud enough so everyone could hear him. I returned the favor, "You ratted out the Family and now you want people to think I'm a Narc?" "What? What did you say, Bailey?" I got in my car and drove away. I could just hear Red, "Hey Bailey, I ain't no snitch. Why you say that?" If there was one thing I knew, a rumor like that could get you killed. It was the last time Red had anything to say to me.

With the Number One Family shut down, there were no more fancy cars, girls, drug boys with gold chains, money throws at Seaside Park, firework displays, nothing. The once-proud Sanchez clan had their jackets seized by the Feds as evidence of a drug enterprise. What hurt the most was the loss of my nephew to jail, for his part in the Sanchez operation, and of course, Suzie Sanchez.

I couldn't believe my eyes. I was driving by Clinton just for old time's sake and there she was. I called to her, but she kept walking. "Suzie, let me help you." She was walking to the corner of State and Fairfield Avenue where girls sold themselves. "Suzie, please." It was the last time I saw her. A few weeks later she was arrested and sent to prison. I looked at her picture, and that said it all. The once-beautiful girl was someone I couldn't recognize. It said one thing to me, the drugs had taken over. Suzie would later pass away so very young in life. God have mercy on her soul.

Maggie wouldn't talk to me anymore. Maybe she found out about Suzie, or maybe she was upset about my part in taking Sanchez down. To get even with me she went to Gumby's one night and cut the tire on my car. I watched her do it. I just shook my head and called to have the flat fixed. Sanchez' sister Maria said it best. "We all loved Sanchez but there's a price to pay for what he did." Each of them was sentenced to 10 years or more federal time. Big Red actually lucked out with me arresting him. He got three years. State level cases don't get as much time as federal. With the chapter on Sanchez closed, it was time to move on.

## Mario Sanchez and More

TNT was now considered the best of the best. Our team earned it. We were on standby until the command staff could figure out our next target. We were told to complement patrol and cover them on the hot calls for a few days. There were still shootings, murders, burglaries, and other crimes that needed tending to.

A call came over the radio that Reggie Rogers and his cousin Ashmore Johnson were wanted for shooting Eric Hopkins. I knew all three. I went to the Rogers home and knocked on the door. Imagine their surprise to look outside and see me on their doorstep. They hesitated at first. "Listen, I can call a whole bunch of cops and surround the place, or you guys can just come out, no drama." They came out. "Bailey we didn't do it." "Okay. Then you can come with me to Detective Bureau and tell them that." When we got to DB, the looks those detectives had said it all. One of them blurted out, "Who does this fuck think he is?" I replied sarcastically, "A member of the Ad Hoc?" I was tired of those fools. My words were becoming harsher.

"Lieutenant DeCarlo, Reggie and Ashmore came in as a favor to me. They're here to cooperate." "Nice job, Bailey. We'll take it from here. Sergeant, go get some coffee and cigs for them." I walked past a small group of older Detectives whose time had passed. They were the Ad Hoc guys, the ones who couldn't stand me. I had to do it. I just couldn't let it go. I'd hate myself in the morning, but I did it anyway. I stopped, turned and stuck my tongue out at them. Much to my surprise Rita's father cracked a smile. I could just hear him at home, "Martha, you know what that nigger did today?"

I was not out of the woods on Cruz and the rumors that plagued me. But I still had my duties to attend to. Officer Tesla and I were told we had to report to court on a drug case. We were on the second floor sitting in the hallway when Cruz got off the elevator. I looked over to Judy. "I could've sworn Inspector Spencer said Cruz didn't work for him. There he is going into the State's Inspector's office." Cruz saw me and blindly ran my way. Just before he got to

## No Black Heroes

me a sheriff stopped him. Was that supposed to impress me? If only he knew where this was going.

When the sheriff returned I thanked her, but she looked at me like she wished me dead and walked away. I asked a second sheriff who she was. "Bailey, the guy that came after you, it's his girlfriend." "Cruz is dating a sheriff? And they say I should be careful who I'm dating." I looked over to Judy. She was pretty shaken up. "Sorry Judy, just another day in the life of Bailey the dirty cop." "Bailey, how do you live like this?"

I went into court while Judy remained in the hallway. I was there on a small case involving a threat. The guy I arrested was James Akins, a well-known cop hater from the streets. Normally, I didn't arrest anyone for threats, but this guy really meant it. It wasn't just mere words, and you could tell he meant what he said. I needed those threats officially in the system for when that day came. So if he did try something, I would be covered, if I had to protect myself.

His attorney was Erol Skyers, a top-notch attorney by all standards. Attorney Skyers drilled me every which way but loose. I was firm that I believed Akins was going to punch me out the first chance he got. I knew some figured I arrested Akins just to give him a hard time with a threatening charge. Attorney Skyers finished his line of questioning, and I was excused by the judge. On my way out, I heard a loud smack, and turned around to see the sheriffs rushing towards Akins. Skyers had just been punched out by his client. I told ya, I told ya!

The next week, Carwin returned to work. He wanted to take on P.T. with the hopes of getting one of the Holmans. I wanted to tell Sergeant Convintito the Holmans were family, but there were still rumors that I was involved with the drug trade. M&M said my older cousin Earnest was the ringleader. He was supposedly running a section of P.T., along with Tyke and Uno Holman.

## Mario Sanchez and More

Carwin had a plan. He wanted to sneak into P.T. and hide in one of the apartments, so we got in early and set up the surveillance. With no takedown cars or backup, I was concerned. It was just the two of us. How is this going to work? Carwin was looking at building three not far from where the Holman's lived, building one. Tyke came out and sat right under our window. He pulled out a large plastic bag with folds of dope in it. Carwin was going nuts, "Bailey, we got to take him now. Come on, we can do this." He took a few pictures of Tyke with the drugs and out the door we went.

Carwin ran down the stairs towards Tyke. We weren't in uniform, and no one knew we were out there. It could turn bad quick. Tyke was up and running his ass off. Was he thinking this was a robbery, or did he know it was the cops? Carwin caught Tyke, who pulled the drugs out of his jacket and threw them to the ground. Carwin ran into the hallway alone and I could hear them struggling. I wanted to stop and pick up the drugs, but Carwin sounded like he needed me. I could hear the fight deaden before the apartment door closed.

The hallway was blocked by two lookouts, and I didn't hesitate, punching one in the face. He fell hard. The other was shoved into the wall so I could get through. I ran up and pushed the apartment door, but it was locked. I could hear a lot of yelling from inside. "The cops are coming, hurry up and let me in." My Auntie mistook me for one of the lookouts and opened the door. She wasn't happy to see it was me.

Carwin was on top of Tyke, bouncing him up and down like a ragdoll on the floor, with the family around him. Carwin wanted to know did I get the drugs Tyke threw down. "I couldn't stop and take a chance on you getting hurt." Once we got back outside, we realized the drugs were gone. Carwin said Tyke made it to the bathroom and flushed something. He must have had more on him. I was hoping the pictures we took were going to hold up in court. Not absolutely sure about Tyke's arrest, we called for a patrol car.

## No Black Heroes

Outside, my cousins and their crew were surrounding us. They were trying to free Tyke. Earnest started yelling police brutality. It was getting ugly. Everyone was upset that we snuck into P.T. unnoticed. They didn't like it. Carwin's plan worked, but Tyke was just a little too fast. Aunt Queen came out of the apartment, "If your mother could see you now." I finished her words, "She would want to know what in the world you're doing, Auntie." Silently, she went back inside.

Someone in the crowd yelled, "You ain't taking Tyke anywhere." Carwin called for backup to pick it up. They were closing in on us, until I pulled my gun and pointed it at Tyke's knee. "Tyke is going with us. If anyone pulls at him, I can just see my gun going off. Now try me." Tyke looked at me, "Hey cuz, this ain't funny, man. Are you nuts?" Carwin looked at me from a distance, shaking his head no. Someone pulled at Tyke, and I pulled the hammer back. Tyke yelled to the crowd, "Don't! Don't!" They all backed up.

Carwin notified radio, "Two officers in plain clothes on scene." He held his badge high in the air so they could see it. Patrol cars arrived and everyone started to scatter. They took Tyke and put him in the car. Angry, Earnest scurried into the hallway yelling back, "You ain't no family, Bailey." Carwin looked at me, "That's your family? Why didn't you say something?" "There was nothin' to say." "You were going to shoot your own cousin?" "It was a bluff, I think." Tyke yelled from the police car, "You think?"

Sergeant Convintito was called in and wasn't pleased. "They said you guys caused a near riot out there, and alone?" Carwin showed him the pictures of the drugs Tyke had, but Sergeant Convintito said it wouldn't fly. "No more solo acts, guys. We work as a team." During our conversation we got a call. Earnest was at the front desk filing a complaint about us. "Good, I'll be right there."

"Earnest, come with me." "What?" "You're under arrest for inciting a riot." "Are you crazy? I'm here to file a complaint!" "I keep hearing I'm crazy over and over again. It must be true. You can file your complaint after you make bail." Sergeant Convintito was waiting for me in the office. "Is this your family, Bailey?" "Yes, they are." With his index finger to his lips, he joked that he would keep it a secret. "Well I think it's safe to say you're not going to get invited to Sunday dinner." "Probably not, Sarge."

Chapter 12

## CRUZ MAKES HIS MOVE

It had been a busy couple of months. I hoped all the arrests in the Sanchez family would have killed the rumors, but they kept coming. Chase finally admitted he was watching me but cleared me of any involvement with drugs. Rita called. "Hey Bailey, thought you should know my father is up to something. He said they were all sick of your bullshit. Something is about to go down." "Rita, did he tell you what?" "No, he was talking to my Mom again. He gets real loud when discussing you. And you owe me a dinner date." "Count on it, Bae."

Willie called. "Hey Bro, it's been a while. Jan and I are going to Gumby's tonight. Come on out and play." "Have you seen Cruz around?" "I ain't seen that guy in a while. Come on, man. The girls have been asking about you." "Okay Will, I'll pick you up around nine." "I'll be ready."

We arrived at Gumby's around 9:30. The place was packed. Jan was at the bar waiting for us. "Ron, I got you something special, here's your milk." They both laughed.

## No Black Heroes

"Very funny." A few hours went by and we were having a great time. Jan looked at me and turned her head slowly, so I could follow her eyes. Cruz was coming in with Griffin. "Well, I guess the party's over."

They both sat by the door to make sure they could see if I tried to leave. Cruz had an unusual slight smile, looking straight at me. We went to the other side of the club and sat down. That night was Willie's night. All types of girls were coming over to chat with him. "Willie, what's with all these girls?" "You can't have them all, Bro, and why are you staring at Cruz? Fuck him." "I intend to."

A waiter came to our table, "The gentleman over there wants to buy you guys a drink." He pointed to Cruz who raises his glass. Willie was about to go cuss Cruz out. "Waiter, can you tell Mr. Cruz thanks, but we're all set." The waiter returned and said Cruz still wanted to buy us drinks. Willie yelled out, "Hey, tell Cruz thanks, but no thanks!" Cruz then had a frozen smile on his face, and I felt like something was going down that night.

It was the end of the night and the club was closing. We were trying to wait Cruz and Griffin out, but they weren't moving. I reflected on how Rita wasn't sure what the Ad Hoc had planned for me. I figured they may have sent Cruz, in the hopes that his constant provocation tactics would cause me to do something stupid. The state, Detective Paul, the Ad Hoc; who else was this fool connected to?

Jan was over by the door and decided to try to get Cruz' attention. She moved over to him and started talking. He was annoyed, knowing she hung with us, but the distraction was enough. Willie and I walked quickly with the remaining crowd out the door. We hurried to the car before Cruz could follow us.

I was on I-95 when my attention was drawn to my rearview mirror. A car was so close I couldn't see the headlights. "Willie, we got trouble." Willie turned around, "What the fuck is this? Ron, pull away from this idiot." "I can't, the

## Cruz Makes His Move

ground is wet." I pulled my gun from between the seats. Willie looked down at it. "Hey man, what's wrong?" I didn't say anything. The car pulled alongside us. Cruz was driving and swerved his car at mine. I lost control for a moment. I guess Jan's distraction back at the club only delayed the inevitable.

Cruz was trying to force me off the road. He swerved at me again but by then my window was down. I pointed my gun, about to shoot Cruz, but Griffin's head was in the way. I had no choice. Bang! Willie yelled out, "Oh shit" I shot at Cruz' rear tire. He backed off, while Griffin ducked down in his seat. He was trying to get control of his car. I looked quickly at Will, "Sorry man, but enough is enough." Willie responded, "You should've killed that motherfucker!"

The sound of the gunfire in the car was so deafening our words sounded warped. Willie was cussing and yelling. "What the fuck is wrong with that guy?" I headed for the police department, and asked Willie to drop down low in case Cruz came at us again. "Willie, duck; he's coming up on your side." I pointed my gun at the opening of the car window. I was going to empty it, but Cruz drove by fast, too fast for me to get a clear shot.

Willie rose up in the seat and stared at me. "You weren't just talking shit, you were going to kill him, weren't you?" "Yeah Will, it was time. Some things ya just got to do." "What stopped you?" "The look on Griffin's face, Will. I'll never forget it. That was the first time I'd seen someone who knew they were going to die. Cruz is the one who has to be put down, not Griffin." Willie didn't say another word.

I made my way to the police department and got on the desk phone. "It's Bailey, send me a supervisor to the front desk. That guy Cruz just tried to kill me on 95." I called the State Police next and identified myself. "I just shot at a car on I-95. A man tried to run me off the road, Markis Cruz Majors. You need to send someone, it's your jurisdiction."

## No Black Heroes

What I had in mind for Cruz didn't go as planned, but close enough. Cruz made the first move. And I knew the state and Bridgeport Police would not be going after Cruz. Even Willie, who witnessed what happened and was considered a reputable person, wouldn't make a difference. No matter what we were going to say, they were going to ignore it. Everyone was out to get me. They would be coming after me, and I was counting on it.

We were at the front desk waiting on a supervisor when in came Cruz. He was there to file another false claim against me and fix his mess, and right on time. The state was too predictable. When I called the State Police to send someone, they were already contacting him, for sure. They told him to come in and file a counterclaim. He was there doing just what I'd hoped for. There he came, pointing his finger and yelling. "Come on kid, just a little closer. That's it, a few more steps."

"Cruz, you're going to be arrested for what you tried to do on 95." Then came one of his lies. "You tried to run me off the road, Bayleeee." He put his hands in his pocket. It was going better than I could have hoped for. I had dozens of reports that Cruz made threats about shooting me. Still, it could've been the real thing. "Take your hands outcha pocket!" I reached over to pat him down. "Fuck you, Bailey. Don't touch me!" He made a sudden move. I kind of lost it knowing he tried to kill us on 95. I backfisted him to the face then pulled back planting a flawless reverse punch with my entire body behind it to his eye. Cruz was knocked back about seven feet and dropped hard.

His shades went flying across the front desk, some 20 feet. They hit the wall with so much force they shattered. Willie yelled out, "Oh shit. Uh huh motherfucker, that's what you get, that's what you get." I heard a female voice behind me. "Ron, stop; what are you doing?" It was Officer Louise Karoli. She was getting off the elevator with a prisoner who had just made bail. Louise stood there motionless.

## Cruz Makes His Move

Willie was asking Cruz, "How's it feel, sucker? You should have left Ron alone. Does it hurt? Looks like it does." Cruz was on the floor, disoriented but slowly coming around. He started to cry, in a fetal position. Willie was smiling. "This is what you wanted. Get up bro, and get some mo'." I wanted to help him but I couldn't. I needed to send a message to him, never come near me like that again. "You told everyone you were going to get me. Stop your crying and get up. Let's finish this." Louise couldn't believe her eyes. "Don't do this Ronnie, this is not like you." "Louise, this guy has been threatening me and my family over a year now. It ends tonight."

Detective Johnson, a senior officer, happened to come in and saw what was going on. He asked Louise to go back upstairs. "Bailey, we all know someone here put him up to this, but you got to calm down." I looked at Cruz and walk away from him. He was on the floor blindly feeling around for his shades. Willie picked up pieces of the shades and placed them on the floor next to Cruz. "Here, just in case you want a rematch. Tell ya the truth; I don't think them shades can protect that eye bro." I looked down at Cruz, "Do you want a medic?"

Cruz eventually got up and staggered over to the pay phone. He dropped coins in it, then spoke. "Inspector Spencer, Bailey just hit me. What do I do?" He almost fell while leaning on the wall, holding his face. Suddenly he put the phone down, staggered out to the door and yelled "Aghhhhhh!" Sergeant Allen Stack arrived. "Where's Cruz, Bailey? I heard he lost the fight." "He just walked out, Sarge." Al looked at me, hunched his shoulders and walked back out the door.

"Willie, can you wait here while I go to patrol?" Sergeant Art Carter was in the patrol office just getting off the phone. "What happened upstairs? You need to write a good report, because they're going to come after you." "Sergeant Carter, I've been making reports for eight months. Maybe they will listen now. Cruz tried to kill me, with a passenger in my car." I sat down as instructed, wrote a very short report and

## No Black Heroes

handed it to Sergeant Carter. "You sure you want to turn this in?" "Sarge, I put down the facts, the truth. I hit Cruz because he was going to hit me. He tried to kill me on 95. I was protecting myself and my passenger. That's all I have to say for now."

A call came in to patrol from the State Police. They told me that if the threat was over, they would come by tomorrow for my statement. All I could think was, "How many cops have had someone try to murder them while their own police department did nothing?" I suspected calls had been made among Inspector Spencer, the State Police, and that special underground group of fools in my department. I was sure of it. Their goal was to get me, but I was ready.

Willie and I went to the diner to eat. He was telling everyone there, "You should have seen it, I never saw anybody get hit like that. That boy will never mess with you again, Ron." Jan was there with some girls, listening to Willie. They were all laughing. Willie talked about Cruz being on the floor, "Boo hoo, boo hoo." Everyone was laughing, but I just smiled. It was going to be rough going because those people were not done. Hopefully, I could discover who and what were really behind Cruz and the conspiracy.

The whole department was talking about Cruz and me. More rumors. "Bailey almost killed that guy." Someone leaked it that the State Police took Cruz into protective custody. They said he was transported to a special clinic in New York with severe eye damage. The newspapers said I broke Cruz' jaw. One officer was heard saying I hit him with a bat because there was no way I could have done so much damage with a punch.

I had done my research on Cruz beforehand. Cruz had run-ins with officers in other towns. His criminal history included trying to run another cop off the road, pulling a gun on an officer, impersonating a police officer, and a whole slew of other serious crimes. All were dismissed. No one can be that wrong without being convicted of something! I had all I needed to expose corruption at every level.

## Cruz Makes His Move

Now I needed to wait for the state and Bridgeport to make their next move.

Chief Walsh was out of town, supposedly. Captain Richard Cummings was instructed to conduct the investigation on Cruz and our, for lack of a better word, fight. Captain Cummings couldn't believe the state wasn't going to do something about Cruz' attempt on an officer's life. He finished his investigation and sent it to Lieutenant George Sedgewick, Commander of OIA.

I reported to OIA the next week as instructed, and Lieutenant Sedgewick asked for my gun and badge. "Bailey, I told you to stay away from this guy." "Lieutenant, I did." Sedgewick knew something was wrong but didn't know what to make of it all. He apologized, suspended me, and said my case would be heard by the Board of Police Commissioners. I thanked him. He seemed genuinely upset, perhaps aware that something wasn't right. Someone tried to kill a cop and no one was saying anything about it.

On the way out of Sedgewick's office, Sergeant Blair Cooney and Detective Paul were standing by the Lieutenant's door. They looked like two kids caught with their hands in the cookie jar. They had to be listening, but why? Curiously, it looked like the two might be involved with Cruz. I was sure I'd be finding out soon enough.

The state called me to meet with them. They took a statement and told me they'd be in touch. What a joke. I knew what they were going to do and waited at home for the call. First the notification came from the Board of Police Commissioners on my hearing. Sergeant Robert Craw delivered it, and as always, he was blunt. "Bailey, not everybody at the PD agrees with what they're doing to you. That dirtbag tried to kill a cop and they aren't doing anything about it." "Thanks Sarge, I appreciate that, but I might be done with being a cop." Sergeant Craw looked upset by my comment. He shook my hand and patted me on the shoulder. He didn't know what else to say and walked back to the car. I had to make people believe I had given up. It was essen-

## No Black Heroes

tial, if I had any chance of beating the system and finishing Cruz off.

Little Ronnie was visiting when suddenly I heard him scream from the living room. I ran in to see what was going on. He was pointing out the window. "Daddy, Shades, Shades." I was glad I had the Stranger Danger talk with him. Cruz was in a yellow cab smiling, then sped off. "Ronnie, don't be afraid. Go get your things so I can take you back to your mother's. Okay?" I got my backup gun and headed for the door. Luckily, the department didn't try to take it when they suspended me. With Ronnie now at his mother's, I headed over to the cab company. Chet was the dispatcher. He saw the gun in my hand and became nervous. "Chet, where is he, where's Cruz?" "Bailey, what are you talking about? Cruz doesn't work here anymore." "Chet, don't lie, he was just at my house in your cab." "Bailey, calm down and look at the schedule. He hasn't been here for months." "Chet, I just saw him." "He may have been in a cab, but it's not ours. Bailey, what's with the gun?" "It belongs to Cruz. I want to give it to him."

Was I going crazy? I knew what I saw. He was in a bright yellow cab. Where did he get it if it wasn't the cab company's? The papers said he was in New York under state protection. Guess they were wrong. I called Leak to make sure Chet wasn't protecting Cruz. "Hey Ron, Chet's not lying. Cruz can't drive for us anymore. He came in the other night to tell everyone he got you and you're done. You all right?" "Yeah, I have a few things to do before I get Cruz off my back, for good. At least I know he's still in Connecticut." "Hey man, don't do anything stupid." "If you see Cruz, let him know I came by looking for him. Tell him Smith and Wesson were asking about him."

Then the call I was expecting came. "Bailey, this is Sergeant Cuminotto, we have a warrant for your arrest." "What's the bond and what about Cruz?' "That's not our problem, that's the state's jurisdiction. There's no bond for you." I turned myself in. They fingerprinted me then took my picture. Sergeant Cuminotto asked me to put my home

## Cruz Makes His Move

address down. I was concerned about giving my address, because it would become public information. That meant anyone could find out where I lived. "I've always used the police department's address." He ordered me to put my address down or there would be an additional charge. "No problem, Sarge." I had to make it look like I was beat. There was no doubt he would tell the others that I was humbled.

Sergeant Convintito came to booking before I left. "Bailey, I know you're going through a lot, but for now, you're out of TNT. Sorry." "No problem, I understand." He tried to console me, and I wished him luck with the unit in the future. He sensed I was done being a cop. That's just what I wanted everyone to think. I was just about out the door when booking personnel handed me a note. It said I had to call the State Police in Westport. They had a warrant for me too.

The next day, I went to the State Police barracks in Westport. "Officer Bailey, we have a warrant for your arrest for the shooting on I-95." "I assume you're not going to arrest Cruz, right?" "We only have a warrant for you." I looked at him, "Thank you." He looked confused by my thanking him. I almost forgot myself. I needed to look beaten. I remained quiet during the rest of the process.

What a bunch of crooked cops. Little did they know I had an ace in the hole, Karen Hill. They had no idea. Karen was my first cousin, working at Troop G. She recently got hired and was very aware of what they were up to. She called me after my release. "Ronnie, they were all laughing after you left. They were saying you had to be kidding. There's no way they were going to arrest Cruz for someone like you." "Thanks Karen. I was counting on their stupidity." Unsure of how it would turn out, I really needed to be careful. If Mom were alive she wouldn't have been happy with what I was up to, but my back was against the wall.

As if I didn't have enough trouble, Jan needed to meet with me right away. When I got there, she chimed in quickly, "Ron, promise me you won't get mad. I was just

## No Black Heroes

speaking with several of your so-called friends from the department. They're glad you got arrested and can't wait for you to get fired." "Hey Jan, I know." "Ron, this may surprise you, but it was several black cops saying those things. They kept saying you're too much with your 'black and I'm proud' bullshit. What kind of friends do you have there?" "Scared ones, Jan, scared ones. It's got to be awkward having only a few fighting what's going on in that building." Jan asked me what it was really all about. Sarcastically, I responded, "The Klan works in mysterious ways at the department."

I needed an attorney for the criminal case; Attorney Burton Weinstein came to mind. He had sued so many crooked cops, he was a star of sorts. They hated him. He was very blunt with me, "Officer Bailey, I have pissed off so many in court with my courtside manner you may want to reconsider hiring me. I would be honored to represent you though, if you need me. It sounds like someone crooked has a hired gun." I thanked him for his honesty.

Officer Jesus Llanos called me after learning about my arrest. "Bailey, go see my friend Attorney John Gulash. He can help you." "Thanks, Jesus." I made an appointment to see him. We spoke about everything that happened to me from day one with Cruz, the state and Bridgeport PD. Attorney Gulash asked me to get all the information I could on Cruz. I placed a huge five-inch folder on his desk. "I'll say this for you Officer Bailey, you come prepared." He read through it. "It looks like there's enough here to bury Cruz, the state, and your department."

I was home preparing for my hearing before the Board of Police Commissioners when Margie called. She needed to see me and was on the phone crying. It couldn't be about Little Ronnie because when she told me Cruz had been watching him, I took him out of the school. I went to Kossuth Street and she jumped into my car. "Bailey, I know this could mean my life, but I have to tell you this. Cruz had a few of the girls on the block make statements against you. He had us say you use drugs, paid us for sex, and that you have been sleeping with kids." "Margie, how do you

## Cruz Makes His Move

know that and what do you mean, "us?" Did you make a statement too?" "Bailey, I had to. Cruz told me if I didn't he was going to put cocaine in my house and have me arrested. The state would take my kids from me. I'm sorry Bailey. I didn't know what else to do." "Don't worry Margie, it's alright."

Margie wanted me to know how dirty Cruz really was. She told me Cruz had set her brother Danny up. How he did it was actually clever. Cruz had Danny drive a car for him to Cooper's Auto on East Main Street. There Danny delivered the car to a guy waiting for it. The guy gave Danny $500 for what he thought were repairs Cruz had made on the car. Danny came back and gave Cruz the money, and Cruz gave him $50 for dropping the car off. Turned out the guy at Cooper's was an undercover state trooper working for auto theft. Cruz set up Margie's brother with a stolen car just to do it, no reason other than the money I guess. Cruz kept the remaining payoff for the car and Danny went to jail. In the end, what could Danny say? He took money for a stolen car. "Bailey, my brother is in jail for selling a stolen car he had nothing to do with. That's what you're dealing with." "Margie, do what Cruz tells you, this conversation never happened." I was thinking ahead. Cruz will be dead soon.

The letter from the Board of Police Commissioners arrived informing me to appear before the Board. I went to the police department and emptied my locker. I took everything out and left it open on purpose. Word got around I cleared out my things and was going to resign soon. That's just what I wanted circulated, that I was quitting.

It was the night of the hearing and many thought I wouldn't show. I came into a packed room. I guess they wanted to hear that I had quit. There were a few surprised looks when I walked in. You would have thought it was a murder trial. The first one to speak was Police Commissioner Robert Buccino. His statement was pretty much what I expected, "These are very serious charges, any one of

## No Black Heroes

which could result in this officer's termination." Yeah, and Santa's black, driving a Mercedes.

The police department hired a special attorney to make sure I would be terminated, Attorney Vernon Maxwell. The way he looked at me was worse than Cruz' cold stares. Maxwell called his first witness, "Officer William Bailey." All his questions had one theme; to make me look bad. Suddenly, he took a new approach. "Officer Bailey, did you know your friend Janice Rodriguez was in club Gumby's and she's underage?" I sat there for a moment confused. "No, actually I had no idea." I was thinking, what does that have to do with Cruz.

"Didn't you bring her to the club?" "No, I didn't." "But you met her at the club, didn't you? What's your relationship with her?" Attorney Maxwell wanted to make it a point that I was dating someone and married. I guess he didn't get the memo I had been living alone until the divorce was settled. "Look Attorney Maxwell, I don't know Ms. Rodriguez' age. We aren't dating if it's any of your business." Attorney Maxwell was upset at my response. He continued asking questions about my character, attacking my sudden brashness at the hearing. Finally he asked me why I shot at Cruz on the turnpike.

"Attorney Maxwell, he was trying to kill me." "Why didn't you just speed up and get away from him, Officer? Weren't you driving a Corvette?" "The turnpike was damp from the dew on the road. We could've been killed if I tried to accelerate." I continued with my answer, "Why didn't Mr. Cruz Majors just stay away from me?" "I didn't ask you that Officer Bailey." "Sorry, I thought you asked me why I didn't run from Cruz. I didn't know police officers were supposed to run away."

Attorney Maxwell was furious. He walked over to a pile of papers and pulled out a weather report for the night Cruz tried to force me off the road. He told the Police Commissioners there was no rain that night and I was lying. I was two seconds away from standing up to ask him who he was

## Cruz Makes His Move

calling a liar when Attorney Gulash objected. "Honorable Commissioners, Officer Bailey didn't say it rained that night. He said there was dew on the road from the dampness of the night. This is an elevated portion of the turnpike we're talking about. There's no reason to infer my client has lied." Maxwell most certainly didn't like Attorney Gulash's objection or my testimony.

Maxwell entered the weather report into the records as evidence. The commissioners ignored the objection of Attorney Gulash. If I didn't know better I would say the police commissioners had their minds already made up. It was near the end of Attorney Maxwell's questioning. He couldn't get what he wanted from me, an outburst. His questions were consistently answered with unemotional straightforward answers. I had testified in so many drug cases, this was nothing to me but amusing.

He was asking the same questions over and over again, in the hopes my answers would change. It's an old trick useful when dealing with nervous witnesses. I wasn't. "Attorney Maxwell, you asked me that question before. The answers won't change." "Just answer the questions, Officer." It was time to counter his nonsense. Every time he asked a repeat question, I asked him to repeat himself. Everyone was getting annoyed.

He asked me again; how do you know Ms. Janice Rodriguez. I responded, "Can you repeat that, please?" Then he was getting upset. He told the stenographer Shirley Sambrook to read it back to me. I answered with a purposeful slowness. The slowdown caused Maxwell to lose momentum, which began to bore the commissioners even more than his repeat questions strategy.

Finally Attorney Maxwell got upset and started yelling his questions at me. I remained calm with no expression. He was so frustrated his last question was a made-for-TV antic at best. Then it came, "Officer Bailey, you shot at my client for no reason, didn't you? You beat him up to get even with him, isn't that right?" He was yelling so loudly, it was hard to make out what he was saying. "Attorney Maxwell, I can't understand your question, you're yelling so loudly. Was that two questions? Can you repeat them? Which one do you want me to answer first?" I give him a slight smirk of arrogance. He was about to explode and responded to my question, "Both." I answered, "Attorney Maxwell, I had no choice but to fire my weapon at Cruz' car. He was trying to kill me. I protected myself and my passenger. At the front desk, Cruz tried to sucker-punch me. He tried before in a court hallway. You have my files documenting his behavior for months."

Then he tried to do damage control. I had just implicated the police department's failure to act on my reports and requests for help. He ended his questioning by yelling once more and posing a sarcastic question. "Officer Bailey, do you expect this police commission to allow you to keep your job after you shot at and beat up an innocent civilian. A civilian who came in to file a complaint against you? Who do you think you are, Clint Eastwood?" I didn't answer his question, ignoring his remark. His comment about actor Clint Eastwood was in the papers the next day.

Commissioner Buccino stopped the hearing before it went any further. On the way out, Police Commissioner Ramon Larraquente motioned to me. Everyone was so busy talking after the hearing they didn't notice us. He was trying to help me. "Officer Bailey, you came before this commission looking and sounding a bit arrogant. You do know you're facing termination?" "Commissioner, I haven't done anything wrong other than protect my family. As for my being arrogant I apologize, you're right. I have to tell you I'm not afraid of losing my job." Commissioner Larraquente looked confused that I wasn't afraid.

At home the next day Sam Palmer and I were outside talking. He was the best neighbor you could ask for. He had the greatest stories from when he was a cop. And I thought I was cocky! He told me he survived 11 suspensions and punched out more cops than anyone in the history of that department. "I don't know what you got up your sleeve Bai-

## Cruz Makes His Move

ley, but fuck 'em. Don't let them stop you, don't let them win." "Hey Sam, let them do their worst. I have an ace in the hole."

Sam and I were still talking when Cruz drove by, slowed down so I could see him, and then peeled out. Sam looked at me, "Don't do it, Bailey. Don't let him win that way. Call the police. I'm a witness." Sam could see me turning towards my car to chase Cruz down. "You're right, Sam; I'll do it your way and call." "Bailey, you can't do what I used to do, those days are gone." "Not if I can get to him and nobody sees me." We had a good laugh over it.

I called and filed another report. Sam was a viable witness, a retired cop. My case against the police department was getting stronger. And Cruz' stupidity was helping me, as he inched closer to being dealt with once and for all.

At the next hearing, we reported to the commissioners that Cruz had been coming by my home, and we had a witness to bring in. The commissioners denied our request. They said it had nothing to do with the pending case. According to them, Cruz had a right to drive anywhere he wanted in Bridgeport. I overheard them ask each other hypothetically, "How would he have known where Officer Bailey lived?" Don't tell me there isn't a concentrated effort to get me. I had to keep up my sense of humor or I'd do something everyone would regret, especially me. I muttered to myself, "It's official, the department has been infiltrated by aliens posing as imbeciles."

I had a point to make and spoke with Attorney Gulash just ear shy of the board. "Attorney Gulash, I have no choice but to arm myself 24/7. If he comes to my home again, I **will** protect my little boy." I went to my chair and sat, looking disgusted with them. They not only heard me, they were clear about how I felt. Someone was sure to call Cruz or his contacts to tell him what I said.

The next one on the stand was Willie. He was straightforward, "I was in the car and if it wasn't for Ron's actions,

## No Black Heroes

we would've been killed." Attorney Maxwell brought his usual character attacks, "And Mister Bailey is your close good friend isn't he?" "Officer Bailey is my friend, but I didn't come here to lie for him." "You're dismissed." Willie got off the stand and looked my way. He mouthed the words to me, "FUCK THAT ASSHOLE." All I could do was smile as I choked on my laughter.

It was now our turn. Next to the stand we called Carmen Ortiz. She was a friend from the Panic who got in touch with me when she heard about Cruz. She was the witness Maxwell and Cruz didn't want. Maxwell tried to have her excluded. The board went into executive session and was about to rule for Maxwell's objection to dismiss Carmen. Because the stenographer couldn't record in executive session, it was the one time I took out a pad and began writing everything they had to say. My note taking gave them the impression that their words were going to be heard later, and they were right. They suddenly allowed Carmen to testify.

Cruz had tried to date Carmen who went out with him only once. It was that date I wanted the board to hear about. She told the police commissioners about Cruz and his drug use. "He wanted to date me. We went out and he used cocaine in the car. That was the last time he and I saw each other." Attorney Maxwell tried to cast doubt on Carmen's testimony. "How do you know Cruz was using cocaine while you were in the car with him, Ms. Ortiz?" "Well, first he offered me some. Then he sniffed it. It's white, and going up his nose. What do you think it was?" Frustrated, Attorney Maxwell did his usual. "You expect this police commission to believe this wild allegation?" "I have no reason to lie. Cruz is an asshole and you're going after the wrong person. Bailey's a good cop. Cruz is a cokehead." "You're dismissed!"

We called Jan to the stand. She told the police commissioners how Cruz ran to his car after we left the club, following us up on the turnpike. Under questioning she testified she couldn't understand why the police department

## Cruz Makes His Move

wasn't doing anything about him going after a police officer. Attorney Maxwell then had the floor. "When Officer Bailey left the club, and you say Cruz chased after him, how do you know that? Do you know what happened on the turnpike?" "No, but Cruz left in a hurry." "I didn't ask you that." "Oh, well. Sorry, but he left in a hurry to get Ron. That's my testimony." "I didn't ask you that either, Ms. Rodriguez." "Oh well; sorry again."

Then it came. "So Ms. Rodriguez, what is your relationship with Officer Bailey?" He was not expecting her answer. "I'm an informant for Ron." "What? And just what information have you given to Officer Bailey?" That's when Attorney Gulash objected. "That's privileged information. This line of questioning could endanger Ms. Rodriguez' life." Attorney Maxwell responded, "Ms. Rodriguez, you're dismissed."

I glanced over to see the disgust in Commissioner Buccino and Commissioner Marsha Goodman's expressions. They hated me, and their minds were made up. I had no doubt they were going to fire me. Commissioner Larraquente was the only one who felt something was wrong. The board was waiting for me to resign, and I had sent out all the signals that I would, but when? Perhaps I was going to quit right after the hearings were done. I was certain that was just what they were thinking.

The hearings had been delayed for about six weeks. Cruz must have been told what I said about being armed and protecting my son. He had not come by since the last time I saw him. The day of the final hearing came, and it was time for me to make my move. I arrived for the hearing earlier than usual. "Commissioner Larraquente, you look worried. It seems you're the only one who is. What's wrong?" "Officer Bailey, you are looking at termination. You don't seem to care." I took a deep breath and spoke to him so he would know why. "Commissioner, six months ago the Board of Police Commissioners brought back Officer James Halen and Officer Robert Cray. If I'm not mistaken, these were two police officers who almost killed an unarmed man on the booking roof." Commissioner Larraquente paused and reflected. I continued, "I have the documents from that beating. This board allowed those officers to remain out for two years while they cleared their criminal case. When I say cleared, they pleaded out to a lesser charge. When they had their hearings two years later, this board didn't fire them."

Commissioner Larraquente responded, "Officer Bailey, one thing has nothing to do with the other, but I do understand what you're saying." "Commissioner, if I may, this department is under a federal court order. The court is watching this place closely, due to a history of blatant racism. Sir, what do you think the court will say when they hear about my case compared to Halen and Cray?" I wanted to make sure Commissioner Larraquente knew all the facts.

I told him how Officers Halen and Cray beat a man by the name of Colquit so badly that Officer Ted Meekins was assigned the hospital detail to protect him. "Mr. Colquit was beaten in handcuffs within an inch of his life. With all due respect, I'm looking forward to this board firing me." Commissioner Larraquente smiled, in obvious agreement. He shook my hand before joining the rest of the commissioners.

Then came Cruz. It was his time to testify. You could see the anger in his eyes, as he limped with a cane to the stand. Give me a break. I punched him in his face, not his leg. OIA escorted him in. They were giving the board the impression Cruz needed protection. That's when I was certain who his main contact in the department really was, Detective Paul from OIA. I should have known. Was Paul a member of the Ad Hoc too?

Commissioners Goodman and Buccino were adjusting their seats but looking my way. Their facial expressions looked as if they had just swallowed a live cockroach or something. My guess was Commissioner Larraquente just told them what I had said. I could only imagine how they felt when I threw the Colquit case in their laps.

## Cruz Makes His Move

Attorney Maxwell was about to start his questioning. He was so kind to Cruz the victim. I was waiting for him to give Cruz a big sloppy kiss. Come on already, I have more in store for you. Cruz had on new shades to hide his all-white eye and scar. He still had remnants of the hit he took to his face from me. Then came the contradictions Cruz was famous for. Maxwell started, "Mr. Majors, did you attack Officer Bailey?" "No, he attacked me." "Did you try to run Officer Bailey off the road?" "No, he tried to run me off the road." "Do you use drugs?" "No, but some of the girls I went out with do." "And isn't it true you came to the police department the night you were attacked to file a complaint?" "Yes, but Officer Bailey beat me up."

Missing from the witness list was Terry Griffin. He must have gotten word that Cruz was a snitch and was using him to locate his brothers Bret and Rodney. This was working out better than I had hoped. Under cross examination, Cruz began to tell the commissioners so many lies, they couldn't keep up!

Attorney Gulash asked, "Mr. Majors, did you ever try to take a police officer's gun?" "No." "That's not what this police report says. Mr. Majors, did you ever impersonate a police officer?" "No." "Well please take a look at this file from Westport." Cruz turned, snapping his head and eyes towards me. I looked away and smiled. Yes sucker, I did my homework.

We were about to produce more on Cruz when Attorney Maxwell objected. "Commissioners, I don't see the relevance of my client's arrest record, or these files. Officer Bailey is facing termination for what he did. This isn't about my client's past." The board refused to hear anything else about Cruz. We put the last nail in the coffin. "Mr. Cruz Majors, have you filed multiple claims of injuries that you are now making claims to here tonight?" Cruz was stuttering, not sure what to say. His answer made no sense. "I don't recall." "You can't recall if you filed injury claims or not?" Cruz wouldn't say anything else. Attorney Gulash handed the Board of Commissioners a stack of injury claims I found

## No Black Heroes

from his previous jobs, accidents, and insurance claims against cops from all over the state. "Honorable commissioners, I'm done with this witness." Yeah, but I wasn't.

It was late, but the board decided they could finish the case before the night was over. I sat there confident. I threw them completely off. They really thought I was going to resign. Even Rita had heard talk about my taking all my things out of my locker, and that I was going to quit. Her father and the Ad Hoc were excited to finally be rid of "that cocky nigger cop."

The board returned not even an hour later. Commissioner Buccino began to speak, "This was one of the most difficult hearings I have ever had to undertake. Commissioner Larraquente was smiling and gave me a nod. Buccino read their decision, "Officer Bailey, you are hereby suspended from this department and ordered to go through retraining as a rookie police officer. You are to have a psychiatric evaluation and cannot carry a firearm." He rambled on for a while before concluding with, "Do you have anything you wish to say?"

Attorney Maxwell was bright red with anger. Cruz stormed out of the hearing. Funny, the cane he used for his entrance, he didn't use to exit? Commissioner Buccino was waiting to see if I would accept the terms or not. I looked right at him, so he knew it was my turn. "Commissioners, I asked this department for help to protect me from Cruz. He wanted to, and tried to, kill me. I told this department Cruz was an informant working for the state, and that he's dangerous. This department did nothing to protect me or my family. I will accept your decision, but this is wrong." They were just the right words the newspapers would print. The whole state could read that Cruz was an informant, a snitch, a rat!

The next day news was about the hearing, but more importantly about Cruz being a state informant for Inspector Spencer. It was getting close to time to let the dogs loose. I wondered if Cruz was mindful that his being exposed made

## Cruz Makes His Move

him useless and could get him killed. The beauty of it all was the board asked me if I had something to say, and I did. They couldn't even come after me for exposing their snitch. They asked.

My phone was ringing off the hook. It was Rita. "Congratulations, Ron. I just heard." "Rita, let me guess, your father, no, the Ad Hoc, baked me a cake?" "Very funny. I'm so glad you get to keep your job. I heard Dad talking. He was upset, and so are his friends. Be careful, babe." "Thanks, Rita."

While returning my things to my locker, I was met with angry faces in patrol. Stuffed in the door of my locker were two letters. Neither had return addresses but had been postmarked Bridgeport. I opened the first one. The letter simply said "Thank you," signed Terry Griffin Sr. It was a letter from Terry's father who was in jail at Bridgeport Corrections. Obviously, he'd figured Cruz had been working on his son to find Bret and Rodney Griffin. I guess I had inadvertently exposed the plot, and so it went up in smoke. I opened the second letter. It contained several pictures of Cruz. On the back of each picture were the words, "MARKIS CRUZ MAJORS, POLICE INFORMANT." It was time to let Detective Bureau know about the pictures I was receiving. I decided to have a little fun and went to see Rita's father.

"Excuse me, detective. I thought you should know that I got this letter in the mail with pictures of Cruz." He gave me that look of how dare you speak to me. "It advertises Cruz as a snitch." He still wouldn't speak. "Detective, I wouldn't want anyone to think I sent these pictures out. You know I would never do that." He remained silent. "I'll just file a report that I spoke to you on it. Have a nice day." On a positive note, it was over for anyone using Cruz.

Out of work until the next class for retraining, I needed a job. My ex-wife was making her usual comments, "Why did you mess with these people, now what are you going to do? You almost got killed for nothing." I couldn't let that

161

## No Black Heroes

type of thinking get to me. I was raised right and no one was going to break me.

I went to see retired officer Charlie Smith, father of NBA player Charles Smith. Charlie was a past Guardians President and knew a lot about the workings of the police department. I asked what he knew about the Ad Hoc Committee. He couldn't believe they were still around. "Bailey, they are a deep-rooted group of white detectives who have no use for black officers. They especially hate the Guardians. If they are out to get you, then you need to watch out. It may not be over." "Charlie, do you know who the head of the Ad Hoc is?" "Bailey, all I know is he's said to be Chief Walsh's right-hand man. They say he was the one who protected Walsh when the Melody Law scandal took place." "Mclody Law?" "She was the madam who ran an upscale prostitute house in Black Rock. Someone supposedly accused Walsh of being a regular at the house, or having had some kind of involvement in it. Walsh had only a few people he trusted. The rumor was Commander Lou Fugazzi took care of it." "You mean Fugazzi who runs Detective Bureau?" "Yep." "Well, just so you know, I'm dating the daughter of one of the Ad Hocs." Charles looked at me with his mouth open. "Don't let them find out, Bailey. There a nasty group of guys."

I asked Charlie if he knew anyone who could offer me a temporary job. Before I could get up from the chair, he told me I could work with him. He had a part-time job for me working dispatch at the Wilton Police Department. I worked nights with him, but it was short-lived, one week. "Bailey, someone made a call. They said you can't work here because you're a cop on suspension." "No problem. I'll find another job, Charlie."

Over the next few days, I searched the want ads. There was an opening for an investigator at a security company. I got hired and worked one assignment. "Mr. Bailey, I have to let you go. The State Police came here and said you can't work for us." "Did they say why?" "No, but I'm licensed with

## Cruz Makes His Move

them and have to let you go." "No problem, at least I know who's messing with me."

I happened to read an advertisement for a daycare opening. I thought back on how I'd worked with my mom when she had a daycare in Greens. I could open one up in my home and the state couldn't do a thing about it. I placed an ad in the papers, Daddy's Day Care. To my surprise, the first customer was Officer Thomas Lula. He had his two kids he needed me to watch. Tom figured they couldn't be any safer than at a cop's house. "By the way Bailey, when you get to federal court, don't forget about me." "You got it." How did he know I opened a daycare? Maybe he saw the ad and recognized my number.

I could only imagine, if the state was watching me, what they were thinking. I took great pleasure in that thought. It was actually humorous thinking the state was most likely watching all the people coming in and out of my house. I bet they were going nuts thinking I was selling drugs or something. And they couldn't shut me down, it was my own business. With an income, I then had money for my next hurdle, the court case.

Chapter 13

# THE LEGAL BATTLES

I figured once the Board of Police Commissioners completed their process the court would then move forward with the criminal case. My only concern was how the criminal case would turn out. No matter what, the federal court would be my next move. My first court appearance was a postponement, as with most cases.

The next night at the Guardians meeting, I explained the Board of Police Commissioners' decisions compared to how so many others cases were handled, especially the Halen and Cray case. There was a double set of standards for all to see. I asked the Guardians to back me in federal court. What they told me next was a shocker, "Bailey, you don't have a case. You assaulted someone." I countered, "And what happened to Colquit and the beating he received in handcuffs from two white officers, what about that?" Anyone could see the cases were similar, but Halen and Cray received preferential treatment from the board. They refused to help me on the advice of the Guardians' law firm Koskoff and Beider. "Bailey, we talked to them. We have a perfect record in court. They don't feel your case is a winner." "No problem, I'll do what I can on my own." I was not going to let anyone stop me.

I couldn't get over the Guardians wanting to protect their perfect winning record. The board had a history of allowing white officers' cases to be delayed with far less discipline administered while we were punished frequently and more severely. What happened to me was something I knew the federal court would not be happy about. I couldn't wait to see the court's reaction that a man tried to kill an officer, and nothing was done about it.

I left the Guardians meeting pondering how to enter federal court on my own. The next day, I went to the legal library on the top floor of the Main Street courthouse. I studied the legal books on motions, discrimination, and previous cases that were won in court. It was a real eye-opener for me. I was going to take on the City Attorney's Office, the Police Commissioners and the Bridgeport Police Department. The one thing I had going for me was no one would expect it.

I was about to lose everything I'd worked for. My home, cars, and all my savings would be gone. Was it worth it? I remembered how my father suffered for taking a stand when we weren't treated right. And how Mom cried so hurtfully when she got that letter calling us niggers. I proudly remembered how they both remained dignified through it all. I had a legacy to live up to. My choice was clear; people were going to see someone standing up for what was right.

I filed a basic motion for the federal court to hear my case. Charles Smith told me to send it to Judge William Clendenen, appointed by U.S. District Judge T.F. Gilroy Daly. It was his task to resolve discrimination issues in the police department. He was overseeing the department and would ultimately decide if my case should be heard. It would be the first time someone filed a case on discrimination under the federal court remedy process without the Guardians' backing. At least I had that right.

## The Legal Battles

I thought about calling attention to the Ad Hoc Committee in court and what they were doing behind the scenes. Charlie said it wasn't a good idea. There was no way to prove they existed. "Bailey, you can't even bring in the girl who's been feeding you information. She only told you what she had heard. You need to stick with the facts." Charlie was clear about what I had to do. "Tell Judge Clendenen about the state and Cruz, but focus on the Board of Police Commissioners and how the police department takes care of white officers compared to black officers." "Thanks, Charlie."

Judge Clendenen received my complaint and ordered the city to prepare for a scheduled hearing on it. Rita called. She overheard her father say his friends in the Ad Hoc were going to lay low because the federal court served notice on the Bridgeport PD about my complaint. The wording on the notification said the court would investigate and remedy, which meant Judge Clendenen could inquire on just about anything. It was a wonderful process in fighting racism, and swift.

My criminal case was now moving forward as well. A few weeks later, after several delays, Attorney Gulash called. I had to be in court at 9:30 because my case was going forward. I wanted to take it to trial and expose a crooked system, including the state and Bridgeport PD. They were all part of a devious scheme. Attorney Gulash said I needed to apply for a special form of probation that would clear me of all charges with no arrest record.

I followed his advice by applying for the accelerated rehabilitation (AR). If I were granted the AR, my case would be dismissed, as long as I completed a two-year probationary period with no further offenses. The lead prosecutor Joe Marcello fought hard against it. Finally, Marcello told Judge Richard Damiani he would call Inspector Spencer in to paint a picture of what really happened between Cruz and me. He told the judge I had planned on killing Cruz, and Spencer had it all on tape.

## No Black Heroes

After court, Attorney Gulash said if I had threatened to kill Cruz we would lose the case. "I never threatened anyone." I explained about the file I wrote when Cruz confronted me at Scruples. "I told him he was going to get an ass-whipping on top of getting arrested if he didn't leave me alone." Gulash said if that was the case I had nothing to worry about. "You got some balls to put something like that in a file, Officer Bailey." "It was what I said."

At the next hearing, Inspector Spencer testified I threatened to kill Cruz by blowing him away. He used hand gestures to illustrate me holding a gun and pulling the trigger. Cruz must have gotten lessons from him on threatening hand gestures. Attorney Gulash asked the judge if we could hear the tape. They stopped the hearing and went into the judge's chambers. A short time later they returned to court and rescheduled a hearing for the next week. Attorney Gulash said we would be fine and the tape had nothing on it like what Inspector Spencer had said earlier.

After court, I was more relaxed and took a stroll downtown to see a few friends hanging out. While walking by Jimmy's Army & Navy store, City Attorney Mark Anastasi happened to walk my way. Mark was the main attorney for the city of Bridgeport. He walked up to me and politely said, "Officer Bailey, I got to tell you, this can be easy if you want it." I hesitated for a moment, "What are you talking about?" "Well, we know you filed a complaint in federal court asking Judge Clendenen to look at your case." "Yeah, what's that got to do with anything?" Attorney Anastasi thought for a moment stroking his fingers on his chin, "I'm not supposed to tell you this, and if you repeat it, I'll deny it. Drop the complaint in federal court and you'll get your AR." "What does my complaint in court have to do with my AR?" "Bailey, this is a matter that would be best put behind us and we all move on. You know what I mean?" I thanked him for his candor and called Gulash. I asked him if the City Attorney's office had filed any papers to object to my case. He said no but they could appear if they wanted to.

## The Legal Battles

At the next hearing, Gulash and I were in the hallway when a parade of attorneys showed up: Attorney Frank Riccio for Cruz, Prosecutor Marcello, and three city attorneys. Then the big Hispanic guy I had seen with Cruz at club Scruples moseyed in. I asked one of the sheriffs if they knew him. "Oh him, that's an undercover trooper. That's Trooper Valentine." Oh my God, that explains a lot of the rumors Cruz circulated, and the State's part in it. Looked like Cruz had someone credible to back up his allegations, an undercover state trooper. Could this Valentine character have been fooled, or was he trying to make Cruz look good? Something smelled like a crooked cop to me. I would find out about Valentine later. If he wasn't straight-up honest about the whole scenario, he would be going down too. But that day was about making headlines.

Attorney Gulash informed me that Judge Damiani was holding our case over until early afternoon, due to so much opposition. I drove over to Charles Smith's house and told him about the City Attorney's Office opposing my application for an AR so the case could be dismissed. He was visibly upset. "They can't do that. They've never done that with white officers who've been arrested. You need to notify the City Attorney's Office in writing before they return. They shouldn't be there. That's going to be an additional lawsuit for you if they do show."

I went home and wrote a short letter advising the City Attorney's Office their appearance at my court case exhibited a difference in treatment for all officers, and therefore had a discriminatory effect. "Your office has never appeared in cases involving white officers. So I am compelled to inform you, if you continue, I will be forced to file in federal court on your blatant discriminatory practices." I took a copy of my letter to the mayor's office so he would be aware of what had transpired as well.

I returned to court with minutes to spare as Judge Damiani came in. Several people I arrested happened to be there trying to figure out what was going on. My thoughts were troubling me. How ironic the justice system was. The

## No Black Heroes

court was filled with blacks and Latinos. Then it just became so obvious, blacks lived in crime, were the major victims of crime, yet the judicial system jailed more blacks than any other race. The court speaker stood up, "The people vs. Bailey." I whispered cynically, "Not my people."

Attorney Riccio was the first to speak. He asked the court to deny my AR and force me to plead out. Then came City Attorney Zeneski with two more city attorneys standing by. He told the judge that Cruz was going to sue the city, and if I were granted an AR, my records would be sealed. That would hamper the city in fighting the lawsuit. He then told the judge the only reason he was there was to keep those records open for the civil suit. Guess they got my letter, I could see where this was going.

Zeneski then switched from his so-called "I'm only here for justice" speech to his real intent. "Judge Damiani, I just received a letter from the mayor's office that may be of some importance to you. The letter is from Officer Bailey that infers some kind of threat. He surmises the city has never appeared in court for white officers' hearings, and that we are discriminating against him." Zeneski had hoped the judge would be offended by me professing whites got treated differently. I was not about to back down. He continued, "Your Honor, it appears that if Officer Bailey doesn't get what he wants, he will file a lawsuit. I take offense to his letter that implicates the City Attorney's Office is acting in an intentionally discriminatory manner. If I thought that were true, I would be standing right next to Officer Bailey." How many times have I heard that statement, 'I would be standing right next to him?' He then handed the letter to Judge Damiani.

Judge Damiani looked at the letter, then asked Attorney Gulash what his thoughts were on it. While Gulash reviewed the letter, the judge spoke. "It looks to me if Officer Bailey doesn't get what he wants he could be filing a complaint against me on discrimination as well. What do you have to say about this, Attorney Gulash?" Attorney Gulash didn't have a response. Judge Damiani was being swayed

## The Legal Battles

by the City Attorney. Prosecutor Marcello stood up and told the court I should not be granted the AR. He told the judge I should be held to a higher degree of accountability as a police officer.

I was literally twisting in my seat with a desire to speak on my own behalf. Boy did I have something to say. Every black person in that courtroom was looking to me with approval. One black woman mouthed with her lips, "Keep fighting. You're right." The People vs. Bailey? These were my people and they weren't against me. I glanced at the woman who had that look of approval for me, and suddenly I felt ashamed and confused. People were going to jail over the so-called war on drugs. And those same people were standing in my corner supporting me. The stenographer, who was also black, nodded her head in approval at what she heard in my letter to the city.

Attorney Gulash's response was about the history of the Bridgeport Police Department and discrimination. It was all he could do in his effort for damage control after the way Attorney Zeneski made my letter appear. I was about to stand up and yell when Judge Damiani looked my way. "Officer Bailey, would you like to comment on this?" "Yes I would, your honor." Attorney Gulash shook his head as discreetly as he could. He didn't want me to say anything that would ruin all his fine work.

"Your honor, I'm here with one attorney fighting three city attorneys, the state, the state's informant, and the prosecutor." Judge Damiani looked at every one them as I literally pointed each one out. It had to have gotten his attention, how unusual it was having so many there opposing one person. "Your Honor, the city wants me to back down and keep quiet. They know they're not supposed to be here. They've never done this to any other officer before, never."

The judge looked clearly interested in what I was saying. I repeated my assertion, "Your Honor, I have a pending case in federal court on discrimination against the city. They have never shown up for any other police officer's criminal proceedings before. But here they are today interfering in mine." Attorney Gulash was looking down with his lip tightened, hoping I didn't say anything stupid. Judge Damiani looked at the letter I wrote and said, "It looks like if you don't get what you want, I could be the next person you say discriminated against you." "Your honor, I wrote that letter at the direction of Charles Smith who was the President of the Guardians at one time. He told me I should notify the mayor and the City Attorney's Office that they have no right to interfere in my court case." I then elevated my voice slightly while looking at the city attorneys. "They will have a lot of explaining to do in federal court. And for the record, Your Honor, you're the only one here conducting himself in a fair and impartial manner. I would not file anything against you. I'm not here looking to get my way, I'm here looking for justice. I'm fighting for what I believe in."

Attorney Gulash lifted up his head and looked at me as if to say, I can't believe you said all the right things! He then spoke, "Your Honor, Officer Bailey has a right to file a complaint if he feels he has been discriminated against. The city of Bridgeport has had many complaints of discrimination to deal with, and Officer Bailey is exercising his rights." He continued, "The City Attorney's Office has said that they have dealt with problems of discrimination and have gone a long way in solving them. Not true. The city still has problems that have been recognized recently by the federal court and Judge Gilroy Daly."

How I wish I could have taken a picture of the courtroom that day. You could see all those sitting around smiling, and with pride. People I had arrested reached over and patted me discreetly on my back. I could hear someone behind me whisper, "Damn right, don't back down. Tell 'em like it is." It was at that very moment I realized those plaques and citations I had received didn't mean a thing. I looked at the smiles of pride on black and Latino faces in court. It was then I forgot about being a cop; I was an African American fighting for my rights.

## The Legal Battles

There was silence for a long period. Then Judge Damiani looked at me with a straight face. "I'm going to grant you the AR over the objections of all here today. I listened to the tape and could find nothing to show you threatened Cruz as the state has alleged. Not that you didn't say it, but I did not here it on the tape presented to me." Judge Damiani continued, "As for the city attorney's request to keep your records open for a pending lawsuit from Cruz, that will be granted as long as your attorney has no objection." Judge Damiani told me I had to stay away from Cruz and his family. "Your Honor, I never approached Cruz or his family." Judge Damiani responds, "These are just my orders. You are not to carry a gun until you are cleared to do so. And I do consider you an officer 24 hours a day. Lastly, you are to see a probation officer until your probation period is completed in two years."

Prosecutor Marcello took one last shot and asked Judge Damiani to deny the AR because the I-95 shooting and the assault at the police department were two separate incidents. Judge Damiani said he considered the incidents one and the same and closed the case out. Judge Damiani knew something wasn't right. That's why he ended it. Cruz was mad as hell walking hard into the lobby. I gave him the thing he hated most, no expression. Trooper Valentine looked my way seemingly upset as well. I gave him a smile, knowing I'd be looking to see what part he played in the scheme.

In the hallway, Attorney Zeneski walked over to me. He smiled and reached out to shake my hand, "Sorry about all this. Hope there's no hard feelings. I was just doing my job." I looked at him and smiled, "Absolutely no hard feelings. I hope you won't be angry when I file my complaint against you in federal court." Attorney Zeneski's smile quickly disappeared and he abruptly pulled his hand back. He stormed off with the two other attorneys in tow.

Cruz walked by with one more look for me. It was long and hard. If only he knew how much danger he was in. I ignored him and spoke with Attorney Gulash. "You really

## No Black Heroes

handled yourself well in there, Bailey. Judge Damiani realized something was wrong after you pointed out a few things. Attorney F. Lee Bailey, I guess we can meet next week to discuss your payments."

Outside court, Cruz was being interviewed by the news. The next day the papers reported that Cruz admitted he was an informant working for the Chief State's Attorney's office, Donald Browne. Why he would do such a thing was beyond me. If it was fame he wanted, soon he'd have all he could handle. Word on the streets was Cruz' picture was everywhere. I was still not convinced Cruz' involvement was limited to the state, Ad Hoc and Detective Paul. It had all the markings of something much more sinister and deeply rooted. No matter, I was going to finish it, once and for all.

Things were going as planned. Cruz had been exposed as a lowlife paid snitch. Even Inspector Spencer knew he had to back off with all the publicity. The Ad Hoc Committee had no choice but to crawl back under the rock they came from. They knew the federal court was about to investigate my claim. The one thing that had me ecstatic was in knowing that no one would dare try fixing any more of Cruz' arrests. Every single superior court judge now knew about Cruz, and the publicity it garnered.

I wanted a little added insurance to keep the state and Bridgeport PD in check. I mailed copies of my investigation on Cruz, with the news articles, to Congressman Christopher Shays' office and Senator Margaret Morton. I made an appointment to see Congressman Shays to slam-dunk the conspiracy with Cruz. His administrator happened to be a close friend of mine from high school, Snoopy. Snoop got her nickname from wearing her pilot hat in high school so many years ago. When I arrived, she discussed my complaint with me. She wasn't happy with what happened to me at the hands of the state and city. "Ron, this will not get buried, I assure you." The state would surely have some explaining to do. Even if they could somehow make it all look proper, they couldn't go any further with their witch-hunt of me.

## The Legal Battles

Shortly after my complaint with Shay's office, Karen called. She said all you could hear at the State Police barracks was my name. They weren't laughing anymore. Karen said they were having closed-door meetings for weeks, and Cruz was nowhere to be seen. I figured the upper command at the State Police had to stop using Cruz. You could best believe they had a grudge to fulfill now that I had exposed them. Just wait until they saw my next move.

The rumor on the street was Cruz' picture was everywhere and the boyz in the 'hood were waiting for him. If he turned up dead, he had no one to blame but himself. All he had to do was go away. Just to make sure, I dropped by the cab company to see if Cruz had been around. Leak hadn't seen him but told me the cab company was sent a picture of Cruz. He wanted to know if it was me circulating his picture. "Leak, I would never do anything like that." I rolled my eyes upwards with a sarcastic grin. He couldn't stop laughing. "Oh well, he got what he deserved. I told him to leave you alone, Ron." "Guess what, Leak? I'm not done."

The knockout punch came when the State Police did a raid at Bert's Place East Strip Club on Barnum Ave. They found Cruz' picture blown up in the manager's office. I was told the picture had "Cruz the Snitch" on it. On his picture was his address in Fairfield. So people knew where he lived! Cruz was going to be killed if he remained in Connecticut much longer.

Karen was still interning for the state and called again. She told me the State Police were desperately trying to prove I circulated Cruz' picture. "Karen, I know you're worried but Cruz told the news he was an informant. He made it a public matter, not me." I'd have to be a fool not to know Inspector Spencer was pushing the state to come after me. "Karen, let them spin their wheels." "Be careful, Cuz. They hate you." "They let Cruz try to kill me, and they're upset? Good. Guess who's laughing now?"

With no other choice, Cruz was finally pulled. Word was he was back in New York hiding out. Before Cruz left the

175

## No Black Heroes

area, he went back to the cab company to deliver a message to Leak, "I'm going to get Bailey if it's the last thing I do. I know he put my picture out there." Leak, always the good friend he was, "Listen, Ron wouldn't do something like that, but if he did, could ya blame him?" I figured someday Cruz would indeed return and I'd have to finish it.

With Cruz out of the way, I concentrated on my complaints in federal court. I filed a second complaint against the city for appearing at my court case. I kept it simple; "Your Honor, when Officer Halen and Cray were arrested for almost killing a man in handcuffs, the city didn't appear to object to their court proceedings. Curiously, they appeared in opposition to mine. For the record, my charges were not anywhere near as offensive as Halen and Cray. And for the court's knowledge, Halen and Cray are white, the plaintiff is black."

Their first response to my complaint was comical. The City Attorney's Office declared they had nothing to do with the Police Department and that Judge Clendenen did not have a right to hear my complaint. They asked that the complaint be dismissed, but their motion was denied. An informal hearing was scheduled on the merits of my case. My first complaint against the Board of Police Commissioners was on hold to be assigned a trial date later.

I asked Attorney Beverly Carswell if she would accompany me in case there were legal terms I wouldn't understand, and she agreed. City Attorney Thomas Jackson appeared to defend City Attorney Zeneski. He started citing law then suddenly began yelling at Attorney Carswell so loudly, you could hear him in the hallway. She quietly responded, "The city had never appeared for a criminal proceeding involving an officer before. Why now?" Attorney Jackson said it was an outright insult. He said Attorney Zeneski was a pastor, a man of the cloth, and an honorable man. Judge Clendenen was still waiting for a reason why they interfered in my court case. With no reasonable explanation, the city got creative, "Judge Clendenen, this is a new policy we have started. When an officer gets arrested

## The Legal Battles

we will henceforth be sending a letter to court notifying them that the city is an interested party." He said my case was the only one that the city appeared in because they had just enacted the new policy to protect the city. What a crock!

The new policy angle worked and my complaint was subsequently dismissed. Judge Clendenen did state that if I could show a pattern by citing other court cases involving white officers I could reopen the complaint. He knew the city's excuse was bull. I moved on and concentrated on my complaint to expose the Board of Police Commissioners' lack of dealing fairly with all officers.

It was time to make my move in returning to work. The daycare was doing well, but I couldn't take a chance on something else going wrong while out fighting the city. I was sure Commissioner Buccino thought my being ordered to go through a second rookie class would belittle me into resigning. I would make sure he and the other commissioners would regret what they had done.

One of the stipulations before my return was that I have a psychological evaluation. I made an appointment with the same physician the city used to screen new officers before we could take the job of a police officer, psychiatrist Lazaro Pomeraniec. We talked about what had happened, including the court cases. He put me through the same series of tests all over again. After the tests and interview, he cleared me for work. "You're fine, Officer Bailey, it sounds like a bunch of people down there are trying to make your life hell." "Thanks, Doc, I won't tell them you said that." "Go back to work and I'll send them the evaluation."

I called Union President Sergeant Cuminotto to inform him of the evaluation and sent him a copy. He called me a few days later to say the board wanted a second opinion. "Matt, sorry but I'm done taking orders from anyone out to get me." I paused and chose my words well. "Please tell the board I'm not taking another evaluation. The two officers who beat up Colquit didn't have to. From what I under-

# No Black Heroes

stand, they didn't take one, never mind two." I abruptly hung up. An hour later he called back. "Bailey, return to work Monday in the record room until the next training class. Remember, you can't carry a gun." "Like I said, I'm not listening to you or the board." Click!

I called the parents of my daycare kids and let them know I was closing. I referred them to a friend who had plenty of openings. At the police department, I was greeted by Sergeant Bobby Lindquist, in charge of records. He asked if I had my weapon. "It's in the car, Sarge." "Bailey, you were told not to carry a gun while on duty." "I'm not, it's in the car." "Officer Bailey, you're going to get brought up on charges again." I pulled out a copy of the transcript from court and read the judge's orders. "Once I'm back on the job I can carry my weapon and will be considered an officer 24 hours a day. Those are the judge's orders. If this place wants to disarm me while on duty, that's fine. But when I'm off, I will be armed."

The Board of Police Commissioners sent me a notice days later, reminding me of their orders. Sergeant Lindquist handed it to me. "Do you understand, Officer Bailey, you are ordered not to carry a gun?" "With all due respect Sergeant, Cruz threatened me and my family. He admitted working for the state, and this department did nothing to stop him. He tried to kill me and he still has his pistol permit. If the board wants to disarm me under those circumstances, good luck with that!"

Just so he could better inform the board, I cited law. "Sarge, if you need me to, I can go before the board and tell them about state statute 29-35; it states that a police officer can carry a gun without a permit. I don't need a permit or the board's permission to carry. I'm an officer certified by the state, not them. The statute is clear. Please tell them the subject is closed."

I thought back on how Sergeant Whelan of the State Police Pistol Permit Division had revoked my permit. He ignored my request to take Cruz' permit away after what he

## The Legal Battles

had done. I contacted him by letter so he would know I was carrying. You could best believe he'd contact Inspector Spencer. I could only imagine how Whelan and Spencer would take that letter, but I didn't care!

Chapter 14

## FEDERAL COURT/RACE ISSUES

I was at home on weekends preparing for my case. It was my hope the city would anticipate that I would hire an attorney for the discrimination complaint. Not this time. This time I would represent myself. It had been my experience that attorneys were always careful how far they would proceed. At the end of the day, once a case like mine was over, any attorney knew they had to return to the regular grind of the legal circuit. I had a lot that needed to be said. I didn't want a tactful attorney who couldn't step on anyone's toes saying it for me. My words were about racial issues and there's no polite way to talk about it. I was going to say what most did not want to hear, and bluntly.

The day of the hearing Carwin arrived to show his support. It meant a lot to have the Guardians president there. They all looked stunned when I entered without an attorney. Their surprise turned to a glint of delight, until my opening statement. "Your Honor, I am here today because the police department and its agents failed to take reasonable, necessary, and appropriate action to protect my rights. They treated me differently from white officers." Those noticeable specks of cheerfulness quickly disappeared from the faces of my adversaries.

I began presenting my case. "Your Honor, the city ignored my complaints and requests for protection from their informant Markis Cruz Majors. The court has in its possession as evidence approximately 11 months of files, reports and documents submitted to the police department. They did nothing to protect me and my family." I continued, "Your Honor, for comparison of the different treatment I endured compared to other officers, may I cite one for the record? Officer Lou Cristello received threats by way of a letter from someone he arrested. Just one! The police department provided him with police protection at his home for two months, day and night. As this court knows, I filed numerous reports with the police department, and I was ignored. The court also has other cases I forwarded for its review."

I then pointed out the most obvious case similar to mine, Halen and Cray. "Your Honor, Officer Halen and Officer Cray beat a man in handcuffs who almost died, John Colquit. They were arrested, but allowed to clear their criminal cases before their return. That process took them two years. Once they pleaded out to a lesser charge, they were brought before the Board of Police Commissioners and welcomed back with open arms."

I continued, "Your Honor, I have in my possession a case in which three white officers fired their weapons improperly in Father "Panic" Village almost killing an innocent motorist in a nearby car. I used my weapon on I-95 because their informant tried to kill me. Those officers in the Panic were never brought up on charges for using their weapons improperly. The reports on that shooting indicate one of the officer's rounds ended up in the headrest of a civilian's car! There is a set of double standards going on here."

The next case cited even I knew took some nerve. "Your Honor, Chief Walsh threw a loaded gun on the table in the

## Federal Court/Race Issues

presence of Police Commissioner Buccino during a hearing. It was done so during a heated debate. The chief who is white was also not disciplined. Commissioner Buccino did nothing about it." After the evidence portion of the hearing it was time to call witnesses.

I called Police Board President Buccino. He was incensed about my forcing him to appear and haphazardly smiled, taking the stand. He told Judge Clendenen he and the board had been completely fair with all officers. When asked about Chief Walsh and the gun-tossing event, he replied, "Your Honor, I've been second-guessing myself ever since that happened." That was a comment, not an answer! I questioned him again. "Mr. Buccino, isn't it true that you and Chief Walsh had a disagreement and Walsh threw his weapon, a loaded gun, on the table where you were sitting? And sir, isn't it correct you did nothing about it?" Commissioner Buccino looked to City Attorney Jackson for help. With no objection, he finally said "yes." "Thank you." Buccino's remaining testimony was nothing more than excuses about why this and that had happened. I was sure Judge Clendenen was unimpressed with him.

My next witness was Attorney Maxwell, who answered my questions with long-winded evasiveness. He refused to provide a straightforward answer to anything I asked. Judge Clendenen seemed tired of his caginess. It was time to end my questioning. "Attorney Maxwell, one final question. Did you spread a rumor I was involved in an affair while married?" He just sat there. I continued, "Wasn't that you getting personal on your part?" He was dumbfounded and unable to speak. "Sir, we're waiting for an answer." Maxwell started to speak, "Well, I believe that if you look into—" I interrupted his smugness. "Excuse me, but I would love a yes or no answer, if you please." He looked like he wanted to choke me to death. "Attorney Maxwell, answer my questions, yes or no? We're all waiting!" My thoughts kicked in, payback's a bitch. Isn't it, you pompous ass? He finally answered with a slow and discreet "Yes." "Thank you sir, and you're dismissed!"

## No Black Heroes

Judge Clendenen began to ask questions that opened my eyes. "Does the Bridgeport Police Department have a policy in place to protect its officers from citizens like Cruz? Is there anything in place to ensure the police department provides assistance for an officer in distress? Officer Bailey was asking for help, and he was ignored." Commissioner Buccino said it would be something they could look into. That hearing was a real eye-opener at getting people to admit to failure and get to the truth. Carwin pulled me to the side later. "Bailey, you made us proud here today. But you best believe you're a marked man." I looked at Carwin, "Yeah, so what else is new?"

After the hearings, I took a few days off. When I returned, I saw Officer Halen in the record room. He looked upset. I guess he heard about my hearing. He came over. "Bailey, how much longer am I going to have to relive this shit? Enough already, can we stop talking about it?" "Halen, I'm not after you. I needed your case to show I was treated differently. Just so you know, there are no more hearings." "Good!"

The papers reported the hearing, "Officer Cites Race In Cop Board Discipline." Officer Travis James had a few words for me. "Bailey, the Guardians should have backed you on this. I hope you win. You got some nerve though, talking about Chief Walsh and his gun-tossing thing." "He's a cop, too. If I'd done that, what do you think they would've done with me?" "You better hope he isn't mad about it. You don't want to be another Ted Meekins."

A few weeks later, I was ordered to report to the police academy. The new class was beginning. The board was unquestionably disappointed I didn't resign, opting to go through another rookie class. I arrived to class early with 30 new police officers drifting in. Lieutenant Dave Boston was in charge and stopped me before I entered class. In his office, he asked that I abide by the rules. "Sure Lieutenant, I won't cause any problems. I'm looking forward to taking it easy for a few months." "Officer Bailey, you have to participate in these classes." "Lieutenant, I will participate. But for

## Federal Court/Race Issues

the record, I don't have to pass classes to keep a job I passed to get on." His expression let me know, I had a valid point.

The first day was a "get to know you" kind of thing. The new guys had heard about me through the papers. That "Clint Eastwood" comment Maxwell made stuck with a few. One of them stood out above all the others, Officer Dave Daniels. He was a tall, brown-skinned cop who had lived in P.T. housing most of his life. Dave was another project, battle-tested kid like me. "Officer Bailey, it's a pleasure to finally meet you." "You too, Dave, and the first chance you get, join the Guardians." "Already have, my brother."

It had been several weeks of class and I was keeping a low profile. After class, I went to Duchess for a quick bite. White Boy Louie, a low-level drug dealer, was there. I met him by chance at the Tae Kwon Do school a while back, sporting a black eye. White Boy seemed impressed with my breaking five boards with a punch in a demonstration. He was surprised to see me and asked if I could give him private lessons. I politely declined. I could hear the department on that one; he's teaching drug dealers how to fight.

He wanted to speak to me outside the restaurant. In the lot White Boy leaned towards me. "Bailey, Sergeant Cooney from the Office of Internal Affairs contacted me about my drug case in court. He said he could help me out if I could tell him something about you." "Why would he ask you about me?" "That's what I'm talking about. We don't hang out. I thought you should know." "Thanks for the 411, Louie." That's when it dawned on me. OIA had to have been watching the Tae Kwon Do school. They must have seen me talking to White Boy there almost a year ago. They've been watching the school all that time?

Take care of one problem, another one crops up. I had to think what my next move would be. It was Friday and there was a new club in New Haven everyone was talking about, Montego Bay. I needed a break and headed out. The club was packed. No need to worry about Cruz, he was out

## No Black Heroes

of state. I was hanging out hoping no one recognized me. To my surprise I see Officer Lisa Lees. She had just gotten the job and fired a few weeks into her rookie class. Word was it had something to do with drugs.

Lisa walked over. "Bailey, I need to let you know something. They're after you, big time." "Lisa, what's up? Who's after me now?" "Sergeant Cooney and Detective Paul are out to get you. They called me in after I got arrested. They said if I gave them something on you my case would disappear. Hope I didn't ruin your night." "No, you just gave me a little something to think about." OIA, an investigative unit of the police department offering deals to White Boy Louie and Lisa. You couldn't make that stuff up.

It was Sunday and I was on my way to church. I needed guidance and strength. God had been sending me messages all throughout my ordeals. Bishop J.C. White spoke just as I sat down, "No one can harm you when God takes up your cause. Go and be fearless." I hadn't even had a chance to get comfortable and got the word right then and there. I thought back on the old woman at Bradlees who told me no harm would come to me. She said God told her to tell me that! Again and again I had been reminded of what needed to be done.

At home, still reeling from God's word, I sat down and wrote a detailed report. It reflected what I had been told by Louie and Lisa. Detective Paul and Sergeant Cooney were making deals with felons to get me. OIA isn't a criminal unit, it's administrative. Filing a detailed report would stop them from attempting any more deals was my guess. I couldn't wait until the next day.

Monday morning, I handed my report to Lieutenant Boston. He looked at it and wanted to know what I needed done with it. "Can you send it to Chief Walsh? I'll be sending a copy to the federal court and Congressman Shays' office." Lieutenant Boston raised his eyebrows. I knew exactly what was going to happen next.

## Federal Court/Race Issues

I was finishing lunch and in the hallway talking to Dave. Then came Sergeant Cooney. "Just so you know Bailey, I will be calling in Louie and Lisa to make statements about what you said in that report you wrote." "Sergeant Cooney, you got some nerve. How long will it be before someone makes up something about me, if you keep offering them deals? Do me a favor and stay the fuck away from me. I won't tell you that again."

Cooney forgot himself and walked right up to my face. I grabbed him by the collar and pushed him up against the wall. I was about to take him down but Dave grabbed me. "Bailey no, don't do it. Don't fall for their bullshit." I looked hard at Sergeant Cooney. "Don't ever come near me again. If you do, you got nobody to blame but yourself for what'll happen next. Now get the hell away from me." I turned him loose. Sergeant Cooney stormed off with short stomping steps like a spoiled toddler who didn't get his way.

Grabbing a supervisor was definitely a suspension in the making. Still, I had no intentions of letting anyone get in my face like that. After class, I went to Lieutenant Boston's office. "Lieutenant, Sergeant Cooney just confronted me. Don't I have the right to file a report?" He told me to calm down. I was calm, but enough was enough. I was firm about one thing; no one was going to intimidate or railroad me.

That night I was on my way to train at the Tae Kwon Do school. The fire damage to the school had been repaired. I drove by the police academy en route to the school when lo and behold, there was Attorney Riccio getting out of his car. I pulled over just in time to see Lisa pull up. They both went inside OIA. It didn't take a rocket scientist to figure out Cruz probably set Lisa and White Boy up. Attorney Riccio must have been the point person among the three. It was all making more sense. I could only hope they all had some kind of an idea what they were up against. I'd been pushed to where anything goes.

## No Black Heroes

Lieutenant Boston told me later Lisa made a statement to OIA that I lied about our meeting at Montego Bay. My response was a classic, "That's curious, Lieutenant. Why would they go to such lengths to prove Lisa didn't tell me anything? And OIA has White Boy Louie's number? What's even more curious, tapes don't lie." I immediately clinched my lips tight and looked down like I had slipped. I got up from the chair looking angry and left the office. Lieutenant Boston looked a little put out about my "tape" comment.

It was a street-smart move. Drop information to rattle someone and see what happens next. Now they had to wonder if I'd been recording them, perhaps watching their every move. And just like that, no one in the department would come anywhere near me. That was just what I wanted. Even Lieutenant Boston stopped having meetings with me after the tape comment. A few weeks later, I saw White Boy who turned and looked the other way. "What's up Louie?" "Hey Bailey, what I told you was for you only, man." "Louie, I'm sorry. I should've told you first." He walked away angry, and rightfully so. That would be the first and last time I would betray someone's confidence.

Back at the academy Sergeant Cooney happened to walk by, and he looked angry. I whispered to him, "Didn't I tell you to stay away from me?" He stopped and looked my way. "You heard me. Now get out of my face." It was all about intimidation on his part, and I wasn't having it. There was no reason for him to be anywhere near my class. Unbeknownst to me, Dave was standing close by, shaking his head. "Bailey, you don't make threats to a supervisor, especially one from OIA." Dave looked like he was about to burst out in laughter. "There's definitely something wrong with you, and it ain't drugs." "Why Officer Daniels, you know me."

Shortly thereafter, the ruling came down making headlines, "Officer's Bias Claim Upheld." Judge Clendenen ruled that the department failed to act on my behalf. The entire penalty was set aside. The department was ordered to re-evaluate my case and report back to the court. Commissioner Buccino's comment to the papers said it all. "We will

## Federal Court/Race Issues

appeal, and we will take the next step." They were not going to follow Judge Clendenen's orders. Their arrogance was obvious in Buccino's statement.

With the ruling in my favor, OIA made their move. "Officer Bailey, you are to report to the Office of Internal Affairs. You will have to make a statement. Bring a union rep." When I arrived, Detective Paul had a look of disgust on him. "I have to ask you some questions about your involvement in drugs." "Sure, why not?" Officer James Remele was my union rep. Detective Paul was peering at my clothing. The rumor I wore a wire was making its rounds. I remarked, "Funny how you guys call me just after I win my case in court."

I had seen that look Detective Paul had on many a foe in the streets. He wanted to take a swipe at me. I was hoping he would. "Officer Bailey, we have been investigating you for about two years. Please answer the questions." Was that supposed to rattle me? He read me my rights before the questions began. I was thinking, they wasted two years, and it all came down to a statement? Where'd they get their investigation skills from, a Ouija board?

Here we went. "Have you ever sold or used drugs?" "No." "Have you ever slept with minor children, or prostitutes?" "No." He paused and had the nerve to say they'd seen me coming out of a prostitute's house. "Then you should arrest me, if that's a crime. I don't live with prostitutes." He was getting angrier. The questioning lasted about an hour. So then he started with the repeat questioning, "And you never used drugs, Officer Bailey?" "I answered that question." Frustrated, he ended with the catch-all, "Do you have anything to add?" "Yes. I don't mess with drugs or children. I will submit to a drug test, but it has to be by my physician. I don't trust you or this place." Officer Remele had a broad smile. Detective Paul had nothing else to say. I got up, smiled and walked out.

Coincidently, the newspapers were reporting on a major investigation in Hartford, Connecticut. The head of the

State Police, Commissioner Lester Frost, was under fire. The Connecticut Legislative Committee and Review Board were investigating the state's improper use of informants and looking to hold Commissioner Frost accountable. The news reported that a state informant tried to pressure Judge Anne Dranginis to drop a pending case against him by going after her husband. It was perfect timing. It was my goal to let that review board know about Cruz and OIA. The best way to challenge corruption is to expose it.

After contacting the Legislative Review Board I was invited to attend and testify. As I entered the chambers, there was a heated argument ongoing about the informant going after Judge Dranginis. The State Police were looking really bad, and hints were evident from those in attendance as to who would ultimately be held responsible. It would likely be the top management that would have to pay the price. They called me to the stand to speak. "My name is Officer William "Ron" Bailey. I'm here to tell you about an informant the State Police is using, including my own department, the Bridgeport Police."

There were gasps in the room once they heard testimony detailing how Cruz tried to kill me, and the State Police refused to arrest him. I told them about the allegations I was selling and using drugs, sleeping with prostitutes and children. They were extremely attentive to what I had to say. "Honorable Board, these are rumors spread by people within my own department, and promoted by informant Cruz, the state, and State's inspector's office." I then told the review board how odd it was that Detective Tony Paul of OIA would question me after a two-year investigation on rumors. The whole thing reeked with the stench of corruption. "Honorable Board members, those accusations are all echoes of informant Cruz who works for the state and my department." One member of the commission asked a simple question, "Officer Bailey, for the record, you do not use drugs?" "No sir, I do not." "Officer Bailey, thank you for your candor."

## Federal Court/Race Issues

I had just implicated my department, OIA and the state in a conspiracy. Someone was sure to call them about my appearance. When the hearings were over, as suspected, the Legislative Committee criticized the state and the use of its informants. State Police Commissioner Lester Frost resigned. The new mandate required sweeping changes in the use of informants. The pendulum was now swinging my way. If the state lost control of an informant, aka Cruz, there would be hell to pay.

Didn't these people ever give up? The secretary for OIA said to report immediately for an interview. And there he was waiting at his desk, Detective Paul. "Sit down. You're going to answer some questions about your comments in Hartford." "Detective Paul, let me get this straight. You're going to question me on your own complaint?" "Yeah, sit down."

Detective Paul was a huge man who needed a wakeup call. "Listen, Farmer John; I'm not doing anything you tell me. Got it?" He looked like a bus had just hit him. "You are ordered to sit down." I was sure no one ever refused to follow his instructions before, so I ended the nonsense. "If you want to make the papers, keep fucking with me. I'm done with you, and Cruz." He was angrily bouncing some papers he had in his hands on his desk as I walked out and slammed the door behind me. You could get fired for refusing to make a statement when ordered by OIA. My thoughts were clear. He was wrong in trying to force me to submit to questions, when the investigator was also the complainant. He had no right and I wasn't buying it.

I headed to the third floor, Chief Walsh's office. I walked into his office and was stopped by Union President Cuminotto. He looked at me somewhat sad. "Matt, where's Chief Walsh? Detective Paul just tried to question me on a personal complaint." "Not now, Bailey." I turned only to see Chief Walsh walking by with a small box in his hands. "Bailey, what do you want?" "Chief, I just told Detective Paul to fuck off." "That's not my concern anymore, so get out." "What the hell is going on?" Matt pulled me to the side. "After 27 years the Chief is retiring." I stood there completely caught off guard. They couldn't force him out. He was leaving on his own terms, and you had to give him that. "Bailey, you better leave before you piss him off." I whispered to Matt, "Just so you know, if Detective Paul is downstairs, I'm going to deal with him my way. I've had enough with this place and the nonsense."

Walsh spoke to Matt just before I was about to exit the office. Matt called me to the side. "Walsh will call Detective Paul on this. Please go back to the academy." Many at the department didn't like Chief Walsh. Regardless of what they said about him, he seemed to be a cop's cop to me. Sergeant Cooney called me soon afterwards. He told me Detective Paul was pissed about the testimony in Hartford and my using his name. "There won't be an interview, Officer Bailey." "Good, now if both of you can just leave me alone." I slammed the phone down.

There was still a furor with the Board of Police Commissioners over the court's decision to set my penalty aside. The board had to reconsider my case and their ruling. I knew that wasn't going to happen. They called a special meeting and invited me to attend. The entire board made it clear they had done nothing wrong and there was no need to reconsider anything. "In the Bailey matter, how say you?" They polled each commissioner for the vote, one by one. "No. No. No. No. No. Nay. No." All seven agreed they had treated me fairly. Shocker.

They tried to protect their decision by using the same ploy the City Attorney's Office used in my first complaint. "Henceforth, we will have swift and firm justice in dealing consistently with all police officers, starting with the Bailey matter." The smugness on the commissioners' faces was surreal to me. The city informed Judge Clendenen of their decision and promise of a new beginning. I knew it was just a matter of time before they'd slip up again. I had the perfect saying as I thought about their latest maneuver, "Patience is a Virgin." All I had to do was wait.

## Federal Court/Race Issues

I returned to the academy the next day, smiling. Just before I got there, Dave had read about the board's decision in the papers. He asked if I was alright. "Dave, that was round one. I have more in store for them." "Yeah, I figured you weren't going down without a fight. I can't wait to see what you do next."

A month or so later, Lieutenant Boston went before the board to ask that I be put back on the streets. He told them it made no sense for me to be there, but they refused, as expected. It was payback if you asked me, for my embarrassing them in court. Just to stick it to them, I booked off on an injury for two weeks, then returned and passed all the tests I missed. Lieutenant Boston informed them of my missing classes yet passing the required testing. No rookie had ever missed class without being terminated. I was provoking and daring them to.

Four months of classes were coming to an end. The guys were about to graduate and wanted to know what name to put on the class plaque. So the board would see and remember the persona they had learned to hate about me, I chose for the plaque: Wild Bill Bailey. The last day of class, Lieutenant Boston said I could now carry my gun. "That's funny, I never stopped." Lieutenant Boston looked so relieved I was returning to the streets. And what a surprise, someone from the state called to warn me about carrying a gun without a permit. I didn't ask for his name nor cared who put him up to it, "Call me when you take Cruz' permit away. Until then, I'm carrying." Clearly the state and BPD were still in touch with each other.

Fresh out of the academy, I had a few months left before the bank would take my home. I sold the cars, motorcycle, and salvaged what I could. Being restricted at work with no overtime, court costs and attorneys' fees took its toll on my finances. I kept track of everything I lost. The city was going to give it back, I'd see to that.

My ex-wife was still asking me what the point was. It was a period in my life when I had no answers to that ques-

## No Black Heroes

tion. I wasn't a Malcolm X, a Jackie Robinson, or a Dr. Martin Luther King, nor was I trying to be. I was simply someone fighting a hate that had resurfaced throughout my life time and time again. I was tired of it all. I answered her sarcastically, "Yeah, what was the point?" The one thing I did know was, if you can't stand up against wrong, then what good are you?

I was ready to hit the streets but needed a place to live. I still had the second home for an investment on Willow Street. It had been up for sale but no one was buying. The bank seemed more concerned with my home on Platt Street, so I moved to Willow, turning it into a rooming house for extra income. The ad in the papers called for women only. I figured women would bring less drama. Although they were skeptical at first, they saw it was about rent only and started moving in.

The girls were glad to have me around. They felt safe. Talk about a movie in the making! When they couldn't sleep they'd come to my room and we would talk. They cooked for me, danced with me, and sometimes we watched TV until I fell asleep. The guys at the department heard about the all-girls home and drove by occasionally out of sheer fascination. Anything the department had done to me was becoming a long-lost dream.

With Walsh officially retired, the city was conducting a nationwide search for a new chief of police. The Guardians were concerned about who would be coming next. We were hoping for someone fair. We needed a chief who would end the divide at the police department. It would be a plus if the new Chief could shut down the Ad Hoc Committee's reign of hatred.

Rita called to say her father was worried. The Ad Hoc had gotten away with so much under Chief Walsh. Their methods were mostly about backroom deals and opposition. But they did have one avenue that was to their advantage. They controlled the Detective Bureau and all the warrant requests. So when a white officer committed a crime, there

## Federal Court/Race Issues

seemingly was never enough evidence to get a warrant. If one of us had any run-in with the law, no matter how slight, a warrant was issued immediately. We had seen many Guardian members arrested under their system. We were hoping for an end to the Ad Hoc and its one-sided schemes.

After months of speculation the announcement came through; the city hired a new Chief from New York, Chief David Irving. His swearing-in gave us hope. He said it was a new day and he would not tolerate violations of policies, and especially discrimination matters in his police department. At the Guardians meeting, we all asked the same question; was he for real or just making a proclamation for Judge Clendenen and the federal court to buy into? Only time would tell.

Chapter 15

## BACK ON THE STREETS

I was off for a few weeks due to time earned while assigned to the academy. As expected, I lost my spot in TNT. I had a lot to consider and wasn't sure what to do. If I returned to patrol, most officers there weren't going to cover me. My stopping Officer Pitch from beating up that kid was still resonating with officers. So my options on being safe were limited. Being in a unit gave me some protection, compared to being out there alone. In a unit, the accountability of a team is monitored and reviewed. Luckily, and faced with a huge problem in crime, Chief Irving solicited requests for a new unit called TRAP, Tactical Response and Patrol.

From the start, it was made clear that there was no overtime in TRAP, before anyone bid for the unit. I assumed the "no overtime" clause was the reason many officers didn't apply. I put in for it and luckily got the assignment. The TRAP unit was a quasi version of TNT that focused more on crime suppression. The scheduling was centered on evenings in high-crime areas. We had 12 officers who got

## No Black Heroes

reassigned, including Sergeant James Honis. It was going to be activated in two weeks.

While at home relaxing, I was called for department overtime. It was an East Side, two-man car. I took it just to see who they would force to ride with me. It was Officer Jeanie Cabana. Great, she and I never had any problems. Once I knew she was working with me, I relaxed. She was curious because they pulled her from a one man car at the last minute and reassigned her with me. "Jeanie, these guys don't want to work with me. You're probably assigned with me because you don't complain."

We were riding down Connecticut Avenue when we got the call, "Red 42, go to Marina Village on the South End. We have no cars and you're the only one free. A woman's throat has been cut." Jeanie spun the car around. I was impressed. When we arrived, I saw my friend Pearl Sharp lying on the ground in a pool of blood. Someone had cut her throat and just left her there. Officers were arriving but wouldn't approach Pearl. Jeanie said, "She might have AIDS, Bailey"

I ignored the AIDS concern and ran over to her. She had a five-inch slice partially covered by her hand. I moved it, and a long spurt of blood shot right into the air. Jeanie began to look a bit pale. "Jeanie, call the ambulance and have them pick it up." "What are you gonna do, Bailey?" "Hurry Jeanie, I don't have much time." She called for the ambulance, while I put my fingers into the cut and felt a pulsation. That's where I applied pressure to stop the spurts. "The ambulance is almost here, Bailey."

"Bailey, your cross!" At that moment, Pearl had noticed my tiny piercing in the shape of a cross. Was she thinking it was a sign she'd die? "Please Bailey, help me." "Pearl, you're not going anywhere, I got this." The ambulance arrived a short time later, and the EMT asked me to step aside so they could handle it. "Guys, if I move my hand, she's gonna bleed out." They looked at me, figuring I was making something out of nothing. "We'll handle it officer, just move back." "Okay." I pulled my hand out. "Holy shit, wait, wait. Put your hand back, back!" Jeanie was now looking ivory in color. Blood was spraying all over Pearl before I put my hand back in the cut. The EMT maneuvered around so he could put direct pressure on it and stop the bleeding. "I'm so sorry officer, thanks. You can let go, shit."

Back at the car, Jeanie asked, "Bailey, where did you learn that? I'm impressed. You did great out there." Pearl was a good friend of mine. I could only hope she wouldn't die. I needed to change the subject, and try to get back to my right frame of mind. Jeanie had always been straight with me. I had to ask. "Jeanie, can I ask you a question?" "Go ahead." "I know it was a while ago, but I need to know. Before we first got on, the court rescored the police test. Black officers moved up on the list ahead of white officers. What were they really saying about us after that?" "The guys were upset, Bailey. They said the test was fair but the Guardians used the color thing. It caused a lot of resentment. Why?" "It's been bothering me, the things I've seen and heard here." It was important for me to hear, from someone other than us, about how officers really felt, and Jeanie spelled it out. I didn't want to push it; she was one of the few who would still ride with me. I decided to leave well enough alone.

The next day I got called and assigned with Jeanie on overtime again. "Hey, are you asking for me by name?" She just laughed. We weren't in the car two minutes, "Amber 23, go to an unwanted person call. It's Joey Manero." Joey had a reputation for fighting with the police, and winning. It usually took four officers to handle him. The family asked that we remove him from the house.

Joey got into his fighting stance. I touched Joey's arm in an attempt to talk him down, and he quickly pulled away from me. Jeanie called for backup. No one over the air said they were coming. I walked over towards Joey, but Jeanie stopped me. "We should wait for backup." Suddenly, Joey started swinging wildly at me, but I blocked his crazed punches. "Joey, stop fighting." He took a wide swing at my

## No Black Heroes

head but missed. I gave him a stern straight left to his jaw, down he went.

"Joey, knock it off!" We struggled until he got up and lunged at me. With no other choice, I gave him a devastating punch to his head, bringing him back down. At first, he wasn't moving. Slowly, he began to sit up but remained on the floor. He just sat there staring at the kitchen, dazed. The family was yelling, "See what happens when you fight?" I was concerned, because Joey had a blank look on his face. "Jeanie, call for an ambulance. He's not acting right, something's wrong." The ambulance soon came and took him to the emergency room.

I looked at my middle knuckle, which was swollen. That had never happened before. Jeanie looked at my hand, "What happened?" "I don't know. I must have hit him wrong." At the hospital the nurse came out, "You can take your prisoner. He's alright for now, but he will need to come back later for more tests." "Nurse, what's wrong with him?" "Mr. Manero has a metal plate in his forehead. It's dented." "What?!"

Back in the car, Jeanie looked at my hand, shaking her head. "Jeanie, I didn't know. All these years, I don't think anyone knew." At booking I filled out the paperwork. Everything was in the file, including Joey's injuries and how it happened. I hit him in his forehead in the hope it wouldn't cause him too much injury. Guess I was wrong. At the end of the night I told Jeanie it was a pleasure working with her. She wished me good luck with TRAP. "Hey Jeanie, did you notice one thing, no one showed up to cover us?" She stopped and looked at me like a light bulb had just come on. "I'm outta here, Jean. Be safe."

My last assignment in patrol before my transfer took me completely by surprise. I got called to work overtime in a solo car. The assignment was to patrol East Main after store owners complained about crime and no police presence. I wasn't there a minute when the call came in over the air. "Shots fired at Benjamin Franklin School." *A shooting in a*

## Back on the Streets

*school; what next?* I was two blocks away and arrived just in time to see a young kid in the hallway with an Uzi-type weapon. I walked straight into a bad situation.

This kid wanted to show me he was a badass with a gun, but there was something in his eyes that just didn't fit his "gangsta" look. I raised my gun and pointed it in his direction. Students in the hallway were ducking and running for cover. I knew I couldn't take the shot without accidentally shooting one of them. Suddenly, he took off running with me right behind him. "Don't do it kid, drop it, DROP IT!" He kept looking back and I could see he was about to turn on me. He ran to the parking lot and threw his gun under a car before I caught up and handcuffed him. School security arrived and filled me in on him. *Great, he's just a 14-year-old kid.* The news crews arrived in numbers from across the state and had a field day with the story. It was the first school shooting in Bridgeport, and I hope the last. At that point I just knew I was done with patrol.

A 14-year-old shoots up a school. Just another day in the 'hood.

It was my last night of freedom before my assignment to TRAP. Grand Master Eddie Mezerewski, who was the head instructor from the Tae Kwon Do school, called me. They were planning a night out and wanted me to come with them. I volunteered to be the designated driver. It was a Saturday and we all headed to a new club, the White Parrot, in Waterbury.

I arrived at the school by cab to drive the rented van. They were all asking me where my Corvette was. "Home,

## No Black Heroes

safe from you guys. You didn't think I was gonna to let you all pile in that, did you?" Everyone was laughing and looking forward to a night out. At the club, we were having a good time. One of the black belts, Eugene Soars was at the bar talking to someone. She was a brown-skinned female with long black hair, Lillian Santiago. She looked at me and said, "Hi, I'm Lil." Eugene offered me a soda. Lil chuckled at the soda offer. She smiled and continued talking to Eugene.

The bartender placed my soda on the bar. I reached over to get it when a woman sitting by Eugene spoke. "Excuse you." I looked at her, "Sorry, I was just getting my drink." Eugene turned around, "Oh Ron, this is Lil's sister Yvette." She looked Italian but with Chinese-looking eyes. Lil, on the other hand looked all the part of a Latina. I repeated my apology to Yvette. "I'm sorry; I didn't mean to offend you."

We struck up a conversation and danced a bit. At the end of the night Yvette asked for my phone number. She surprised me by pushing me up against a mirror and kissed me in front of everyone leaving the club. Her sister pulled her out of the door. To my surprise, she called the next day. We talked about her running away from Providence, Rhode Island and an abusive boyfriend. We discussed my job and what it was like to be a cop. If only she had known what I had been through. She probably would have run the other way.

Short conversations went into hours and hours nightly. I finally confided in her about what happened to me. She was shocked to hear what the Bridgeport Police Department was really like. "The racism, crooked cops, and the hate between officers, it's shameful. But that's how it really is." It was nothing like what she thought. Yvette, like many others, was under the impression cops took care of each other. I joked with Yvette, "Yeah, we were told that in rookie class. I was also told that all cops are honest and virgins. So much for that claim, too." She laughed.

I began to worry. Cruz could still be around and this would be a perfect way for him to get at me, through Yvette.

## Back on the Streets

I gave her a picture of Cruz with details of the sordid events. "If you ever see this guy, pretend you don't know him and call me. I'll take care of it from there." Cruz was infamous for going after others to get at someone. I had a feeling Yvette was about to change my life. Cruz had better stay gone if he knew what was good for him.

The first day in TRAP was fairly simple. We were assigned to the hot areas in Bridgeport and told to make our presence known. Sergeant Honis was straightforward, "Go out and arrest somebody." We began shutting down the streets, saturating the high crime areas. It forced the drug trade inside. The Special Service Division took advantage of what we'd done. With the drug trade inside, they were making controlled buys and conducting raids weekly.

TRAP members devised a second plan of attack. We all knew that drug users who came to buy drugs always had something wrong with their cars. No lights, wrong plate, cracked windshield, no seatbelt and so on. People on drugs don't care about their cars, just getting high. So we started taking out the buyers.

The dealers couldn't have cared less if the buyers got arrested or not and kept selling from inside. Always in a hurry, the buyers would park halfway in the street and run in. When they came out, we were waiting for them. Everyone we stopped either had the drugs in their hands or tossed them as soon as they saw us. It was like shooting fish in a barrel. We took their money and drugs; and got information on the dealers. The buyers were offered drug rehabilitation services, but most just wanted to be released so they could go buy somewhere else. We did save a few.

I got a call from Carwin. "Bailey, you're not going to want to hear this, but the police department is having its annual citation awards event. The entire TNT team is being honored. All of its members are to receive a unit citation. You were left out." "Carwin, what does the notice say?" "The TNT members are being honored for over 1300 arrests. Your

## No Black Heroes

name was not mentioned or the fact that you made the first major arrest with the Number One Family."

Clearly, the Board of Police Commissioners were not about to give me anything. This was a stab back at me for what I put them through. Carwin said he wasn't going to accept his award. "Why?" "Bailey, when you get yours, I'll accept mine. Not until then." I appreciated his gesture but begged him to reconsider. He wouldn't say anything. Once he made up his mind that was it. I was very proud of him. It seemed silly to file in court over what many would consider trivial, but it was the principle of it.

I filed in federal court and served the Board of Police Commissioners with papers. I was sure they would be insulted to receive papers from me, independently. Having an attorney represent you provides distance and a sense of professionalism. It probably seemed personal to them, and it was. I cited their arrogant, biased behavior. I even provided the dictionary's description of bias in the writ; "an unreasonable hostile opinion and prejudice towards another." I'm sure that went over well.

As the weeks passed, TRAP actually made a huge impact in Bridgeport. We shut down drugs in certain sections of town by taking care of the little things; traffic, drug buyers, and other small nuisances. Taking on the smallest problems kept the big ones from growing. Unfortunately, TRAP was a temporary assignment, and we were about to be shut down after six months.

It was the last week and things were going as usual. We were assigned to the Panic when it happened. I pulled up and stopped this guy for not having his seatbelt on. As I got out and walked towards the car, the car's reverse lights came on. He backed up trying to run me over. Bam, bam, bam. I fired three shots into the trunk of his car. He put the car in drive and floored it, headed for I-95. I was about to give chase when it dawned on me; I had just gotten suspended for shooting at a car, Cruz. I stopped right there.

## Back on the Streets

Sergeant Honis was parked in the grassy area across from the Panic to keep watch over the team. We all knew he had a sense of humor, but I hadn't seen it yet. He got out of his car, standing there watching me, in total disbelief and silence. He walked to the trunk of his car and opened it. I figured I was in trouble for sure. With his head pulled all the way back, he pulled out a large bottle of liquor, turned it upside down, and pressed it to his lips!

It wasn't until I crept closer that I realized he had not removed the cap from the bottle. He scared the bejesus out of me. I thought he really had lost it. All the officers looked my way and began laughing. Even a few drug dealers came out and had a good laugh. Officer Feyk looked at me with a smile, shaking his head, "Some people never learn, Bailey." They all got back into their cars and drove off. "Hey, where're you guys going?" "Sergeant Honis put the bottle back in the car, shook his head one more time and drove away. They left me standing there alone. It was one shooting no one was going to report.

Chapter 16

## TNT Out of Control

Just as my assignment in TRAP was ending, an opening in TNT came up. The guys I worked with on the first team had been reassigned. There was a new crew in TNT assigned by seniority, compared to the first team picked by Sergeant Convintito. The names of the officers had me feeling uncomfortable. Most of them had faced criticism from Guardians about their community efforts and rumors of callousness when dealing with people. I had a choice to make. If I returned to patrol, isolation would be my reward. In TNT, there was no telling what those guys would do or how they would treat me. I decided to take my chances with TNT.

My bid for TNT was accepted, but once in the unit, I realized something was wrong. Cynical overtures and under-the-breath comments greeted me. "I hope he don't start his shit here. Guess we got to watch what we do now." I thought back to how the first team had worked together. Sergeants Convintito and Samatulski made sure we were a team and righteous in what we did. The obvious difference

## No Black Heroes

was that the first team members were chosen, while these guys got assigned by seniority rights. Officers with more time on the job weren't necessarily the best qualified. My only saving grace was Tony, he was still there.

The new supervisor was Sergeant Rob Copeland, a wide, stocky man who spoke with a high nasal twang. He reminded me of the old-time sheriff Ray Stuckey from the movie *Mississippi Burning*. His racism wasn't supposed to be visible, but the real person he'd been hiding was obvious. Copeland always had a story to tell about how great he was in the armed services. The team loved listening to him. The military exploits he boasted about had me suspicious though. Whether bragging or lying about his heroics, it wasn't a good sign.

The first to make an open comment to me was Officer Rob Frost. With other team members standing by, he told me he didn't care about my fight on the racial issues, the informant, the state, or the rumors. "Bailey, are you gonna be a team player?" I knew exactly where he was going. He was referring to Officer Pitch, and that kid in cuffs. "Bob, I came here to work. I'm sure you guys won't be disappointed. There's no Officer Pitches here, right?" They all slowly drifted off in their different directions.

The new team seemed uncomfortable with me around. I wasn't seeing the things I had heard from people on the streets. The rumors of beatings and the other things were not taking place, at least not while I was out there. Unsure about those guys, with their constant whispers and side huddles, I decided to take a peek at what they had done before I got there. I reviewed the pictures of prisoners arrested over the last year. A great deal of them had a common theme; bruises or marks on their faces. Drug dealers were known to run, but fighting was something they usually tried to stay away from. It was a given on the streets; you don't fight with a cop. If you did, it was an excuse for a beat-down and your drug business suffered. All the officers' buddies would then be constantly messing with the "cop

## TNT Out of Control

fighter." So why were there so many pictures showing injuries?

What a wakeup call to grip me next. The surveillances were being done by hardnosed Officer Brad Simon. Running late, he asked if I could get him an undercover car. I couldn't believe what I saw next. I pulled back the curtain that kept prisoners from viewing the fleet of cars TNT had. In the front row was a bright yellow taxicab. All I could do was stare at it. Officer Simon commented, "I'll bet you never thought we had a car like this one, right?" "No, I had no idea." I had no doubt it was the cab Cruz used to come by my house. They let Cruz use an undercover car to come after me? I was convinced the people in control of the place were from an insane asylum!

Officer Simon decided to take the cab out instead. I rushed into the office and pulled the signout sheets for the undercover cars. It wasn't hard to find what I was looking for. The log had the informant's number cosigned by none other than Detective Paul. I thought about going over to OIA, to punch him out, but as I calmed down, it dawned on me that it was clear evidence of Cruz, the department, and a conspiracy. They allowed Cruz to come by my home using one of the department's cars! With the police board's decision refusing to reevaluate my suspension, and the new revelation, it was another nail in their coffin. Maybe I could write a book someday about all of it! Yeah, right. No one would believe it.

After working with the team for about a month, they were running low on arrests. We tried the old Rambo Roll-ups, but no one ran or dropped drugs anymore. They had seen those tactics before. Desperate to make more arrests, Sergeant Copeland came out of the office. "Head over to Jane and Brooks Street. I just got a call there's a crowd of kids hanging out on the corner. Check 'em out and see what you can find." I didn't like the sound of it, 'See what you can find?'

## No Black Heroes

We got there only to see a bunch of frightened kids walking away from us. What caught my eye was the church where they were hanging out. "Hey guys, these kids are from the church. It's not what it looks like." At the time, I was riding with Officer Dave Raddison. "Hey Bailey, I know you're supposed to be this great Narc and all, but we've been doing this a while, too." I got out of the car and watched them throw those kids up against the church. Officer Raddison looked back at me, "You gonna help out or what?" "They haven't done anything, I'm not touching them." "We'll see what Sergeant Copeland has to say about that."

That's when the minister of the church came out. "What are you doing to my kids, officers?" "Father, these kids are hanging out in a known narcotics location. We're checking them for drugs." The pastor looked at Raddison, "These kids just came out of church. It's dress-down day!" I was standing by the car door, slowly easing back into the car and sinking down low. How embarrassing.

I could just about see over the dashboard as the team let the kids go. Officer Raddison got back in the car. He slammed the door shut, upset. He didn't say anything as we drove back to the base, swerving the car all over the place. Back at the office, Sergeant Copeland was led into his office by Raddison. When they came out, Sergeant Copeland called me in. "Officer Bailey, we have a little problem. The guys don't trust you. They're concerned that when they need you, you won't be there for them." "Sergeant Copeland, what they did today was wrong. They rolled up on a group of church kids. They were searching for drugs and had no reason to. That's not drug enforcement, that's stupid." "Officer Bailey, that's what I'm talking about. I was told you didn't even get out of the car. What if someone got hurt and those kids were dirty?" "Anyone could see those were church kids, Sarge. Shaking down people to find something is not a part of my job description." Sergeant Copeland didn't like what I had to say. He ended the conversation. "All right Officer Bailey, but you're isolating yourself."

## TNT Out of Control

Tony waited for me to come out of the office and pulled me to the side. "Hey kid, these guys are gonna mess with you. You got to make it look like you're a part of the team, even if you're not." "Tony, I didn't see you shaking anyone down." "No, I was looking in the alley for drugs." Tony looked at me and smiled. He was old school and knew the ways of the world at the BPD.

The next day, we were at State and Clinton Avenue. It used to be the Sanchez Number One Family's spot. We had gotten a call about someone selling drugs there, and just as we pulled up, a sale was going down. It was Wilfredo Sanchez and Tommy Perez, and right away, they both started to run. They ran for the rear yards, with Perez lagging behind. The guy who was buying from them took off in his car.

I used the patrol car to cut Perez off. It slowed him down, but he ran around and made it to the rear yards. I got out and caught up to him. That's when he pulled out a gun. I yelled out, "Gun!" so the team knew what we had. Perez threw it down and kept running. I could hear Sanchez running through a series of broken fences one yard over. Perez went over a fence and back towards the street, as the team was yelling for him to stop.

Knowing they were on Perez, I focused on Sanchez. I ran, ultimately forcing my way through a clump of fences with my arms up. My right arm started bleeding as I got closer to Sanchez. The razor wire on the fence slashed a 13-inch long cut on my arm, near the shoulder. I tackled Sanchez, who got up to fight. I landed a kick to his head, and down he went. Officer Simon came over the fence just in time to see it. "Bailey, that just made up for all the shit you put us through since you came here!" I handcuffed Sanchez and picked him up. As we walked back, we retraced his trail, finding the drugs he tossed. I walked through the adjacent yard and retrieved the gun Perez had thrown, a Titan .38 caliber handgun.

We returned to base with our prisoners. At the Stockade, a table we crafted with cuffs bolted on top to keep prisoners immobilized, a kid Officer Castro "Short" Rodriguez arrested was handcuffed to it. I guess he must have mouthed off to Rodriguez on Clinton, so he arrested him. When I came through the door, I caught a glimpse of Rodriguez slapping the kid while in cuffs. "Hey Short, do that again and I'll knock your ass out, got it?" "Aw Bailey this kid's an asshole." "Touch him again." Rodriguez walked off. I went into the office and told Sergeant Copeland what happened, and he said he would handle it.

Sergeant Copeland contacted the parents to come pick up their son. When they arrived, I watched as he let the parents take their kid, but he never said anything to them about my complaint. Talk about déjà vu! I decided it was time to take notes, if that was the future of things to come. Oddly, the reports for Clinton Avenue arrests were written by Sergeant Copeland. It had Perez with the gun on him instead of where he threw it. For some reason, the report stated that Sanchez was arrested by Officer Simon instead of me.

Why Sergeant Copeland was writing the report was a mystery to me. The arrests were good ones. I didn't see a need to say Perez had the gun on him. I saw him throw it. The only thing that was correct in the report was my getting cut on the fence. What are these guys going to do next? Maybe I should have taken my chances in patrol. The team was proudly saying Wilfredo Sanchez was a member of the Number One Family. I didn't want to burst their bubble, but he was just a guy we arrested on Clinton who happened to have the same last name as Mariano Sanchez! He was just another low-level dealer.

Over the next few weeks drug arrests were fewer and fewer. They had run out of options and ideas. This was my chance to get away from Radisson. I was tired of his fat ass. "Hey Sarge, let me give surveillance a try." Sergeant Copeland looked at me and smiled as if I were kidding, "Okay Bailey, go see what you can do." He puffed on his pipe, turning away from me, and then looked up at the ceiling, rolling his eyes so the team could see it. Those guys really thought a lot about themselves.

My surveillance resulted in several drug arrests. Sergeant Copeland was surprised and caught off guard with me insisting on writing the reports. If I were going to swear to something, it had to be accurate. Over the next few weeks, the number of arrests began to surge. Sergeant Copeland would occasionally walk in and say, "Great job." As he walked out, he would look at the guys and roll his eyes as before. He had no idea my peripheral vision was extremely sharp. I saw his antics every single time.

We were making good arrests but you could tell the guys were uncomfortable. Doing my own reports meant that whatever I saw would be included. They didn't trust me, and that was fine. It kept them honest and away from me. All I had to do was make sure no one on the team got hurt. One thing was certain, there were no more pictures of injured prisoners. If my doing surveillances avoided that, fine with me.

Sergeant Copeland decided it was time to break the surveillances up between Officer Simon and me. I noticed when the arrest numbers were up, Simon would go out instead of me. If they slipped a bit, I was put back on surveillance. Officer Simon had done a good job on surveillances. I figured his numbers were dropping because his surveillances were forced from a distance away. Simon knew he couldn't walk into the 'hood without standing out. There was no doubt I could get in and up close.

It was my turn to do takedowns. I was working with Officer Raddison in a rare pairing between us. God, if only this guy would stop chewing for a minute. We went to Shelton Street to check out a tall brown-skinned black male near a drug spot. When we got there, everyone started walking away slowly, and no one fit the description of who we were looking for. A local drug dealer from White Street was hanging out, John Boy. He was leaning on a fence, saw us approach, and remained where he was. Raddison got out

## No Black Heroes

of the cruiser and threw John Boy up against the car. I walked over. "John Boy, what's up?" "Hey Bailey, I ain't doing nothin'. Wassup witcha boy?" Raddison patted him down with me standing close by. John Boy wasn't an angel and could've had a gun. Raddison pulled a wad of cash five inches thick out of John Boy's pocket. He looked my way. "Hold on to your buddy while I check the rear yards." I asked John Boy to turn around and stand up, then patted him down again.

Raddison returned from a yard and told John Boy he was free to leave. He gave him his money back, but I could see the fold was nowhere close to what he had when we arrived. I walked over to him. "John Boy, I can't file the complaint, you have to. If you do, I'll back you. You got my word on that." Raddison was yelling for me to get in the car. John Boy looked visibly upset, "Hey, Bailey, I can't file no complaint. You know his buddies won't leave me alone if I do. It's the price you pay for doing business out here. This is some fucked-up shit, Bailey." "John Boy, you have to do this. It has to be you because the money taken was yours." "Thanks anyway, Bailey."

I walked back to the car and got in. Raddison started in on me, "So you and your buddy know each other?" "What the hell is that supposed to mean?" "Nothing, except I'm out here doing what I was asked by the Sergeant while you're striking up a conversation." "If you knew anything about what goes on out here you would stop talking. Take me in."

Back at the office, I told Sergeant Copeland what I had just seen. "Sarge, I know John Boy had a larger fold of money than what Raddison gave back." "Bailey, where is this guy if an officer took his money?" "He didn't want to come in." After speaking with Copeland I didn't feel remotely comfortable with the unit. Here was a crooked cop taking money and another who liked to slap kids around. And Copeland wasn't doing anything but giving lip service.

I was on surveillance at Main and Whiting Street the next day. I tried to do the surveillance from the rooftop and

## TNT Out of Control

was on the oldest house built by African Americans from the Freedom Trail, Little Liberia. The house was so old, the roof was giving way to my weight. I moved to Murphy's Moving company roof next door. We had made 10 arrests when I called out one more; a white male with a beard, grubby looking. The guys told me they had him but let him go. Officer Frost called over the radio, "Bailey, there was a problem with this arrest." He didn't tell me what it was. I reminded the team that anyone getting rid of the drugs was to be charged with tampering. No one responded.

I returned to base and asked who stopped the last buyer. It was Officer Frost and Officer John Ramos. Ramos pulled me to the side. "Hey Bailey, we let the last guy go because it was Butch." "Butch who?" "You know, Butch, who got fired for drinking on the job." "Let me get this straight, you had Butch under arrest and you let him go because he was a cop?" I got the fellow officer thing but they should have made the arrest. We could have released him to appear in court, no bond. "Did you guys forget he was fired for beating his wife and selling his gun?" Ramos just looked at me. "What if the Feds sent Butch in to buy, looking for crooked cops and you just let him go?" I figured that probably struck a chord. "Hey Bailey, we didn't find anything. Put it in the report that way." "Tell you what; I'll put what I saw, what you did, and anyone who reads the report can ask you what happened if it comes up."

More complaints from the team were being lodged with Sergeant Copeland than anyone could imagine. "Bailey won't search the prisoners. He isn't a team player. His friends are drug dealers." Copeland was looking for any reason to remove me from the unit. The only thing stopping him was the federal court monitoring the treatment of minority officers at the department. I couldn't be removed from the unit unless there was a justifiable reason.

I called Rita and asked if Sergeant Copeland was connected with the Ad Hoc Committee. She wasn't sure. She was telling me she heard her father say its members were keeping a low profile due to allegations that white officers

## No Black Heroes

were receiving preferential treatment. They somehow knew Judge Clendenen was looking at the figures. "Bailey, I don't think Sergeant Copeland is connected with the Ad Hoc. He's friends with my father, but I never heard his name mentioned."

I kept meticulous notes on anything having even the slightest hint of crookedness with those guys. The team's complaints against me so far were their opinions. I hadn't violated department policies. On the other hand, Sergeant Copeland still hadn't acted on Raddison taking money, or "Short" Rodriguez slapping a kid in cuffs. If the team leader was keeping a blind eye on those types of conduct, that was the real root of the problem. I began to focus more on Copeland.

It was a slow night and for some reason Copeland decided the office needed to be cleaned. Here it came. "Hey Bailey, it's your turn to do a Felix Unger, hop to it. You were late coming in." I wasn't sure what he was talking about. "Hey Sergeant, I don't know what these guys have been telling you, but I've been coming to work on time." "Well, the guys have been saying you haven't. They all can't be wrong." He left the room momentarily but came back in for some reason. He caught me writing in my notebook. The look he had for me wasn't pleasant. "Officer Bailey, can you come into my office?" I walked in but put my notebook away. "Officer Bailey, what were you doing in there and what were you writing?" "Sarge, what are you talking about?" "Officer Bailey, are you keeping notes on me?" "Why, Sergeant Copeland? Do I need to keep notes on you?" "Bailey, you're dismissed."

After leaving Copeland's office I knew what was next. He was so one-dimensional and predictable. There was no doubt he would tell the team about the notepad. The next day, no one except Tony was speaking to me. I didn't have to be a genius to figure out why I was assigned a solo car. I was actually happy about it, but knew it wouldn't be long before they tried something.

## TNT Out of Control

Not long after, we were doing a takedown on William Street. I was the third car to get there. Officer Ramos was out holding someone against the car, searching him. Officer "Short" Rodriguez was looking around for drugs. I watched them search the guy twice. They didn't find anything on him. Tony was looking on the ground for drugs nearby when Officer Ramos asked me to hold onto their prisoner. I walked over and held him in place. Officer Simon called over the radio for the team to arrest the guy. Ramos and Rodriguez, who hadn't walked but a few steps away, immediately turned and took their prisoner.

Once we were all back in the office, Rodriguez entered the office with a gun in his hand. He looked at me and asked if I checked the prisoner. I looked at him, "What are you talking about? When I got there you and Ramos were searching that guy. I held onto him for seconds before you guys took him. Did you search him again before you put him in your car?" Rodriguez walked into Sergeant Copeland's office. Tony came over, "This is where they're gonna come after you, kid. Be careful." "I know Tony, but it's Sergeant Copeland who will be leaving, not me." Tony looked confused.

Copeland called me into his office. "Bailey, how did you miss this gun?" "I didn't put him in their car, they did." "Bailey, this is a result of you're not searching prisoners." "That's not true and you know it." Sergeant Copeland took the gun from the desk and put it near my face, "Then how do you explain this?" I grabbed the gun and his hand, "Get that out my face if you know what's good for you." He moved closer and whispered, "Go ahead, hit me. I dare you, so I can have you fired." I looked him in his eyes, "You and Rodriguez can kiss my ass. This won't work."

I walked out of Sergeant Copeland's office. Officer Raddison walked past me in a hurried pace, as I walked down the hallway. I guessed he heard the arguing. I could hear Sergeant Copeland from a distance, "Tell the guys to stay away from this asshole." I responded loudly, "You're the

217

## No Black Heroes

only asshole here!" I knew what was next, but I was way ahead of them.

The next day, I went to the commanding officer and handed him a large legal package. He asked what was in it. "This is a detailed complaint on discriminatory treatment by Sergeant Copeland. It also details TNT members who have conducted themselves in violation of department policies. It chronicles Sergeant Copeland not doing anything to stop corrupt behavior after being informed." He had nothing to say and looked absolutely astounded. I turned and left his office without saying another word.

A few days later, I was called to Chief Irving's office to confirm my complaint and allegations of crooked cops in TNT. "Are you sure about what you think you saw, Officer Bailey?" Here we go, 'Think I saw'? "This looks like you are retaliating against the TNT officers. I was told about the gun you missed." "If you look at the package, Chief, you will see my documents go back four months. My paperwork and notes were taken long before Sergeant Copeland and his 'Band of Merry Men' made up the story I missed a gun."

Chief Irving seemed to brush off the fact that cops were stealing and abusive in their conduct. I reminded him of the recorded dates and times Copeland allowed belittling and derogatory behavior that he himself also took part in. I urged Chief Irving to authorize an investigation on my complaint of money being taken by Raddison, as well as the abusive conduct of Officer Rodriguez with a defenseless kid in handcuffs. Everything was all laid out for OIA to follow up on. If they called people in to verify what I had documented, it would be a wrap.

Chief Irving's response was more than enough for me to realize he was next on my list of things to do. "Well, Officer Bailey, perhaps Sergeant Copeland felt you were not being truthful." "No offense, but Sergeant Copeland knows the number to Internal Affairs. Why weren't they notified when I first complained? If my name had surfaced about a theft or abusive conduct, he would have called." Irving said my tim-

## TNT Out of Control

ing was curious, just when Sergeant Copeland was in the process of writing me up for failure to search a prisoner, and threatening. "Threatening who?" "Sergeant Copeland. Officer Raddison saw the whole thing." "Fat boy Raddison is a liar. He wasn't in the office when Copeland put a gun in my face. He was in the back eating a bucket of Chinese food!" I then reminded Chief Irving my delay in filing the complaint was due to my efforts to gather more information. "Officer Bailey, I will make my decision after the investigation has been concluded." "Chief, everything in that package is the truth. And for the record, it was Rodriguez and Ramos who missed that gun." I whispered as I turned to leave, "Or planted it."

Back at the unit, things were intense. The whole team was either looking the other way, or attempting to stare me down. Tony was the only one speaking to me. Officers Rodriguez and Ramos passed me in the hallway. Rodriguez spoke to Ramos in passing, but for me to hear. "I can't wait until that guy is outta here." I stopped and turned around, speaking in a quiet

The turmoil and death of a once-good unit.

tone, "Uh, guys, excuse me. I'm not going anywhere. Both of you lied on me. When no one's around, I'll deal with ya my way. "They both looked at me, seemingly afraid to speak. I pointed down to my right foot, and they understood what it meant.

Tony came up from behind, after observing our exchange. "How do you know they won't go back and tell the Sergeant?" "Because they know I meant it, they're cowards." Tony looked at me and shook his head. "You're dangerous, boy; but I love you." Big man Tony Brown always had a special fondness for me.

**No Black Heroes**

The complaint Sergeant Copeland lodged against me was on the fast track. Chief Irving, for some reason, decided he would handle it himself. I figured either the Board of Police Commissioners wanted nothing to do with me, or Irving wanted to keep a lid on the crooked cop thing. I guessed only time would tell if I had beaten Sergeant Copeland and company.

Chapter 17

## POLICE BOARD CITED FOR RACISM

As I had figured, the Board of Police Commissioners returned to its old ways. Cases against white officers were on hold while black cops were going before the board at an astonishing rate. Their promise to treat all officers equally starting with "The Bailey Matter" didn't happen. The Guardians soon realized black officers were being brought up on charges twice as often as white officers, who outnumbered us three to one.

We were in amazement that the board did nothing about two white captains punching each other out in the Detective Bureau, or the white officer who intentionally hit a man with his police car during a chase, causing him to lose part of his leg. Amazingly, not one person in authority raised the significance behind such a depraved and reckless act. A man's leg was severed for a motor vehicle violation, and the officer got away with it? The straw that broke the proverbial camel's back was when a group of white sergeants took Carwin's hat he had left in the car and stomped on it in the patrol office. Carwin went to patrol and confronted Sergeant

## No Black Heroes

Dennie about it. Dennie, the only one in the office at that time, became enraged, pulling his gun catching Carwin off-guard. Officer Candito happened by and overheard Carwin telling Sergeant Dennie, "Go ahead and shoot, but you better kill me." We were told Carwin reached for his gun and Dennie ran out of the office.

Always the fighter, Carwin filed in federal court about the clash in patrol, and the motivation behind what they did. It was a deep-seated hatred for Carwin, our Guardians president. No one knew for certain if Carwin had reported everything that happened between him and Dennie in patrol to the court, and especially the gun thing. But suddenly, without so much as a peep, Dennie retired. I'd bet anything Carwin was waiting until his day before Judge Clendenen to tell him about the confrontation and the guns being drawn. With so much at stake, and not sure what Carwin was going to do, he bailed out.

Could anyone imagine, officers in patrol pulling their weapons on each other? Dennie was a supervisor! The hostile, and at times antagonistic, conduct of white supervision had worn thin with black officers. Things were escalating. Guardians were in contact with African American officers on a national scale, and found that many of them were also subjected to some of the same biased and shameful behavior. The Guardians were about to file on the "disparity in treatment" against the Board of Police Commissioners, but something else was going on.

Ted called. Somehow he knew; "Brother Bailey, Judge Clendenen is looking at the backlog of police cases pending. Remember the board said starting with your case they would pursue all cases thereafter, immediately, and with evenhandedness? We knew the board said that just to keep from doing what they should've, reevaluate your case." "Ted, what's goin' on?" "Judge Clendenen is about to come down on this place. You're about to see what the court can really do."

## Police Board Cited for Racism

The board was hearing a case against Officer Hiram Jimenez. His case was brought before the board, ahead of all the other pending cases. Some actually understood why. Hiram was accused of cutting the tires on Police Commissioner Marsha Goodman's car. Rumor had it that he did it because of a previous ruling against him. Many thought he had the opportunity and motive, due to his living close by Goodman.

I went to listen in on his case. The commissioners were not happy to see me. I sensed their contempt for me as I sat down. Union Attorney Lander was worried. Jimenez was about to testify and was known for saying what was on his mind. The board advocate asked questions on behalf of the police commissioners. Then came the question of all questions not to ask Jimenez, "Officer Jimenez, how do you 'feel' about Commissioner Goodman?" "I think she's a piece of shit." Oh no, he didn't! There were gasps from even seasoned police officers. He was asked to repeat his answer. "I said I think she's a piece of shit, but that don't mean I cut her tires!"

Attorney Lander continued, "With all due respect, you asked Officer Jimenez how he felt, and he answered you truthfully." It was a moment of truth Attorney Lander capitalized on. The board was furious over Jimenez' answer, but they asked the question. The case was ultimately dismissed, and Commissioner Goodman was seen turning two shades of purple. Hiram had a new title, "Hiram 'The Truth' Jimenez." I figured they'd never ask his opinion again.

The promise of change Chief Irving swore to wasn't happening. The Board of Police Commissioners failed in their promises as well. Judge Clendenen had conducted an investigation most were unaware of. He came down with a ruling that made front-page news; "Cop Board Discrimination Found." The ruling said the Board of Police Commissioners willfully and intentionally disregarded the rights of the Bridgeport Police Department's minority officers in handling disciplinary cases. Judge Clendenen ordered the board to clean up the backlog of pending cases. His new

## No Black Heroes

ruling kept referring back to the "Bailey Matter." My name was becoming more and more synonymous with challenging inequality.

The court clearly acknowledged that the "new beginning" they claimed would take place didn't happen. He ordered the board to explain why they should not be suspended from their duties. To top it off, the city was fined $1,000.00 a day until they cleared up the backlog of cases. The news reported that the board had 33 cases pending, including one over a year old. How stupid can you be citing change only to return to your old ways? It was time to make my move. I hired Attorney Gerald Gaynor and sued the city, police department, and Board of Police Commissioners. They treated me differently from other officers, and I had a ruling in support of that claim.

"Hey Ted, did ya hear, the papers said the Board of Police Commissioners discriminates?" He just started laughing. "Brother Bailey, now listen well. You're a target for every white officer who has something to lose over this ruling. Remember, they had it their way since God knows when, to their advantage. They will blame you for their punishments. You gotta watch yourself."

Soon afterwards, a second bombshell dropped. I went to the TNT office ready to be ignored as usual. Every officer except Tony Brown walked out of the day room when I came in. Tony smiled. "Kid, I don't know how you did it. This is something that has never happened before. No supervisor has ever been removed from a specialized unit. They removed Sergeant Copeland from TNT." Tony spoke matter-of-factly, "Copeland is out, kid." I hunched my shoulders, "Hey Tony, there's a first time for everything."

A notice came down from the Chief's office just after Copeland's exit from TNT, but not about Copeland. Chief Irving took seven holidays from me for threatening Sergeant Copeland, and missing a gun. You could best believe I'd respond to Irving and how he handled things. But first, I requested the commanding officer to give me all the state-

## Police Board Cited for Racism

ments made by TNT members. A few days later, I got a large package from the Chief's office detailing the entire investigation.

What a joke. I asked Tony to listen to the questions they were asked. "Officer, have you seen or engaged in beating anyone in custody? Officer, have you stolen any money or know anyone who has?" That wasn't an investigation; it was a shitty attempt to make it look like one. "Who did the questioning, the Ad Hoc Committee?" Tony motioned for me to quiet down. "Well kid, you knew that was all they were going to do." "Tony, here's the killer. They asked Officer Rodriguez did he ever hit a kid in handcuffs as alleged by Officer Bailey. His answer was 'Absolutely not.' When I hear that 'absolutely not' answer again, I'll know it's probably a bald-faced lie."

The formal order came down from Chief Irving's office. Sergeant Copeland was reassigned due to improper supervision. He stayed clear of my assertions that it was a racial issue, opting for a mismanagement excuse. Chief Irving sent down a third memo, which would push me for that head-on collision we were destined to have. Irving's memo said I threatened Copeland, but as the chief, he was restrained in what he really wanted to do to me. He mentioned the court that was still involved with the monitoring of the department, and he emphasized that in the future he would not tolerate threats, harassment or intimidation from officers. He sent Judge Clendenen and the Connecticut Post copies! I responded with my own memo, "Chief Irving, you had two captains involved in a knock-down drag-out fight; I sure hope you're going to take that seriously. It's been sitting on your desk for over a year." I attached his memo to mine, and sent it to Judge Clendenen.

Judge Clendenen began sending down rulings on complaints from the Bridgeport Police Department on a regular basis. Just before the court was about to hear my complaint on the TNT citation they refused to give me, the board decided to award both Carwin and me. We were sent a notice to attend a special session. Commissioner Goodman was the Board of Commissioners President and would do the presentations. Police Commissioner Buccino resigned after the federal court criticized the handling of my case and its racial implications.

I was extremely proud of Carwin. He refused to accept his citation until I received mine. Not many would do something like that, nor have the courage to make that kind of statement. Commissioner Goodman had the nerve to say she recalled how great that tactical unit was, and she was sorry we had been inadvertently overlooked. Carwin and I just looked at each other with a smirk that brought a dimple to the corners of our mouths.

Eventually, the court ruling against the board gave way to more resignations. They were forever linked to the word discrimination. Commissioners Goodman and Streets were the last holdouts to step down. Commissioner Larraquente was the only one left standing in the end. I was sure he tried to tell them about the racial implications of their actions or inactions, but they obviously didn't listen. I remembered Commissioner Streets' comeback at a board hearing on one of my many issues, "It ain't over 'til it's over." He was right about that.

Chapter 18

# TNT Team Three

With Sergeant Copeland removed from TNT, things took a turn for the better. Sergeant Samatulski was returned to TNT. Finally, we had someone who knew what he was doing! Slowly but surely, over the next few months, the guys who had served under Copeland were asking to be reassigned back to patrol, if not rotated out. They returned to patrol and told officers I couldn't be trusted and had kept notes on them. I was labeled a turncoat who used race to get Copeland out of TNT. Tony was still in disbelief. "Damn boy, you cleaned house."

The bids for new TNT officers went out, and guys who wanted nothing to do with me refused to bid in. I had hoped that it meant honest cops would be coming instead of what he had before. The first round of bids was all minorities. The second go-around saw a few white officers join who had the right demeanor for the job. They had a confident walk about them while laughing and joking about their being the

## No Black Heroes

real minorities. We were going to rock the town, doing things right.

One of the new members was Officer Juan 'J.J.' Gonzalez. He knew the street players better than anyone else, and was the first to make a joke. "Bailey, looks like some good guys here. I guess they don't mind working with someone who would rat 'em out." I shot right back at him. "Yeah, we got some good guys now, so don't take any drugs or money while you're here." We both started laughing. Like me, rumors had followed J.J. that he had sold drugs at one time. He said it started behind a hooked-up Lincoln he drove when he came on the job. Talk about stereotyping. Guess cops can't have nice cars without something being wrong.

In the beginning, Sergeant Samatulski assigned the target locations. Our first couple of assignments resulted in good arrests. We were seizing large amounts of money and drugs. The Panic was a standby due to its size. It was a huge area divided into six or seven drug spots owned by different street gangs. We could always go there if nothing else was shaking. Samatulski was still not fond of solo surveillances but knew I could handle them. When I told him I was going in the Panic alone, he almost choked on his coffee. "Hey Bailey, those guys over there don't play. I know you've done this before, but the Panic?" "Sarge, I got this."

I went to the housing office and got keys for an apartment in building five. The apartment was empty. I spoke only to the head manager about it, because no one else in that office could be trusted. The dealers were known to pay housing workers for information on us. The crew selling at building five was well organized. Information had linked the Jeffersons to that spot. I happened to see old lady Grandma Jefferson keeping watch over it the day before. I guess selling drugs has no age limitations.

To assist me sneaking into the apartment, Sergeant Samatulski called on patrol. They were told to come into the area and ask around, "Where's the guy with the gun?"

# TNT Team Three

While the 'hood watched patrol looking for a man with a gun, I walked right past them into building five. The dealers never paid attention to vacant apartments that were locked. I took a spare lock and hung it on the latch for appearance. The apartment looked locked and no one noticed otherwise.

It was 4:30 in the morning. The first bundle of drugs hadn't come in yet. They usually came in by 8:00 or so, and never in large amounts. The risk of getting caught and losing a whole load on a traffic stop was too risky. Also, rival drug gangs looked to rip off their competition. If you lost a delivery, you had to pay for it. If you couldn't, someone was getting shot. That was the drug business.

The TNT takedown team was close, but hidden well. The first bundle came in around 9:00am. Ed Valentine brought it in. This case was going to be a new beginning. The targets were known to be organized, and guns were always on the set. The dealers were giving each other handshakes used by the Nation gang. I had to wonder if the Jeffersons joined them for added clout and protection. Those guys were known for guarding their spot with a vengeance. No matter, everyone was going down that day.

The first call, a TNT arrest, was for Isidro Rosa. He was standing in the courtyard and pulled out a silver handgun, making sure everyone knew he had it. He was the enforcer for that location. He walked to a blue Malibu and put the gun in the rear seat, like it was no big deal, and drove off. Rosa was out checking the entire Panic area. I had the team arrest him and take his .357 handgun. The stop was so fast, he never knew what hit him. I asked the Sergeant to contact the court to seize Rosa's car as part of a drug enterprise. It looked like we were in store for a long day.

Business was good. I began calling out every buyer sold to. There were so many sales I couldn't keep count. I gave out descriptions of buyers, cars and license plates. The chase team got every one of them. I wrote down anything said on the set. "Give me six, you got eight? Hey man, I saw Narcs not too far from here. You need to be careful." Even

## No Black Heroes

though word got back we might be out there, the selling continued. Everyone felt safe inside the hallways. There was so much money, it was no wonder selling drugs was so widespread. All you had to do was hang out, sell, and collect.

It turned out to be as first thought, an all-day event. We had 11 dealers ready to be arrested and 11 buyers in lockup. I had lengthy and multiple charges ready to shut down the operation. If they collected money, looked out, or warned anyone by yelling "Five-O" or "Narc," they were going down. I called in a detective to type up a search warrant for me. The dealers were going in and out of building 5, apartment 314. It was their safe haven, and I was shutting that down, too.

Someone in the hallway standing next to my door said Rosa had been arrested with a gun. Whoever was listening reacted with a heavy southern accent, "Lawdy, Lawdy, what in the world is goin' on dis mo'nin'?" I had to chuckle, with my hand over my mouth. People in the courtyard were passing word about Rosa's arrest, and I could see the concern over their lookout/enforcer being out of play. I let the team know the set was wise to us out there.

The man with the southern accent told the next buyer they were out and waiting on a bundle. I knew then we could make a clean sweep and had the team come in slow. No one was going to run, they were out of drugs. The team came in as I walked out of the apartment and down the stairs dressed in a hoodie and raggedy jeans. I walked out of the hallway and into another one across the way for a better view.

From my new location, the team was directed to James Banks, William Hamilton, Anthony Davis, Sonia Harris, Michael Brown, Guy Fecto and Pablo Perez. All were to be charged with conspiracy in the sale of narcotics. I then sent TNT to apartment 314, but in a slow relaxed-like approach. They were told to knock and see if someone would open the door. No one had drugs on the set, so why not? Sure

## TNT Team Three

enough, the door opened and everyone inside was handcuffed. The team brought down Andre Bruce, Tracy Moore, Ed Valentine, and Brian McGee, so I could confirm the right persons had been arrested.

It was a department record with 22 arrests off a single surveillance. Even though they ran out, we had all the drugs we needed for our case through their buyers. The message was out, TNT was back to doing things with purpose and taking everyone in under a criminal enterprise. I petitioned the court to take Valentine's car along with Rosa's. Imagine Valentine's surprise to hear we knew he brought the first bundle in. Drug spots were being shut down and the communities were ecstatic.

The Panic had gotten too hot for the Jeffersons, so they moved their operation to a small apartment complex at 129 Black Rock Avenue. It was a West Side location, and no one could get into the tightly guarded building. The drugs were tearing the neighborhood apart and people were begging for help. Statewide Task Force undercover detectives tried unsuccessfully to infiltrate the Jeffersons. Sergeant Samatulski heard about the new location and wanted it shut down.

After a few weeks of observing their new spot, I could see their defense was tight. We couldn't arrest the buyers because no one could see the sales. Drugs were sold exclusively from inside. The door only opened long enough for someone to enter or leave. My plan to shut it down was to knock on the door; buy drugs, and ask if I could use my stuff upstairs in the hallway. It was a risky thing to do for sure. Officer Earnie Garcia was my point man and direct cover. He didn't like it at all. "Hey Earnie, almost everyone in Bridgeport still thinks I'm this tall dark-skinned cop. If Walter or Howard Jefferson aren't there, I'll get in. They know me, not their crew." You'd best believe Earnie would be a whisper away until I gave the all-clear sign.

I walked up to the door and knocked. They let me in while eyeballing me closely. "Who da fuck is you? We ain't seen you here before." I spoke in a raspy voice imitating someone who lost theirs to crack. "Hey man, I just want 10 dollar's worth and a place in the hallway. I need it, come on." After a long hard stare and someone else knocking on the door, they took my money. Someone pushed me to the side, "And don't stay up there all day, mothafucka!"

I scrambled to the second floor, set up and watched buyers come and go. Peaking from the stairwell had to be the hardest surveillance I'd ever undertaken with so many nearby. The team had a hard time hearing me communicating in a whisper, but they got 12 buyers. It was a oneway street and easy pickings. The dealers had forgotten about me, and business was good. They'd never been hit before and had no reason to worry. Drugs were coming out of the first floor apartment, and the sales took place right at the door.

My plan was to get the team inside before any of the dealers could make it into the apartment. I called the team and told them to come in quickly when they saw the door open. They parked just out of sight from the doorway. When I walked down the stairs and towards the door, Kai Weaver and Denise Gorham looked at me, "Hey man, what the fuck were you doing up there all that time?" I staggered to the door "Hey, I'm dope sick, sick man, look out." I stumbled to the door, opened it and made gagging noises like I was throwing up. "Hey motherfucker, shut that door before I put a cap in your ass. I don't care how dope sick you are." The team came in running past me, placing everyone down on the floor.

Debbie Bass tried to walk by me unnoticed, but I turned and grabbed her. It must have been confusing to see a crackhead helping the narcs. With Bass' back to me, I put her in cuffs. She asked, "Who the fuck is you?" Without saying a word, I started punching Debbie in her face over and over. The guys stood there, shocked. Finally, I kicked her in her face with her back still turned to me. It brought her to the floor.

## TNT Team Three

One of the team members shouted, "What the hell are you doing, Bailey? Are you fuckin' crazy?" I started jumping up and down with Debbie on the floor. I was jubilant, but the guys all stood by motionless. I had to wonder if they were thinking if Copeland's TNT team ways had somehow rubbed off on me. I could see it in their eyes as I seemingly jumped for joy. Then I yelled out, "She grabbed my private, my dick and wouldn't let go, you fools. Oh my God it hurts!" They paused, looked at each other, and started laughing, barely holding onto their prisoners.

I was up against the wall in agony, and they were cracking up. "Hey man, this ain't funny. She wouldn't let go." I was holding it, rubbing it, and the guys were falling all over themselves. "We thought you had lost it." "Yeah, I almost did!" The prosecutor read the report and called the next day. They had a ball with the report. "So Officer Bailey, was that a simple assault, or an invasion of privacy?" "Very funny, ha ha ha, very funny." Click!

By then, Yvette and I had been seeing each other for some time, and we had moved in together. We had a baby boy shortly thereafter, Brandon. There were times when Little Ronnie and Ashley were living with us as well. It was kind of crazy at times, but the kids loved each other. At home we discussed what Bass had done to me. Yvette was surprisingly upset, "Hey, tell your 'street friends' hands off; that's mine. You could hear the kids in the room laughing about her declaration.

TNT was hurting the drug trade, no doubt about it. Drug gangs were forced into concentrating on countersurveillance, like the Sanchez Number One Family had done years earlier. They drove by our office, checked to see what days we worked, and even tried following us. As time went on, their regular intrusions had revealed almost all the undercover cars. Our office, unfortunately, could be viewed from the street, and we had no legal means of stopping them from spying. It was a constant game of counterintelligence and we were losing.

## No Black Heroes

Except for a few cars kept for informants at a different location, we were out. With no other choice, I decided to use my older Jeep Cherokee for surveillance. It was a car I used for hauling junk, and no one had seen it before. There was no way it would draw attention. Sergeant Samatulski said he didn't want to know anything about me using my personal car. But it was the only way to get back in the game.

To keep the streets guessing, I altered my surveillance tactics. Sometimes I got out of the car a distance away from a drug spot and hid nearby. I used dumpsters, grass areas alongside I-95, abandoned houses, and even the roofs of high-rise buildings, sometimes 10 stories up. When I could, I blended in with a crowd of people just to hear what was going on in the streets. It was risky, because some out there knew me, but most didn't. I had that look and just fit in. "Where's Bailey?"

TNT's success had its drawback, homicides. We were costing the streets thousands in drug dollars. Any loss of drugs or money meant that someone had to pay. With TNT successes, drug dealers' costs were rising, so they began using junkies. They were cheap labor, paid with drugs instead of cash. If they got arrested, they were left in jail. If any of them took money or drugs, they were the next day's news, "Another shooting in Bridgeport." Drug life was cold, no two ways about it.

It was never made public, but our sources informed us that a huge amount of drug overdoses were taking place. Some said the dealers used untested cuts to stretch out the drugs that killed folks. Others were telling us that instead of paying the junkies, they just gave them a hot dose and moved on. Who knew or cared? They were junkies. God, what were the streets doing to people?

With street gangs pissed about TNT, word was the boyz in the 'hood were out to get me. Officer Santi Llanos reported to Chief Irving's office that there was a contract out on me. Santi filed a report that several of his informants had firsthand knowledge. I was to be killed at any cost.

## TNT Team Three

Chief Irving ignored the threats on my life, and I was at a loss for why. Perhaps his inner circle were badmouthing me, or even making light of the situation. Maybe he wasn't happy with the Sergeant Copeland thing. Whatever his reasoning, he wasn't stepping up.

While at court, getting a search warrant signed, William Carrasquillo was walking in the hallway. I had arrested him several times and he wasn't happy about it. On my way out, he intentionally walked into me. It was a street challenge that needed a response only someone from the streets understood. "Hey, let me tell you something. If you're looking to get your ass handed to you, fucking with me is the way to go." It took him completely by surprise. Cops didn't talk like the street boys, especially when alone. He had nothing to say for a moment.

He chose his words, "Well I guess we'll have to see about that, Bailey. I have a reputation for killing motherfuckers." "I'll be waiting, Carrasquillo. In the meantime, step the fuck off." I placed my fist in his chest and pushed him hard enough to make him stumble into his boys that were standing nearby. He regained his footing and moved towards me. I walked right into him, jolting him so hard he fell back into his boys who stumbled to regain their footing. I kept walking and refused to turn around. It was the ultimate street disrespect.

I notified Chief Irving's office of Carrasquillo's threats to the familiar tune of silence. I had to wonder if Irving just didn't give a damn and why. Imagine my surprise, a few weeks later, when I saw Carrasquillo in the news. "Latin King Arrested For April 26 Shooting." Carrasquillo fired more than 40 rounds in an all-out commando style assault at the Mills Memorial Housing Apartments in Meriden. Who knew; Carrasquillo was a regional Latin King leader. If he hadn't been arrested, my guess was I would've been next. He was sentenced to 12 years for shooting multiple people in the project. It was the nature of the beast, but I had work to do and moved on.

## No Black Heroes

Back at the office we received a call someone was selling drugs at Evergreen Apartments by building 20. The description was a tall black male. We all headed out, but Tony rolled up before we got there. That's when all hell broke loose. Arthur Corbett was running towards a hallway holding something, with Tony right behind him. Corbett pushed his way into an apartment, and a woman was heard screaming. Tony opened the door and Corbett jumped head-first out the window holding a MAC-11 assault weapon. Tony said over the radio, "In all my years I ain't ever seen anything like that."

We quickly relocated our cars to Andover Street just in time. No sooner had Tony spoken when Corbett ran right toward us. We didn't even have time to pull our guns, he came at us so quickly. I cupped my hands bending forward like I had my gun out. "Drop it or you're dead." Corbett dropped the gun and ran past us. I suddenly felt an urge to pee. Talk about a close call!

I chased Corbett from Andover to Pine Street and leaped on his back. Corbett was about 6'1", 210 pounds, and in great shape. With me on his back he just kept running and dragged me along. He began elbowing back at me to shake me off. I slid down a bit and grabbed his waist, finally pulling him down. He tried to get up while I held on and hoped the guys could catch up. Corbett pushed me off him and stood up. As he turned to run, I managed to pull him back down. We were off balance and went down with him landing on my knee. I yelled out in pain while the team caught up to us.

They dragged Corbett off me, and I literally screamed out in agony. A woman came out of a nearby house to see what was going on. Her facial expression exhibited just what I was feeling, pain. The team handcuffed Corbett and picked him up. He was bleeding from his mouth, and they all turned to look at me. "I didn't touch him guys, I swear." They took two large bags of dope from Corbett's pocket. At the hospital, the physician said I pulled ligaments and had a large contusion on my knee, but no serious damage. Corbett, on the other hand, needed stitches for his lip. The team all looked at me again, "I swear he fell on the pavement, guys. I didn't touch him."

Sergeant Samatulski was very pleased with the arrest and recommended a citation for Tony and me. I was delighted for Tony. He had been a good and faithful officer for years. So it was about time. A few weeks later, Sergeant Samatulski let us know the award request had been denied. "Who denied it, Sarge?" "I was told Chief Irving. Sorry, Bailey. I tried" I quickly called Ted. "Brother Bailey, so far Chief Irving has not lived up to our expectations. As I told you before, no two black officers have ever received an award for their collective efforts at this department." Ted informed me that the complaints in federal court against Irving were mounting. So much for his "New Day" promise!

Chapter 19

*Couldn't anyone see how we were
being treated? Didn't anyone care?*
—Ron Bailey

## CHIEF IGNORES RACISM

The Guardians had always been a force to be reckoned with. Racial complaints were mounting, but sadly, there were only a select few black officers filing in court. The majority of African American officers were avoiding court under fear of retaliation. Most black officers were convinced that white officers, especially supervision at the department, could easily make life difficult for us. So the unwritten rule was to shy away from fighting, even though everyone should be entitled to being treated the same.

There was no word on the Ad Hoc Committee or what they'd been up to. After Judge Clendenen's investigation, and the critical rulings against the Board of Police Commissioners, things were strangely quiet. I was watchful of sleeping dogs. What were they up to? Rita called and said her father remarked, "Anyone in this family who's a nigger lover has no place here." Rita was embarrassed by her father's words. She and I were concerned that he somehow knew about us. We kept an even lower profile.

## No Black Heroes

When it rains it pours. Just when I thought things couldn't get worse, reports were coming in that Dave witnessed a police beating. Word was he saw a veteran white officer beat a black man in handcuffs. Dave was on his way to report it when he kind of lost it in the locker room. I heard he began knocking over lockers and punching the walls, when the commander heard the commotion and went in. Dave just straight and outright told him what happened; he witnessed a helpless man being beaten in handcuffs.

All I could think was that the "Officer Pitch Thing" was going to be pale in comparison to what Dave was in store for. He made a formal statement. Not even the Ad Hoc could stop that warrant from being issued! The state had been called in, since it was a cop who officially reported another cop. It took a while, but Officer Joseph Brenner, who had been arrested, was sent to prison. Brother Dave Daniels was in for a long ride, alone.

When the dust settled and with Officer Brenner sent to jail, Dave was returned to patrol. It was no surprise that no one would cover Dave on calls after that. If he called for help over the radio, his transmissions were blocked. Offiers keyed their mikes to make sure anything Dave would ask for could not be heard. This went on for months, and not one supervisor did a thing about it. Essentially, Dave's life was in constant danger. The final blow came when Dave's car was keyed, the tires slashed, and a hangman's noose was found on the hood of his car. The news broke, and all eyes were on the Bridgeport PD.

We all knew what would happen next. White officers were saying that Dave left the noose on his car for attention. They were saying it was all about a lawsuit, and he wasn't in any danger. I went to him, knowing what he was going through. "Hey Dave, if you need someone to ride with you, I will. I'll leave TNT." "No Bailey, I'll be alright. They're gonna transfer me out of patrol."

Dave had been through a lot but turned his frustration into a personal mission. He was tired of the "Don't cross that blue wall of silence" rhetoric and decided to go after that culture the best way he could. He decided to run for Guardians President. It was his hope to change an establishment that had been the center of racism for as long as anyone could remember.

Dave ran for office, and won. He was the new kid on the block and the Guardians president. After the election, some white officers were incensed. Officer Halen, whom we all knew to be a racist, had the nerve to ask how it felt having a rat for Guardians president. I played along. "I have no idea how he won. This isn't a good thing, I can tell you that." Officer Halen smiled, thinking I was now on his side. Yeah, right. Dave had plans, and I figured he was about to make changes I couldn't have predicted.

Dave was soon reassigned to the Community Service Division. Strangely, or perhaps *not* so strangely, there were no signs of an investigation over the hangman's noose. No word of an investigation as to who keyed his car, nothing. It was evident we were experiencing a great deal of hate and nothing was being done to stop it. It was the same excuse as always, "The department is looking into it."

At the next Guardians meeting, Dave told us he was going to petition the court to force the Bridgeport Police Department to get a new radio dispatch system with a tracking system that could identify who was keying the mikes. It would put an end to officers endangering other cops blocking their transmissions. Officers were infuriated by the notion. Why, I'll never understand! It would keep all officers safe, black, white or otherwise. The cost for the system was in the millions, but the city had no choice. Once the court formally heard what happened to Dave, a new dispatch system was ordered.

It never ended. I was in patrol, sniffing around, shortly after the ruling, to see what the mood was like. I happened to hear officers talking. They were laughing about a comment Captain John Lyons was rumored to have made. They were talking about a joke he had made about Detective Ray

**No Black Heroes**

Sherwood's wife. Lyon's was rumored to have joked about Mexicans coming over to America illegally to get work, including Ray's Hispanic wife. I couldn't believe what I was hearing. And they thought it was funny.

I immediately contacted Officer Roberto Melendez of the Hispanic Society. I asked if he was aware of Captain Lyons' racial jokes about Hispanics. He told me they had spoken with Chief Irving about it a while ago. The court had just criticized the department for the unnecessary delays when it came to officers in violation of department rules. Here we go again! Chief Irving had been sitting on information about racially insulting comments made by Lyons. I knew he and Captain Lyons were buddies, so it was no surprise that nothing was being done. "Melendez, I'm not a member of the Hispanic Society, but that's not right. You guys need to force Irving's hand." They were waiting to see what Irving would do. I had the answer to that. Nothing.

After the ruling by Judge Clendenen chastising the pervious Board of Police Commissioners, a new more diverse board evolved. Its new members were taking care of business. If a matter was sent to them, they dealt with it swiftly. They had a few Latinos serving on the board, so I was curious about how they would feel about Irving's "inactions." It would be interesting to see how the new board would deal with racial issues.

I wrote a complaint about the comments Captain Lyons made in regards to Hispanics and sent it to the board. They were informed that Chief Irving had been holding on to the matter. Not a week passed since my contacting the board when a memo came down from Chief Irving's office. Captain Lyons had been suspended for three days. I remember that the memo curiously left out the reason why. Not divulging the reason why an officer had been brought up on charges was something out of the norm. Irving was still trying to shield his friend after the board forced his hand.

Commissioner Larraquente was the last remaining member of the old board and caught up with me. "The board would like to thank you, Officer Bailey. We had no idea about this until you contacted us." "Commissioner, it was my pleasure. You don't have to be Hispanic to be offended by those types of comments" "I just wanted you to know the board appreciates your taking a stand."

Meanwhile, Captain William Chapman had been transferred to the third floor to work with Chief Irving. Chapman was an older black supervisor who stayed out of controversy. He wanted to make a difference, his way, and focused more on the community. He was looking out for me and pulled me aside. "Officer Bailey, Chief Irving is upset with you and so is Lyons. Your name has been mentioned repeatedly on the third floor." As always, I made light of the situation. "Thanks, Cap. Guess I won't be getting a Christmas present from the Chief this year!"

Things were so bad under Chief Irving that even black officers who were reluctant to file complaints were filing. At the next Guardians meeting, Officer Bryant told us something I really thought he was joking about at the time. "Did you guys hear? Sergeant Carol Lakes came to work with a ruler and measured all of the black female officers' nails." "What? Why would she do such a thing?" Keith said Lakes was saying she would make sure all the female officers' nails were in compliance with department policy.

"Keith, let me guess. Not one white officer had their nails checked. Why doesn't Lakes take her fat "Betty Cracker" donut-eating ass to the gym and leave our womenfolk alone?" Officer Earl King was laughing hysterically but chimed in, "Brother Bailey, didn't Sergeant Lakes go after a Hispanic woman from records not too long ago, Laura Azevedo?" "Yes, she did. I see what you're saying, it's a pattern."

I informed the membership how Laura Azevedo had been driving her father's car that was registered in Florida, where he lived. Laura was just using it. Sergeant Lakes took it upon herself to confiscate the license plate from the car, saying it was not legally registered in Connecticut. I remember Laura crying in front of the police department. Ted got involved and went to see Chief Irving. Sergeant Lakes was ordered to give Laura back her license plate. The court was made aware of what Lakes had done and we had trouble with her ever since.

Dave told us the female officers were going to file complaints in federal court against Sergeant Lakes. Others at the meeting began to share their own personal horror stories about white supervisors. There were numerous complaints mounting, but one thing was clear, Chief Irving had created a culture where it was safe to treat African American officers in a biased and degrading manner. I was convinced that Irving was the one we needed to haul into court.

I listened as Guardians complained about black officers being excluded from specialized training, assignments, and even overtime. Oddly, the police union's excuse for why we were being shortchanged on overtime was absurd. They said it was a first-come first-served thing, because the jobs had to be filled. Carwin kept records and knew we were not being called for those extra jobs. He was not having it and filed on the overtime problems with Judge Clendenen.

We were also concerned with the way Chief Irving had been handpicking certain disciplinary cases. Irving would decide if an officer's violation of policy was a routine matter. If he decided it was routine, he dealt with it. If he considered it a serious matter, it was forwarded to the board. It was a low-keyed form of institutionalized racism. We were being murdered. The whole process was one big mess the new commissioners had no way of knowing about. If you combined that with how supervision targeted us, anyone could get the picture.

The good news was many of our concerns sent to federal court were having positive results. Just days after the court had been notified about Sergeant Lakes measuring only black female officers' nails, a formal order came down for supervision to refrain from embarrassing officers under their command. Needless to say, Chief Irving failed to for-

## Chief Ignores Racism

mally notify the department that Sergeant Lakes' conduct was humiliating to African American officers. His lack of effort on certain issues spoke volumes about his character.

I was very vocal about Chief Irving and Sergeant Lakes at our meeting. What an eye-opener it was when Captain Chapman pulled me to the side sometime later, "Officer Bailey, Chief Irving was not happy about your comments at the Guardians meeting. I trust you to keep this between us." "Thanks, Captain. My lips are sealed."

Who was telling Chief Irving our business, and why? Someone in our organization was a Judas. The city was desperate to get rid of the federal court process, so it made sense to befriend someone in the Guardians to keep watch over us. In the meantime, the city hired what they considered the best law firm in the state. Curiously, that law firm had ties to Bridgeport's Democratic machine. Does the word "kickback" come to mind? And this law firm's mission was clear; remove the federal court oversight at any cost. I considered it a waste of money during that time period. The city had more racial complaints under Irving than ever before.

### *Protests/Civil Disobedience*

Chief Irving had been writing new policies since his arrival in Bridgeport. The Guardians noticed those policies were harming mostly black officers. There was no other way to say it; we were exceptionally outnumbered, yet African America officers were constantly facing departmental charges. It just didn't add up. Was it the policies or how and who was applying them that had been causing us harm?

Our first of many challenges was the new sick policy. We couldn't prove being targeted, but the numbers clearly showed a disparity in how the policy affected us. The way the sick policy was written made no sense. If an officer missed more than five occasions in a year due to sickness,

## No Black Heroes

it was considered excessive. The officer was subsequently removed from the overtime list for 30 days. So on top of suffering from being sick, you could be punished with the loss of extra income on your return. Overtime was how cops got by. Talk about double jeopardy.

The way the sick policy was being applied made matters even worse. The policy gave some officers an out. If you had an old injury that caused you to miss work it was an excused absence. White officers started booking off with old injuries instead of sick with no questions asked. Their buddies in supervision took care of them. But when black officers booked off with old injuries, they were rejected. The sick policy was apparently the subject of interpretation by supervision. With white supervision as the majority at police departments nationwide, we were the ones taking the hits.

We tried to raise the issues with Chief Irving. His response was in the form of a question, "How can a policy be biased?" I knew everyone was tired of hearing black this and black that. I was tired of saying it. But couldn't anyone see how we were being treated? Didn't anyone care?

Having injured myself a few times, I missed work on several occasions. I always returned with a physician's note stating I had been out due to an old injury. My operations proved I wasn't making excuses. To my dismay, my notes were rejected by the department clerk. They were going to take me off the overtime list for 30 days for chronic sickness. I went to the clerk's office to discuss the matter. Some things never change. It was another sergeant I had never seen before, in all my years on the job. We talked about my absences and as expected, he flat out refused to reverse the rejection of my doctor's notes. My comments were kind of in your face, "Tell Irving he's messing with the wrong person."

I took my issues to the union, explaining that my absences from work were due to either medical procedures or injuries. "The department removed me from the overtime list for being out injured!" Their response was that the pol-

## Chief Ignores Racism

icy had to be appealed and it would take several months. "It's Christmas. You want me to wait on an appeal. What do I tell my kids?" As expected, the union was useless when it came to us. They were too busy fighting the Guardians on having the federal court process ended.

I returned to the department clerk and requested a list of all the officers who had been removed from the overtime list. He handed it to me with a smile, clearly knowing that I was on it. My comment didn't go over well. "Here's a big surprise, only black officers are out sick. We're the only ones who don't come to work, I guess. By the way Sarge, how do you guys stay on the job and no one ever sees ya?" Suddenly, his smile disappeared.

I requested a special Guardians meeting to talk about the disparity in how the sick policy was being applied. At the meeting the focus was more about Chief Irving and the attempts at having the court oversight removed from the department. I blurted out, "Let's do a protest calling attention to the problems we're having with Irving." Officer King spoke up, "Bailey, I know you mean well, but no one will protest the Chief. He'll come after us or anyone who challenges him." "That's all the more reason to, Earl." In court, a retaliation claim is easier to pursue than discrimination claims.

I had one more thing to say before leaving the meeting. "Hopefully I can get a few more people to protest with me." No one had a clue what I was talking about. At home, I told Yvette what I had planned. As always, she was supportive. She was a little concerned but realized it was important. "You're going to make front-page news Ronnie, make sure you take pictures of my kids."

I waited for Ashley and Brandon to get out of school. Little Ronnie had returned to my ex-wife's for a while. When the kids came home, I sat them down, "Kids, remember me telling you why things were going to be a little rough for Christmas?" "Yes, Daddy." "Well today, if you want, we can tell the Chief what we think about his not allowing me to

## No Black Heroes

work. Do you want to come?" Both said yes and even drew up their own signs to carry. I found it amazing how my children understood it wasn't right what the department had done to me for being out sick. They said it was so unfair. It was even more upsetting to them after having been taught that Christmas was a time for kindness towards others.

We got to the police department just in time for the shift change. I parked my car across the street and took out my 3 by 6 foot cardboard sign, placing it up against my car. It was facing directly up to Chief Irving's office. It read, "Chief Irving's policies hurt minority officers." Ashley and Brandon were walking in a circle in front of the department. Ashley's sign read, "Let my Daddy work, it's Christmas." Brandon's sign said, "Chief unfair to my Dad." I was so proud of the kids.

Connecticut Post reporter Beth Fisher came and asked about the protest. She seemed amazed at my nerve but loved talking with the children. I kept a baseball cap on and down low, to cover my face. I still had to work in the streets undercover. I could hear yelling from the third floor and listened more carefully. Chief Irving was screaming near his third floor window. Fisher looked up, smiled, and then asked about the policies harming minorities and the number of complaints in court. "I have been told the federal court received 11 complaints against Chief Irving and supervision under his command so far. Clearly his policies are hurting black officers."

During the protest, several officers were walking by snickering. Officer Olivia Bell stopped, "Bailey, now you know you shouldn't have made these kids come out here." She began to laugh, looking at Ashley and Brandon. Ashley looked up at Bell, "Dad didn't make us come. We came because it's not fair." Bell raised her eyebrows and snapped her head back, "Well scared of you!" Bell shook her head and said she'd see me in church Sunday.

## Chief Ignores Racism

We walked about two hours and were about to leave. Deputy Chief Hector Torres, the highest-ranking minority officer on the job, had an officer ask me to come inside. I walked the kids into the lobby and asked Officer Cliff Cunningham if he could watch them for me. Torres had a straight face. "Officer Bailey, the Chief wants a report on your protest." "Deputy Chief Torres, please tell Chief Irving I'm off duty and don't have to give him anything. I'm exercising my first amendment rights." Torres looked at me, "What about these flyers you handed out? These are an insult." "D.C., what's on those flyers are facts and opinions. I can explain them to Chief Irving if you want me to." Torres looked at me quickly and with purpose. "Bailey, please take your children home if you're finished. Do *not* go upstairs."

The next day, the newspapers printed a lengthy article with pictures of the children and me. They reported what we spoke about and the disparity at the department. Chief Irving was caught completely off-guard. His response in the papers was to say that he had done everything possible to try to ensure everyone was treated fairly. The best part of my protest; whoever was telling Chief Irving Guardian business had no idea what I had planned.

Guardians were shaking my hands telling me what a great thing I had done. Keith said it best. "Too bad the Guardians don't have the balls to do what you did. We wouldn't be having all these problems." "Thanks Officer soon to be Detective Bryant. Much appreciated and congrats." "By the way Ron, bringing your kids to the protest was sheer genius." I could imagine the community was also paying attention. Now, all I had to do was wait. Surely the chief would react, and I was counting on it.

I received a rare call from my good friend Rita. It had been a long time. She read the news and told me how crazy I was. I asked her if she had any idea who put the rope on Officer Daniels' car. "Bailey, my father said they didn't know who did, but it was long overdue." Then Rita said something to me I had no idea about. She told me that according to her father the Ad Hoc was giving way to a new

## No Black Heroes

group. "Rita, what are you talking about?" "Bailey, haven't you heard? There's a bunch of officers working hard to get you guys off the job. They call themselves the K-5." "What?!" I asked Rita what K-5 stood for. Was it a reference to the Klan? "I heard my dad say something about the name K-5. It comes from the black silhouette on the targets police shoot at. When these guys hit the center K-5 mark, they think of it as killing a nigger." All I could do was thank Rita one more time. She had been a blessing in our fight to end racism. The Ad Hoc was passing the torch to another hate group. I was seeing firsthand how racism was kept alive. Welcome to the AmeriKlan way.

I immediately called Dave and Ted about the K-5. They were just as astonished as I was. "Look, I'll do some checking around with a few guys I trust." I pulled Sergeant John Rockwell to the side and spoke with him. He had always been one of the few straightforward guys on the job. "Bailey, if you say anything about what I'm about to tell you I'm done here." "Sarge, you can trust me." The K-5 is a group that at first got together to fight you guys. It's gotten way, way out of hand." "What do you mean, Sarge?" He kept looking around before he'd speak. "They originally got together to get at black officers, but now they're doing beatdowns on the streets. And they are being rewarded for them." I couldn't believe my ears. And right under our very noses.

According to Rockwell, when members of the K-5 beat someone up, they were given comp time. "Are you telling me they get comp, free time off, for beating up on someone?" "Officer Bailey, I'm sorry, but some of the patrol supervisors have no problem with these guys. The better the beating, the more time off they get." I asked him if I were to somehow get a look at the comp. book and files, could I assume it would be only blacks getting those beatdowns? "The ones getting beat are mostly black. But Hispanics are not off their radar. Please leave me out of this." All I could think of was a supervisor just confirmed a hate group was attacking the community and being rewarded for it. Thank God for Rita and Rockwell.

## Chief Ignores Racism

I went back and told Ted and Dave what I'd learned. Dave wasn't surprised. He was aware of the increase in use of force complaints from the community. We just didn't have an idea how bad things had become or what we could do about it. "I can't tell you the Sergeant's name Dave, but he's not one of them." Ted responded, "He might as well be." Ted had a look of disgust about him. "Brother Bailey, it seems the old Ad Hoc has given way to the new and improved K-5." The dilemma we were faced with was how to expose a hate group no one would confirm existed. We had no proof. For the time being we decided to keep quiet until we could learn more.

Chief Irving was still reeling from the protest. He had D.C. Torres bring me up on departmental charges. The memo from his office said I brought the department into ridicule. They took two holidays from me for violating department policy. Captain Chapman said Irving and Captain Lyons were in the office for a long time before the memo came down. They must have thought it pretty cute to use a minority to bring me up on charges. Where was it written that you're shielded if a minority does your dirty work?

Sergeant Jack Donald was the union president. He said the union would appeal my loss of holidays. I looked at him with a smile. "Chief Irving wants to test me. I guess I'll have to get his attention." "Officer Bailey, whatever you're planning, please don't. You have a right to protest. The union is going to appeal your loss." "Sergeant, no offense, but the union hasn't been the greatest when it comes to black officers' complaints. I appreciate your concern, but I can handle Irving."

Sergeant Donald didn't know, but what really had me in a tizzy was knowing that the union had just chartered a bus to take Bridgeport cops to Hartford for a protest. They were going to march on behalf of an East Haven officer who shot and killed an unarmed man, Malik Jones. I was not happy with my dues being used in support of such a thing. Sergeant Donald was telling the membership it was on behalf of a brother officer. The brother officer thing was not

## No Black Heroes

something I wanted to hear. Malik Jones was killed over a motor vehicle stop. That just didn't sit well with me.

At the next Guardians meeting my desire was to convince them it was time for a second protest at the Bridgeport Police Department. "We have the facts, figures, and Irving's years of ignoring our complaints. What else do you need?" Some agreed while still others were not sure. I decided they needed a wakeup call, so I told them about the K-5. "This group wouldn't exist if not for Chief Irving. The K-5 must've felt comfortable enough forming a group under his command."

The membership was in shock at the existence of a hate group and had no words. A few hardcore members were still not convinced about the proposed protest. Others questioned how we knew about the K-5's existence. I took another shot at their conscience, "By the way, Chief Irving just promoted Lyons to Deputy Chief. Correct me if I'm wrong, but wasn't Lyons just disciplined for his insensitive remarks about Hispanics? Now he gets promoted?"

Lyons' promotion was the ultimate slap in the face, bar none. With Chief Irving's policies harming black officers, Lyons' promotion, and so much more going on, I knew it was the tipping point. Officer Jeff Brown wanted to know what the union was saying on Lyons' promotion. I had raised that very issue with the union and received a letter with their response. I read it to the membership. "It says they do not consider the issue a clearcut case of discrimination. If I get further evidence of a discriminatory nature, they will reconsider the matter. In other words, they're not gonna do a damn thing."

Dave began to tell the membership how the union was beginning to oppose anything we asked the court to approve. The union told us its membership was concerned about their contractual rights. We all knew the decisions to oppose us in court weren't made by the complete union membership; they were made by the union's executive board. The irony was in the union using our dues to fight us in court. "Mister President, we have 21 complaints against Irving in federal court, and counting. I'm requesting we show our displeasure with a group protest." All in attendance said "yes."

We showed up in numbers and made our discontent known. "There are 21 complaints in court against Chief Irving. He protects white officers, while coming after us. No justice, no peace." We called Mrs. Emma Jones, the mother of slain youth Malik, to protest with us. Her attendance was the message we needed to send the union as well. "Don't use our dues to charter a bus in support of a cop who shot an unarmed black man."

At the window of the second floor we saw Captain Robins. He was filming us. Someone in the crowd yelled up to him, "Kiss-ass!" Captain Robins was another follower of Irving. The Guardians showed strength in what we were about. The membership was finally getting to understand. If racism exists in the police department, then what chance do people of color have in a community whose department tolerates such behavior?

We protested for over an hour and knew something was wrong. The Connecticut Post had been called several times. No one came. It was rumored Chief Irving and the editor of the paper had become fast friends. Word was they were in agreement that the protest didn't need coverage. No matter, the court was notified of our protest. We had an abundance of complaints pending, and Judge Clendenen was listening to our calls for help.

Two weeks after the protest, I received a notice from Chief Irving's office. He brought me up on charges and took two holidays without a hearing! There were over 20 other police officers who protested, but I was the only one brought up on charges. The Guardians were informed about what he had done. The comment from Dave was, "I guess you're gonna get paid big-time, Bailey." Irving was slipping. He had become fixated on one thing, getting me.

Chapter 20

## CRUZ DEAD; A SHOOTING; THE FOX AND NEWS

My cousin Wilbur "Luck" Lary called. He sounded upset and surprisingly afraid. That wasn't like him. Something was very wrong. "Cuz, we got to meet right now." Luck had taken the day off. I didn't know at the time, but he had been contacted by Inspector Spencer from the State's Attorney's Office. I met Luck, who was in a frenzy, at Seaside Park. If Spencer threatened him, he was about to become front-page news. Luck was like a brother to me.

"Ron, I just met with some guy, Inspector Spencer, at the courthouse downtown. He said if I wanted to help you, to come talk to 'em. They asked me about you using drugs and said you were a dirty cop, and they could prove it." Luck said they questioned him for over two hours. Spencer was out of options and reaching for straws. How desperate could you be, questioning my family to get something on me? "Luck, you've known me my entire life. I'm not about what they're saying. And I'm for sure as hell not a crooked cop." "I had heard the rumors, but left it alone. Why are

## No Black Heroes

they after you?" "I fought them and now they look like fools. It's that simple." I told Luck the whole sordid details about Cruz.

Luck gave me the impression they'd do anything to get at me. He said a guy working with Spencer clearly hated me. My guess, it was Scanlon. "Hey Luck, let 'em do their worst. I beat them, and their snitch." I reflected on how things had changed since Luck and I were kids. We both grew up afraid of the cops, after our family's warnings about them. "Luck, you forgot one thing. You know our moms taught us God takes care of us. They don't concern me at all."

I told Luck about Bishop White and how he told me no harm would come to me. Luck seemed to relax. Surprisingly, Spencer had the nerve to tell Luck he couldn't talk to me about the interview. It was one of the oldest tricks in the book. Tell a person not to talk knowing they would. This latest move was meant to worry me into doing something stupid. That's when my suspicions kicked in; was Irving behind this? He and Scanlon were pals.

Even I was dumbfounded at how desperate Spencer was. One thing was certain; they had been following Luck. I had to comfort him. "Hey Luck, don't worry about this. It looks like they've been following the both of us. I caught them following me over by Washington Park, after making a sudden turn. That's when I saw Detective Paul with some of the guys from the Statewide." I joked, "He's too big and ugly for undercover work." Luck began to smile. "Let them follow us all they want. We're not doing anything wrong. They can just kiss my tutti fruity!" Luck laughed, we hugged and went about our day.

I drove straight to the police department and called for a car. Officer "Shorty" Rodriguez showed up. My, my; if it isn't Sergeant Copeland's liar in the flesh. I asked him to write a file about the meeting Luck had with Inspector Spencer. He was definitely pleased to hear about the investigation but didn't want to write a report. I was right in his face, "You

## Cruz Dead; A Shooting; The Fox and News

can write it now or I'll catch your short ass later; your choice, brother." He wrote the report.

Never a dull moment. A few days later the City Attorney's Office called. They said a lawsuit filed against me was ready to be settled. I had no idea what they were talking about. They informed me Cruz had filed a lawsuit against me a few years back. They said if I signed off on it I wouldn't have to pay any damages. "First you tell me there's a lawsuit I had no idea about, now you want me to sign off on it? Wouldn't that make me look like I had done something wrong?"

I was about to go ballistic. First, Inspector Spencer tried to get Luck to say I was involved with drugs. Suddenly out of nowhere, there was a lawsuit the city wanted me to roll over on for Cruz? Don't these people have a life? It's no wonder I'm always at church asking for forgiveness. I can't stop cussing these fools out!

I tried the calm approach. "Tell you what. I want the court to know about the state and what the Bridgeport PD has done to me. Oh, by the way, I found the cab Cruz used to come by my house. It belongs to the police department. See you in court." Click ... The next week, a letter arrived at my house from the City Attorney's office. I was dropped from Cruz' lawsuit so it could be settled. I yelled out sarcastically, "It's a miracle. They've all forgiven me!"

I had a feeling Cruz was about to make his comeback. The schemers were running out of options, so Cruz was sure to be brought back. I asked God to have mercy on me for what I was about to do. Getting prepared, I sent a letter to the State Prosecutor's Office, Inspector Spencer, the State Police and Bridgeport PD. I wanted the world to know how "afraid" I was for my life. The letter detailed the desperation in having to protect myself from Cruz and the likelihood of what could happen. I was sure they figured it was a setup to kill him. If it was, it didn't matter. They couldn't or wouldn't keep him away. I prayed on it again, and then waited for him. I was carrying my gun at all times, and thinking about different scenarios of what Cruz might try. If he showed his face anywhere near me, they knew what was next.

Captain Chapman called. He said Chief Irving wanted to remind me I didn't have a pistol permit to carry a firearm. According to him, I couldn't carry my weapon unless I was on duty. He said the state refused to give back my permit. "Capt, I never asked them for it. They want Cruz to take me out. That's why Irving wants me disarmed. Tell him I'm carrying and he can arrest me. I'll be waiting." "Officer Bailey, you need to calm down." "Capt, I'm done with this. I won't disarm, and Cruz can never come near me again. Tell Irving that's it, end of discussion."

Captain Chapman didn't want to tell Chief Irving what I said, but he had no choice. He told me later Chief Irving kicked his desk so hard he thought the man had broken his foot. The whole thing was certain to come to a head soon. I went out and bought special bullets, Teflon coated, cop killers. Cruz could be wearing a vest, and his time was near. It was going to be him or me.

That very week was a shocker in law enforcement, and especially for those who wanted me dead. All eyes were looking closely at me, but ever so discreetly. The newspaper article said it all, "Fire victim was drug informant ... against Bridgeport Police officer and dies under mysterious circumstances." I read how a New London house caught fire with the informant inside. He died on a mattress face up. That was kind of curious in itself. Who lies in a bed while it burns? The papers didn't release his name until much later. Cruz died in a fire that appeared to be accidental. You could bet your last dollar the state was investigating his death, and I was the prime target. I'd just told everyone to keep him away from me or else. Then he was dead. On the streets, they called that "smoked."

For the next few weeks, I remained home to myself. Yvette was frightened not knowing how or who killed Cruz. I sensed she wanted me to give up being a cop. Then the

## Cruz Dead; A Shooting; The Fox and News

news reported something I didn't know. Apparently, Cruz had been working on Officer Lee Lawrence, who was involved in drugs. Lawrence was one of the few black officers that had been a Bridgeport police officer well before my arrival. It was said Officer Lawrence had a stash of drugs hidden in his police car. How they found them in the air vent of a police car was a mystery to us all. Cruz was said to have had something to do with knowing where the drugs were hidden. If you asked me, he planted them. It reeked of a setup. If Lawrence had indeed kept drugs in the police car, it was an ingenious spot. I would've never looked there. The papers said an informant was responsible for Officer Lawrence resigning from the police department and going to jail. I guess that made both of us prime suspects.

With the mysterious death of Cruz, new and more intriguing rumors surfaced. It was said that Officer Lawrence found out Cruz set him up years ago, and that was that, smoke! Some said I knew about Lawrence and Cruz, which made it the perfect murder no one could link to me. Still others had a more believable story, that I circulated Cruz' picture knowing he would end up dead, and he did. No matter how it happened, it was his destiny. My guess was the state would spend an eternity looking closely at me for his death. Good luck.

I was about to focus on Trooper Valentine, Cruz' occasional partner and the one person I missed, who may have tried to frame me. Coincidently, and not too long after Cruz' death, Valentine was arrested on 18 felony counts, including drug charges. He was the only part of the puzzle I never got the chance to finish looking into. Through my investigation, I had found papers linking them both, but Valentine was headed down another path, jail. Who knows, maybe he and Cruz had been scamming drug dealers for years. Maybe having me go down as a crooked cop would have given them room to expand on their "dirt" as Mom would have put it. In the end, Valentine was sentenced to a very long term, and I never heard about him again.

## No Black Heroes

In the meantime, Sergeant Samatulski noticed a drop in TNT arrests. Dealers had changed how they were doing business and weren't out on the corners like they used to be. My assignment was to find out what was going on. I walked into Marina Village dressed like a bum, doing my "picking up cans" routine. But the streets were dead. The boyz in the 'hood were off to the side of a building taking a close look at me. They'd never done that before. At first, I figured they were on to me. Then one of them spoke. "Man, that ain't the Fox. He's dark with crazy eyes and cracked out. He just robbed me. If I see him again he's dead." Who's this Fox they're talking about killing?

I returned to my office and made a few calls. My girl M&M would know what it was all about. "Bailey, Rodney "The Fox" Rollins is sticking up drug dealers. They're all scared of him. Everybody got guns out there, because he's a high-ass stickup kid." "You mean to tell me no one is selling out here because of one man?" "Hey, Fox rolls up on them day and night. They say he wears a bulletproof vest and even wrapped his arms and legs with vest cutouts. He's fuckin' crazy." I was so embarrassed. One man did what the whole TNT team couldn't for years, clear the streets!

That explained the increase in shootings no one had been talking about. "Bailey, be careful. Fox is caught-out crazy. Last night he was in a tree and dropped down on these guys. He took their guns, jewelry, money, and made them strip down to nothing before he ran off. He even shot one of these boys in the leg for fun." "Thanks, Bae. I'll get on this."

I told the team what was going on in the streets. They all agreed, let the Fox shut the dealers down. Earnie was even colder in his thoughts of the Fox, "Hey, we could kick back and let street justice do its thing." "Man, you guys are hard core!" My cousin Billy Gant, who lived in Marina for years, called. "Hey Cuz, thought you should know the Fox came out here last night." Billy said he never saw anything like it. "Cuz, Fox was walking across the street and hit a passing car with his hand for a sound, to fake his being struck, and

## Cruz Dead; A Shooting; The Fox and News

then he dropped to the ground. The boyz didn't know it was him. Some of the fellows came over to see how hurt he was. The motherfucker jumped up with two guns in his hands and robbed them. He shot one kid for nothin'." The Fox had some ideas, a faked accident? "Any idea what car he's driving, Bill?" "Naw Cuz, I saw him from the window. He picked up some jewelry and drugs they threw to the ground and walked off like it was no big deal." "Billy, stay off the streets 'til we get this fool."

I asked Sergeant Samatulski to pass the information over to Detective Bureau. He made sure not to let them know it came from me. The Ad Hoc still had a few detectives left in the bureau upset with me. Once the Detective Bureau knew who was doing the shootings, a few victims began to talk. People tend to cooperate more when the police know what's going on out there.

Warrants were issued for the Fox's arrest. Meanwhile, he just kept on robbing and shooting over the next few months. M&M called to let me know the Fox had a beef with some guy named Bo, and somehow, the Fox found out Bo was at a Little League game in Stratford. Fox got out of his car, and in the middle of the game, he started chasing and shooting at Bo, while the game was in progress! Children and parents were ducking for cover. He didn't seem to care about anything. The Fugitive Task Force worked with Detective Bureau and stayed after him. They were going door to door and watching the streets. A call came in, the Fox was at a house in Stratford hiding out. The Task Force responded surrounding it but came up empty. It was a cat and mouse game the Fox was playing, and he was winning.

Then came that word cops hear a lot, luck. TNT was helping patrol one night because of a shortage in manpower. Officer Ron Henderson was making a motor vehicle stop by the Sheehan Center downtown, and he had the driver out of the car for driving erratically. Luckily, J.J. and Earnie happened to be in the area and showed up to cover him. The Fox was standing there, high as a kite. J.J. and

## No Black Heroes

Earnie immediately recognized him, and that was all she wrote.

Any other time, that stop would have been a shootout for sure. We all imagined catching Fox and having a battle made for the movies. Instead, the Fox was so high, he stopped his car, did what he was told, and didn't even pull a gun. The bad news was drug sales were back to normal on the streets. As they say, "Be careful what you wish for." Earnie commented we should have left well enough alone. "Someone please go bail the Fox out!"

After so many years undercover, the bad news was people on the streets were finally getting to know who Ron Bailey was and really looked like. It was time to change my way of doing things. After some careful thought, I drove to a theatrical store in New Haven. I had a feeling my idea would work, and I figured it was worth a try. I bought fake beards, glasses, mustaches and wigs. All the disguises were top-notch gear actors used. On my next surveillance, I'd give it a go. But I had one real test to try first.

I was on my day off and patrol happened to call, asking if I wanted to work overtime. They had to be desperate to call me. Everyone was on vacation, and it was one of those rare occasions when they called TNT. I went in with my tactical gear and made sure I had my extended clip. Patrol guys may still have been reminiscing about some of the things I had done. With Dave recently turning a cop in, it wasn't a good time for "honest" police officers.

The lieutenant on duty was Art Carter. He had moved up in rank and was one of the very few black supervisors on the job. Having challenged the department for years, he was only too familiar with the hate many officers had for me. "Bailey, I got you in a solo car on the East Side. The surrounding cars are guys who don't have any problem responding." "Thanks, Lieutenant." "Call for cover if you have to. These guys will cover you."

## Cruz Dead; A Shooting; The Fox and News

It was a quiet night compared to all the shootings, rapes, fights and burglaries patrol had the previous months. Then a call came in about a man threatening a woman at 47 Bell Street. When I got there, the woman was waiting on the sidewalk. "Officer, there's a guy up the street, he's crazy. He said he's gonna kill me, my dog, and burn my house down!" I turned to see a tall black man standing in a yard, just a few houses up. She said his name was Trevor. She seemed terrified and repeatedly asked me to be careful, because he was crazy and capable of anything.

I walked up the street towards him. "Trevor, can I talk to you?" He turned and walked away without saying a word. The turn was spooky and slow, while walking towards the rear yard. What caught my attention was how he kept looking directly at me. His head didn't follow the path he was walking; it remained steadily towards me, as he walked off. He continued looking my way until he disappeared into the shadow of the house. It felt like I had just entered a scary movie of sorts.

I called over the radio to let them know what was going on and where I was headed. Out of habit, I didn't ask for cover. To my surprise, Officers John Roach, Gerry Bonaventura, and Santi Llanos showed up. Officer Roach and I were fellow martial artists, so I felt comforted with him there. He was new on the job but could handle himself. Gerry, on the other hand, was old school but someone you could count on. Officer Llanos was still fairly new and anxious to make his mark. He had done some great things in the streets so far. They were all good guys.

"I guess I lucked out tonight. I never knew I could get so much cover." Gerry looked me with that sly smile of his. "Bailey, knock it off, will ya? We only came here because we had nothing to do." We briefly all laughed at each other, as I told the guys what we had on our hands. Our walk to the back of the house was eerily quiet. I called out to Trevor again, but he didn't answer. That's when we heard it. Crash!

## No Black Heroes

We had to duck into the walkway to avoid the glass raining down on us. I pulled my gun out to be on the safe side and was about to go up the stairs when Roach asked to take the lead. "Go ahead John, but be careful." The hallway was dark, so we were feeling our way up the stairs, almost blindly. Even with flashlights, the hallway was so narrow with sharp turns, we couldn't see much. The hallway was probably illegal and built by someone who didn't know much about carpentry.

Then came the sounds of a woman's screams and more crashing. We scrambled up the makeshift stairs, and at the top we could see light shining through from the apartment door. I let the others go first, in case Trevor might come up from behind us somehow. The door opened and John asked the woman if she was alright. Terrified, she responded, "A tall black guy just broke into my house! He walked past me staring and out the front door!" "He walked?" "Yes, it was the creepiest thing."

We all figured the guy had to be family. Who would break into an apartment for no reason, with four cops behind him, and just walk through? So we did a quick check of the apartment. "I'm telling you he went out the front door!" "I know Miss, but we have to make sure he didn't drop anything or hide something. Are those your kids in the room?" "Yes officer, they're fine, but a little scared." Was she and Trevor somehow related? Was this staged?

John took the lead down the stairs. The front hallway was a little wider but dark. "Don't they have lights in this place?" I was next in line followed by Bonaventura then Santi. John got to the second floor landing and was about to make the turn for the stairwell. That's when things went bad.

John made his final turn to descend, using his flashlight to guide us out. At his first step down, we heard running and stumbling sounds heading up towards John. It was Trevor. John tried to hit him with his flashlight but struck the railing instead and dropped it. With the flashlight roll-

## Cruz Dead; A Shooting; The Fox and News

ing on the floor, we could see the silhouettes of John and Trevor. John got slammed back against the wall. The rolling flashlight gave a strobelike effect making it even harder to see clearly.

Trevor was making stabbing motions at John, and as I moved towards them, the fight intensified, as they drifted back towards me. I moved back quickly to get some space. I could see Trevor's silhouette making stabbing motions towards John. They both fell hard against the wall. It all happened so fast when John screamed, "Get him off me, get him off me!" I fired two shots at Trevor, low. John is right under him and if I missed ...

Suddenly more gunfire came from over my head. I got hit with a hot shell casing and ducked. Bonaventura and Santi were firing their guns just over me from the stairs. While crouched on the floor, I got hit in the face with another hot shell. I could see muzzle flash coming from John's gun as well. We were all in each other's line of fire, and it was a dangerous set. Trevor fell back and on the floor. He'd been hit and was using his leg to push himself back from John, as he slid head first down the stairs.

"Everyone, holster your weapons and stay put! Don't move until we get an evidence team here." "Bailey, we had no choice." "Guys, settle down. I'm going downstairs to see about this guy." Officer Bonaventura called for backup while I called for an ambulance and a supervisor. Downstairs, Trevor was lying on the floor, breathing hard but still alive. He looked up at me but didn't move. I asked him where he'd been hit but he didn't answer. God, please don't let this guy die.

I couldn't find the knife and wasn't about to move him, he'd just been shot. There was a large rock next to him. I knew the drill; it had to stay where it was for evidence. As I heard the sirens approaching, I couldn't help but feel uneasy. I knew I had to shoot the guy, but that didn't make me feel any better. When officers arrived I asked them to

265

watch Trevor. "I didn't move him, because he's been shot. There may be a knife under him."

I headed back upstairs. John wasn't hurt, shaken, but not hurt. Bonaventura was solid. Santi on the other hand, was staring at the floor. "Hey, Santi, you alright kid?" He nodded yes but something in his eyes was wrong. Then a yell came from downstairs. "Bailey, you up there?" It was Captain Richard Petite." "Yeah Capt, I'm protecting the set." "Okay, you can all come down. Detective Bureau is here. Just watch where you guys walk."

We were ordered to report to patrol. I told Captain Petite what happened, and he ordered us to hand over our weapons to the Detective Bureau. It's mandatory; in a police shooting the department has to take your gun as evidence for the investigation. "Captain Petite, Officer Santi Llanos needs to go to the hospital. He looks pretty shook up." Patrol took him to the emergency room.

Outside, a crowd had gathered and someone yelled, "You couldn't wait to shoot another black man. Now you're just going to leave him on the floor. That's fucked up. He ain't got a gun." We just saved an officer's life and did our best not to kill someone. How would anyone know what just happened if they weren't inside with us when it all went down? I stood at the doorway looking at the crowd and yelled out, "You might want to hold off on that we shot him for nothing bullshit. If you don't believe me, then ask that poor lady upstairs how she felt about a man breaking into her apartment with her kids." Captain Petite called to me from the hallway, "Bailey, don't argue with them. It could cause a riot." "No offense Capt., but they're out of line." I turned back to the crowd. "Now, are we done here?"

Slowly. the crowd began to walk away. Captain Petite looked at me in disbelief. I didn't want to hear the "We shot him for nothing, just 'cause he's black" bullshit, not then. Bonaventura and I got into the car and drove to Detective Bureau. On the way, Bonaventura looked at me. "You know what, you got some nerve, I'll give you that. That crowd

## Cruz Dead; A Shooting; The Fox and News

could've torn us apart." I didn't respond, as I reflected on how bad things could have gone. If those guys hadn't shown up to cover me, who knows what could've happened.

Bonaventura shook his head, "Yep, you're a 52." I looked his way and laughed. Fifty-two was police code for a crazy person. You could see Bonaventura was dealing with the shooting in his own way, by telling jokes. Some would have figured he was happy about shooting someone. The fact is most cops who face a life and death situation deal with it in their own way. Many cops use humor to get their minds right. It wasn't a disrespect thing, it was a survival thing.

At the bureau, the detectives were looking at me strangely. It was if they knew something I didn't know. What's this place up to now? I was beginning to write my report when Detective Billy Perez approached me. "Bailey, can I talk to you?" "Of course, what's up?" Perez began to ask questions about my filing bankruptcy a while back. "Hey, I filed bankruptcy because this department suspended me without pay over the Cruz thing. I hope this isn't about him." "No Bailey, this isn't about that. You defaulted on a loan from the Police Credit Union." "I feel bad about that, but there was nothing I could do. Contrary to popular belief, I don't sell drugs, or have a pot of money stashed somewhere." Detective Perez said he needed a statement. "You want me to make a statement on a bankruptcy?" "No, the statement is about your forging your wife's signature to get a car loan."

Here we go again. "Chief Irving put you up to this, didn't he? Tell ya what; I'll be happy to make a statement." We went into a private room where I began to answer his questions. "Did you sign your wife's signature for the car loan?" "I don't remember." "Why can't you remember, Officer Bailey?" "You're asking me about a loan well over five years ago. I've signed my then-wife's signature in the past, like all husbands do. I don't recall." I paused for a moment. "Tell me you're not going to try and arrest me over a husband signing his wife's signature? Say it ain't so." Perez was not

267

## No Black Heroes

amused and looked a bit disturbed at my relaxed attitude. I guess I was supposed to fall apart or something. They were going to get a warrant. I knew the Ad Hoc Committee would see to that. I smiled, "Are we done? I have a shooting to attend to."

Detective Perez got up and walked out of the room. He seemed upset. I was the one who should have been upset. Looking to arrest me, the department just questioned me about signing my wife's signature five years ago! I had just been involved in a shooting and they couldn't have cared less. Even a few veteran officers who didn't care much for me heard about it and considered that low. As Perez walked by, I smiled again, "You should ask Officer Willie Samuels about the loan, by the way. He was the one that notarized it. I don't remember going to his home to sign any papers, so I think my ex-wife did sign them."

What a group of dopes. I just helped to save an officer's life, and they were talking about car loans and signatures. A quick look around while doing my paperwork revealed disappointment. The guys in the Detective Bureau must have hoped I would break down or something. I shook my head, smiled and continued with my reports.

The preliminary reports on the shooting came in. We fired 16 times between the four of us. People on the streets were saying the shooting was excessive. They didn't understand that four officers shooting simultaneously to stop an officer from being killed wasn't excessive. What was really terrifying was shooting at Trevor with John right under him. We could have killed John. To make matters even more surreal, we learned later that John and Trevor were not up against a wall as we had originally thought. They were up against an apartment door. Thank God we didn't kill someone in the apartment.

We were all assigned inside on desk duty until the investigation was completed. I was concerned and called the hospital to see how Trevor was doing. They said he was sta-

### Cruz Dead; A Shooting; The Fox and News

ble but might not ever walk again. I hung up and prayed for him.

Officers were talking about the shooting. The comments were not what one would have expected to hear. Guys passed by the front desk and made comments like, "That was your chance to take someone out. You blew it," and "I would have shot him in the head up close. He deserved it for attacking a cop." "Anyone who tried to hurt a cop is supposed to be dead." It took a lot of restraint for me not to tell them to just shut up. It wasn't a winning situation for anyone. Not only would Trevor and his family's lives change forever, but all of the officers involved would never be the same either. No matter what, it was a tragic event for everyone concerned.

Several weeks later, we were cleared of the shooting by the department and told to return to our regular duties. The commanding officer of TNT was waiting for my arrival. He was funny. "Bailey, you finished with shooting up the God damn city? I have an assignment for you. Channel 12 news is here. They want to film you selling drugs on the reverse sting you had planned." "Commander, that sting was scheduled for next week." "Sorry kid, we're doing it today. It's good public relations."

I quickly drew up the site location, plan, and conducted the briefing. "Guys, we're doing Steuben and Pembroke Street. The set is owned by the Latin Kings, so we got to be tight. We are taking over the block so I can start selling crack cocaine."

The news reporter wanted to know why we were selling drugs at a corner instead of arresting the dealers. I explained that the location was hard to shut down. No matter how many arrests we made, it kept going. By posing as a drug dealer, we would arrest all the buyers. When word got out that cops were posing as drug dealers, the corner would shut down. No one will take a chance on buying drugs at a spot where an undercover might be.

## No Black Heroes

The reporter liked what he heard. "Just one thing, can you blot out my face on the news? It will keep me from being exposed on the streets." "No problem, Officer Bailey." The takedown team set up near Steuben and Pembroke, but out of sight. We told everybody on the block we would be taking over, to leave. They were pissed. "We live here." "Okay, the first one of you who interferes with this operation, you're done. By the way, I hope you like your picture on the news." That was all they needed to hear. Gone with the wind, they turned their faces away from the cameras.

The undercover van with audio and visual was put in place. I was standing in the hallway ready to make my sales. My cover was Detective Ester Ramos. If anything went down she was my weapons point person. I was on set without a gun, to be less intimidating. The cue the deal went down was the Latin King handshake after each sale. It was the visual signal, in case the audio failed. It also gave the buyers the sense that I was the real deal. I had learned the King's hand sign from watching them selling on the block.

Two hours into the sting we had 14 drug arrests. The buyers ranged anywhere from young women who looked like they used to be attractive, to elderly folks. Drug addiction doesn't favor people; it could be anybody. "Hey man, you got dope?" Some who were suspicious asked, "Where's my boy at, what you got?" The news was eating it up. We were so overburdened with arrests, we had to shut it down. One more buyer and that would be it. The last guy bought from me, and I gave him the handshake/signal. The team moved in. He saw TNT cars coming and took off running. It was the last sale, so I decided to run after him. I used a push takedown technique in the hopes of having him fall without me going down with him, but he kept his balance. I tried it one more time. He stumbled while looking back at me, and I closed my eyes. I couldn't watch.

By the time he turned back to see where he was running, he hit a cement pole head first. His head struck the edge of the pole, knocking him out. You could see the in-

## Cruz Dead; A Shooting; The Fox and News

dentation in his forehead. I thought the guy was dead. He was taken to the hospital where he was admitted. We were informed he was alright but oh what a headache he was going to have.

The news couldn't believe the footage they had. On the way back to the office to debrief, the guys started their nonsense. "Did you see Bailey push that guy into the pole? He tried to kill him. Mess with Bailey and he'll push ya into a car, bus, or even a train. He don't care." "Aww come on guys, give me a break, will ya?" I kept a copy of our surveillance video just in case.

The news team thought it was hilarious. The next day, the newspapers had a field day. "Fifteen arrests in two hours. Business was brisk." I wasn't happy about what I saw next. They put my picture in the paper. I turned to the Channel 12 news, and they did the same.

A few months later, the show *Narcs* and *Emergency Call*, both spinoffs of *Cops*, came to town. They all wanted a piece of the newfound TNT fame. We accommodated them with a few raids, and a second reverse sting at a house with the signage "Crack Heads Only" posted on the porch. The camera crew thought the sign was hilarious. "Hey, they put it there, not me." They even had footage of me kicking in a door with a turnaround backkick. I wasn't showing off, we actually forgot to bring a second ram for the two doors we had to break through. We were the focus of cop shows and national news. With my face a matter of public television, it was time. I had to change my appearance in ways people wouldn't expect.

Chapter 21

# MY ARREST; LOST IT; SHOTS FIRED

I was at home contemplating new ways to be effective in TNT when the phone rang. It was a call from Sergeant Cuminotto asking me to turn myself in on a warrant. Didn't we do this once before? "Sure, no problem, I'll be right down." I didn't ask what the warrant was for on purpose. I was sure it would upset him over my lack of concern. He hung up without saying another word. When I told Yvette what the call was about she wasn't the least bit concerned. "You beat' em before, and you'll beat 'em again" "Be back in a few."

Sergeant Cuminotto was waiting for me in Detective Bureau. I signed a few papers and was escorted to booking. Several of the Ad Hoc guys were standing by smiling as I walked out. I smiled back while reminiscing. I was having thoughts of the beating I took as a kid years ago at the hands of McKegan. Their expressions oddly reminded me of him.

## No Black Heroes

In booking, my memories plagued me. I wasn't smiling anymore and had my fists balled up tight. I was grounding my right foot to stable my stance. The flashbacks about McKegan had me visualizing myself hurting those guys. I was tired of it all. Shaking my head a bit, I looked up and saw Officer Joann Meekins behind the desk, Ted's wife. At that moment, I remembered Ted telling me I was destined for great things; fortunately I snapped out of it.

Funny how you could go in a completely different direction until something like a friend's face could change your mindset. Joann looked so confused and disappointed when she was ordered to picture and print me. "Is this some kind of a joke?" I smiled and asked her to just do her thing. "This is ridiculous, Bailey. Forgery?" "Just do what they say, Joann. I'll be back soon." Deputy Chief Lyons was standing by in booking. He was there to gloat and report back to his boy Irving.

I was about to sign some papers when a prisoner recognized me. "Bailey, I know you got some pull. Can you help me on this shit?" I glanced at his papers. Patrol had arrested him for drugs. "I'll put my number in your bag. Give me a call in a week or two." Lyon's became enraged. I was ignoring him and the arrest. "Bailey, you mind signing these papers so you can leave?" "Sure thing, it's not like I'll be gone long." He was pisssssed.

I was about to leave when Lyons said I had to go to the Office of Internal Affairs. "Sure thing D.C. I promised Yvette I would pick up a few things on the way home, but I can drop by there first." He stormed off without saying a word. I told Joann not to worry and I would be back soon. Outside booking waiting was Sergeant Viadero. He said I should leave my car and let him take me to OIA. "Sure, why not?"

The Office of Internal Affairs had changed over the years. The new location was a donated office at the University of Bridgeport in the south end. The only original person left after the Cruz mess was Detective Paul. He was in his office and closed his door on my arrival. Sergeant Robert

## My Arrest; Lost It; Shots Fired

Studivant and Detective A. J. Perez were about to do my interview. They set up the recorder, and I answered the questions with the same answers I previously gave Detective Perez. "I don't remember signing my ex-wife's signature, it was years ago when we were married. All I can tell you is to speak with Officer Samuels who notarized the application." The questioning was completed.

As I was about to leave, Sergeant Studivant asked for my gun. "Hey Sarge, this is my gun. I paid for it. It belongs to me." "Bailey, the Chief ordered me to take your gun." "Sergeant Studivant, are you aware there are death threats out on me? My gun is all I have to protect my family. That's why I bought it." We kept going back and forth about it. "Bailey, you are ordered to turn in your weapon, or else we will seek to terminate you." I had sold my backup, and without my gun, I would be at the mercy of anyone who was after me.

"Irving is so obsessed with getting at me he would risk my family being killed?" I was furious. "He knows there's a contract out on me. He's not a real cop; what a piece of shit." "Bailey, calm down." "Tell that to my fiancée and kids." I turned to leave with no intent of giving up my weapon. Suddenly, I realized I was playing into Chief Irving's hands. I turned back around unexpectedly and pulled my gun. Both Detective A.J. and Sergeant Studivant leaned back and froze. It was at that point I realized how stupid I was. I just looked at them stuttering to speak, "Hey, come on guys. I would never do anything like that. I'm so sorry." Sergeant Studivant just looked at me, "Bailey, what were we supposed to think? First you said no, and then you pulled your gun on us." "Guys, I'm so so sorry. I wasn't thinking." Detective A. J. looked at me, "Jesus, Bailey." I handed him my gun and walked out. "Baiey, come back. Calm down. Come back, brother." I started my long walk back to the police department.

Sergeant Viadero had been waiting outside and saw me walking away. He pulled alongside me. "Bailey, what happened? Come on man, get in the car. It'll be alright." "They

## No Black Heroes

took my gun. It was my gun. Tell Irving I'm gonna give him what he wants." Sergeant Viadero continued to follow me. I walked a few blocks over to Marina Apartments where the Latin Kings were running the show. Viadero asked me not to go in there. "Chief Irving wants me dead. Let's do it."

I walked into the project and yelled out, "Hey guys, it's me, Bailey. I don't have a gun. Here's your chance!" They all looked at me not sure what the hell was going on. I pulled up my shirt so they could see I didn't have anything. "Remember what I'm saying guys, **Chief Irving** wants me dead, so let's do this." One of them replied, "Bailey, if that's really you, we know you're up to something. We're not falling for your bullshit. Leave us alone." "No guys, really, do me a favor and tell Irving I said thanks." "Tell him yourself." I looked at this kid and suddenly realized how right he was. I walked out the project and saw Viadero who was pleading with me to get in the car. If he had heard what I just said, he probably would have taken me to Bridgeport Mental Health. I asked him to take me to patrol.

He tried to talk to me but I remained quiet. Once we arrived, I jumped out of the car. "Hey, where're you going?" I ran past the office and day room in patrol. The supervisors were stunned, watching me run by. I made it to the third floor with no one in sight and walked through the double doors. What a pleasant surprise. Standing by the Chief's door was recently promoted to provisional Captain Scanlon. My, how time flies. I had no idea he had moved up in rank so quickly. Scanlon was listening in on whatever was going on in Irving's office. Startled, he began to look at a book he had in his hands. "Well, well, well; fancy seeing you here. You got nothing better to do than listen in on others?" "Bailey, the Chief's busy." "Well, he can just get un-fuckin' busy. By the way, that book you're reading is upside down." He shut it quick. "Get out of my way." He shuffled off to the side.

The office phone rang as I was about to enter Irving's private office. I stopped briefly, "Answer it, Scanlon. It's patrol calling to tell you I'm on the way up to see your buddy."

## My Arrest; Lost It; Shots Fired

I slammed the door behind me. Chief Irving was sitting at the table with Officer Ken Welk and Sergeant Nina Thomas. It was a disciplinary hearing I had interrupted. Irving noticed how soaked in sweat I was, as I stared straight at him. Caught off guard, he tried to play it off. "Bailey, I—" "Shut up, I have something to say." He turned pale and could see I wasn't myself. No officer had ever barged into the chief's office before, unannounced. What I was there for was suddenly paramount to him. "Shut up, sit there and listen." He remained motionless with Welk and Thomas frozen in their seats.

"You have a lot of nerve. You know there's a contract out on me. You ordered OIA to take my gun? My gun is the only way I can protect my family. I knew you were dirty, but I had no idea." He tried to interrupt. "Officer Bailey, —" "No, you listen. Shut the fuck up! I've had it with you. You're an abomination to anyone black in America. And if anything happens to my kids or fiancée you'll be the one I hold responsible. You're not a real cop and never will be. Got it? **Now** you can continue with your fuckin' meeting."

Both Sergeant Thomas and Ken Welk sat there speechless. I just cussed the police chief out. Had I crossed the line? You bet I had. I exited the office and slammed the door behind me. To my left was Scanlon still holding his book, looking at it again upside down. "By the way, you're a real piece of work, too. Enjoy this now, because I'm far from finished with you. You're next on my list of things to do." I walked out of the office, glancing back at Scanlon. He was nodding his head up and down rapidly, but in a frightened manner. The only reason I didn't punch either of them out was because they both had the faces of cowards. I walked back down the stairs past the patrol window and stared back at the supervisors who were getting up and walking slowly towards the elevator. They saw the anger in me and didn't say a word. I could hear a few more chairs shuffle as I got to the exit. It sounded like people rushing out to head for the chief's office.

## No Black Heroes

Sergeant Thomas called me at home later. "Bailey, you shouldn't have come to the chief's office. You put us on the spot. He called the meeting off. Patrol walked him to his car and escorted him home. He was scared." "Hey Nina, what did I say that was wrong or threatening? Yes, I used a few curse words, but that was it. I told him how I felt, the truth." "Bailey, it wasn't what you said but how you said it." "That's not a policy violation."

I told Yvette what happened in the chief's office. She couldn't stop laughing. Suddenly she blurted out, "Good, he needs to be afraid after what he's done to this family." I couldn't remember Yvette being deep in laughter while showing rage. It was absolutely frightening to see her that way. I couldn't help but wonder how my life had affected hers. She was tasked with maintaining a normal as possible family life; keeping watch over me, all while trying to maintain her own sanity. With so many trying to harm us, and a concern for our kids, it had to have taken a toll on her.

The years of dealing with racism, crooked cops, and all I'd done in the streets was catching up to me. Rest was hard to come by. Although I was faced with so much, I had the audacity to ponder about the complaints Guardians filed in federal court. It was painful to watch the department getting worse by the day. I truly believed the Klan would've been proud of Irving and crew.

I needed to stay focused. My gun was gone and there were folks looking to get me. I had to stay sharp for Yvette and the kids. I was so exhausted but stationed myself on the couch by the door just in case. Worn out, I drifted for a moment and suddenly woke back up in a sweat. My heart was racing so fast, I had trouble catching my breath. I called Yvette but spoke calmly. "Yvette, can you come here a minute" "Ronnie, what's wrong?" "Look, I have to go to the emergency room. I'm just not feeling well." She looked so worried. "Hey, I'm fine. I just need to be checked out. You know how I am about my health." She calmed down and called for an ambulance.

## My Arrest; Lost It; Shots Fired

The ambulance arrived and took my vitals. "Ms. Bailey, we're taking Mr. Bailey to the hospital as a precaution." Ronnie and Ashley had just returned back to my ex-wife's. I wanted to call her so she could keep them inside with so much going on. Worried and weak, I was pretty sick and compelled to get over to the hospital. "Yvette, you and Brandon need to leave here, it's not safe." Yvette looked at me, "Hey, we'll be fine, don't worry. If anything happens to you, your chief is dead. I'll kill him myself." I had never heard her like that before. I asked her to please go stay with my cousin Luck, but she didn't want to leave home.

At the hospital, the physician was very concerned. "Mr. Bailey, we've detected some unusual heart rhythms. You need to stay in the hospital while we do more tests. They took me to a room, and I asked to speak with security. "Hey guys, I need to make sure no one knows I'm here. My name is Bailey, and I work for the Narcotics Division. There're contracts out on me." The head of security returned later and said the hospital had put a news blackout on me.

The doctor was telling me I would be there for at least a week. Yvette called the next morning. I could tell something was wrong. "Okay, what is it?" "Ronnie, there were gunshots in the front of the house last night." "What? Are you and Brandon okay? What did the police say?" "I didn't call them. They don't care about us, so why bother?" "Okay, look, I'm leaving now. I'll be home as soon as I can." Before she could say don't leave, I hung up. The physician was called and reluctantly released me after being told what was going on. He said I needed to take it easy, and something about an irregular heart rhythm. Hurriedly, I rushed out without calling anyone in my family for a ride. I couldn't chance them getting hurt, so I had to go it alone. I walked three miles home. All I could think of was getting home to Yvette and Brandon.

When I got there, I could see the porch had taken a few hits. The house was up high from the street, so luckily the porch was all that got shot up. Whoever did it must have been driving fast. There was a wide spattering of small

## No Black Heroes

holes across the front porch. It looked like someone sprayed shots in a drive-by. We lived on East Main near Beardsley Park, a quiet area, but not anymore.

Yvette called our friend Lucy from the Tae Kwon Do School. She and Brandon needed a place to stay. Lucy told her she would be right over. Yvette was worried that I was staying there without a gun. "Why are they doing this to us, Ronnie?" She couldn't understand my so-called brother officers. "I should stay here with you." "Yvette, out!" Lucy arrived, and they left with a few things.

I called patrol to report shots fired at our home. My family was in danger, and I had no way to protect them. When the sergeant answered, I didn't even give him time to say his name. "Hello, this is Sergeant ..." "This is Bailey. Someone shot up my house last night. Can you send a car?" He said he'd call dispatch and have a car respond. Curiously, the way he spoke was so matter of fact, it was like it was no big deal to him, and then he hung up. I was hoping he abruptly hung up to notify dispatch and the department that an officer was in danger. I then called to tell my ex-wife to keep Ronnie and Ashley out of sight for a while. "Don't trust no one!"

A day later, no one from the department had come. Suddenly, there was a hard knock on the door. I had a pair of steel throwing stars on my forearm. They would have to do. I peered out and saw a UPS truck parked. I looked to the right side of the porch, "Package for Mr. Bailey." Cautiously, I opened the door with the sharpened steel in hand. "Mr. Bailey, package sir, special delivery." I glanced to see where it was from, Florida. I didn't know anyone from Florida. He put the package down and told me it was a rush delivery. The driver asked for my identification, looked at it and left the package. I just knew it was gonna explode. I looked closer at the return address before picking it up. It was from Mr. Gee. Only one person used the word Gee, and that was Detective Billy Chase. How in the hell did he know where I was staying?

## My Arrest; Lost It; Shots Fired

Chase was forced to retire years earlier. The drug dealers somehow recognized him and tried to kill him. Someone had struck him from behind with a pipe wrench. Caught off guard, he couldn't even lift his gun up. The attack had left his arm useless. It was sheer luck I just happened by. When I got out of the car, everyone scattered. Must'a been my gun cocked and pointed in their direction, that had folks looking for higher ground. Then again, it could have been what I said. "That's right, run motherfuckers. Somebody's gonna die on this, trust me!"

I remember visiting him in the hospital after his attack. You could tell he had more than just a dislocated shoulder. He was smoking cigarettes down to the filters, one after another, rambling on. Chase was messed up. "Bill, you need help. You know what I'm talking about." You'd think that anyone who had been deep undercover for so long would've received better care. The department hadn't watched out for him. He needed protection, and more importantly help, so he could get whole again. To my utter disbelief, he was forced to retire and moved out of state. Chief Irving had said they couldn't protect him. The department used him, and then tossed him aside like he was nothing.

Wow, so that's where he was laying low, Florida. I opened the box and couldn't believe my eyes. It was a fully loaded automatic 9mm MAC-11 assault weapon. I called him, and before I could say a word, "Yo Bailey, I was expecting this call." "Chase, how in the hell did you get this through UPS security? How'd ya know where I was? You do know the government don't allow the shipment of 'rigged' guns through the mail, right?" His MAC was jimmied for fully automatic fire. "Hey Bailey, I told ya I got pull, Gee." "How in the world did you know Irving took my gun?" Chase, always the elusive one, "Hey, protect yourself, my brother. Get it back to me when you're done. Peace." "I owe you, Bill."

My aunt Betty Fogel lived next door. She was leaning out of her doorway the next morning reaching for her mail. I asked her if she knew they shot at the house two nights be-

## No Black Heroes

fore. She said she had heard the shots but was too afraid to look out the window. "Well did ya call the poleece?" "Yeah Auntie, yesterday." "Baby, they still ain't come? What's wrong with that place?" "Auntie, stay away from the front of the house for awhile." "Boy, you know if your Mom was alive, she'd tell you it's time to leave." "Hey Auntie, look." I smiled and showed her a small portion of the MAC-11 under my jacket. She saw it, looked at me, and raised her eyebrows, "Well, alright now. They best leave my nephew alone."

Now armed again, I drove myself to the police department. There was no sense in going to Detective Bureau because D.C. Lyons was in charge there. He was so far up Irving's ass you could only see the soles of his shoes! I could actually envision that. I went to patrol and met with Captain Petite to let him know what happened at my house. He was shocked. "Bailey, are you telling me your home was shot at and no officers or command staff has come by to check on you and your family?" "That's right, Captain." "I am absolutely appalled. A cop's family in distress and no one took the time to check the fucking bullet holes or look after one of our own?"

Captain Petite said to go back home and he'd send a patrol car immediately. He wanted to speak with the chief about it. "No offense, Capt., but he's not going to do anything." I drove back home, and just in time. Two officers arrived, Officers Chris Lamaine and Paul Ortiz. They were both new and not sure what was going on. "I'm Officer Bailey. The other night someone shot at our home." I asked them to take the report to Detective Bureau, confident that no one was going to do an investigation anyway. Lyons would most likely call Irving for a laugh, was my guess. Still, I had to follow procedure.

Shamefully, I realized I was gradually losing my sense of decency. I was trying to figure out how to get Irving before anyone could stop me. I wanted him dead and gone, and was willing to do it! I knew in my heart it was wrong, but my thoughts were about my family and how he had put

## My Arrest; Lost It; Shots Fired

them at risk. I began to understand how a person could cross the line and do the unthinkable. Victims of domestic violence, sexual assault victims, people who'd been bullied or tormented over time; I could see how they could snap. With no relief in sight, I had fallen to damn near the point of no return. Was it some sort of Post Traumatic Stress Disorder veterans are prone to? My wife, my kids, God, don't let me fall.

Two weeks passed and not one officer had come by. If people on the streets ever found out the department had abandoned me, it would have been open season on me and my family. I heard the sound of a car stopping in front of the house and was stunned a police car showed up. This can't be good. It was Officer Doc Hill.

Doc was a loyal supporter of the Guardians and a good friend. "Bailey, you got a minute?" "Sure, Doc." He came in with a package. "Bailey, this is all news to me. I just found out you were suspended and arrested. The only reason I know is because I was assigned to return your gun." "The city attorney must have told Irving he shouldn't have taken it." Doc wanted to know why they took it in the first place. "That's the million-dollar question, Doc. Irving will answer for it later." When I told Doc my house had been shot up, he was speechless. His reaction had me thinking the department took the route of a news blackout.

I needed to explain myself. "Doc, I didn't reach out to anyone, because I thought it best to stay low and protect my family, my way." I didn't want to offend Doc, and I certainly trusted him, but I wasn't sure who to speak with under the circumstances. We still had a mole in the Guardians, and the walls had ears. Doc was upset and said there was no reason for the department to leave me out there like that. He asked if there was anything he could do. "Doc, I'll be moving soon. Yvette and Brandon are not living here for now. I'll call the news on this later. I'm sure Irving will have his excuses ready when I do. For now, I'll keep low." Then he gave me some bad news. Officer Sheila Peeler had

## No Black Heroes

passed away from cancer. The funeral was a few days away. I asked Doc to give my best to the family. I couldn't make it.

Luckily, a real estate friend of mine told me about a house that was cheap but needed a few repairs. I could move in right away and work on it. My credit was shot over the bankruptcy, but Yvette's was fine, so she applied for the mortgage. I had the keys and moved in while the bank worked on the closing. It was a house on the North End. Hopefully, we would be safe there. My real concern was my state of mind, which was holding on by a thread.

Once Yvette and I settled into our new home, I asked her to marry me. When I thought about how she managed all the changes that took place in our home for years was beyond me. It was long overdue. I asked her if we could elope, and be married, just us and God. She loved the idea. We were married in Florida, away from the nonsense of the police department and the insanity associated with it. I called Chase but he was away on something he couldn't discuss. He wished me well and said I was back on track. "Don't let them keep you down, Gee." "Thanks Chase, love ya, man." With the kids safe; we made the trip and exchanged our vows. It was such a wonderful time in our life we didn't want to return. But, with my arrest still pending, it was time to go back for someone to face the music.

Chapter 22

## CHIEF'S SLIPPING AND THE KINGS

Chief Irving was feeling cocky. It was a David versus Goliath situation. He had all the city's assets to back him, but I was counting on my resolve. Once the court heard my case, I was convinced it would be thrown out. My former wife was completely confused by what they had done. Why would my own department arrest me for signing her signature, five years ago? The answer was simple; they wanted me at any cost. If you added in the Chief's motivation, his hatred; it was the catalyst behind it all. They wanted me forced out or dead.

"Lord, it gets better." Officer Bobby Moss called. A devoted man of the Muslim faith, he also had no fear of Chief Irving. He was famous for speaking the truth. "Brother Bailey, I was at Sheila's funeral. Chief Irving threatened Officer Willie Samuels." Bobby said that Willie had gone to the Office of Internal Affairs and made a statement. Willie remembered my ex-wife coming to his house and signing the papers he notarized. OIA was informed I didn't sign her signature. I asked why Irving would threaten Willie. "The Chief

## No Black Heroes

told Willie he had lied in his statement for you, Bailey. Willie was ordered to make another statement. And Irving warned Willie that if he lied again, it would be out of "his hands." "Let me get this straight, Irving is forcing Willie to change his statement?" I wanted to be clear before my next move. "So Willie has to change his statement or get fired?" "Yes." I would gamble a black man's chicken, mac and collards as soon as Willie changed his statement, Chief Irving would fire him anyway.

"Bobby, I know this is a stupid question, but can I count on you to make a statement on this?" "Bailey, do you have to ask? So what are you going to do?" "I'm gonna apply for a warrant. Chief Irving has to be arrested." "You're gonna do **what**?"

I called Willie and asked him if he was okay, but was careful to not say anything that would make it look like I was trying to influence him. Chief Irving had just made that mistake. "Willie, I want to tell you how sorry I am for what you're going through. I will be taking care of this soon." "Bailey, don't do anything stupid. Chief Irving is hoping you'll do something dumb." "Yeah, he's close to getting his wish." It was a lazy attempt at a joke. I wasn't pleased with myself for the things I'd envisioned for Irving and a few others.

It would be my boldest move yet. No one had tried what I was about to do. I called the Detective Bureau and made an appointment. "I'll be coming in to apply for a warrant for Chief David Irving's arrest." I could hear the laughter in the background, as the message was passed on to Deputy Chief Lyons.

"Bailey, what's this all about?" I had a sarcastic tone. "Hi, D.C., how are you?" He asked, "What's this about a warrant for the Chief?" "Okay, listen very carefully, D.C. Lyons. I'm exercising my rights just like any other citizen in the United States. I'm asking for an appointment to swear out a warrant for David Irving's arrest. That's all you need to know." He didn't say anything. "So we're clear; I'll be in

## Chief's Slipping and The Kings

touch with the Justice Department if my request isn't taken seriously." Lyons handed the phone to the call taker, and she made the appointment.

I came in early the next morning and met with Captain James Resta. He wasn't sure what was going on. "Bailey, I understand you want to swear out a warrant for someone's arrest?" I guessed they didn't tell him. "I'm here to get a warrant for David Irving." It went right over his head. Captain Resta was setting up and ready to take the statement. "That's funny. You want to apply for a warrant for someone who has the same name as the chief." "No Captain, the warrant is for the chief." He just sat there trying to take it all in. "Captain Resta, the Chief tampered with a witness in a criminal proceeding. I want him arrested." "But Bailey, he's the chief." "And?" "But Bailey, he's the Chief." "So what, Captain. Chief Irving threatened Officer Willie Samuels. Officer Bobby Moss is a witness. He heard it, and I want him arrested."

Captain Resta sat back a bit, unsure what to make of my request. He kept saying over and over, "Bailey, he's the chief. Bailey, he's the chief." I couldn't have cared less if he were Chief Sitting Bull. I politely asked Captain Resta to please take the statement, "Captain Resta, you're a good man. You need to know, Irving and I are going to court over this. Please protect yourself and do what has to be done. I'm not backing down, and you should know, this will probably make national news." Captain Resta took the statement and I went home. It was Friday and my weekend was looking better. I had just walked into that valley of death you hear about in church. My intentions were to bury Irving in that valley.

Sunday came and I was in church thanking God. I needed forgiveness for my thoughts, the cursing, and for not being a better person than I was. But that's what God is all about, forgiveness. Bishop White was preaching like there was no tomorrow. What a message. "You have God's authority, he gave it to you. No one can stop you with God

## No Black Heroes

by your side." Every time I went to church there was a message for me. I went home feeling good about the word.

I was seemingly back on track being the kind of person I had been raised to be. Home, I opened my Bible and looked at the very first scripture that caught my eye. Psalm 64:7-8. "But God shall shoot at them with an arrow; suddenly shall they be wounded. So they shall make their own tongue to fall upon themselves: all that see them shall flee away." There was no doubt; Irving was going down.

It was Monday afternoon. I was on the couch relaxing when Yvette came in and handed me the phone. She said it was the chief's office. Someone wanted to speak to me. "Officer Bailey, this is Captain Chapman." He began to joke in his deep most southern accent. "Hey Offsir Bailey, who eis yo 'turney?" "Captain, how are you? So what did I do now?" "Whoever your attorney is, I needs da hire him." He continued, "Your court case was dropped this morning." "What? No one called me from court." "Officer Bailey, you have been ordered back to work, immediately. The Chief just signed the papers. Just so you know; he wasn't happy with whatever you did." "Yeah, he never is, Capt." "Well, welcome back. You are to report to patrol in three days." "Captain, I'm supposed to report to the Narcotics. That is unless he's taking me out, which would be a mistake on his part." "Brother Bailey, I'll call you back."

A few moments later, Captain Chapman called back. "Officer Bailey, report to TNT after your days off." "Captain, do you know anything about the warrant I applied for?" "What warrant?" "I applied for a warrant for Irving's arrest for tampering with a witness." There was a long pause on the phone. "You did what? Boy, they're going to burn you at the stake." Captain Chapman said he was unaware of a warrant but said I should check with DB. Happy with my return, Chapman chuckled, and hung up.

I called Captain Resta, who had been notified that my case in court had been dismissed and he welcomed me back. "Officer Bailey, I know why you're calling. I was told

## Chief's Slipping and The Kings

not to apply for the warrant on Chief Irving." "Why?" "Well, your case has been dropped. There's no tampering with a witness, because your case is off the docket." Irving had committed a crime. Dropping my case must have been their only way out of the mess he made. That had to have hurt! Captain Resta had one last comment. "Don't kill the messenger, sorry Bailey. For the record, you got balls."

I reported back to TNT, and the guys were happy to see me. "Bailey, the place wasn't the same without you." "J.J. what's up?" "I wanted you to be the first to know, I'm going to the FBI." "Get out of here J., that's great news!" I looked at J.J., "You know I sent requests to the Chief's office for an assignment to Statewide, DEA, FBI, hell, even Gang Task Force. I guess I'm not qualified." I asked J.J. jokingly if he was aware that he might have been chosen because I questioned Irving not sending minorities to specialized units. His response was always with a quick wit, "Well thanks for the assignment, Brother Bailey." We laughed at ourselves.

I needed a few days before I could get back out on the streets. My face had been exposed by the news. I had the theatrical gear, but it needed testing. I took out the beard first. It had a mesh backing so your skin color would come through once it was glued to your face. I was amazed at how completely natural it looked. I put on the glasses, makeup to change my skin color, and even a wig. It looked good at home, but it needed a real test. It was time to take the Pepsi challenge! I snuck out of the house and back in to get Yvette's attention. Wow. She screamed and reached for a knife, about to stab me. I yelled out, "Yvette, no, it's me!" I pulled off the glasses and wig fast. "Ronnie, are you fuckin' crazy?" I joked with her, hoping she'd calm down. "Puerto Ricans and their knives, what's up with dat?" She slammed the knife down, "Never do that again!" Wow, almost got sliced up by the only one who still liked me, hopefully.

I tried my first outfit, a hoodie, long dreads, beard and a walking cane. I went into the projects like an old Jamaican man looking for cans and bottles, and no one paid me any mind. I came out, and went back in again. That time I went

## No Black Heroes

in as a young dark-skinned guy with a thick gold chain, beard, NY Mets cap, jeans and Nike sneakers. Again, other than a few looks from the girls on the set, no one paid me any attention. I decided not to let the team know what I was doing; word had a way of getting around.

We were just about ready to go out when my nephew Benji called. He had completed serving his time for his part in the Number One Family and Sanchez enterprise. I couldn't believe how fast the years had come and gone. "Uncle Ronnie, they threatened me." "Who threatened you?" "Orko from the Latin Kings said he was gonna have me killed. They said I was selling drugs on their block, and that I'm a snitch working for you. I don't sell drugs anymore, Unc." "Benji, I'll take care of this. Get off the street for a while." I told the team I had something that needed to be taken care of and drove to the Latin Kings' storefront on East Main Street. I was still amazed they had an office with their name on the door. "Almighty Nation of the Latin Kings."

Word on the street was the Kings had shot up my house. This was a good excuse to shake the tree. I parked the car and went inside. A few members started moving around. "Hey, where's Orko?" "Who wants to know?" I wasn't in disguise, and for that moment, not concerned. This was about family. "I need to speak to Orko. Can you get him here?" "Tell us what you want and we'll tell him when he comes in." I looked at the biggest one standing by the doorway. "Let me see if I can get you to understand. My name is Bailey. I'll make a deal with you. You go get Orko and bring him here, or we can get it on right here, right now." I counted four of them before I turned back to the big one. He needed to know I was for real. So I yelled out, "Stop fucking with me and call him!"

The big guy started walking my way. I put my hand on my gun. He stopped. "Oh, you gonna shoot me, cop?" "Come closer and find out. There ain't a judge in the country that would say I didn't have the right to shoot your big ass." I yelled louder, "Now get Orko down here. I ain't leav-

## Chief's Slipping and The Kings

ing 'til I see him." Then I changed the subject. "By the way, which one of you motherfuckers shot at my house?" I cocked the trigger on my gun. The smallest one looked at me, "Hey Bailey, calm down, he's on the way."

Fifteen minutes later, King Orko walked in. He looked at me, grabbed a chair, dragged it over, and sat down. He motioned with his hands for his crew to back off. There was no doubt they were upset with me. "Bailey, what's up with you coming into my place disrespecting me?" "I got two questions, Orko. Why are your guys shooting at my house, and why are the Kings trying to kill my nephew Benji?" Orko paused. "Look, nobody here gonna touch your nephew, you have my word." "That doesn't answer my question." Orko looked at me and smiled. "Damn man, what's up with you?" "I didn't come here to disrespect you or the Kings. That's not my way. Why are the Kings shooting at my place? Did you know my fiancée and baby boy were in there, and not me?"

I let him know it wasn't a joking matter. "Someone's gonna get capped over that, trust me." Orko leaned back and was about to speak when he peaked at what was under my left arm. He could see my backup, the MAC-11. He leaned forward and whispered. "Bailey, we didn't shoot at your place." "Orko, if I had a problem with you, I would've taken it to you. Not your girl or ya kid." He wanted to clear the air. "Look Bailey, it wasn't us. I heard it was the Kings from New Haven. Someone told me they were upset about you dissing the Kings, wearing our colors and selling on the block using our sign of the crown." I countered, "Someone must have told them where I lived. By the way, I didn't disrespect. My job was to shut down Steuben Street. Not the Kings, the drugs."

I was talking but thinking hard at what he had just said, so I repeated it, "The New Haven Kings were at my house over colors? That ain't right." Orko nodded in agreement. I wasn't sure if he was confirming the Kings had shot up my place, or that it wasn't right. I calmed down. "Orko, I'm glad we had this talk. But if anyone else shoots my way,

## No Black Heroes

I'm gonna return da favor. And I won't be a cop when I do." "Bailey, I'll relay the message." We shook hands, and I headed for the door.

The big one was at the door blocking my way. "Listen, here's the deal. If this goes down we're all gonna be standing before God, and he'll be upset. Upset because I brought a small crowd with me. I'll be the one in the front telling him I had no choice but to bring y'all with me." Big boy was listening and smiling. "God will want to know why I did such a thing. My answer to him will be because your dumb ass got in my way." Orko walked over and placed his hand on his boy's chest, moving him back.

The next day at the office, I got a call from New Haven Officer Ralph Sagarra. "Bailey, can I meet with you?" "Of course, Ralph. Make it the Wonderland of Ice by the park." I was surprised to see Ralph in plain clothes. "Ralph, what's up?" "Bailey, you are by far are the craziest son of a bitch I've ever known. I thought they were going to kill you yesterday." "Are you following me, too?" "Hey man, I work Gang Task Force. The Kings' office is wired. We thought we were going to have to come in guns blazing. You're fucking nuts." "Sorry Ralph, I hope I didn't mess up things for ya." Ralph looked at me and smiled. "Actually, we're glad you went in. After you left, they started talking 'bout some things that will help us." What he said next floored me. "By the way, the Kings in New Haven may have killed a cop's son, Phillip Cusick. Word is the kid was involved with the Kings and someone found out his father's a cop. So now he's dead. We aren't sure it was a sanctioned hit." "Ralph, I'm so sorry. If I can help, please let me know." "Like I said, Bailey, you're one crazy son of a bitch." "So I'm told."

## Explosion; K-5; Chief is Out

Over the next few months, the drug trade had taken a turn for the worse. The TNT team was making an average of 20 arrests a day with no end in sight. The East Side of Bridgeport was becoming an unbearable place to live. The Panic had so many sections doled out we could never shut the whole thing down. We were looking to hit The Nation's part of the project. They had returned to the Panic and were even more dangerous than before. So we went in by the numbers.

I set up a surveillance point at the abandoned Remington gun factory across the railroad tracks from the Panic. It was so busy, I called out one sale while letting three go so the team could keep up. I decided to go in disguised for a closer look. It was risky because The Nation had a habit of checking out anyone who came onto their turf. I needed to hurt that spot. Risky or not, I went in on foot.

I walked in and saw Kim Hamlett making a sale right in front of me. I walked past her, called the team in, and they took her down. She had 13 small bags of crack cocaine on her. While still on the move, I saw a kid walking away quickly when the team came in for Hamlett. He was trying to hide a gun. I walked up from behind and threw him up against the wall. Everyone out on the set was watching the takedown team and never noticed me. I pulled a .38 Smith and Wesson revolver from the kid and cuffed him. He was so scared he must have thought it was a robbery. I looked like an old street urchin. I called to the team while putting the kid down on the ground.

"What's your name?" "Felix Rodriguez. I live in building 27, the Panic." I kept his gun and told him not to move. He was so afraid he laid there like I told him to. The team came over to where the kid was, picked him up and arrested him. I called over the radio, "I'll bring in the gun later." You could see the confusion on the team members' faces. There was this kid on the ground cuffed and I'm nowhere in sight. They took him in.

I saw Earnie, who was the last to leave the set. I wanted to have a little fun and got his attention from a distance while flashing my badge. He squinted his eyes and smiled, still unsure who I was. Then he got right up on me, "Damn, Bae Bae. You look fucked up, man. Let us know next time you come out like that." Earnie, for some reason, liked call-

## No Black Heroes

ing me by my code name, Bae Bae. "Earnie, don't let the guys know. I want to keep this under wraps for now."

I moved quickly around the corner of the building making sure no one saw me. There was Wayne Calvin Williams looking at a plastic bag in his hands. You could see the small bags of dope in it. "Yo man, you trying to cop? I got what you want." I glanced at him, "Naw, I'm good." I rounded the building and called the team back in. They came back as Williams tried to walk off and arrested him right next to me, taking in 30 bags of dope. No one on the team except Earnie noticed I was standing there.

"Let's keep it going." I moved to another side to try for a few more. There was Eugene Walker walking. He had made a few sales with me staggering close by. My disguises were working. The team was called in and grabbed Walker with 54 bags of crack on him. The packaging had changed over the years. Crack cocaine was now in tiny little bags instead of vials. They must have had Munchkins somewhere packaging the stuff. The baggies were that small!

As I walked around looking to do one more hit, I observed a few more buyers. They had a habit of looking at their dope in hand as they walked off the set. I guess they were making sure they didn't get ripped off. Some out there sold chips of soap or crushed aspirin that looked like crack. The team came and took Betty and Francis Beasley, Mike Carmello, Lloyd Sanders and Otis Bohannon for possession. Walker sold to them just before his arrest.

Sergeant Samatulski called over the radio, "Bailey, that's enough, stop." TNT was overwhelmed. I left the set and removed my disguise. The guys had so many arrests some of the team members were waiting with prisoners for cars to return. Sergeant Samatulski was about to call patrol when I got on the air. "Hey Sarge, I can transport some of the prisoners. No one will get a good look at me. I have a regular unmarked car and my hoodie up around my face." "All right Bailey, but be careful."

## Chief's Slipping and The Kings

Some of our unmarked cars had been seen so much, they were burned anyway. I grabbed two of the prisoners from the team and drove the long way back to the office up Pembroke Street. With prisoners in the car, I figured no one had a reason to take notice of us. We drove past Pembroke and Ogden Street. It was the Green Top Posse spot run by Padoto. I drove by slowly and was shocked at what I saw next. A guy was standing on the corner gesturing to me he had cocaine. He gave the street sign by thumbing his finger under his nose.

We all looked at him with our mouths open. I pulled over and told the prisoners "Don't even think of leaving this car. An escape charge is worse than what you have now." They both looked at me and smiled. "Are you kidding, we know what's up. This is better than TV."

I moved the car to the side of a house. The guy walked towards us. You could hear the snickering inside the car. "Come on guys, cut it out." They were trying not to laugh too loud. I got out and looked over. It was Lee Best. When he got closer I pulled my badge from under my shirt with handcuffs in hand. Best looked like he had just seen a ghost. He looked all around from side to side then took off.

We got about half a block where he dropped the drugs in a sewer, but it didn't matter. I arrested him for the attempt to sell to me. Back at the car, he was upset. I told him I had witnesses in the car who saw him try to sell to me. "Hey, Bailey, that ain't right. You can't use them. They're under arrest, too." "Yes, they are, and they saw what you did." All the way to the TNT office, they enjoyed a hilarious moment at Best's unfortunate slipup.

The team was still trying to catch up on all the arrests and paperwork. They were so overwhelmed, I decided to help by taking some of the prisoner's downtown to booking. Officer Jose Bahr and I did the transports. We were on our last of three runs. Jose had a heavy Spanish accent and was hard to understand. "Jose, you ready?" All I could get from him was a quiet mumble and a nod.

## No Black Heroes

We took the last four prisoners in the car. On the way, he asked me, "Howd chew dooen, Bailey?" He wanted to know about Chief Irving and the shooting at my home. By then everyone knew about it. "I'll be in court soon with my lawsuit against Irving." He smiled. "So, chew ala-right ten. Dat's goud. And da famalee's safe?" I kidded with Jose a bit. He and I were close friends. "Thanks, Jose, they are fine. So, how chew dooen." "Vaey funey, Baileee."

We arrived at booking, and the process to book the last four prisoners took about 30 minutes. We walked out of booking, and Jose opened the driver side door to get in. That's when all hell broke loose. BOOOOOM! The noise from the blast was so loud you could hear it five blocks away. Jose ducked. The explosion was only 15 feet from where he was standing. He was lucky to be alive. All I could see was a thick white and gray cloud of smoke coming from a red van. It had been parked there for months.

Jose stood up, covered in glass. There was no doubt someone had waited for us to come out before detonating an explosive device. From the looks of things, it had been planted on the rear door of the van. The explosion was so strong it blew the back doors and frame of the van inward. It was at that very moment I heard something I'd never heard before. Jose stood upright, looked over to me and yelled in perfect English, "What the fuck is going on here?" I was so amazed at Jose's accent change all I could do was look at him. Could the explosion have me so messed up I'm not hearing right? He spoke again, "This is not funny. Someone is playing a stupid game and needs to cut the shit."

I stared at Jose who no one on the job could understand for years. I completely forgot for a moment about the explosion and just started laughing hysterically. I had to say something. I just had to. "Jose, don't you mean 'Whot da foc us gooen oon hare?' It's a miracle, you've been healed, my brother." I extended an imaginary microphone towards Jose, "Brother Jose, say something for the fans." He spoke again. "Someone is looking to get their ass beat, and I am not playing." Oh my God, I thought I was going to need a medic. I was laughing so hard anyone would have thought I was shock or something.

Sergeant Joseph Gaudett opened the window to his office from the third floor and looked down at us, "Hey, what the hell just happened. You guys alright?" I looked up at him, "Sergeant, it looks like someone tried to take us out. The van just had its doors blown in. Call the FBI. By the way, Jose's been cured." I was serious but still couldn't get over Jose. Sergeant Gaudett just looked at me, probably thinking I was in shock. "Hey, Sarge, I'll be at TNT if anyone needs me. We took a quick peek at the van then left without touching anything. "Oh, tell Irving he missed." Gaudett was not amused at my comment.

The explosion took place on police property and wasn't a joking matter. Then TNT called me over the radio. "Hey, Bailey, bad news, someone just shot out the window to your car." "Okay, I'll be right there." Jose was still upset but speaking very clearly. "Someone is looking for trouble. I am very upset about this." I paused, and then started laughing so hard I could hardly breathe. "Bailey, do you realize we could have been killed?" "Oh my God Jose, please stop, stop talking."

We drove to TNT base and it dawned on me, the explosion, my car; that was no coincidence. Someone was trying to send me a message or take me out, and missed. The one thing that really concerned me was that day I drove my BMW instead of the Jeep. My cousin just gave me that car, which made it all the more unsettling. Who could've known about it? I made the mistake of parking on the side street instead of in the rear where it should have been. My window had been shot out alright. It looked like someone used a .22, which doesn't make much noise when fired.

I wrote my reports on the explosion and the shooting and sent them to the chief's office. He didn't disappoint me. He kept the whole thing quiet. There was no investigation, and no news of it in the papers. The only story I read was

## No Black Heroes

for Lee Best's arrest in trying to sell drugs to me with prisoners in the car. I had to admit, that was newsworthy, but more newsworthy than an explosion at the police department? It reeked of an effort to downplay anything that had to do with me, or what I was enduring.

Chief Irving was no doubt an evil man. He wanted me dead. I mean come on; any other police officer in America would have received protection for his family. At the very least they would've offered it. I saved the files and reports sent to Irving. Someday, I knew I'd have a story to tell that no one would believe. But it was not a time to look past what needed to be done.

I had more than enough evidence to prove Chief Irving was out to harm me and my family. It was time to push my case in federal court. Yet, taking on the chief and the city would surely have them using every resource available, and then some. This time I was going for broke, so I contacted Attorney Gerry Gaynor. Gerry was a longtime friend and attorney of mine. He was very well respected by his peers. The city of Bridgeport had long arms of corruption. Their constant attacks on me, the false arrests, the shielding of a crazed informant, and the trumped-up charges against me were just the tip of their treachery. I needed someone who couldn't be bought, and that was Gerry.

Attorney Gaynor took my case and said it would be his pleasure to expose a crooked system. We discussed Chief Irving's failure to provide protection for my family, Cruz, and the department refusing to arrest Irving for tampering with a witness. My ordeals had Attorney Gaynor reeling. He almost fell on the floor when I told him about my arrest for signing my wife's signature on a loan over five years old.

"Officer Bailey, you're kidding, right? Everyone signs their wife's or husband's signature if they're married. What is he, a moron?" He said the icing on the cake came from Chief Irving taking my gun, knowing there were contracts out on me. "The fact that someone shot at your house, your car, and that explosion at the police department, that tells

## Chief's Slipping and The Kings

me it was all about you being killed. And this guy Irving not doing anything for you screams that he wanted you at any cost." Attorney Gaynor wouldn't say the word dead but he knew. He filed motions requesting an expedited hearing for an immediate trial.

Gaynor asked me for a wish list when we got to court. What did I want? I gave him a dollar amount, and more importantly, that Chief Irving be removed from the Bridgeport Police Department. I also wanted any negative reports or records in my personnel file erased. "Officer Bailey, if this goes to court you will be paid handsomely. My gut tells me the city will settle." He filed the motions to move the case forward.

The first court date was a discovery hearing to see if my complaint had merit, and it did. Attorney Gaynor said we were now moving forward on a fast track. Gaynor called me about the discovery hearing. It wasn't about my case but curiously about what took place at the hearing. "Officer Bailey, I just thought you should know I have very sensitive ears. A certain lead city attorney was making racial jokes at your hearing. If you get a copy of the recording you'll hear what I heard." "What kind of jokes, Gerry?" "He was making jokes about a white officer and the Klan. I suggest you get a copy of that tape."

I requested the tape of the hearing. What a shock to hear City Attorney Jackson. It was just like Gerry had said, Jackson was joking about an officer and his connection with the Klan! I notified the court of my displeasure and what was on the tape. Shortly afterwards, Attorney Jackson resigned from his position. One by one they were knocking themselves down. All I could do was think about a quote from the bible repeating itself again, "So they shall make their own tongue to fall upon themselves: all that see them shall flee away."

The city was scrambling to recover from their embarrassment. A top city attorney was on tape at a hearing on discrimination matters making insensitive jokes. You can't

## No Black Heroes

make this stuff up. Should I take it to the news, or wait and play it in court revealing publicly what that place was really like? I was visualizing Attorney Gaynor's opening statement, "Your Honor, the city takes racial issues very seriously. In fact, we ask that you listen to this tape from their former lead attorney." I couldn't wait to be heard.

Back on the streets, the community was in a state of chaos. They were repeatedly calling the Guardians with their concerns. Community members told us white officers with skinhead haircuts and tattoos similar to members of an Aryan supremacy group were tearing the place up. We were told horror stories of beatings and false arrests of blacks. We knew it was the K-5, but so far no one in the department would acknowledge their existence. The blue wall of silence was holding firm.

The Guardians met to discuss the K-5 to see what, if anything, we could do. Only a few members showed up. There was no doubt about the fear some of them had about those guys. Even a few white officers were afraid of them. It was scary having cops on the job who took pride in beating African Americans. And they seemed to dare anyone to challenge them.

We had gotten wind that the K-5 were going to have an emergency meeting that would take place in the police garage. I was a little skeptical about the information. They had a lot of nerve, but a hate group meeting on police property? It made no sense, but it was our first real lead. We discussed filming the meeting or perhaps calling the FBI. Over my objections, the Guardians decided to tell Chief Irving. "Come on guys, really?!" This was our chance to show the K-5 existed. "I'm telling you guys, this is a bad idea. Don't tell Irving anything. Let me stake out the meeting." Over my objections, they told Chief Irving about the K-5 and the meeting.

A city that never acknowledged discrimination was going to expose an underground hate group? I didn't think so. No way. The next day we received a call from Captain Chap-

### Chief's Slipping and The Kings

man. "There was no meeting held in the police garage." I truly believed Chief Irving didn't have anyone check it out. More than likely, the whole thing was a scam to see what we knew about them.

The Guardians met again, and we decided it was time to tell certain members of the community about the K-5's existence. It was too risky to make accusations about what we couldn't prove. But the least we could do was have others in the community keep an eye out as well. Unlike the old Ad Hoc Committee, which was subtle, these guys were an in-your-face yet guarded group.

After we notified the chief's office about the K-5, certain white officers began using the staredown routine with many of our Guardian members. I just knew a leak came from the third floor that we were onto them. It was as if they were daring us to try anything. But who exactly was really in this group, and who were their supporters? Skinhead haircuts with tats wasn't enough to identify them, we needed more.

I dropped by lineup in patrol every now and then looking for something to indicate who those guys were. I took notice that certain white officers became arrogant when I was around. But that was something common Guardians were accustomed to. After lineup, you could see several of them gravitate around this huge cop, newly hired Officer David "Stretch" Stacks. They gave the impression that he was their go-to guy, their champion. They took pride in being around him.

Officer Stretch looked like a WWF wrestling champ. He was tall, well built and always looked my way with an overconfident grin. I made it a point to waltz by patrol occasionally to show him and his buddies I could give a "you know what" about his superior act. Stretch was their symbol of supremacy, and my presence was the brashness they all hated. My fleeting fantasy was about a shin kick to Stretch's head, ending the belief that someone is superior due to size.

## No Black Heroes

Slowly but surely, the K-5 were revealing themselves through their arrogance. What I had in mind was risky, but I needed to attach names to that arrogance. I needed proof as to who they really were. Having been told that every time one of them busted someone up, they got time off, I knew I needed to see the comp. book. If I pulled the files on those arrests, the patterns of abuse would be there. It wouldn't be easy. The captains kept the comp. books in their office in patrol. God only knew if any of them were somehow involved with the K-5 too.

I began to wait every night and watched for a time when the patrol office was empty. Several times a week I was able to sneak in the patrol office and look at the comp. books. I looked silly climbing through the patrol window, but I needed to know. I checked and discovered only a few officers getting time off for so-called good arrests. The files associated with the comp. awards showed patterns of prisoners being injured or brought to the hospital. Any cops worth their salt could figure out those were the ones, the K-5. The names that stood out were Officers Stretch, Rosa, Strep, Rome and Cue. All of them were steroid-taking muscle boys. But not all of them had the skinhead haircuts and tats the Guardians had focused on.

We still didn't have enough to prove what we suspected. The supervisors who were rewarding those guys would never admit to their existence. We told our membership what they needed to do. "We have discovered a pattern of abuse in the community. All Guardian members need to show up at any hot calls." What we wanted were our guys at the foot and car chases, fights, and motor vehicle stops in our neighborhoods. It was the only way to stop, or at the very least cut down on, the abuse on the streets. Who would complain about a cover car? That was the beauty of it. They could think whatever they wanted, but we would be there to help. It had an immediate impact. The beatings went down to a minimum. And we looked like the good guys, showing up to cover their Aryan rumps.

## Chief's Slipping and The Kings

The news I had hoped would come someday arrived. Dave called, "Bailey, I thought you'd want to know Chief Irving just resigned." For a second, I thought about running through the streets naked, in celebration. "I beat him, Dave." "Yes, you did. You chased him out of town." I was extremely drained. Attorney Gaynor called and said the lawsuit had been postponed. The city didn't have an explanation for the delay either. I told Gerry of Irving's untimely departure, while singing, "Yes, Jesus loooooves me. Yes, Jesus loves me, for the Bible tells me, sooooooooo!" Gerry was in stitches.

Chief Irving's reign of terror lasted almost seven years. In the end, he left town without fanfare or celebration. No formal acknowledgement, dinner in his honor, nothing. The city had no comment on his sudden ride into the sunset either. What could they say? His legacy would be that of a chief who tolerated racism, corruption, and spawned an all-white hate group. That was his parting gift to Bridgeport.

As dumb as it may seem Chief Irving left one last standing order before he resigned. He ordered all officers to stay away from McDonalds on the West End! Unbelievable. We were ordered not to eat there because the manager refused to charge us. What many didn't know was that the manager was a recovering addict we had arrested years earlier. She felt the arrest helped get her off drugs, and ultimately turn her life around. Her way of thanking us was to allow us to eat at her place, no charge. What I was about to do was wrong, but I did it anyway. I mailed Chief Irving a Happy Meal with a note, "McDonalds is our kind of place, and it's such a happy place." It was the McD's old slogan, and the perfect reply to his departure.

After years of oversight by the federal court, it was clear the City of Bridgeport was still up against the ropes. Under Chief Irving's command, racism flourished. His resignation left the city with no choice but to postpone all pending discrimination cases. The good news was, a search was underway for a new Chief of Police. With a new mayor about to come in, we were hoping for a new beginning. Sadly, I had been down that road before, having hopes for a new beginning. There was little optimism left for me in that daydream.

The years were flying by. The new mayor-elect was Joseph Ganim. He defeated Mayor Moran, who had the distinction of being nationally recognized as the mayor who filed bankruptcy in the city of Bridgeport. She was possibly the first mayor in the United States to do such a thing. For a time, the banks didn't want to cash officers' checks! We had to wait in line while they called the city to check on our status. Mayor Ganim promised to drop the bankruptcy suit if he were elected. Once in office, he did just that.

The City Attorney's Office was in discussion with Attorney Gaynor. They were very concerned about my case, and rightfully so. I was demanding they bring back Irving to testify. Just as Attorney Gaynor predicted, the city settled. We turned down the first two offers. Finally, they made me an offer I couldn't refuse. Attorney Gaynor asked me to meet him at Murphy's Law, a small place where attorneys went to unwind after a long day.

"Bailey, your ship has arrived. You got enough money to replace the house you lost, your cars, and then some. They did stipulate you cannot discuss the amount you received." "Good, I don't need anyone to know how much I got anyway." "More importantly, they agreed to purge your record. All the things Chief Irving, Sergeant Copeland and Lyons did to you have been erased. Your file has nothing in it to represent those guys ever existed." I looked at Attorney Gaynor, "Gerry, I've been waiting for this day a long time." I signed the papers, shook Gerry's hand, and went home to celebrate with Yvette. She decided it was time to move. We bought a new house and furnished it, cash. I then flew to Canada and bought a new BMW X5, cash. Of course, as the commercial said, "What are you going to do now?" I took the kids to Disney and Universal Studios. To top it off, Yvette was able to complete her schooling, earning her Master's degree, courtesy of Irving's idiocy.

## Chief's Slipping and The Kings

Upon reflection, things were not as jubilant for me as some would've thought. Vindication was mine, and it felt good. But the ones who had done so much to me got away with it. How I wished they would have been forced to pay out of their own pockets for what they'd done. If people had to pay for their actions, instead of the taxpayers, the unfair treatment of others would drop significantly or end. I looked forward to seeing them again, to look them in their eyes. Not to gloat, but so they could see the dignity they couldn't take away from me.

Chapter 23

## Major Drug Gangs

The news had spread like wildfire. The new Chief of Police was Wilbur Chapman. It was the day we had hoped for. What a surprise, Bridgeport now had its first African American chief from New York City. We had heard great things about Chief Chapman. Always watchful, I had a question. Why did the city choose a black Chief of Police? It was not their style.

It wasn't a time for worry, but a time for celebration. Chief Chapman brought the New York style of policing to Bridgeport. The higher-ups were learning the Comp-Stat model of policing. The shocker was in Chief Chapman holding upper management accountable for crimes in the city. They were running around like chickens with their heads cut off! We had never seen this type of policing before. Furthermore, the chief took care of the guys in patrol. All he asked was one thing; keep Bridgeport safe.

TNT had its new marching orders. Chief Chapman wanted us to start taking down all the drug gangs in

## No Black Heroes

Bridgeport. With Sergeant Samatulski promoted to lieutenant, we were getting Sergeant Ralph Villegas to oversee the unit. "Bailey, from Chief Chapman, get out there and shut it down. His words, 'whatever it takes'." It was a tall order. We still had the Latin Kings, Green Top Posse, The Stack Boys, Bush Mob, The Brother Hood, the Jones Family, and Frankie Estrada and the Terminators. TNT was gonna need some help.

My disguises were still working. I had the 'hood confused, showing up clean shaven in uniform one day, and then returning as a bum, project worker, telephone lineman, whatever, the next. The image they always had in mind was the clean-shaven Officer Bailey I let them see. While in disguise, I even heard a local drug dealer say in fear, "Look, look over there. The old white guy sitting on the milk crate drinking a beer, it's Bailey." Wow. They were getting desperate to find me.

Chapman's orders resulted in a whole new set of assignments. The drug factions the department wanted shut down were considered the best and hardest nuts to crack in the city, the Jones family. They owned most of P.T. followed by the Terminators and Holmans. The Joneses had their sections of P.T. on lockdown. Interestingly, the Jones brothers all had names that began with the letter L. There was Luke, Lyle, Lance, Lonnie and Leonard Jones. Luke was a huge problem. Word on the street was he had killed several on behalf of the Jones empire. If you ever turned your back on him, you were a done deal. And he didn't care about cops.

I still had my main informant who knew the Jones family well, M&M. My new info kid was Casanova, "Cass." Fresh out of jail, Cass refused to sign up to get paid. "Hey man, that's how you end up dead, Bailey; no thanks." "Why are you doing this?" "Because I've changed, and it's the right thing to do." Cass was clear about one thing; the Jones family was not the kind of people to mess with. "Watch out for Luke." Cass had seen Luke murder several on the streets, and even my department had no idea about

## Major Drug Gangs

them. It was risky meeting with informants who weren't registered, but it was my only solid link to the streets. And I had to hold onto the intel until I had proof that would keep Cass out of it.

The DEA had recently been assigned in P.T. to keep watch on TNT's work, and of course, the Joneses. Agent Milton Tyrell contacted me. He needed a good spot to set up and observe P.T. all day, if possible. "Absolutely. I'll take you to see the manager at Twin Towers. It's a high rise for the elderly that overlooks the entire project."

We met with the manager and she provided Agent Tyrell with an apartment. "Agent Tyrell, this one will give you all the views you'll need on the Jones family." He looked at me curiously, "Bailey, how do you know about these locations?" I had just done a series of raids with Statewide in the complex. "We raided six apartments every weekend for two months, to clean this place up." I was familiar with all the apartments I hit, and the views.

Agent Tyrell, still curious, wondered why a place for the elderly needed to be raided. What he was seeing was the clean version of the Towers. Months earlier, the place was a drug-infested scene out of the movie *New Jack City*. The truth was, the elderly men living there wanted companionship. Many of them allowed the local prostitutes to live with them in exchange for free sex. From there, the drug dealers came in and began selling from the apartments. It became a drug haven. "By the time I got here, Agent Tyrell, the whole complex was infested. When I hit these apartments a few stood out as good places to watch P.T. from." He brought in his equipment. Tyrell commented, "I was told you were the man."

Over the next few months, I concentrated on the Joneses. I glued on my beard, put on some raggedy clothes and walked in. I was dragging a large plastic bag with cans rumbling inside for effect. In the bag were my gun, surveillance equipment, radios and supplies. Early at 5:00am was the best time to sneak in. The Jones family was mostly out in the afternoon or evenings, never the mornings. The morning crew was not too sharp, especially after selling all night.

"Here comes that bum again. Yo man, get a life. We don't want you 'round here." I was picking up more cans, playing the part. It was a dangerous thing to do. Those fools were known for kicking street people around unless they were buying dope. It was my only way to get by them and up close. I hoped I wouldn't get jumped.

I walked through P.T. still picking up cans, with a limp like I had a bum leg. I was out there about an hour before the lookouts started to ignore me. One lookout sniffed his dope right by me and threw down the empty fold. They were selling heroin with the Batman logo stamped on it. The Jones family liked the Marvel Comics markings on their product for some reason.

I walked towards the empty apartment, trying to sneak in, when someone spoke. "Yo, you looking for Batman?" I hawked up some spit in my mouth, heaving it out and wiped my nose with the sleeve of my hooded sweat shirt. I didn't look up, but it sounded like Fat Boy talking to me. He was a major player in the Jones family. He responded to my disgusting behavior, "Damn, you a nasty motherfucker. Get away from here."

I limped over to building seven and entered the apartment while no one was looking. The team watched me from the outskirts of P.T. making sure I got in safely. Detective Angel Llanos waited until I was in the apartment, "Bailey, you should get an Academy Award for that performance." All eyes were on me from Twin Towers while Agent Tyrell filmed it. It was time to get to work.

Once inside, I took the drill from my bag and started drilling holes in the boards covering the apartment windows. Next, I used roach spray to create a circle on the floor around me. Those things were not going home with me! Roaches were known for climbing into your clothing, and

## Major Drug Gangs

even your pockets, if you were there too long. I pulled out my food and drink, set up the radios and waited several hours for the sales to start.

Hours into the surveillance, I called out several buyers, and TNT arrested them. No one knew we were out there. I had my eye on the dealers, the stash location, and the ones holding money. The person who oversaw the drug operation was Eugene Rhodes. Rhodes was important to my case. He ran the street business for the Joneses, and they trusted him. M&M told me he was the key to the Joneses' operation. During the surveillance, Rhodes had taken money from the sales while telling everyone what to do. I meticulously documented his every move, including all his instructions by hand or head motions.

My case was ready. John Lewis and Lavita Jones were making sales. In order to make a solid case, it was important to get Rhodes. TNT officers were called in, and the 'hood didn't know what hit them. Back at the office, Rhodes looked at me. I was no longer in disguise. He turned to Lewis, "When this goes down, we had nothing to do with each other." I wrote what he said in the report. Rhodes was trying to avoid being linked to the Jones family operation. I got a call from M&M, she said Lavita wasn't related to the Jones I was after. "Hey Bae, it's a good start."

We took in $1300 from Rhodes, and he gave the same excuse as everyone else we took money from. It was always money from a job. "Rhodes, when you get to court, just bring your check stub. Otherwise that won't fly, my brother." Rhodes had been a street dealer all his life. I had a feeling he knew where it was eventually going to go, but how could he stop then?

A few days later, I returned to P.T. using the same surveillance tactics. I had a different disguise, walking around with a hoodie on, looking in dumpsters. I was picking through the garbage and talking to myself. People looked at me, turned and walked the other way, thinking I was crazy. This surveillance wouldn't take long. Rhodes was back out

## No Black Heroes

again trying to make up for the money he lost. That meant he had to take chances he normally wouldn't.

Rhodes was at building 12 speaking to a beautiful woman, Jasmine DeJesus. There was the mistake dealers frequently made. Rhodes wanted to impress DeJesus. You could see he was all over her. They spoke briefly, and Rhodes walked away after taking DeJesus' money. He came back and gave her several folds of dope. Suddenly, Rhodes ran out of sight. Not sure what happened, I gave TNT a description of DeJesus and her car.

I left my spot and started walking around, until I saw Rhodes getting into a blown-out, top-of-the-line BMW. The team notified me they had DeJesus and the dope too. I asked them to come into the project and stop the BMW with Rhodes in it. "Bailey, we got Rhodes in the car. Guess what? Lonnie and Lyle Jones are in it too. Lonnie has a bulletproof vest on." "Okay, arrest Rhodes and I'll call you later."

I didn't want the Joneses to know we were watching their operation. It had to look like it was all luck. So I told the team to let the Joneses go. "But Bailey, we got Lonnie with a vest on; he's a convicted felon. We can arrest him for that." I asked them to step away from the car so they couldn't hear us talk. "Hey guys, I know, but it's better to let the FBI handle that later. Document all you can, so when these guys go down, they stay down." Arresting one of the Joneses then was too early in the plan. They would back off and set things back for months, if not years. That time, Rhodes had $3000 on him. We got lucky. It was the money pickup we interrupted. Rhodes then had several cases and lost a lot of money for the Joneses. In my mind, Rhodes was close to turning witness for us. I needed to do just a few more things before he would come on board.

Lyle and Lonnie thought we missed our chance to arrest them. I did a detailed report on the BMW, the $3000 rims, the $10,000 blowout kit installed on the car, and of course the bulletproof vest Lonnie had on. It was all forwarded to

## Major Drug Gangs

the FBI. Once we had enough to take the Jones family down, those reports would be overwhelming evidence in court of the Joneses' drug life business.

Over the next few months, P.T. saw new faces working for the Jones family. Rhodes had so many cases pending, the Joneses had Glenda Jimenez running their business. Glenda was as street smart as they came. She had been on the streets dealing since she was a kid, according to M&M. Glenda was good at watching out for us, so I had to be where she would least expect, right in front of her.

Wearing women's clothing and a wig, I was sitting in a car and imagining the laughter if someone saw me in this get-up! It was pretty well known that for some reason, drug dealers didn't feel threatened by a woman's presence. Glenda, as street smart as she was, also paid no attention to me. My hope was to do a quick hit before one of those fools came over and asked me out! God help me if the team sees me like this!

To make sure they believed I was a woman, I got out of the car and took a baby's bag out of the trunk. Anyone looking would think I was waiting on "my man" to meet me. Glenda glanced my way and paid me no mind. She was selling dope at building 18. It was a different location the Joneses had moved to in order to throw TNT off. Cass warned me the Jones family was feeling the heat and were changing how they did business. They had moved their business location and even switched the logo on their dope from Batman to Superman, then to a Red Bull insignia.

The last sale Glenda made took me completely by surprise. Oh my God, it was Officer Davis Dee! He bought several folds from Glenda. I followed Dee out but had the team arrest him a ways off. I couldn't believe it. We had just delivered drugs to his house in an undercover operation a few weeks before. That case was still pending, while he was on suspension. I had figured he wasn't the major drug dealer the state thought he was. He had fallen on hard times and

313

violated the cardinal rule, "Don't get high on your own supply."

Glenda was selling with a few helpers hanging out. TNT chase units did their thing and took down any buyers I called out. Glenda, for some reason, had a habit of selling and then running into her apartment close by. I was not leaving there until she came back out. I knew this arrest was going to be the start of the Jones family downfall. Glenda was not about to go to jail for anyone, I could just feel it.

I took off my dress, wig, and high-heel shoes after parking a few buildings away, and boy were those high heels murder! My feet were pulsating. I walked comfortably with my sneakers on towards building 18, while people were out watching, and surprised to see me. It was no secret, and everyone on the streets knew if they saw me, it was about to go down. You could hear voices in the courtyard, "Yo, that's Bailey. Oh shit, somethin's up."

I called for TNT to roll in making a lot of noise when they arrived and began my run towards building 18. On the way, I saw Eugene Rhodes walking. He froze when he saw me. I ran up to him, gave him a palm shake and hug. When I pulled him in closer I whispered, "Gene, it's time for you to do the right thing. The FBI can help you, but you got to help yourself first. Let me know. You got the number." He whispered back, "I can't talk bout this right now." I pulled back, patted him on the back, and finished my run. The look he gave me said it all; he was going to make the call. At building 18, the team was just starting to get out of their cars. Glenda came out of her apartment to see what was going on. By then she had nothing on her. The commotion did just what I needed, drew her out. I pointed the team at her as she tried to walk off, and she was caught completely off guard. "What the fuck, I should've stayed inside."

Back at base, we processed everyone and took them to booking. Glenda was held over under the ruse that we had lost her paperwork. I brought her into my office. "Glenda,

## Major Drug Gangs

you might want to do the right thing before it's too late." I had enough to send her away for a long time. She didn't even hesitate, "Call them, Bailey." Things were close to an ending of the Joneses. It had been months and months of surveillances and arrests, all linked to their family.

The FBI showed up with J.J. and took Glenda to their office. "J.J., just so you know, Rhodes will be coming on board soon. Could you let Agent Tyrell know?" "No problem. I'll call him for you when I get back to the office." The ball was now in motion. Glenda was major in the FBI investigation. She not only worked for the Jones crew, but she had ties to Frankie Estrada and his Terminators. It was one step at a time, Glenda first, then Rhodes. The Joneses were on their way down.

With all that was going on, Cass called. He said a recent rash of murders was due to the Joneses being suspicious about some of their workers. He said Luke was on a roll. "Bailey, you know the drug factory where Chub and Shanice Green were killed a week ago? Luke did it. He walked in and executed them." "Cass, how do ya know that?" "I was there when he did it. I was hanging out when he rolled up. I knew what was up, so I left before he came back out." Cass went on to tell me about a hit a few months before. David "A-Whack" Clemons had just gotten out of jail, completing a six-year bid on a case of mine. Cass said Luke killed A-Whack because they had beef with each other. "Bailey, Luke followed him in a car one night and killed A-Whack at Park and Vine Street, and his passenger Rijos." Cass said he saw the car crash into the store on the corner. I knew Park and Vine was a Jamaican hangout, and Cass loved Jamaican girls. So he probably was there innocently enough. It seemed Cass was always at the wrong place at the right time. I told him he needed to chill on the streets, but he just repeated his assertion that he saw Luke do it.

Funny, I would have put my money on A-Whack taking Luke out. A-Whack was a polite, low-key killer no one had a clue about, according to my sources. I was told, by the time

315

you thought he was coming for you, it was too late and you were dead. Word was, A-Whack killed everyone, including any witnesses, so he didn't have to worry. He was like a ghost. Luke, on the other hand, was known for being ruthless, in your face see-ya, period. He wasn't worried about anyone snitching on him because he had that street cred. The rumor was he did kill a few witnesses, but the streets had plenty of stories to tell, so who knew.

Cass had one more thing to tell me. "Bailey, Luke said he has his sights on a judge, and your name came up. We all told him it was suicide to kill a cop and judge. We talked about it for awhile. I think he had second thoughts about you." "What?" "Hey, Bailey, we heard about you, the Kings, and that shootout on the turnpike. Luke kinda respects you." "Cass, you need to watch yourself. It sounds like the Joneses are more dangerous than I thought, especially Luke."

P.T. had become too hot for the Jones Family. They were using junkies to sell, instead of their main boys. We had to back off for a while, until they could get their confidence back. I concentrated on another spot away from P.T. for a while. TNT had received a report from patrol that Sergeant Louis Piccirillo had been hit from behind with a brick by a local drug dealer in Marina Apartments. Someone called the office and said Big Ears had done it. If that wasn't bad enough, Earnie said his father lived across the street from Marina, and local dealers tried to set his father's car on fire! We all knew it was a message meant for Earnie because he was in TNT. "Give me a few weeks, Earnie, and we'll take them out." "Okay, Bae Bae." "Stop calling me that!" He just laughed.

Hector "Big Ears" Martinez was the new leader of the Latin Kings. After checking with a few of my peeps on the streets, it was clear to me who authorized Earnie's father's car to be torched. I learned later it was Big Ears who hit Sergeant Piccirillo in the face with a brick, too. It was no secret the FBI was cleaning house, going after the Latin Kings for the murder of a cop's kid in New Haven, and

## Major Drug Gangs

probably the shooting at my home. The Kings were hiding their colors while the FBI indicted many of them under the RICO statutes for organized crime.

One thing about Big Ears, he was smart. I remember him calling a news conference touting that the Latin Kings were about Latino pride, community, and helping others, not violence. He kept the FBI at a distance with his community rhetoric. He even organized a community cleanup. They painted and spruced up abandoned buildings and the railroad underpass on Main Street. He made sure the press saw the new Latin Kings as a community activist organization, improving the quality of life. Big Ears was a great public relations guy. He was also a kid I watched grow up in the projects where I had lived. I knew him well and wasn't buying it.

The drug business in Marina Apartments was next to impossible to infiltrate. Four buildings took up an entire block, but if you didn't live there, the crew wouldn't allow you in. They were using the "keep the community safe" nonsense they were selling in the news to justify hanging out while keeping a close watch out for us. Ironically, Marina was located right next to a major beach front where families looked to spend quality time, Seaside Park. Not even a block away from this drug haven was the University of Bridgeport, an international student based college with a large campus. Talk about irony. Well organized, anyone coming in to buy drugs knew just where to go, into the building hallway on Whiting Street. All the other buildings had lookouts to keep law enforcement at a distance. It was a fortress. We had stayed away from Marina for weeks so they could get cocky, and they did. "Earnie get ready, we're gonna take these guys out." He could hardly wait.

I finally told the team we were shutting Marina Apartments down. They all looked at me, wondering where I could possibly hide. The empty apartments were closely watched. You couldn't just hang around without one of them coming over to check you out. Parking a car to watch them wasn't going to work; the buildings blocked any view

## No Black Heroes

from the streets. They even kept an eye on Earnie's father's house. So where could I go?

I wasn't sure it could be done, but I had an idea. "I'll call you guys when I'm in. Don't come anywhere near Marina Apartments until you hear from me." I had a spot in the back of my mind, but it was sheer madness. I went out and took a look. Hey, why not? "Guys, I should be in soon. I want you to stay out at least one mile from the set." "Bae Bae, how we gonna take out the buyers from that far out?" "Leave it to me."

I drove over to the United Illuminating building and spoke with the manager. He looked at me and smiled, "You want someone to take you to the top of the candy cane, the smoke stack? I hope you know that thing is a lot higher than it looks. You got nerve, officer." I looked at him curiously, "Why would you say that?" "The candy cane is the highest straight-up point in Bridgeport, and not the sturdiest of places to sit. Are you sure about this?" "We had a drug dealer mess with a cop. It's our turn."

The foreman put me in a small cage on the side of the stack. It was just enough room for two. It shot up the side, taking about 10 minutes to reach the top. When we got up there, I stepped out onto a metal grate that circled around the stack. It was only two feet wide. "You're right, not the sturdiest of places." I cautiously looked down. Cars looked like small specks. The foreman asked, "How can you see anything from up here?" I pulled out my scope. "Good luck officer. Call me on the radio when you want to get down."

I sat down and carefully put my bag to the side. I set up the scope and looked. Oh my God, this thing is moving. I called the foreman and asked if it was normal. "Officer, it has to have play in the structure otherwise it would collapse." "Okay, just checking." Looking through the scope made the movement just that much more pronounced. I had to concentrate. "Hey guys, saddle up, we're about to take this place down." Earnie got on the radio, "Bae Bae, where are you?" "Let's just say I'm nowhere to be seen."

## Major Drug Gangs

Looking down at the corner hallway it felt like I was falling. The movement was terrible, but I could see every sale those guys made. Big Ears' brother Ernesto "Little Ears" Martinez was in charge. I start calling out the sales. "Bailey, how are we gonna see where these guys go after they buy?" "Trust me, I can lead you to 'em."

The first sale I called out to the team, they missed. I saw where the car was going and told them to go up to Saint Vincent's Hospital. It was about three miles away. "He's at the light by the hospital right now." I could see the team arrive at St. Vincent's hospital on Main Street. They got the buyer and drugs. "Bailey, how can you see this guy's car from Whiting?" "I'll tell you later, right now we need to focus on Marina. We got more sales."

We had been at Marina Apartments for some time and had enough buyers for a solid case. I was about to call the team in when Little Ears came out of the hallway. In his hands was an Uzi assault weapon. He walked over to a car and put it in like he had just gone grocery shopping or something. I almost fell off the smoke stack staring so hard at the car. It was time to call the team in.

Almost all of the crew was standing in the doorway entrance to the building. I had to let the team know there was a gun on set. "Hey guys, Little Ears just put an Uzi in his car. One gun means there might be more, so heads up." The team came in and put everyone down on the ground. "Bailey, you won't believe what we just got." "I'll be there in about 30 minutes." "Man, where are you?"

It took me a while to get down. I had to wait for the foreman and take the 10-minute ride off the candy cane. When I got to Marina, they took me into an apartment Little Ears was caught coming out of. They said he tried to run back in but couldn't shut the door in time. Once inside, the team had the right to arrest for anything they saw. There was money scattered all over the place. We also took three more guns linked to the crew. Then we walked Little Ears over to his car and got his Uzi.

319

**No Black Heroes**

In the hallway, we had Frankie Cora. He was under arrest for drugs, and a warrant out for him in connection to the murder of a 14-year-old kid. We took in 1200 packs of dope, 30 folds of cocaine, 120 bags of crack cocaine, and $4000 in cash. We hit them hard and shut them down. Although the Kings was a Latino-based group, that day we had some of everybody under arrest. In the drug business it wasn't a surprise to see different factions working a drug spot. It was all about money. The bottom line was anyone working that location went down for drug and weapons violations. And yes, especially for messing with a cop and his family. When all was said and done, dealers Wilbert Henderson, Anthony Broadnax, Roswell Menefee, Orlando Rios and Little Ears were done.

Back at TNT, Earnie was walking around with a big smile on his face telling everyone in the cell, "You don't ever mess with a cop or his family, remember dat. That's why you're all here." He made sure they all knew this was payback for the fire to his fathers' car. "Tell Big Ears, when and if you get out, his days are numbered too." I was in the office writing my reports when Earnie came in. He hugged and kissed me on the cheek. "Thanks, Bae Bae. Now, where the hell were you?" "On top of the candy cane, the smoke stack. It's a long way up, my brother." Earnie stared at me not knowing just what to say. With his mouth open the words just came out, "Bae Bae, you're fucking insane! Only you would think to go up there."

I was about to return to P.T. but got sidelined with information about a gay club in Westport linking drugs to Bridgeport. I put on some tight jeans and a tight shirt, and drove to the Cedar Brook Lounge. I wasn't too keen on the role I had to play. When I entered, all eyes were on me. I had the look and walk down pat. Unfortunately, I was the new meat on the hook for a night. If one more man asked me to dance, I was gonna scream. I hung out for a while but no one seemed involved with drugs from what I could see. Women were kissing women, and men kissing men, what the heck.

I was about to leave when I saw the one person I had no idea would be there, it was Officer Carmen Ramos, wife of recently replaced ex-TNT Officer Ramos. I had heard she was a freak of the week with other cops, but that wasn't my business. Oh my God, no way. Carmen is kissing women, gay men, sticking her tongue in places I would never think you should or could. With the things she did in the club, what was she capable of in private?

I was trying to sneak out when I got cornered by a guy who tried to hit on me. I had to get out of there before Carmen saw me. I told Sherman to give me his number because I had to go. He wrote it down and asked me to please call him. He's about to kiss me. Oh God, help me out of this. "Not on the first date, Baby." He smiled, grabbed my ass and squeezed it. I felt so violated! I just wanted to go home. I winked and touched his chin with a smile. It was enough for me to get past Carmen without being seen.

At home, all I could do was laugh. Officer John Ramos had lied about me in TNT for Sergeant Copeland. I knew it was wrong, but I found it so humorous knowing he was kissing a wife whose lips had been places no man would ever have dreamt of going. It gave new meaning to the term, "If you suck a pole, you'll eat a hole." And he was kissing lips that went to both, and then some. Have mercy. Whenever I saw him, all I could do was smile. Payback is sweet.

It had been several weeks, so I returned to P.T. On my return, I made sure they saw a clean Officer Bailey in a marked patrol car. After driving through, I planned to return back to base and get my disguises but decided to take another pass. I drove to the rear of the project towards building 18, since it was a perfect way to get in if you didn't want to be seen right away. No one ever drove in that way because there was no road, just tall grass and weeds. I had no idea what was about to happen.

At the far end of building 18 was a white Nissan Maxima parked and running. The doors were wide open, like someone had just run away from the car. Eugene Rhodes was

## No Black Heroes

walking by, looked at me and just shook his head. I asked him if he knew who the car belonged to. He didn't say anything, shook his head again "No" and kept walking.

If Eugene was close by that meant something about that car was a good thing, it had to be dirty. I radioed the team and gave them my location. I walked over to the car and peered inside. On the front driver's seat were a bulletproof vest, ski mask and cell phone. The keys were still in the ignition. I pulled my gun and held onto it down low. On the passenger's seat were more keys. The rear panel behind the driver's seat had been pulled out exposing a hidden compartment, but it was empty. The car was no doubt rigged for transporting drugs. It looked like whoever bailed out of the car, was ready to do a hit if need be.

I was desperate for cover and called patrol. No one was responding to my call for assistance. I didn't want to take a chance on being shot, so I called TNT to let them know I was out of there. There was something about that car I knew was important to the Jones family. I asked the team to pick up the marked car in front of building 18 and I took the Nissan back to base.

Earnie was getting nervous, "Bae Bae, what's going on?" "Nothing Earn, I'm leaving now." At base I could do an inventory of the car safely. I began the search and took notes on everything in the car. As soon as I looked under the driver's seat, I knew it was game over. This would be the break the DEA and FBI were waiting for. Under the driver's seat were 272 folds of dope marked with the Superman logo. It was broken down into nine large plastic bags. I had to admit, those guys had a sense of humor, I gave them that. The bag containing the drugs had a happy face on it.

While at TNT searching the car, a cell phone on the seat rang. I answered it. The woman on the other end told me she was Pam, Lyle's mother. She wanted to know where Lyle was. I blurted off the top of my head, "Mrs. Jones, the police are up on us. Lyle's busy right now." She frantically said "Okay" and hung up. A second call came in asking for

## Major Drug Gangs

Lyle. It sounded like John "D.C." Foster, another member of the Jones crew. I told him Lyle was busy and would call back. All the while, I was taking notes on what was said, the numbers and times.

I needed to make a case. So I called Mrs. Jones back, using Lyle's cell phone. I got a recording. "Hi, you have reached the Jones residence." This was getting better by the minute. I returned to my inventory and began looking at details more closely. That's when I noticed the World Gym cards on the key chains. I took the keys from the ignition and the keys on the passenger seat and drove to the town of Orange.

A World Gym employee ran the codes from the cards. The code on the card from the ignition keys belonged to Lyle Jones. That put Lyle as the driver of the car. In a court of law, Lyle would be responsible and own whatever was found in it, case closed. The other World Gym card belonged to Lonnie Jones. That put him in the passenger's seat.

I returned to TNT and continued the inventory. In the glove compartment were pictures of Lyle and his family in P.T. The nail in the coffin was a summons arresting Lyle for speeding in New York. The date on the summons indicated Lyle had possession of the car for a long time. More evidence: papers with his name, receipts substantiating Lyle being a regular in New York, and even pictures that showed the crew at a cookout with strippers. It doesn't get any better that that.

I applied for an arrest warrant for Lyle, and a search warrant for all records for the cell phone left in the car. The records showed Lyle was in contact with the who's who in drugs, including members of Frankie Estrada's Terminators. The FBI was going to have a field day on this one. The link was complete.

I already knew Lyle was going to say it wasn't his car, because it was registered to someone else. It was a well-

## No Black Heroes

*A major break and a link to New York. This is how it began.*

known fact that drug dealers used cars registered to someone else, or stolen ones. If there was a chance of getting caught in those cars, the drug dealers would bail out. The line was always the same, "Hey, man, that ain't my car, so I don't know what's in it."

With the warrant in hand I returned to P.T. to pick up Lyle. He was on the basketball court trying to make three-point shots. He was making them, too. I had heard that at one time, he was a standout basketball player in high school. While watching Lyle, his brother Luke happened to walk by slowly. He didn't say a thing. Luke was definitely one scary dude.

TNT cover units were on the outskirts waiting for my call. I figured if I came in alone, I could arrest Lyle and not have to hunt him down. If he knew we had a warrant out for him, he would have skipped town. Lyle walked off the court and I met him halfway. I told him about the warrant and cuffed him, without incident. The team came in and took him to base.

Back at the office, Lyle asked how I could charge him with drugs from a car he didn't even own. I looked at him, "Who said I was charging you with drugs from a car?" He tried to cover it up. "Not that I know anything about a car I don't own." Too late! Everything he said was added in the report. I asked Officer Bahr, who was nearby, if he heard what Lyle said. Bahr nodded yes, and I put him in the report as a witness to Lyle's comments.

## Major Drug Gangs

It was up to the Feds at that point. I gave J.J. and the FBI all I had on the Joneses. There were months and months of surveillances and arrests. My case on Lyle was exceptionally strong. Glenda was working with the FBI, and I got the call Rhodes reached out to them too. If I knew anything about drug cases, it was for certain the FBI was going to build a case linking anybody and everybody connected to the Jones Family. But I had no idea how far my work was going to take the FBI.

J.J. called to give me a heads-up. The FBI did just as I had figured, they linked the drugs and other evidence I took from the car linking the Jones family, their crew, and even Frankie Estrada and the Terminators. "Just so you know, Bae Bae, get ready to testify for months to come, maybe even a year or two." I thought he was kidding. "J.J., can you leave me out of this? Thanks." He just laughed.

While waiting for the FBI to close any loose ends before the roundup, we were asked by command to take on a few more cases to stop the violence in the city. The DEA from Boston was called to give us a hand. They sent the Mobile Enforcement Team (MET) to help clean up Bridgeport. The MET team brought in a helicopter with cameras that could view a license plate number from 20 miles out. It felt like we were a part of a Seal Team or something. I did the spot surveillance from the ground, and they used the copter to zero in on the targets. It was an amazing time. I was back out there in disguise.

With the arrest of Lyle, the 'hood was tight. They had the nerve to try and keep things going. Everyone was looking out for Five-O. At building 5 in the courtyard, I was watching Eddie "Fat Boy" Lawhorn and Jermaine Jenkins talking. Those two were also important players in the Jones organization. Jermaine stopped talking for a moment to see what I was doing. In role, I kept walking with my cane, pushing a carriage. It slowed me down a bit but made a great cover. Jermaine turned and looked at the New Jacks working for the Joneses. If one of them got caught it didn't matter. With TNT and the FBI lurking about, it was just too hot out there to use the main boys.

Jermaine looked at the new crew still glancing my way. "Y'all sit tight. Don't start up 'til I get back. I'm goin' out to take a look for Narcs." He got in his fancy blown-out SUV and began to check the area. If you know the police are onto ya, wouldn't you have the sense to get out of the business? At the very least go away for a while. I called the chase team and told them to pull out of the area. "Jermaine is on his way to look for you." I started talking to myself to cover up my transmissions on the radio. People who heard me figured I was nuts and kept their distance.

The MET team took over the surveillance from the helicopter hovering from neighboring Stratford. They could see where Jermaine was driving, and they even verified that his car was legally registered, from his license plate insert! I was impressed. Once Jermaine was out far enough, the team took him down for conspiracy in the sale of narcotics. He kept asking, "What I do?" Earnie just kept responding, "Bailey don't allow anyone to be looking for us. Get used to being in cuffs if you're gonna keep that up."

I made my way back to where Lawhorn was. He had become impatient waiting for Jermaine. "Where the hell did he go?" Then he said something I had never heard before. "I thought Bailey only came out here on Tuesdays and Thursdays." They were trying to figure which days I was out there? Impatient, Lawhorn told the crew to start up but to watch out for me. I was sitting on the pavement drinking soda out of a beer bottle, hanging close to my carriage. Eddie was telling the crew to walk away after making a sale. It was a smart move, that's for sure. "If Bailey's out here, it'll be harder for him to spot up on you if ya on the move."

So then we had to adjust. I had seen a rip done by the Broward County Florida police task force. If they could do it, so could we. The rip was simple enough, and we had a van with a sliding door to make it easier. I could target the dealer once he made the sale and follow him out. If I

## Major Drug Gangs

couldn't, the helicopter sure enough could. Once the dealer was far enough out, the van could pull alongside and snatch him up. The van door would close and that would be it, end of story.

"Okay guys, the dealer just sold and has on blue jeans, a bright red shirt and a Bulls baseball-like cap. He's right by building 12 headed for 18. The team pulled up, yanked him in and slammed the door shut. The guy screamed in such a high-pitched voice, you would have thought Mariah Carey was being kidnapped. "Ahhhhhhhhh." Poof, he was gone. A few people came out when they heard the scream and the van door slam. When they didn't see anyone, they just went back into their apartments. We did it four times before we shut down.

The MET team was so impressed with our work their commander decided to federally indict everyone we took in. Chief Chapman was extremely happy with the team's progress. The MET team had seen drugs before, but not on the scale we were operating with. The DEA and FBI investigations were known for lasting years under their process. We produced big numbers in a day. But that was street sales, while their targets were much "higher profiles."

Their team worked with us two to three days a week. With their help, we made over 700 drug arrests in less than six weeks. We took in cars, money, drugs, guns, and served warrants on other fugitives, including a murderer. At the end of the MET operation, we were brought to Boston, Massachusetts by the DEA. TNT members and MET agents all received citations. I remember when the numbers were read, some uttered, "Oh my God." We were given a standing ovation. With the MET team reassigned, it was time to refocus.

## *K-5; Jones; Estrada; Corruption?*

Chief Chapman was an extremely intelligent man and African American police chief. The K-5 weren't stupid and were forced into maintaining a low profile. Unlike Chief Irving's reign where they flourished, Chief Chapman was not someone to mess with. No sooner did he arrive, he made it clear he would not tolerate what he called stupidity and foolishness. Do what he told you or you were on his shit list.

He was well aware of the federal court oversight and made it clear he would not tolerate any forms of discrimination under his watch. Any hint of a problem had the officer, including the whole chain of command, in his office. That meant the sergeant, lieutenant, captain, and the deputy chief were all held accountable. And you could best believe somebody better have an answer when he asked a question. High-ranking officers who didn't have an answer to the chief's questions were sent to answer phones in dispatch. It was a New York thing.

With no way for the K-5 to continue what they had been doing, they slowly started to unravel. My mother had many sayings, but "God don't like ugly" was the one that fit them best. One by one, members of the K-5 were being arrested or forced to resign. Not for the beatings they'd committed, which we would have been pleased to see. No, their downfall was in the cockiness they had grown accustomed to. They had been allowed to do whatever they wanted for such a long time, they couldn't adjust to going by the rules. The ones we suspected were K-5 folded just as they had begun, without much fanfare.

The first one to lose his job was Officer Cue. Officer Joey Choi had just bought a new Harley-Davidson motorcycle. It was stolen right after he got it. Shortly after, Officer Cue contacted Choi and told him he knew where it was and could get it back for him. Rumors had circulated about it, but many thought it was something someone at the PD circulated as a joke. Come on, a cop stealing another cop's Harley? It had to be a joke.

The rumor was Officer Cue was going to get Choi's bike back, but for a price. It sounded like a shakedown to me!

## Major Drug Gangs

Then it suddenly wasn't a rumor anymore, because the department issued a warrant for Cue's arrest. With Chief Chapman in charge, not even what was left of the Ad Hoc dared taking a chance running interference on the warrant. Officer Cue was arrested, the motorcycle was returned, and he quietly resigned.

The next K-5 junkie to go down was Officer Rosa. He got caught stealing and parting out cars to collect on insurance money. Officers couldn't help but wonder if he and Officer Cue had been working together on insurance scams. Who knew, but Rosa went to jail and we never heard about him again.

The so-called champion of the K-5 crew went down really hard, Officer Stretch. I will never forget finding out how he was about to go down. I stopped at Mercado's liquor store on East Main Street to buy some wine for Yvette. I also needed some for cooking. No sooner had I gotten home from Mercado's when J.J. called. "Hey brother, I need to see you in the office tomorrow. Can you come by?" "Sure." Before I could ask him what was going on, he hung up. I couldn't ever remember J.J. being so serious with me before.

The next day at the FBI office, I met with J.J. He looked a little upset. "J, what's wrong?" "Ron, I need to ask you something. Have you started drinking?" "What?" "Do you drink?" "Of course not J, you know I don't drink." He looked at me with more worry in his eyes. "Can you tell me why you were in Mercado's buying liquor?" I looked at J.J. and smiled, thinking it was a joke. "What are you doing, following me?" He was expressionless. His partner was standing close by looking busy, but wasn't. "J, I stopped by the store to get wine for Yvette, she drinks. I also cook with it. What's wrong?" He had a look of relief. I was so confused. He put his arms around my shoulder and took me into another room where he pointed at a few monitors on the wall. "You know we trust you, but we had to be sure about why you were at Mercado's." Someone was in trouble, but it wasn't me.

## No Black Heroes

The FBI was watching Mercado's Liquors. That's when J.J. showed me a picture of the owner, and a picture of Officer Stretch. "You really scared us, Bae Bae. When you went into Mercado's, we didn't know what to think." "Jesus guys, you scared me. So what's up with Stretch?" J.J. looked at me, "Who?" "That's what the Guardians call him, Officer Stretch." "Okay, just so you know, Officer 'Stretch' has been selling drugs. We set up cameras at Mercado's." "Does this have anything to do with the K-5?" "We heard about them, but this is about drugs. Just keep this under your hat for now." "Are you kidding? I don't know anything, and I'm never going there again!" J.J. laughed and walked me out of the office. "I got to tell ya, you really scared me that time. I should've known." "Hey, we both thought the PD was an honest place to work. What did we find? The K-5, Ad Hoc, cops on drugs, selling, and stealing. I'm out."

Not long afterwards, Mercado's crew got indicted. The papers said Officer Jess "Stretch" Stacks was arrested, along with a former corrections officer and members of a high-ranking mobster family. In all, there were 29 arrests by the FBI and the Safe Street project. What surprised the hell out of me was reportedly Officer Stacks was allowed to retire with a pension.

All that remained of the K-5 were Officers Step and Rome, both steroid-taking boys. They slowly faded away, eventually retiring on disabilities. The Guardians were ecstatic to see those guys gone. The K-5 was supposed to be the answer to their issues on race; instead they became the poster children for a supremacy crusade that failed. With the K-5 gone and the Ad Hoc on the wheelchair list, things were a bit more comfortable. But many officers, black and white, dreaded racism would find a way to carry on.

Back on the streets, information M&M was providing was so detailed the FBI was at a loss for words at what I was giving them. But Cass was so close to the Joneses, I just knew someday he would be found dead. Again, he had the 411 on another murder. "Bailey, I was in the courtyard in P.T. when Dingbat got killed. Pablo did it while Fat Boy

## Major Drug Gangs

and Dashiki stood by." "Dashiki?" "You know, Willie Nunes. They work for the Joneses." "Just so you know, Fat Boy gave Pablo the gun that killed Dingbat." Cass had some incredible information, but I couldn't pass it on. If he was found out, he would be killed for sure.

My worries about Cass intensified because of the news the Fed's had passed along to us. Russell Peeler had his brother Adrian kill Karen Clarke and her eight-year-old son, Leroy "B.J." Brown Jr. The news reported that the little boy was expected to be the key witness against Peeler in the upcoming trial for the fatal shooting of Clarke's boyfriend, Rudolf Snead Jr., a former drug associate of Peeler's. If an eight-year-old boy could be murdered for being a witness, anyone was up for grabs. Adding insult to injury, Russell and Adrian were the children of Officer Peeler who had passed away years ago from cancer. I remembered playing with them when they were children. What in the world happened to those kids?

I returned to P.T. with J.J. who was there to monitor our radio frequency. We were looking to take out the other drug factions. I happened to walk right into a sale. It was Isaiah Soler. This was the break we had been waiting for, Frankie Estrada's Lieutenant selling drugs. He seemed in a hurry, made several quick sales, then ran to his car. I guess he figured he'd make a fast buck and get out before anyone was the wiser. I could hear someone yell, "Yo, you don't sell on this side, what the fuck!"

I called the team to have Soler arrested. They tried to stop him, but he drove wildly onto I-95 and crashed the car. Somehow he got away. M&M called, "Bailey you know who that was and what he means to Frankie?" How did she know about Soler so fast, it was just minutes ago? "Baby, I'm on my way to get a warrant as we speak."

J.J. called. "Hey Bae Bae, Soler is Frankie's right-hand man. He just murdered Rafael 'One-eye June' Garcia for him." "J., I got him on sales and escape charges. Give me a week and I'll have the warrant." But I had to ask, "J.,

## No Black Heroes

what's with the one-eye and dead-eye nicknames out here?" He laughed, "These guys miss a lot when they shoot at each other." "Wow."

The next day at the gas station, wouldn't you know it; right next to me was Edward "French Fry" Estrada, Frankie's little brother. He was playing that "stare him down" routine on me. I had to make sure he knew I wasn't someone to mess with. "What the fuck are you looking at?" He was enraged at what I said. "The big bad Narc everyone's afraid of, Bailey. The Terminators aren't the Joneses, bro." I was about to punch him in his face but stepped back to give him a wakeup call. "Look, French Fry, Ketchup, Onion, whatever your fuckin' street name is, you really don't want to fuck with me." I pulled my sweat shirt up so he could see my gun. These guys knew only one thing, you had to talk the talk and be ready to back it up "Your move, motherfucker!" French Fry pulled the nozzle out of his car with gas pouring all over the ground. He jumped in and drove off. I yelled at him one last time, "Later Relish, Mustard, Mayo, whatever."

I got the call from J.J. with the news I expected. He said they had linked my cases not only to the Joneses, but Frankie Estrada, the Terminators, Quintin Powell, Aaron Harris and their Q&A Mob. The car with the drugs I took in was additional hard evidence and a major piece to the FBI investigations. People were turning state's evidence and about to testify in the largest drug case the State of Connecticut had ever seen.

The FBI began the massive roundup, and the newspapers said it all; Drug Murders Linked to Trafficking, Grand Jury Charges 13 with Drug Crimes. The names were a laundry list of Jones associates involved in drug trafficking. I had either arrested or provided intelligence to the FBI on all of them, shutting them down. But the real credit couldn't go to the ones it should've gone to, Cass and M&M. They provided the names and other crucial information needed when I first looked at the Jones operation. Now the papers echoed those same names: Willie "Man" Nunley,

## Major Drug Gangs

John "DC" Foster, Craig "One-eye" Baldwin, Rasheen Lewis, Leslie Morris, and Aaron Harris of the Q&A Mob.

Right after the first roundup a second one took place: Eddie Pagan of the Foundation, Lawson Day, Eugene Rhodes and Glenda Jimenez. Rhodes and Jimenez were already on board with the FBI. An entire empire done in behind one question, "Do you want to do the right thing?" And they did.

A few months later, a third round of indictments came. It was Frankie Estrada and the Terminators. The FBI took the last of the Q&A Mob including Quintin Powell. The news reported Raid Nets 22 Suspects in Drug Trafficking Ring. It was another list of names that mirrored out of the TNT cases, Michael Hilliard, Vivian Jimenez, Yamarr Shipman, Jermaine Jenkins, Eddie Lawhorn, and Isaiah Soler.

It was sad to see how Jermaine Jenkins had been days earlier in P.T. when we spoke. "Bailey, I'm not doing anything anymore." "Jermaine, it's too late for that. You need to help yourself." He looked at me, "They'll kill me." "No, they won't. They're going away for life. You can do this, man." He dropped his head down and went back in his apartment. In the end, he turned state's evidence too. He had no choice. It was that or life.

In the meanwhile, Frankie Estrada was about to turn state's witness as well. He wasn't your average drug dealer. He was ruthless, but also intelligent. He knew what was up. It was a domino effect. J.J. invited me over to hear what he had to say. J said Estrada was in the room talking about politics in Bridgeport, and I listened in briefly. "Who do you think is gettin high off my shit in City Hall?" Oh my God! "J, is he talking about the Mayor?" J.J. nodded yes. "Yo, I'm out of here. I don't need to be involved in that." J started laughing as I made a quick exit, stage right. Was Estrada supplying drugs to Mayor Ganim, or someone high up he thought was the Mayor? Could it have been the Common Council president? I wasn't about to go down that path. J.J. kept laughing. "Hey, I can deal with drug dealers and murderers all day, but politicians? I'm out!" J.J. was cracking up as I abruptly made my way out of there.

When all was said and done, I had testified for about two years on all of the drug cases. It started with the Jones family and eventually progressed to other cases. But the theme from the beginning was the cooperation of Eugene Rhodes, and Glenda Jimenez in making the state's case. They both testified it was my asking them to "do the right thing" that started the ball rolling. The news printed it the next day. One of the family members in court was standing in the hallway, "So you're the one responsible for all this. We should've known." He actually had a smile when he said it. No hard feelings, I guess.

Back in court the questioning was ruthless by a half dozen attorneys, "Officer Bailey, where did you watch my client from?" "Sir, I have done so many cases. I need the reports to refresh my memory. We're talking about hundreds of cases." They all wanted details. So I cut to the chase. "Counselor, I was in abandoned apartments, in the boatyard at Captain's Cove, Twin Towers in the hallways, apartments, roofs, in cars, taxis, a mental health bus, in the projects walking, picking up cans, Longfellow School, a nun's home, a dumpster, and a tree." The attorneys looked at me astonished. "Officer Bailey, how did you walk around the project unnoticed?" "I had disguises, so they never knew." "Did you say you were at a convent? We're talking about P.T., officer, and you are under oath." "Sir, there is a school on Bird Street that's also home to the nuns of a church." "And did you have the right to be there?" "If I was inside they gave me permission. In the parking lot I was on my own." "Did you use information supplied by informants?" "Yes, but due to safety concerns, I cannot reveal my sources." The jury was asked to leave while there was a huge argument. It was determined there was no need to expose the informants I was using. I didn't sign M&M and Casanova up anyway. So no matter what, they were not going to hear about them. After the Peeler murder of a child witness, there was no way I was gonna say their names.

## Major Drug Gangs

By the end of the trials, every single person indicted for drug trafficking was sent away. Eugene Rhodes and Eddie Lawhorn got nine years. That was better than life. For the risks they took coming forward, they deserved time off. All the others who cooperate got about the same or less. What had me shaking my head was what Cass told me about Luke Jones. He was the last of the brothers to get life in prison. He asked Judge Alan Nevas if he could be put to death. He felt death would be better than life in prison. Judge Nevas said it was too late because the sentence had already been given. Could you imagine asking to be killed?

With no shame, Frankie Estrada testified against everyone he knew, including his sister and brother. French Fry was furious at the trial. It was the ultimate slap in the face. His brother turned state's evidence on him. Estrada had been referred to as the Big Dog and Million Dollar Kid. The man who paid $100,000 cash for a Mercedes, $70,000 for a Rolex, bought a nightclub for $1.6 million, and stashed millions away had lost it all. Estrada's Terminators also went down hard. It was their violent history that put them away for life. Estrada had hired the likes of Eddie Mercado and William 'Billy the Kid' Gomez to protect his kingdom. At trial he told the jury it was good business, "Nobody would mess around with you, rob your workers. They're killers."

Estrada elaborated on how the drug trade was a complex violent business that sometimes linked rival drug gangs together in order to be profitable. He then told the jury how Gomez and Mercado killed for him, including a state's witness. He had ordered Sam Colon to be killed for robbing the stash house that his sister was in control of. He admitted Colon was killed by a gun he provided. Testimony revealed he tried to kill a rival drug dealer in P.T., Tyrone 'Ty' Holman, my cousin. I was told Estrada had no idea Ty was family. Not that it would have made any difference to him.

The total shock was to hear him give testimony about his longtime friend Attorney James Ruane. According to Estrada, Attorney Ruane hinted it wouldn't be a bad thing if one of the witnesses disappeared in a case he was defending. According to testimony Estrada then ordered the witness killed. More damaging testimony came from Estrada that Ruane wanted to protect him by having a witness change his story on the murder of Jeremy Jacobs, too. He testified that Attorney Ruane told him it would be better if Charles 'Glass Top' Morey were to change his statement. Estrada told the jury he had Morey do just that. If anyone challenged Morey's change of story he was to blame it on the Bridgeport Police.

Prosecutors chimed in and said with the assistance of Attorney Ruane, Estrada was able to take steps to avoid prosecution, pour drug proceeds into various businesses and other assets, and remain at liberty for more than five years, despite being one of the most prolific drug dealers in Bridgeport. Prosecutors said they sought Ruane's removal from another case after police discovered government documents provided to him in Estrada's apartment. He was accused of being an integral part of Estrada's criminal enterprise that ended with Estrada's conviction.

In the end, Frankie Estrada got 29 years. His cooperation kept him from a life sentence. Not bad, considering all he had been responsible for. Estrada's right-hand man Hector "Junebug" Gonzalez got 27 years. What amazed the jury was Gonzalez had been running the business even though he had a radio transmitting device on him as part of his parole from a previous drug case. Estrada and Gonzalez were responsible for bringing over 66 pounds of heroin and three pounds of cocaine into Bridgeport during their few years together. Missing from Estrada's testimony was what he had said to us about the Mayor getting high off his stuff. I wondered why, but it was time to move on.

I had finished testimony on all the drug cases, but there was now an urgency to refocus on Guardians being challenged. The Guardians were up in arms over union interference. We were concerned about the lack of minorities being hired, especially black officers. After all those years in court battling the city over blatant racism, we missed the obvi-

## Major Drug Gangs

ous. Our numbers were dwindling. The paramount question we were asking was how can you hire a class of 30 recruits with only two African American officers? I reflected on how just after I came on the job we had about 90 black officers. But over the years we were down to about 50. With over 400 cops at the BPD, our numbers begged the question about how we could find a way to get more of us on the job. We were becoming extinct!

Another problem still nagging Guardians was the city's number one objective had not changed in years, to get rid of the court oversight. The mayor, chief, Board of Police Commissioners, and God only knew who else, were all in favor of removing Judge Clendenen. The court was bombarded with appeals and motions. The city, union, and several concerned officers were attacking it at every juncture. The city's new angle was that they had an African American chief of police. The Chief Irving era was over and the city was supposedly heading in a new direction.

We took a more factual approach in court. The department never placed African American officers on special assignment other than one, Chase. The top ranks were severely lacking in black leadership. We challenged the city to acknowledge there were still shortcomings when it came to black officers. The union filed papers opposing our motions. Always the same, it was about their union contract. We asked the union about blacks not being represented fairly across the board at the BPD. As usual, we were met with chirping crickets. I asked the union president, "Does the union contract you keep pushing address black assignments and leadership positions? Don't you have an obligation to represent all officers?" His response should have been recorded and replayed time and time again, the contract, the contract, the contract!

What did I just read? "Mayor Joseph Ganim indicted on corruption charges." Are you serious? Governor John Rowland was urging Ganim to resign. Mayor Ganim was accused of seeking more than $425,000 in bribes, cash, merchandise, services and meals, in return for steering city business to friends and associates. An hour after the indictment was announced, Ganim held a news conference: "I'm being falsely accused. I've done nothing wrong. I've never taken one dime as a part of a conspiracy. Nor have I ever authorized anyone to take money on my behalf."

Eventually, Ganim took his case to trial but lost. He was sentenced to nine years by Judge Janet Bond Arterton. Ironically, others in Connecticut government were also going to jail. Mayor Philip Giordano of Waterbury was arrested and sentenced to 37 years for forcing an eight-year-old and 10-year-old to perform oral sex on him in various places, including a police car, his law office and City Hall! The cherry on top of the insanity was Governor John Rowland. He was charged in a corruption scandal of his own. To avoid trial, he took a deal that got him a one-year jail sentence. It was a sad time in Connecticut. We were the hub of political corruption in America, for a time.

Now it all made sense. The FBI didn't allow Estrada to bring up his assertions about the mayor getting high off of his "shit" for a reason. They were working behind the scenes on Ganim's corruption case. The only bright light to the sad tale was for my friend Lennie Grimaldi, who was Ganim's campaign manager and advisor at the time. He had warned Ganim about the corruption, to no avail. It seemed that Lennie's mistake came by way of association with Ganim. Judge Arterton said Lennie was the only one who seemed to have a conscience and cooperated. He did less than a year, thankfully. There was so much corruption; crooked cops, and crime, a person's head could spin.

I had kept myself grounded during my ordeals, and for the many things to come. One of my pleasures was being on the Connecticut Tae Kwon Do team. My sparring partner and student, Billy Patron was still the middleweight champion of the United States. We were training at the Colorado Springs Olympic Training Camp and preparing for the national tournament in Portland, Oregon. I was far away from the madness and enjoyed the competition. For three years running I had won national titles. The gold medal was on my list of things to do. After our training, we headed to Portland. It was the Nationals and I went prepared. I fought six opponents, making it to the finals. In the end, the winner was the Oregon state champion. My opponent smiled at the end of the last round and said, "Sorry my brother, home turf rules." "Politics here too?" I smiled knowing he got the decision, but the tapes don't lie.

When we arrived back in Connecticut, I hadn't even unpacked, when the call came in, it was Dave. John Fabrizi, who was the interim mayor, and Chief Chapman were clashing. Chapman made it clear he ran the police department, and everyone else had better stand down. How the in-house fighting was going to affect the city's chances at removing the federal oversight was anyone's guess.

The good news was the police department was having an awards night to honor officers for their work in the city. By night's end I had a Tactical Unit citation and three special awards for my work on the Joneses, Estrada, and their affiliates. The one award that was bittersweet was for saving Pearl Sharp's life. She recovered from the stabbing to her neck only to die of cancer a short time later. I had saved this woman's life so she could suffer so much more? I couldn't make sense of it, but God knows. Compounding my feelings was accepting awards from a place that had shunned my achievements before. I guess some things had changed.

As the years rolled on, Dave climbed to the rank of lieutenant. As our Guardians President, he wanted everyone to study for the sergeant's exam. I didn't want to take the test, because I loved working in narcotics. Dave gave me that look, "Bailey, no one can deny you're the best this city has seen in narcotics. But it's time for some of you guys to make rank. You can't change this place unless you're in a command position." I couldn't argue with him, he was right. Dave scheduled several study sessions. We were tutored by him and a few retired captains and lieutenants.

## No Black Heroes

The day of the test came, and we were all prepared. When the test results came out, it was the first time African American police officers in Bridgeport were on the top of the list. Then it came. A large group of disgruntle white officers accused us of cheating. They complained that we had been tutored by the firm that conducted the test. They were making accusations, because the test was administered by a black-owned testing company. Officers circulated a petition accusing Dave of orchestrating and fixing the test so blacks would score higher. More specifically, it was said Dave used his position as the Guardians president to rig the test.

Officer Adolf Hunt, the main person responsible for the accusations and petition, was hauled into federal court. It was determined there was no basis for his allegations that we cheated, or that Dave had done anything wrong. In the end, he quietly resigned. Ultimately, the sergeants test results stood, and we were to be promoted, in spite of the hate we were experiencing. I was high on the list for promotion but still unconvinced about taking the position.

## *TNT Final Raids; Court; Promotion*

After thinking about it, I decided to take the promotion. Then it suddenly hit me; there were several pending cases I needed to close out in TNT. Leaving a unit that had been a part of my life for 18 years was a sad time for me. Where had the time gone? I had some work left to do and called the FBI. I needed their SWAT team for the raid. "Guys, today we're gonna hit 1246 Noble Avenue. My source just bought drugs out the house. He saw five guys in there, handguns, shotguns and rifles. The designated gun person today is Mike Syrax of the FBI's SWAT. Let's do this."

We had 15 TNT members, in addition to the other law agencies. "Hey guys, no marked police cars. We have a no knock and announce warrant. We go stealth to contact." Some of the team wasn't sure what the heck I was talking about. "Bailey, you and your SWAT crap, speak English." "We go quiet until first contact. Jesus, guys." With so much firepower in the house, it would be an advantage to sneak in, if at all possible.

We caught a break. When we got there you could see the door open to the second floor. The owners of the house just happened to be looking at the hallway for repairs. We got out of the cars and moved quickly, single file. At the porch we pulled the landlord and her husband to the side. The second floor targets saw us and started running. We caught everyone inside and put them down without firing a shot. It was a textbook takedown. Agent Syrax was impressed. He wanted to know if our team had SWAT training. "Yeah, some of us trained with the Broward County Sheriff's Department. But only two of us took it, and the other officer who did, he retired." Mike said that my training showed through the teams takedown efforts. "We work hard on our take downs so no one gets hurt."

We finished a sweep of the house, taking in a shotgun and four rifles. My informant called and said the guy with the handgun left just before we got there. The haul was still a good one, $3,000 in cash, a huge stash of drugs, and six drug dealers. On the way out, one of them looked over to the landlord, "Sorry, Ma, I didn't mean for this to happen." There was no doubt, the mother didn't know what was going on, and so we let her go.

My next hit was Whittier Street, Aunt Queenie's house. We got there at 5 in the morning and Sergeant Villegas asked, "Bailey, you sure bout this?" "Let's do it." We knocked on the door. Aunt Queenie opened up. It looked like a furniture store in there. Everything was brand new. I knew Aunt Queenie wasn't into drugs, but my cousins were. They were using her house as a stash location, according to the warrant.

Aunt Queenie looked at me but remained silent. I had to ask, "What's wrong with you?" She just looked on. We finished searching the house, taking money and some contraband. Ono and Tyke weren't there. Sergeant Villegas asked me what I wanted to do on this one. "Auntie, I know who's selling here, and it ain't you. If I come back you'll have to go. Please tell the family, 'enough.'" She looked at me and responded, "Alright, Ronnie, I hear you." I glanced back at her, a little embarrassed about having to speak to my aunt that way. "Auntie, please tell them kids of yours to knock it off. The last thing I need is this."

We got in the van and drove back to base. "Tag the stuff and seize the money. You guys will need new equipment and buy money for your informants when I'm gone." Tyke called the office. "Hey Cuz, don't worry. We ain't never gonna use Mom's place again." I left it at that. "Good enough, Cuz."

I sat down looking for a moment's peace. There on my desk was a court order to report to federal court. Now what? I opened the summons. It was for the Bell Street shooting. I was being sued and had to report for trial. The other officers involved were upset. I took it for what it really was, someone trying to make money off the city, at our expense. We hadn't done anything wrong, but that's how the game was played. It didn't matter if you were right or wrong; someone was always looking to get paid. The city had deep pockets, and it was the American way.

I prepared for trial with Attorney Barbara Massaro defending us. If anyone was good and knew her stuff, she was the one. The first day of the trial started with Attorney Phil Martin from New Haven who represented Trevor Thomas. He didn't waste any time and accused Officers Santi Llanos, Gerry Bonaventura, John Roach and me of violating his client's civil rights. Say what you will, but it was no coincidence that an African American attorney was representing an African American victim. The color theme was still alive on both ends of the spectrum.

The city brought in an expert witness to testify on our behalf. He was very knowledgeable in the use of knives and what could happen to an officer. Even with a gun, it was impressive how he showed a man 25 feet away could kill an officer before he could get his gun out. If it weren't for

## Major Drug Gangs

John's bulletproof vest that night, he could have possibly been stabbed to death! After the expert witness made his point, I was called to the stand.

Attorney Martin began with the basic questions, how long was I on the job, my age, training, and so on. He then went right for the jugular. He asked about my martial arts training. I knew where he was going, having been down that road before. He wanted the jury to think being a black belt in martial arts would have made it easy to disarm his client. I answered his question, "Counselor, if I may? I'm a national champion in Tae Kwon Do. I didn't try to disarm your client in a dark hallway with my bare hands. That's the kind of stuff you see on TV that can get you killed." The jury continued to listen. "In a ring when I fight, there are four corner judges and a referee. When they say stop, you stop. When you're on the streets fighting for your life, people don't always stop on command." He continued, "Officer Bailey, when you shot my client, what did you do?" "I called for backup, an ambulance, told the officers to remain where they were. I then went downstairs to take care of Mr. Thomas." "What else did you do?" "I called the hospital later to see how Mr. Thomas was doing. I didn't want him to die. So I prayed for him."

Attorney Martin dropped the bombshell I expected. "Officer Bailey, didn't you shoot my client because he's black?" I looked at Attorney Martin realizing he had not done his homework. John and Jerry were white, and Santi Hispanic. It was a huge error. "Attorney Martin, if I may state for the record, no one shot your client because he's black. With all due respect, I am an African American, I'm black." Right then and there several jurors gasped, including one woman who had a short outburst, "Ohh!" It was like a bomb had been dropped. They thought I was Hispanic, too! I explained how my folks were from South Carolina, and that some in my family were fairskinned.

Embarrassingly, Attorney Martin had no response to my answer and tried to move on. "Attorney Martin, not one of the officers shot Mr. Thomas because he's black. I would

343

tell you if they had, trust me." He did his best to make a case, staying away from the color angle. But the damage had been done. There was no doubt; I had shut that avenue down.

Attorney Martin's only option was to look for flaws in how we handled the shooting. My only concern was John. He had a habit of making jokes about the shooting. We all knew it was a survival thing. But, Lord, please no jokes today. Luckily, he kept it professional. At the end of our testimony, the jury was out about two hours. They returned with a verdict, not guilty. The case was dismissed. With the Thomas shooting behind me I spent the next few months concentrating on my remaining cases in TNT.

A local drug dealer who called himself "Sir Al" was in my sights. I happened to see him driving a stolen car while I was checking out my last few targets. I was sure drugs would be in the car, so I went after him. I figured he would try to ditch it and run.

Sir Al took off but lost control, ramming into the front porch of a house on Linen Street. Just as I pulled up to get out, I had to duck. All I could see amid the night's darkness were the shots and muzzle flashes. By the time I recovered and made it to the car, he was gone. With nothing to lose, I made a little visit to his home on Central Ave. Of course, I called TNT to back me up. We arrived and knocked on the door. His girlfriend opened the door with Sir Al standing close by in pajamas. Pajamas, on a Saturday night? I explained why I was there, and he of course said he was home and had nothing to do with any shooting. With no proof it was him, I had to let it go. There would be another time. There always is when you're doing wrong.

Not long after, the FBI came to TNT on a mission. Anyone shooting at cops was public enemy number one. Sir Al was no exception. The FBI raided Sir Al's house, with me tagging along. The message was clear; Shoot at a cop or his family and you paid the price. They didn't get him on the

# Major Drug Gangs

gun charge, but he went down for his involvement with drugs. It was payback for what he had done.

I was making my rounds, ready to close down the remainder of the Stack Boys gang in Marina Village, when I was caught off guard. James Pitt was a small-time drug dealer. He was walking across the street, high as a kite! He stopped right in front of my car, forcing me to stop, and daring me to continue. I got out of the car, and Pitt fired six shots at me while running from the crosswalk of Columbia and Ridge Avenue. He dashed into the projects. As I stood in the opening of the car door, I pulled my gun. Kids were ducking, so I couldn't shoot back. A few of the boyz in the 'hood just shook their heads. "He's fucked now!" someone yelled out.

With so many kids out there, Pitt high, running who knows where, and me in my personal car, I decided to take him out another way. I returned to the office where a warrant was typed for his arrest. My guess, he was so high, he couldn't have known it was me. Pitt was always low-keyed and a small-timer. A few days later, after the warrant was signed, word in the project was out that I had been looking for him. Someone told him he had shot at me, so he was hiding. "Hey, tell him to come in, or I'll find him." That night, Pitt turned himself in.

My cousin Billy called, "Hey, Cuz, Pitt turned himself in because he didn't want to end up like that snitch Cruz." "You guys still talking about that? Hey man, I had nothing to do with it." "That's not what I heard." Billy was one of my favorite cousins. He had such a sense of humor and always had a story to tell. The way he was talking gave me the impression people considered me dangerous. I guess a part of me was. "Cuz, whatcha tryin' to tell me?" "Hey, the streets know you're good for shooting at folks coming your way. And everyone's talking bout that snitch you smoked." I laughed my butt off, while he continued. "Cuz, people can read the papers. And the street knows things. That's how it is, you came from this. Everyone knows who took out the Joneses, and Estrada, that's real!" "Bill, it sounds good the

## No Black Heroes

way you tell it. You make it sound like I'm da man." I was kidding. "Truth is Cuz, everybody knows you are."

I hung up and though for a moment on my years as a cop. Bill had me thinking, no lie. I couldn't help but wonder. Had I really been defined by shootings and moments of hell on the streets? The way he said it, the streets pictured me as some kind of legend or story to tell. It felt uncomfortable. How do you live up to that? I'd hoped people would remember the kid from the 'hood who tried to make a difference.

My thoughts drifted back to Mary Morales, the woman was so scared her boyfriend would come back and beat her up. So I hid my police car and stayed a few hours a night with her just so she'd feel safe. I thought about Keith Pierce who put his hand on my gun during a crowd fight. One of the kids was trying to pull it out the holster and Keith stopped him. Yes, Keith! This was the same man I had arrested years earlier, and the same man who may have saved my life that night. So many memories came to mind; the times I gave food to folks on the streets asking for help, rides for people stranded, drug addicts who needed a kind word, and the ones I took to detox so they could get cleaned up. And how could I forget about Felicita who needed a friend to visit her in jail and the halfway house, so she knew someone cared.

There was so much I had done, not because I had to, but because I wanted to. It was unsettling to be considered someone of importance because of a few fights on the streets. It was disturbing if people missed the little things that really defined me; a smile, handshake, or a hug someone needed. I guess action is what people remember, the stuff movies are made of. I could only hope that someday people would realize there's more to me than that.

The unofficial announcement came from the Chief's office, I was to be promoted. Still knee deep in search warrants that Judge Sullivan signed, I got busy. The target was the Bush Mob. I walked in disguise to 644 Pembroke Street

## Major Drug Gangs

and called out a few buyers. With sales in hand, I called the team in. It was a complete surprise to see the Bush Mob working with the Brotherhood. No matter, we took in 100 grams of uncut cocaine, crack, and four guns.

Shakeen Anderson, Marc Smith, Alton Bedford, and Keith Teasley were arrested for operating a drug factory within school limits. The lookout, Samuel Smalls, was getting in a car when the team hit the house. He tried to play it off, covering a gun he had on him. Before he could start the car, I walked up and pointed my gun at his head. I'm sure he thought it was a hit by some crazy old man with a beard. He handed me his gun and sat waiting for my next move. I pulled my badge out and hung it around my neck so the team could see it was me. I also removed my beard. I wasn't about to get shot during my last few weeks in the unit, especially over my own disguise. TNT came down and saw me grabbing Smalls from behind the steering wheel. With his arrest, we called it a day.

Just for the fun of it, I took out the marked car the next day. I wanted to feel a police car in my hands, one more time. Bad move, I guess. That's when I saw him, Martin Moore. Moore was wanted for the attempted murder of a 14-year-old. No sooner had he looked my way when he took off. He drove through Bridgeport like it was his own personal racetrack. I was right behind him. We hit I-95 doing 125 miles an hour. If he hit a car on the pike at that speed, anyone, including him, would have been dead.

We got off exit 32 in Stratford doing about 90. I knew just what was going to happen and hit my brakes. I had no idea a car could slide so far. Moore's car slid the entire length of the exit and crashed at the bottom of the ramp, into the elevated edge of the sidewalk. He jumped out and ran toward a chain link fence to try to escape. He climbed the fence but slipped back down. I had no time to waste, so I drove the car right up to the fence, pinning him against it. It was a risky maneuver but it worked. I got out of the car, handcuffed him, and got back in the car to let radio know where I was. Moore was yelling that I hit him with the car.

## No Black Heroes

There wasn't a scratch on him, he was just pinned down. He wanted me to back up so he could run. I got back out and handcuffed him to the push bar of the car. I pulled the car back along with him. "Tell it to the judge, Moore." I got him in the car and headed to booking, while he continued to complain that I tried to kill him. Of course, the papers made a story out of it.

Looking forward to the next phase in my career, I decided to take the day off to get my new uniforms. Boy, did I choose the right day to take off, perfect timing! A search warrant for Beach Street had to be served, with only one day left before it expired. It was a pretty routine warrant on a low-priority spot. What a shocker when I got the call. The team had just raided and busted a public defender from Bridgeport. Attorney Carol Martin was taken in for possession of narcotics, and immediately started rattling off names of court personnel, even judges. She demanded to speak with me about her arrest. I had no intention of getting into that, so I never called. In the end, the system took care of her anyway. She got into a program, and her case was eventually closed out. I guess the system does work for some. It got back to me that she said I'd be toast for not helping her out. I'd keep an eye out for her in case she ever did try to get at me in some way.

The team wondered why I decided to work one of my last cases alone. My target was Little Man, the shortest person I had ever seen. I swear he was two feet high, if that. Little Man had been selling drugs on East Main near Pulaski for as long as I cared to remember. He was kind of cute, selling from his mini scooter. And he had a habit of taking off on it after each sale.

I parked the unmarked car close, got out, and arrived just in time to see him sell. I ran up on him but he took off, ziiiiiip, ziiiip, zip zip. I caught up to him and snatched him off his scooter before he could get away. "Too late, gotcha." The scooter engine revved down and eventually rolled to a stop before it tilted to the side. I wanted to laugh; it looked like a kid's trike falling over. He even had multicolored flyers coming out of the handle bar ends. "Wow!" Little Man had the nerve to try and fight with me. His arms were too short to connect. "Man, what are you doing? Stop it. Stay still!" In his squeaky voice he responded, "Fuck you, Bailey, fuck you!" I smiled, took his bag of dope and pocketed it. I couldn't handcuff him because his wrists were too doggone small. With no other choice, and him flailing about, I picked up the scooter under one arm, and Little Man under the other.

It must have been a sight. All you could see was Little Man's legs kicking from under my arm and spinning tires under the other. I dropped the scooter in the trunk and placed Little Man in the front seat of my car. I figured he would need a boost, so I brought a baby booster seat we kept at lockup for transporting kids from raids. Back at base, they were all surprised when I walked in. They tried to hold their laughter, as I shook my head at them as discreetly as possible. Please don't! The TNT guys must have thought it was the funniest thing ever, but I didn't want to make a joke out of Little Man. Adding insult to injury, he gave me the middle finger when I placed him in lockup. I guess he didn't appreciate the kiddie stool I gave him. I wasn't being funny; we had small stools for children. Barely audible, he just kept repeating, "Fuck you, Bailey, Motherfucker!"

With my TNT time running out I took a ride in an undercover to take one last look before our last raid. The streets looked sparse with drug activity, but it was still going on. At least we brought it down to a point where there was some peace in communities that had not had any for way too long. I parked a few blocks away from Hallett and Ogden Street and looked through my scope. What the hell is this? Someone's gonna get killed! I had to make sure I wasn't just seeing things. A large young man was standing on the corner trying to flag cars down. I had no time to waste; I drove closer, parked, and walked to the corner with my badge hanging from around my neck.

**No Black Heroes**

I walked up to the kid and tried to reason with him. "Young man, I don't know if you're aware, but this is the Green Top Posse's spot." "Officer, I'm not doing anything, I'm just hanging out." I decided to be blunt, "Look kid, no offense, but you stick out. In all my years in narcotics I ain't ever seen anyone white selling on a corner in Bridgeport. I've arrested plenty of buyers from the suburbs, but not one white person trying to sell in the 'hood." He looked at me not knowing what to say. "Son, do me a favor and leave before you get hurt, or maybe killed. These boyz here don't play when it comes to their turf." He thanked me, got into his car and drove away. Man, was he out of place.

With one week left, I combined my last three pending cases. For months, I had been sending my informants and undercover cops to buy drugs from Bishop Corner, R-Place, and Something Different Café. All three strip joints were the hub of corruption in the Bridgeport sex trade. It was going to be a major hit if I could pull it off. The case was about finished when I sent Officer Nick Malone in to do one last undercover buy. He was supposed to get the girls to make offers while he wore a wire, so we could wrap things up. For some reason, he was in the place a lot longer than usual. I got worried. Suddenly, Nicky's wire stopped working. We held off on running in, hoping for the best. It was taking too long, and we were saddling up. "Nick must be in trouble."

We were getting out of the cars when he came out, walked over to us casually, and asked for a cigarette. "Hey, Nick, what the hell? What happened in there? And what's with the cigarette? You don't smoke." He just smiled. I didn't ask, I did not ask. I walked away. He was supposed to get the deal on tape, nothing else. All he could say was the girls in R-Place are gorgeous. "Nick, why are you out of breath?"

Detective John Andrews was called in to give me a hand with my last major case in TNT. We had worked together on the raids at Twin Towers. It was a major undertaking, and he clearly knew his stuff. It was time. I called lineup. "Okay guys, we're taking out three strip joints simultaneously. It's

# Major Drug Gangs

never been done before, so let's do this by the numbers. John has control of Something Different Café, I got R-Place. Bishop Corner is small, so we can hit them after. Undercover guys go in masked up when we hit. Any questions?"

We had two dozen cops from patrol and the TNT team. I had to enter R-Place first, before we could begin. No need for a disguise, I was leaving, and it was my last hurrah. The bouncer at the door flashed me with his wand to check for a gun. I didn't need to carry with a whole contingent of cops about to come in. This was a soft target, and I knew how to duck if I had to. I got in just in time to see a few sales, a few getting high, but I was looking for a gun. Someone is always carrying. If Sergeant Villegas knew I was in there without my gun, he would have had my head on a platter.

I sat at the bar and couldn't believe what I was seeing. Something had to be wrong with me. The guy next to me was smoking a joint. It had to be laced with PCP or something, because I thought the smoke had me hallucinating. There was no other explanation for what I saw. The team called me on the cell to see if I was ready. I held the phone in my hand barely able to speak. I had never seen anything like that before. "Guys, I'll call you back. Hold on."

On the bar, right in front of me, was a woman. She was smoking a cigarette, and blowing perfect rings of smoke. How in hell was she doing that? I couldn't call the team in yet. I was too amazed. The woman kept blowing perfect smoke rings. Unbelievable, I never imagined a woman could smoke from, her vagina! I was muttering to myself in disbelief. "No way. That's impossible." I didn't know there was air down there." The guy next to me just started laughing. I got up and walked to the door. My mouth was wide open. I'd seen it all. I called the team and told them the door would be open and to start a count of ten, and run in. More drug deals were going down, but I was still looking at those perfect rings of smoke. It was incredible!

I opened the door and told the bouncer I was looking for a friend to come and peered out the door. I casually said

351

## No Black Heroes

"Hi" as the team approached. They entered swiftly, and with guns drawn, "Police with a warrant, no one move! Police with a warrant, everyone stay where you are!" Only a few had time to drop their stuff on the floor. Anyone who tried to move was pulled back to where they had been standing. "If it's on the floor next to you, it belongs to you." I pointed out six people who made sales while I was at the bar. I could only hope if it went to court, the defense attorney wouldn't ask if I had been distracted. That could prove embarrassing.

Anything on the floor was put on the counters in front of the person nearest to it. The girls were everywhere. The woman with the cigarette in her kitty still had my attention. "If you can do that again, I'll let you go." She pulled out a pack of cigarettes. I raised my hand and stopped her. "I was just kidding Lady, Jesus." "That's fucked up, Bailey. I would have given you a private show." I looked at her and asked, "How do you know me?" "I don't, but we all heard about you. We figured it was just a matter of time before you came here." The teams finished raiding the three clubs and brought all the arrests back to base. By night's end we had 34 arrests. It was yet another department record and more front-page news.

I remained to see if we had missed anything. Surprisingly, no one in the club had a gun. While looking through R-Place, we found a hidden compartment that looked like a closet. It led to another room, where we found video equipment and dozens of tapes. Behind another hidden wall was a hallway that led to the rooms in the back. They were set up for sex; there were oils, towels, lotions and condoms.

I called Nick over and showed him the video collections. He stood there motionless, turning pale. "Hey Nicky, looks like someone was filming the sex acts here. I'll bet you anything these tapes were to be sent overseas to make money." Nick began pulling all the tapes out, looking through them. He was a man on a mission. "Nick, tell me you didn't do what I think you did when your wire failed a week ago." Nick looked at me with half a smile in panic, "Come on Bailey, you know me better than that." "Well not for nothing, but if you did sleep with one of these girls, you're going to be a porn star in Asia. Let's hope you don't get resold back to the states."

Nick wasn't smiling anymore. I was just kidding, but Nick was then frantically looking through all the tapes on the counter. "Nick, you can't see what's on the tapes unless you play them all. And don't throw them away, they're not ours. If it's any consolation, we're not taking them. I'm not about to look at hundreds of hours of porn." He seemed to relax a little. The remaining team members were all looking at Nick and chuckled as we walked out.

It was going to be a long night. We had 34 arrests, drugs, money, the three warrant returns to be processed, and all kinds of sex toys taken in as evidence. Earnie looked at me while I listed the charges on the board, "Bae Bae Bailey, the team is gonna to miss you, brother." Everyone in lockup looked over in disbelief. The club owners looked my way, "Bailey, you leaving?" "Yeah, I'm gonna be a Sergeant soon." The prisoners all stood up and gave me a round of applause. I looked over at all those half-naked girls, drug dealers and the club owners and smiled, "Very funny."

The girl with a talent for cigarette smoke rings asked to speak with me. I thought she was going to give me something I could pass on to the team. She wanted to give me a going-away present. I politely thanked and kissed her on the cheek. "That's so nice of you. Thank you for that offer, but I can't." She looked at me, "You know, you're a cop that knows how to treat people. I think ya will be missed." It had been a whirlwind, 18-year ride. After hundreds of raids, thousands of arrests, five shootings, and three TNT teams, I was leaving. I had a feeling I wasn't done completely with TNT, but it was time to move on. And just like that, it was over.

Chapter 24

*Injustice anywhere is a threat to justice everywhere.*
—Martin Luther King, Jr.

## COMMUNITY DISTRUST/INSTITUTIONALIZED HATE

Chief Chapman called me into his office Monday morning. He looked me up and down, and spoke while gazing up at the ceiling. "You're going to start the first community policing effort in the housing projects of Bridgeport. Do whatever it takes to make us look good. You will have 20 officers under your command. Captain William Chapman will be your only supervisor. Don't let me down. You can leave now." Wow, two Chapmans to answer to. I'm glad Captain Chapman is my supervisor, and friend. I walked out of Chief Chapman's office stunned. I just spent 18 years buying, selling and raiding the projects. Now you want me to make friends there?

That night I conducted lineup. I couldn't help but notice I had all minority officers in our community policing unit. Captain Chapman chose officers from the last few classes and the newest ones fresh out of the academy. We had just a few veteran officers on board. The newest group of officers hadn't done a great deal of policing. They were about to go into the 'hood, and they needed me to lead them. "Listen up people; you're going into the projects of Bridgeport. Every-

## No Black Heroes

one will be in a two-man car. Do not leave the project unless you clear it over the radio." The new guys looked a bit confused but ready to get out there. I finished with a statement I'd used at every line up. "Treat everyone out there like you would want someone to treat your family."

The first week was rough. People in the projects didn't want us out there. Officers before us had treated people in the community badly. And it was no secret that many officers had called women bitches or whores. Other cops had used the words spicks or niggers, too. Why would they want us there after officers had acted like that? It was not going to be an easy assignment.

The one thing I had on my side was where I came from, the projects. I knew how things worked in the projects and had gone through what many were experiencing. I knew only too well how it felt to be poor and dependant on welfare. I never forgot the first of the month when Mom got her state check. We were living in Greens Homes, and she told me to go get it out of the box before someone could take it. I got there just in time to hear the postman, "I need to be like these good-for-nothings. Stay at home and collect." He had no idea about us, to say something like that. My father worked all his life. My mother was disabled, so how in hell were we going to get by without assistance?

I remembered how some officers back then felt about us. Their ideas weren't all that different from that postman's. Some thought of us as lazy good-for-nothings, while others enjoyed talking down to us. They looked like they didn't want to be there, as if we were a burden to them. "Why are you people always fighting and carrying on?" There were always stupid comments. "What do you people expect us to do? We can't tell you how to live. Maybe you should move or something." Not my officers. This was a community policing unit, and we were going to do it right.

The communities of Bridgeport didn't want us, and we knew that. But the housing projects were even worse. They hated us. It was a time when the communities were boldly

## Community Distrust/Institutionalized Hate

saying over and over again that the police were stopping only African Americans. Racial profiling and mass incarcerations of minorities was the lay of the land. I was tasked with trying to change that thought process.

I knew a community policing program called for trust. In order to gain that trust we had to get out there and let people know we were the good guys, no matter how long it took. My reputation as a narc that took out drug dealers wasn't the best image for a community policing effort. On the plus side, many knew me to be pleasant with folks, and respectful. The reputation that stood out was the drug raids, and chasing down the bad guys. So how was I going to bridge the gap with a community that had no use for law enforcement?

I knew that having mostly all new police officers could work to our advantage. Those new officers had no reputation or history that could follow them. The community had no reason to dislike them one way or the other. It was perhaps a plus to start with an all-minority crew. Captain Chapman was careful in choosing officers who had work records free of any signs of abuse in the community. All in all, it was a good start.

"Lineup. Today we are going to try something not usually done in the projects. You are to park your cars, get out and walk." I got long stares from a few of them, especially the few senior officers we did have. "Look people, this is what you do. Get out the car, walk around and say hello. Speak to anyone who will talk to you. It will not be your best experience today, I'm sure. At some point, I'm hoping it will turn things around. I'll be out there walking with you." I had walked the projects years ago on my own. It was the best way for a community to get to know you, up close and personal.

Officer Lou Gutierrez had a good question. "Sergeant Bailey, we're going to start walking in P.T. They all know you worked on Estrada and the Jones families. Aren't the families of those guys living out there? I would think they won't be happy to see you, or us." "Understood, but we got to try. I'll see you out there." I walked alone so the officers could see me. If they saw I was out there alone, they could surely walk in pairs. Set the example.

It had been several weeks and things were not going well. I was walking close to building 18 when an older woman standing by had something to say. "Bailey, why are you out here? You're like them white cops arresting our kids. No one's gonna sell drugs while you're here." I smiled politely. "Can you just give us a chance? I'm sure you'll see this is a new day. I'm here to help." I decided to challenge her. "By the way; find one person who'll say I beat up someone, or spoke disrespectful to anyone. I'm assuming your saying I'm like the 'white cops' is what you meant. Find one person that will say I did any of those things and I'll give you $100." She looked at me in disbelief. "You have my word on that." "Bailey, you got yourself a deal, but if I lose?" "You owe me a cup of tea." "Tea, what are you some kind of mama's boy? Tough cop." I smiled and joked back with her, "Shut up." She laughed at me.

On my way to the car, a little girl about 10 years old walked up to me. She wanted to know why we were out there. "We're here to keep you safe and have some fun." She asked me how the police had fun. "Do you know Eenie Meenie?" She looked confused. "It's a hand game like Pitty Pat." I showed her how it was done, but slowly at first. "Eenie Meenie dis-a-leenee ooo-cha cha ma neenee, I owe you two two shampoo. I saw you with your boyfriend last night, how do you know?" She was so excited to play the game with me and laughed hysterically every time she messed up. I had this hand game down to a science. My daughter Ashley and I played it all the time when she was little. Residents looked at me like I was an alien or something. The next thing I knew, four more kids were waiting in line to give it a try. Even the old woman who said I wasn't welcome was there smiling at the kids challenging me. It was a fluke, an accident, a chance meeting with a little girl that broke the ice. A small child and her willingness to have

## Community Distrust/Institutionalized Hate

fun on that day started to change what people thought of us.

What are the chances of that happening in the 'hood, who knew? A child's hand game allowed me into a community where the police had not been welcomed before. After all the kids finished the hand game challenge, they walked with me to my car. They didn't want to see me go. The parents loved it. Soon the housing officers began to know more and more people in the projects, and that was a good thing. Any outsiders who came in were asked to leave unless they had business there. A few tried the, "I'm just visiting friends" routine. "Well that's great, what are their names, and where do they live?" They never had it right and were graciously escorted out.

One older white guy showed up and said we had no right to take him out of the projects. He told me he lived in P.T. "I know my rights; you're harassing me because I'm white. It's reverse discrimination." "Fair enough, sir. Did you say you live here?" "Yes, with my friend, Mr. Geter." I looked at the guy and couldn't believe what he was saying. "Sir, I know for a fact no one white lives in this project. That's not discrimination, that's P.T. Secondly, Mr. Geter doesn't have anyone living with him. I know because I've visited him many times. Here are your choices; get out of the project or it's jail for trespassing. The signs are posted right over your head." He looked at me, "I'm leaving but the mayor will hear about this." "Tell him I said hello."

I knew Mr. Geter well, and that guy didn't live with him. When the community policing program got underway, Geter was the very first person who came up to me. And boy was he brutally straight-up honest. "Sergeant Bailey, I sell numbers in the project to make ends meet. Is that going to be a problem?" I actually felt honored that he would tell me that with no reservations. "Mr. Geter, I have no problem with you making ends meet." He shook my hand, embraced me and went back into his apartment. I loved that man!

**No Black Heroes**

It was a challenge at times, but we were holding our own. The community unit was working Greens Homes, Trumbull Gardens, Marina Village and P.T. Barnum housing. Twenty officers didn't seem like enough for the two shifts of community policing, but we made do. Bridgeport just had too many projects, and crime was still a huge issue. Sadly, over the years, Father Panik Village, Pequonnock Apartments and Marina Apartments were torn down. I guess that was considered progress. There were a lot of good people who lived there, but the poverty and crime had taken its toll in the 'hood.

I continued to find new ways for the community policing efforts to progress. We attended the housing tenants' meetings, their cookouts, and their annual yearly events. Residents were beginning to ask for us to attend other venues. They wanted us at their kid's street basketball clinics, the fairs, and the housing project cleanup days. We continued walking and even visited people in their apartments, just to say hi. Drugs and crime had been reduced by 80 percent in the projects. Our unit even caught a murderer right on the spot. Officers Jose Luna and Gutierrez were just around the corner when they heard shots fired. The guy ran right into them with the gun in hand. He had no choice but to give up. Everyone had nothing but praise for us.

Chief Chapman reveled in our success. The Comp-Stat model of policing he brought from New York was a Godsend for our efforts, and I used it weekly. You could see the difference we were making in our figures. Captain Chapman said at the command meetings I was being touted as a model leader for community policing.

The unit's successes with the community and especially their families got me thinking more about my own. I learned that hand game just so my daughter Ashley and I would have something silly and fun to play. Her brothers Ronnie and Brandon even got into it at times. They were all so young back then. I couldn't help but feel like there was something off about me playing with other children when I wasn't home enough with my own. Ronnie was the glue for

## Community Distrust/Institutionalized Hate

his two younger siblings, but he was a rambunctious teenager, to put it mildly. The job kept me from them so often, and they needed me just as much as the community did.

I'll never forget the calls late at night from police officers in neighboring towns. "Sergeant Bailey, we have your son here. He's been throwing eggs at cars, or he's telling the police to stop harassing him." For years, my son had been rebellious. He didn't have much use for the rules and wasn't keen on school. Still, he was my firstborn son and I loved him. How I wished I could have spent more time with my family. The years were flying by and the kids were getting older. Yvette, always the supportive one, "Ronnie, we love you, don't worry. Do what you have to do."

Then the call I hoped would never come, "Ronnie, Little Ron has been arrested for stealing." "What!" Ronnie had struggled, unable to get a good job. His willingness to take chances caught up to him and he crossed the line. While on probation he got caught taking car parts from a junkyard. With so many previous cases and probation, the court sentenced him to prison. I felt like I had failed him as a father, always working, always looking out for the community. My concerns for Ronnie turned to hurt, and fear. How would he fare in jail, he was a cop's son? What about Brandon and Ashley, how would his imprisonment affect them? Suddenly, my emotions turned to pure resentment. I was doing my best to serve a system that has no use for African Americans.

Yvette saw the effects of Ronnie's going to jail and tried to comfort me. She did all she could to keep some semblance of normalcy for the family. The problem was Ashley was still living between our home and my ex-wife's. Although Brandon and Ashley loved each other, you could sense a separation taking place, especially with the loss of Ronnie. He had always been that older brother who kept them close with his presence.

With so much going on in my life, Yvette said I should call Chase. He and I talked for a good while. "Hey man,

## No Black Heroes

don't lose focus, or your edge on the streets! You don't want what happened to me to happen to you! That place used me, and they left me hanging. God knows, you've done your best. It hurts, I know, but ya family will realize what you sacrificed someday, and why." Chase was right; I had to remain sharp in a job that could get you killed. I prayed on it, asked God to guide me, and continued as best I could. Lord, watch over my wife and children while I do your will. And take care of Ronnie!

A few months later, I did get some good news. An old-timer from jail saw me and said they all knew Ron was my son. At first I panicked thinking someone was going to hurt him. He told me everyone there had a great respect for me and that no one would touch my kid. "Bailey, you got a good boy in there and we're all trying to talk to him, he's still young. Don't you worry 'bout him, he's gonna be alright." Although I was grateful, I was more relieved than anything knowing Ronnie was not going to be targeted in prison because of me.

A year had gone by and Captain Chapman called me into the office to confess he was worried. It was time for the bids into the unit and some officers would have to leave due to the union seniority issues. "Sergeant Bailey, we have a problem. We have two officers that want to join the housing unit. They have a history of hurting people. I don't want them here. I may have to cancel the bids and keep a smaller unit." "Who are the officers, Captain?" "Officers Charles Carr and Dan Geradi." "Captain, I know you said you heard rumors, but that's not enough to keep them out." He wanted the unit to remain all minorities. "Capt, we can't deny someone an opportunity because of their color. If we do that, aren't we guilty of doing what white officers have been doing to us for years? And I'm not really a fan of rumors." He agreed with me, reluctantly. "Okay Sergeant Bailey. You've made your point, but if they beat up on someone, it's on you." "I'll talk to them, Captain. Let me handle it."

## Community Distrust/Institutionalized Hate

Once the bids were complete, both Officers Carr and Geradi were transferred into the unit. I asked for them to come into my office and told them about my concerns and the rumors going around. I let them know rumors didn't mean a thing to me. There were a few rumors still floating around about me! We ended the meeting with my housing request, "Treat people like you would want someone to treat your family. That's all I'm asking you to do." They both said they would, and thanked me for being up front with them and what we were all about, community."

We were headed towards the end of our second year of community policing in the projects. Residents were constantly calling to say how nice and helpful the white officers were. They were very pleased with Officers Carr and Geradi. They were not only good community officers; they were our go-getters for chasing down drug dealers. There was no doubt, Geradi and Carr were my best two officers.

Chapman called me into the office after he received calls from the housing residents. "Sergeant Bailey, you were right. Carr and Geradi are some good guys. Other than those two fools tearing up fucking police cars, I got to tell you, they're all right." I didn't say anything on his comment about the cars. I didn't want him to get upset.

That's when he changed the subject. "Sergeant Bailey, I want you to do me a favor. Tell that Geradi to stop trying to get my goat. He was in the hallway the other day talking loud, so I could hear him. He said to Officer Carr, 'Captain Chapman is gonna be mad at us. We just crashed another police car.' I got up and ran out to the parking lot. He and Carr were out there laughing as they were driving away." I looked at the Captain and smiled, trying not to laugh. "Capt., Officer Geradi is a kidder. You know that." "Well, tell him to find something to do and to cut the shit." I knew he was just kidding and left it alone. "Sergeant Bailey, thanks for keeping me from making a terrible mistake." Giving Geradi and Carr a chance paid off.

**No Black Heroes**

The next day, I was off duty but monitoring the radio for any problems in the projects. "All cars, we have a man holding children hostage with a knife at 187 Bunnell St. He's asking for Officer Bailey." I was thinking Officer Bailey? It had to be someone who knew me from back in the day. "Does anyone know if he's on? All cars in the area respond." "Sergeant Bailey on, did you call?" "Sarge, Officer Collazo states a man is holding his kids hostage and will only talk to you, can you respond?" "On my way." I drove to Bunnell and met with Collazo. He said some guy named Maldonado was on the third floor and wouldn't let his kids go. I went upstairs and met with the hostage negotiator. "Hey Bailey, he's asking for a priest, and that's not a good thing. Bringing religion into it means he may want to end his life." "Got it."

I got to the third floor, but the door to the attic was barricaded. I peaked in and saw Jose Maldonado. He and I used to talk many times on the streets, just hanging out. He always said I was a cool cop, and I hoped he'd remember that. Jose heard me moving around, "Don't come up here or I'll do it," "Hey Jose, it's me, Bailey." He calmed down and we began to talk. "Bailey, my wife is leaving me. What about the kids, our family? How could she do this to me?" He was very distraught and I had to calm him down. The children were not sure what was going on. From what I could see through the crack in the door, they were playing with a few toys.

"Jose, we've been talking for a while. I know you're upset, but look; it's time for the kids to come out. We can work this out, trust me." He wanted to speak to his wife. I straight-out told him that wasn't a good idea. "Hey man, that's why we're here. Let's try working on you." We went back and forth before I took it to the next level. We discussed for a bit what I had been through with my ex. He knew I was telling the truth, because we both identified with the same issues of separation and family. He sensed I was sincere and cared. I gave him my word; if he let the kids go, I'd come upstairs and sit with him until he was ready to leave.

## Community Distrust/Institutionalized Hate

Finally, he handed me the kids from between the widened space he made in the doorway. "Bailey, what am I going to do?" "Live my brother, live." I went upstairs with him over the objections of the negotiator. "I can do this." We sat there and just talked for a good while, until he realized it was time to go. He put the knife down and told me he was sorry. "Hey man, I never doubted you." We hugged each other and walked down the stairs.

"Jose, I'm taking you to Bridgeport Hospital. They can help you." The emergency room personnel were waiting for him, and I drove him there with cars following. I hugged him once more and told him it would all work out. "Have faith, Jose." He cried but thanked me with one last hug before being escorted away. Officer Collazo shook my hand. "Hey Sarge, do you realize you just saved three lives up there?" I smiled, "No Angelo, you did. You kept calm and protected the set and the family by maintaining your cool. You kept Jose calm until you got everybody we needed in place to work this out. I'm proud of you, man." We shook hands and I headed back home.

There was nothing in the news about the hostage situation the next day, but to my utter disbelief, on the front page in huge letters, "Chief Wilbur Chapman has resigned from the Bridgeport PD." I couldn't believe what I was reading. Word at the police department was Chief Chapman and Mayor Fabrizi had a final shouting match. It was said Chief Chapman told Mayor Fabrizi to get the fuck out of his office. That sounded like something he would say.

The Mayor's office had a different take. They said it was a confrontation over Chief Chapman's remarks to Deputy Chief Karen Katlin. Allegedly, at one of the Comp-Stat meetings, he told her she was only as good as the tampon she wore. Still others said Chief Chapman was sick of Mayor Fabrizi and had leaked to the news that Fabrizi had a drug problem.

I would have put money on all the rumors being true. Frankie Estrada told us someone in City Hall was getting

## No Black Heroes

high off his dope. With Mayor Ganim in jail, news he'd entered a drug program, plus Mayor Fabrizi admitting he too had a problem, who knew which one Frankie was talking about, if not both. Either way, the corruption was real.

Judge Clendenen had received word about the tampon comment and called a special hearing on it. The command staff were all expected to appear and explain why no one reported such a derogatory comment to the court. We then heard more rumors that when the command staff took breaks during the meetings, Chapman would say, "Everyone should now go and change their Kotex napkins." A few of my New York cop friends told me that was classic New York style. In New York, their supervisors were considered gods. They could say or do whatever they wanted.

Judge Clendenen was close to having the hearing on the tampon remarks when one of the captains decided it was time to retire. Captain Gary Napoli put in his papers. This was an officer known for being tough as nails. I guessed he was so unnerved at the thought of testifying before Judge Clendenen, he decided to call it a day. We all thought it was hilarious that Captain Napoli cited ear damage as his reason for retiring. If he was going to be ordered to court, you'd best believe he would have said all he could hear were gurgling sounds, especially when the tampon thing was said.

Chief Chapman never made it to court and resigned his position. And from what I heard, he dared anyone to come to New York to ask him to report. With Chief Chapman gone, our concerns grew again. The Guardians were concerned that tensions would return to the days of Chief Irving, the Ad Hoc and K-5. With the union increasing their opposition against our pursuit for equal treatment, some began to say we were headed back to the 1960s and '50s days of Jim Crow!

Sure enough, discrimination had taken on a new, more subtle tone. Our first taste of change was the department implementing a panel of high-ranking supervisors to approve any special assignments to the FBI or DEA. It was no

## Community Distrust/Institutionalized Hate

surprise the panel was all white. Chief Chapman would have never allowed that. The new criterion to get an assignment was an interview before that panel and a review of your training and experience.

Black officers were immediately disadvantaged. Most guys who had special training and experience had been handpicked for years to receive those advantages. We all felt like no matter what, the new and improved system would increase the racial divide. Slowly but surely, the obstacles to opportunities were mounting. Dave called it institutionalized racism. I called it absurdity.

Something was going on. White officers started training in the gyms, running, and coming in with special weight shakes and healthy foods. We had seen this before. There had to be an opening for a special assignment coming that required us to be in good physical shape. We had always suspected someone was giving advance notice on the special assignment openings, and that someone at the top gave certain officers the heads-up. It was my guess it had to be one of two supervisors, Deputy Chief Bobby Frank or Captain Eva Trujillo. Both had been known for their anti-black officer views.

D.C. Frank was a sneaky little rascal. He skulked around the department, always eager to cause problems for any officer who didn't worship him, especially us. He thought of himself as God's gift from heaven in law enforcement. What was disturbing was his layers of excuses as to why black officers had to be excluded. He must have spent hours at a time thinking of his justified exclusions.

Captain Eva Trujillo, on the other hand, rejected her Hispanic heritage with a passion. I remember when she first arrived and announced to her fellow officers that her ethnicity would never play a part in her progressing at the police department. Then she proclaimed for all to hear the Guardians were known for using race to gain position, but not her. We watched curiously as she rose in rank, a cheap

## No Black Heroes

carbon copy of white arrogance. It was a shameful sight to see.

The Guardians suspected Captain Trujillo and D.C. Franks had been working hand in hand to keep black officers out of special training and assignments for years. The problem was we could never get enough on them to show the court of our intentional exclusion. We needed to find a way to expose what was going on and getting worse. The only way to expose that kind of thing was through files, documents or maybe some misplaced reports. But that would be the day.

If there were any written documents we could use, they would be in the D.C.'s office, or locked in the containment area on the third floor. I actually went there one night in desperation, hoping the doors to those files would just happen to be unlocked. You never know, but there was no such luck. While looking around the third floor, I heard someone walking my way. I wouldn't have an explanation why I was wandering on the third floor snooping around. I ran to the corner stairs and up to the fourth floor. The fourth floor was some kind of old storage area where broken department items were thrown. No one ever went up there. The only reason I knew about it was because of the roof access. It had a great view I used years ago to watch Greens Homes for drug activity.

I remained up there until I figured the person walking the hallway had gone. I needed to get out of there. On my way back downstairs, something caught my eye. There were boxes and boxes of paperwork that looked like someone dumped them there in a rush. I couldn't help but notice the words in large red letters, "Chief's Office." No way! I knelt down and looked closer. Jackpot! Boxes and boxes on the federal court intervention papers, reports, files, and what I could have only dreamed of, special assignments and training opportunities. It was a whole slew of papers from Chief Irving's years, with his supporting cast.

## Community Distrust/Institutionalized Hate

Chief Chapman must have had that stuff removed from his office when he first arrived, and someone dumped it in the hallway on the fourth floor. I didn't dare turn the lights on, so I used my flashlight to take a peek. There was no doubt from a glimpse. I was onto something. I needed more time to look at all the documents more carefully.

Every night possible, I would sneak upstairs and look through those boxes. What's this, a letter sent to Chief Irving about an accident with my name on it? I remembered that. I was off duty at Seaside Park late one night and pulled this kid Danny Pizzaro out of a burning car he had crashed. He sent a letter telling Chief Irving how I saved his life. It was folded neatly and stashed away in a blank folder. That should've gone to the awards committee. What a prick.

I then found the Davy Jones' locker of hidden treasure. Look who was sent to traffic enforcement school for training as a specialist in traffic reconstruction. Wow, a police instructor's course that was never announced. Guess who got that gig. Look at this, a second instructor's course no one knew about. Here's a surprise, one of D.C. Franks' favorite boys got that training. On and on, a whole slew of training classes no one ever knew about. Not one black officer received any of those assignments.

This was the smoking gun the Guardians had talked about. Looking at those papers, it all made sense. Send officers you favor to specialized training. Make sure to keep it on the down low. Once an opening came up for a special assignment, guess who got it? Those guys weren't better qualified for special assignments. The game was rigged. How could we compete against such narrow-mindedness from upper management? Those were training and assignment all of us should have benefited from.

I read pages and pages of training classes offered from the State of Connecticut Training Council to the Bridgeport Police Training Academy. What's this, a class for a weapons instructor course announced by the state? Sergeant Gil Cahill went to that class and no one knew a thing about it.

## No Black Heroes

We all wondered how he was suddenly a qualified range master. A look at the approval letter said it all, signed by D.C. Franks.

It would be a bit harder to show Captain Trujillo was excluding us. Trujillo was as "shysty" as anyone when it came to us. As bad luck would have it, Trujillo's duties were administrative, which gave her access to the entire department. Yet, it seemed her favorite place to be was the training academy, always lurking about. She reminded me of Dorothea Puente, the serial murderer with those piercing eyes.

I continued to rummage through the boxes. Now I had the documents to prove how the place really worked. Only one problem with the information, it was old news. Chief Irving was gone, so the court would most likely not want to hear it. There was another problem in bringing the new revelations to light. How would I explain looking through department files out of the chief's office I had no business looking at? What would the consequences be? You could best believe the city would say they were classified documents, even if someone did drop them in a hallway.

I needed to talk to someone who knew about such things. Someone I trusted. "Attorney Gaynor, how have you been?" "Officer Bailey. No way, they aren't messing with you again?" "No, that's not why I called." I explained about the papers I found and how I came about them. As I had assumed there was no way to submit those papers in court without a motion for discovery. I would be compelled to reveal where they came from. In short, I had to leave them where they were. I couldn't even tell the Guardians about them. Loose lips tend to sink ships.

It was bad news, and more bad news. Lieutenant Dave Daniels, the Guardians President was stepping down. After 10 years of faithful service, he was through. He had taken the organization as far as he could and felt it was time for new leadership. To make matters worse, the union was blatantly increasing their opposition towards us in court. If

## Community Distrust/Institutionalized Hate

only the Latino and black officers could unite. Together we could have stopped the union in their tracks.

With a need for new leadership the nominations for Guardians board positions was about to take place. That very night I was on my way to the meeting when I became ill and was forced to go to the hospital. Now what? The doctor said I was suffering from dehydration. "That's it? That's why I'm here?" "Yes, Mr. Bailey, I reviewed your tests. You need to drink more fluids." I felt so stupid. I guess getting older meant I needed to be mindful of things I had taken for granted all those years.

While getting dressed, the phone rang. "Sergeant Bailey, will you accept the nomination for Guardians President?" "Who me, are you kidding?" It was Officer Tresha Parks. "No really, will you accept?" I paused for a moment. The organization was in trouble. Just maybe I could help turn things around. I accepted the nomination. Yvette was standing next to the bed with Brandon when she heard me. "Are you crazy, Ronnie? You don't have enough stress in your life?" "Yvette, the Guardians need my help. They need someone to fight for them." She didn't say anything else and left it alone.

The next month, the votes were in and I won. I stood at the president's table. "I'll do my best to make you all proud. My first step is to get our organization involved with the community, and they with us." I continued, "As for the department, we will be a force to be reckoned with." Dave looked at me and smiled, "Of that I have no doubt." Ted, who we considered the father of the organization, shook my hand. "Take them to new heights, Mr. President." "Count on it, Ted."

Back at the department, acting Chief Anthony Armeno was on temporary assignment while the city conducted a nationwide search for a new chief. He called me, "Sergeant Bailey, we have a problem in Greens Homes. Can you please come to my office?" I could see his concern when I walked in. "Sergeant Bailey, there is a protest of sorts in the

## No Black Heroes

Greens, and people there are upset. One of our cars started a chase with a young African American kid on a motorbike. They broke it off, but it crashed a short time later into Mayor Fabrizi's car. The kid is dead."

He said the community had gathered in numbers, throwing rocks and bottles and blocking the roads. They were refusing to let the police in. "You think you can help us quiet this down somehow?" "Chief, I lived in that project and worked there. I know this sounds dangerous, but I need to go in there alone." "Sergeant Bailey, I don't think that's a good idea, are you sure?" "If I'm wrong, it will be on me. I'm sure I can at least go talk with them." "Alright Sergeant, but please be careful."

It was getting dark out. I drove past Greens to see what the mood was. People were yelling and upset. I parked my car down the block and walked up to the project. You could hear someone yelling, "Here comes Five-O. You motherfuckers aren't welcome here, murderers. Robbie was just riding a fuckin' motorbike." It was getting intense. Someone standing close by saw me, "Yo, that's Bailey. He's alright." I have to admit, I was relieved someone recognized me. Even in uniform, under those conditions things could go bad, and quick.

I continued walking over to a makeshift shrine on Highland Avenue. There were candles, notes, beer and empty liquor bottles, and a t-shirt with the name Robbie on it. It had been set up by friends and family for the kid. I said a short prayer. "Yo, Bailey, they tried to take it down." I asked why. It wasn't bothering anyone. "Bailey, you know how some of these cops are. They killed him, they killed Robbie for nothing. He was just riding a motorbike. The Mayor hit him with his car on purpose." I looked at the shrine and asked, "Who tried to take it down? I know it wasn't my guys." "No, it wasn't the project cops; it was those white cops from downtown. Bailey, they hate us." "I'll go back to the department and tell the chief. No one else will mess with the shrine. All I ask is that you move it back a bit, so it doesn't block the entire sidewalk. Other than that, it stays."

## Community Distrust/Institutionalized Hate

Gary Haynes lived in Greens. He had been a rough rider since he was a kid and knew me well. He yelled out as I was leaving, "See, that's what I'm talking about. Bailey is someone who knows and respects." What I heard next I don't think anyone could have believed. Someone yelled from a third floor window, "Bailey, just so you know, two white detectives were riding around the project playing music over the police speaker. They were playing 'Another One Bites the Dust.' Yo Bailey, you know that ain't right." "Are you for real?" "No Bailey, that's word." "I'll take care of it." I turned to Gary, "Haynes, what did they look like?" "It was two white detectives in a dark blue car. One of them got his ass whipped in P.T. a while back, and they took his gun." "I know just who you're talking about." It had to be Detectives Michaels and Barry.

On my way out, some young kid shouted at me. "You act like you care about us. You're one of them." I walked right up on him. "I don't know you, so I'll let it go this time. Just so you know, I do care. Otherwise I wouldn't be here. So why don't you tone it down before your mouth gets you into somethin' you can't handle." Gary stepped up, "Bailey, he don't know you man, cut him some slack." "I'm just talking to him, that's all. He just needs to know I'm not someone to mess with." "Bailey, trust me, he knows now." Gary started schooling the kid as I walked off. "Yo Youngblood, Bailey has always been one of us, little nigga, trust." God, how I hated that word, even the way kids were using it.

The next day, I went to the chief's office to give him an update. He was upset when I told him what detectives Michaels and Barry had reportedly done. "Chief, I'm not making a complaint. Can you just keep them out the project? I'm out there alone and that song is not going to help things." "Sergeant Bailey, they'll be told to stay away. I will tell the commander of Detective Bureau, and thank you, Sergeant, for all you do."

It was the day I dreaded most, the day of the funeral for Robbie Cohen. It was a day no officer should have been seen in the project, not even me. The family and community

## No Black Heroes

needed to grieve. It was a somber, quiet day, but it was that night that had me worried. I could only hope things would remain calm. Then the broadcast came over the air; "All cars are dispatched to multiple riots in Greens Homes and the surrounding area." By the time I got there, police officers were arresting community protestors.

Sergeant Sherman from Detective Bureau said the protestors turned violent when they entered the project. My look was one of amazement, "The projects are manned by my guys, why are you here? It was quiet all week." His response was as stupid as his logic, "We have a right to go on calls in the projects, don't we?" "What fucking calls? I've been listening to the radio all night."

Here was a guy who never came into the projects unless he had to. It was clear what he and his followers were doing. They wanted to show the community no one could tell them what to do. No one could tell them to stay out. They were looking for a confrontation and got it. The cockiness of some officers, you have to wonder why they became cops to begin with. It was payback, plain and simple. Under the watchful eye of Sergeant Sherman, detectives and patrol officers arrested anyone they could. It was downright shameful the way they acted, like spoiled rotten kids, bullies. They came in and made sure they destroyed the shrine to satisfy their stupid pride. No one was going to tell them where they could or couldn't go. Hell, they were the police.

How hard could it have been to give the project a few more days to return to normal? Instead, they gave the community another reason to hate us. That hate had a good chance of being passed down to their children, for what had been done to them. Over 20-some people were arrested for mourning the death of Robbie Cohen, a kid who died on a motorbike. I was embarrassed to be a cop. I failed the ones I swore to protect, that's how I felt.

My return to the project days later was even more humiliating. Look at what we had done. I made apologies to those who were out on bond. They all seemed to under-

## Community Distrust/Institutionalized Hate

stand, but in my heart, it felt like I'd let them down. I should have stayed in the project that night and not my office.

Tanisha lived in Greens and was another outspoken resident when it came to the police. She somberly walked over with tears in her eyes. "Bailey, why do they hate us so much? We just wanted to walk for Robbie. We weren't doing anything wrong." She fell in my arms openly weeping. I tried to comfort her, when out the corner of my eye a detective's car was pulling up. It was Detectives Michaels and Barry getting out of their vehicle. They hadn't done enough damage? I went over to them before they could get to the shrine the crowd had replaced. "Sergeant Bailey, we told them they can't have this on a public sidewalk." I looked sternly at both of them, "Don't touch it, and leave the area. That's an order." "Oh, so now you're one of them, Sarge?" I moved a little closer and whispered, "Touch it and I'll kick both your asses. Do you understand that?" They got back in their car and peeled out. What's wrong with those guys? Why couldn't they just leave these people alone?

Back at Chief Armeno's office, we discussed what happened in Greens. He said it was out of his hands. Officers were saying the protestors that night were out of control. "Sergeant Bailey, we had calls that needed our attention. The protestors became violent when we responded." "Chief, if you check the tape you'll see there were no calls." He had no response, not sure what to make of my assertion. It was too late. The damage had been done. I turned to leave his office. Here it comes. "Bailey, I know you care. In the community you are very well respected. What happened was not your doing. But before you leave can I ask a favor?" "Sure Chief, name it." "Detectives Michaels and Barry were extremely concerned after you spoke to them." "I'm sorry Chief. They got to me at a bad time. I'll leave them alone." "Thanks, Sergeant."

The weeks that followed saw more of the same old rumors. I was a turncoat and not a brother officer. I was one of them, those people. Someone in the supervisor's office made a comment as I walked by. "He lived there with them, so why not go back to where he belongs." I ignored the comment but let my presence be known. As I walked past the office door, I kicked it so hard someone inside must have dropped a glass, cup, or something. The office suddenly became quiet. I had been down that road before. None of them had the nerve to confront me before. They sure as hell weren't ever going to was my guess.

On my desk at the office, I found a letter from an Attorney William Whitehall. He was representing Detective Michaels and had the nerve to demand an apology in writing. Detective Michaels said I had lied, harming his reputation. His attorney asserted Detective Michaels never played any offensive music in the projects making fun of anyone, especially a dead kid. Well, I gave him an apology he wouldn't soon forget.

I wrote a report to the commander of Detective Bureau and mailed copies to Attorney Whitehall. It was short. "To Commander Lynn Kerwin, here is a letter from Detective Michaels' attorney. It accuses me of trying to harm his reputation, somehow. Please note, I never filed a complaint against Detective Michaels or accused him of anything. I did ask the chief to keep him and his partner out of the projects while I was there alone, trying to restore calm in the community. If Detective Michaels still wishes to pursue this matter, may I suggest this issue be sent to the Office of Internal Affairs for a thorough investigation? He and his partner can then explain why the community voiced displeasure in their playing a song over the police intercom that made fun of someone losing his life. I'll provide the witnesses regarding this matter." That was the last I heard from Detective Michaels or his attorney.

With the community still upset about the police and how they handled the protest, I got a call from Captain Chapman. He was extremely concerned. He said dispatch had not heard from one of my officers for over an hour, Officer Murphy Pierce. "Sergeant Bailey, Officer Pierce was

## Community Distrust/Institutionalized Hate

last heard from in Greens Homes. Please check on him." "No problem Capt, I'm on my way."

When I get there, Officer Pierce was in his police car. He was where he normally parked and everything looked to be fine. I had asked my officers to stay on the outskirts of Greens that day, but maybe Officer Pierce had to go in for some reason. What I liked about Officer Pierce was he was an older officer known for being nice to people. I admired his way of making friends in the community. To my surprise, he had someone in the back of his car. I was thinking it wasn't a good time to make an arrest, with so much going on.

On closer inspection, I could see the person in the rear of Officer Pierce's car reading. I walked over to Pierce, looked at his prisoner, and then asked him what was going on. "Hi Sergeant, I'm just doing a motor vehicle stop. This guy's car isn't registered." I wasn't sure what Pierce was talking about. "Officer Pierce, why is your prisoner in the back of your car uncuffed?" "Oh, he's helping me with the charges. He's a good guy." "What?" I looked back, and sure enough, the guy was reading the red book on criminal charges. "Officer Pierce, how is your prisoner helping you?" "Oh, he's looking for his charges for an unregistered car."

I stood there astounded and had to smile. I opened the rear door and let the guy out. I spoke to him after I patted him down, "Sir, I want to thank you for assisting Officer Pierce with your arrest, but you're free to go." I told him he should get someone to tow his car, but once we were gone, it was on him. He understood what I was saying. It was the least I could do after this man spent an hour in a police car looking up his own charges. How cooperative can you get?

I turned to Officer Pierce and told him it was nice of his prisoner to be so cooperative, but we don't operate that way. Officer Pierce was a really good community officer, but having your prisoner look up his own charges was a bit too much. "Officer Pierce, I hope this was an honest mistake. Never let anyone in your car uncuffed. Oh, and for future

## No Black Heroes

reference, the red book is for criminal charges. The blue book is for motor vehicle. That's the reason neither of you could find the charges." With all the problems I was having, this was that humorous moment I needed. God moves in mysterious ways. With all my sadness, he sent me some much needed relief, Officer Pierce.

Chapter 25

*The writer's gift can make us see ourselves and our morals differently than our reality suggests.*
—Michael Eric Dyson

## THE FIX; I AM SOMEBODY; A NATIONAL PROBLEM

Before Chief Chapman resigned he was in the planning stages of starting a Special Weapons and Tactics unit (SWAT). Not long after his departure, the notice was posted. The department was about to start their first-ever SWAT team. I asked Captain Chapman who was moving forward on it. He said D.C. Franks was in charge of the entrance level process. In the famous words of Private Gomer Pyle, "Surprise, surprise, surprise." It was a no-brainer. The panel to oversee the selection process would be all white. Who knew?

The memo came down requesting that any officer interested in SWAT put in a letter of interest. How I cringed at the thought; Franks was the same guy who tried to start an all-white street unit some time back. But Chief Chapman then wasn't having it. Any bets on who Franks was gonna favor to be on the SWAT team? I was absolutely sure this was going to court, no two ways about it. And Franks was certain to reject me, even if I performed better than Superman himself.

379

## No Black Heroes

It suddenly became obvious why officers had been training and coming to work with veggies instead of donuts. They had been tipped off about the up and coming SWAT testing. I went right to work increasing my running, workouts with weights, and performing competitively at the Tae Kwon Do school. Franks, for some reason, always thought of black officers as inferior, but I was determined to show him he was wrong.

During the first stage of the process, the department conducted personnel file reviews on all candidates. My file was going to be a shocker for them. Then came the news even I didn't expect. The police department couldn't find my personnel file! It was missing. You can't make this stuff up.

I went to the clerk's office to see Sergeant Joey Hernandez. He had been in control of the files for years and didn't play games, like his predecessors. "Joey, I was told my personnel file is missing. How can my entire file of 20-some years disappear?" "Bailey, calm down. This has never happened before, I know. But the department is going to allow you to continue with the process." "So my file just up and walked out? I'll give you one guess who's behind this."

Joey would never have allowed anyone to take someone's personnel file. This was done by someone high in the chain of command. No one had keys to those files, other than the department clerk and a few officers in command. "Joey, I'll have all my records replaced by the end of the week." "What are you talking about?" "I have copies of everything since my first assignment in 1983. I maintain my own files at home." Joey smiled, "Damn, what are you, a psychic?" "No, but Ted Meekins is." By week's end, I had replaced every piece of missing information. Whoever took my file was surely going to be upset. Someone did their best to blindside me, all for nothing. What's more, if no one had reviewed my file, I had an even bigger surprise many in command weren't going to be happy about. I could hardly wait.

## The Fix; I am Somebody; A National Problem

The day of the agility test arrived. We had to run a mile and a half, and I had the second fastest time of the entire department. Not bad for the oldest officer testing for SWAT! We then did weight lifting, a body carry, sit and leg stretch, and sit-ups. All events were timed. Would you believe D.C. Franks had the nerve to try and discount my sit-ups? He said my back didn't touch the floor. I gave him something to think on. "I hope you can explain what happened to my file when this goes to court." He stormed off to another side of the gym, bless his sensitive heart.

Last in the process were the oral interviews. It couldn't have come at a worse time. I was bedridden with a temperature of 103 that week. I had to wonder if Franks had something to do with that too. I waited until the last moment with the hope of feeling better, but no such luck. There was no time left to get properly dressed and arrive on time, when I decided to gut it out. It was a desperate last-minute decision to go. I showed up pale and weak, wearing my sweats and a do-rag covering my head. I was soaked from fever, when I entered the oral assessment room.

Before I sat down, I sincerely apologized to the panel for my appearance. I explained to them the circumstances, having been bedridden for a week. The panel seemed satisfied with my explanation, but not Franks. He looked at me while writing something on a pad. With a soft-spoken voice, I provided them an overview of my training and experience. I was pretty confident that no one looked at the updated personnel file I had replaced. Most likely, who ever took it had no idea it had been replaced.

What a surprise for Franks. As I referred to my specialized training, he had to be wondering what training I had received. Neither he nor Captain Trujillo ever authorized any specialized training for me. Boy, I raised a few eyebrows discussing the classes I'd taken. To their surprise, specialized training had been given to all TNT officers outside of what the training academy offered. We had received specialized training without the police academy's approval. That perk was forged by the original tactical commander, years before my arrival. Like the song says, "Oops, there it is."

Franks looked repulsed while the panel heard about my training at John Jay College, Homeland Security, crime scene investigations, SWAT basic training, and an FBI instructor's course. The panel would be hard-pressed to deny me a position, but I was prepared. Franks was running the show, so no matter what, I expected a rejection. I was also fairly certain, at that point, the first thing Franks was going to do was make sure those classes at TNT ended. And he didn't disappoint in that respect.

The memo came down that due to budget constraints, the department would no longer provide classes to TNT members without Franks' permission. A classic example of institutionalized racism took placed right before my eyes. Change the rules to keep us out. I'll say this much, he sure was consistent, if nothing else.

A month later, the results were announced. I was dead last in the SWAT selection. All officers selected were D.C. Franks' personal friends, those he liked. One name that stood out was Officer Ron Jersey. Make no mistake; Ron was a good cop and someone I'd work with anytime, anywhere. But he just got on the job, so how did he get SWAT? The proverbial icing on the cake for the fiasco was that during the interview process, Ron was on vacation! How did he end up on SWAT without completing the entire process? What a surprise, after checking, I found out that Ron didn't have the time on the job required to join the team. He was a stand-up guy, and I was sure he wouldn't take it personally that I used his acceptance into SWAT to challenge Franks.

Before filing in court, I contacted Franks to meet with him. He was arrogant and reluctant as usual. "Hey D.C., it's your call, but I'd like to give you a chance to explain yourself before my next step." He didn't like my comment and changed his tone, "What do you mean, Sergeant?" I was about to hang up, when he asked me to come by. Once at his office, I calmly asked, "Can you explain how I was

## The Fix; I am Somebody; A National Problem

eliminated from SWAT, Deputy Chief Franks?" Here comes his rationale. "Sergeant Bailey, you didn't have good answers, and you came poorly dressed." I was dead last on the list because I was poorly dressed? He paused before trying to convince me further, "The panel thought you were not qualified to be a SWAT member." It was time to nail him down, "I just want to be sure of what you're saying, Deputy Chief. You're telling me I'm not qualified to be on SWAT?" He wouldn't answer. I repeated the question, and he just sat there unresponsive. "I will assume from your silence, the panel and you have decided I'm not qualified." I smiled, thanked him, and walked out of his office.

I was so certain of Franks, I had written most of the complaint the day after learning he was in charge of the SWAT entry process. That was how sure I was of his racist views. I just had to fill in the blanks. Knowing how the city would react to my complaint, I thought it best to file it later, after collecting a few more nails for the coffin. It would take a little more time before dealing Franks and the city that final blow once and for all.

As the Guardians President, I had a few things remaining to address. We were still fighting to get minorities in specialized units and command positions. My exclusion from SWAT, and how Franks manipulated the process, was a prime example of why we needed the federal court's intervention. And the union was a constant in their interference in the federal court process.

I tried reasoning with the union president one last time. "Why is the union opposing us? Don't you think it's wrong to stop any progress the court might grant minority officers?" Short and stupid looking, he outright lied to my face. "The membership wants us to fight for their seniority rights." What an imbecile. "I don't recall the union notifying the entire membership about anything" He just sat there, smug, with no answer.

He then said the most painful words I could have possibly had heard, "Sergeant Bailey, the Hispanic Society wants

## No Black Heroes

an end to the federal court process and supports the union on this." The words stabbed in the back took on new meaning for me that day. Latino officers wanted to end the federal court oversight? They sold us out and never had the decency to tell us why. I had nothing else to say. Guardians fought hard to get Hispanics on the job, so they could turn around and do that to us?

The National Association of Black Law Enforcement Officers (NABLEO) was holding its regional meeting in Hartford, Connecticut, and I needed some thoughts from our out-of-state brother and sister members. Perhaps they were going through what we were facing and could provide some insight. Our fellow Latino officers were pulling the rug right out from under us, while the union stood proudly by. It just didn't make any sense.

While looking for help at the summit, it was clear that the Bridgeport Guardians were the only regional Guardians organization that still had court oversight to monitor the police department. NABLEO leadership began discussing the fact that black officers were losing their quest to increase our numbers nationally. Our numbers in supervision were even more disappointing. It was disturbing to learn that complaints filed across our region had risen more than in any previous year.

The senior officers discussed the Ronald Reagan years, which had not been kind to minorities or the support mechanisms African Americans once had. Under the Reagan administration, Affirmative Action was gutted, the Commission on Human Rights and Opportunities weakened, and it was next to impossible to file discrimination claims in court. The new rule of thumb was, discrimination had to be clear-cut, and for a lack of a better word, blatant. No one was that stupid anymore. Well, almost no one. Racism was now subtle and harder to prove. It was the northern way of things, replacing the "in your face" southern style of racism.

## The Fix; I am Somebody; A National Problem

NABLEO members spoke about how reverse discrimination claims were the new norm. There was no disputing the belief that Reagan's Supreme Court appointments were turning a blind eye to discrimination issues and the civil rights gains we had made. Over 400 years of black people suffering had a new response, "That was the past, so move on." Yeah, move on right into ever-changing rules, the good old boys club, and roadblocks meant to obstruct.

While at the conference, I listened to Attorney James Young of the Right to Work Foundation based in Springfield, Virginia. He spoke about many things. What had my attention were the police union issues he spoke of. For years, our union had insisted that we were required to be members or couldn't be police officers. Imagine my surprise to hear, not only could we resign, but the union still had to represent us. I was determined to know more about the process. "Attorney Young, what do I lose by resigning from the union?" "Sergeant Bailey, the only thing you lose is your right to vote on union issues, and you can't attend their meetings." I retorted, "The union didn't ask for my vote when they entered federal court to fight us. No loss there." Someone was going to be angry with what I was about to do.

The following Monday, I went to see the union president. I stood by the door this time, enjoying his usual smugness. I would be brief. "Mr. President, I want the union to remove itself from the federal court process. I shouldn't be paying dues to an organization that impedes our right for equal opportunities." "Sergeant Bailey, we've been through this already." "I know. I just wanted to make it official." Wearing a smug smile, I walked off.

It was hard going back and forth between the Guardians' issues and my own. I needed to get my denial from SWAT filed in court. But first I had to do something no one had ever done in the department's history. I was going to secure my own SWAT training. That's right; my own training, and the best SWAT training possible in the country.

**No Black Heroes**

I called the FBI office and spoke to agent Syrax. "Mike, I need advanced SWAT training. Can I get it through the FBI?" "Ron, I can think of no one more suited for our training than you. The problem is you have to be FBI." Agent Syrax then told me about an organization considered the best worldwide, some place called Blackwater. "You can find Blackwater in North Carolina." "Thanks Mike, I owe ya." I looked up their information and called. The director of Blackwater said any certified police officer could take the classes. But he was adamant, "Sergeant Bailey, we don't just hand out SWAT certifications. You must pass the course, no exceptions. I'll send you the information."

Blackwater was run by the military elite, Army Rangers, Special Forces and retired Navy Seals. This was not a place to train unless you meant business and could handle it. I scheduled the dates for the training, paid for the classes and took vacation time to attend. At such a late stage in my life and career, I was going to do what no other Bridgeport officer had ever done before, train with the Blackwater elite.

I packed my bags and drove to Moyock, North Carolina. The training was from 7am to 7pm. There were SWAT teams from New York, Virginia, Minnesota, and a few guys from South Africa. The South Africans had guns none of us had ever seen before! They were some pretty cool white dudes with British accents. Nothing like what I had envisioned. Everyone there was a part of an established SWAT team. I was the only one who attended solo.

The first day, we reviewed the ops plans and tactical maneuvers. From there we went to the gun range. We conducted shooting drills at moving targets, firing while on the move, then cover and concealment. In all, we fired over 2,500 rounds. The weather was a blistering 100 degrees plus, and we were in full SWAT gear. At the end of each day, we took our fatigues off and wrung the hard-earned sweat out of them.

Next were the building entries. In full gear with flak vests, helmets and gas masks, we entered the tactical

### The Fix; I am Somebody; A National Problem

house. The building interior had movable walls, so every entry was changed, and we had to adapt. The trainers walked on scaffolds over the rooms to make sure if there was a problem we could be stopped on a dime. Blackwater training was live fire. Nothing I received over the years came close, or compared, to that training.

The toughest part for me was hitting the targets accurately while on the move. All SWAT members had special assault weapons. My training was with the department-issued Beretta 9mm. Bridgeport SWAT was still in the early stages of forming. The instructor said it would be twice as hard for me to compete compared to the guys who had assault weapons, but it could be done. He told me about a German SWAT team that used only the Beretta handgun as their assault weapon. I was determined to make it through the course and do well.

To keep all of us on point, we were told if we missed a target, you had to run a mile in full gear to base and back. In 100 degree heat that was an "Oh, hell no" for me. I hit all my targets with a handgun. The SWAT team members on hand were impressed. Unfortunately, a few of them missed. I actually ran for support with one of the team members from Albany who missed his target. You could tell the weather was getting to him as he staggered at times through the course. "Hey man, I know it's hot but we're gonna make it." He thanked me for running with him.

The bus raids proved to be challenging. We had to breach, then break and rake, before we could enter. A raid on a school bus with children had to be tight and precise. There was no room for error. Just when we thought we had done it all, they sent us in the TAC house and gassed us. Thank goodness for my gas mask. For a while, I was beginning to think the instructors were having flashbacks of their times in the Gulf War! They were running us through the mill.

Finally, it was over. I completed the Blackwater course. It was Friday, and I was returning home with my SWAT cer-

## No Black Heroes

tification in hand. After returning to Bridgeport I had just one week to recuperate. There was one more accomplishment to make.

My new destination was Op-Tac in Hagerstown, Maryland. It was a Tactical Commanders course run by Stuart A Meyers, an expert in the field of SWAT management. My intentions were to be taught how commanders ran a SWAT unit, but also how to select team members. We were informed you needed to look at an officer's work record, arrest record, absenteeism, and any abuse complaints. Then it was necessary to get recommendations from the supervisor of the officer and interview his peers to hear their feelings on the candidate's selection. The SWAT selection process I was taught was detailed and structured. Franks' selection process was a joke. With the management course completed, it was time to return home.

After a series of exhausting weeks, I walked into the Bridgeport Training Academy. Standing there was a pleasant surprise; it was Captain "crazy eyes" herself, Trujillo. She was standing next to the receptionist and not very happy to see me. This was a first, I was glad to see her. My hello was met with her usual smirk. I turned to the receptionist. "Excuse me, but I have some documents I want placed in my training file. I took a SWAT course at Blackwater and completed a course at Op-Tac in Maryland. It certifies me to manage a SWAT team." I thought I was going to burst, watching Trujillo, who was listening intensely while pretending to be looking at some papers on the receptionist's desk. If she cuts her eyes any more to see my papers, they're going to get stuck!

I started to hand the receptionist my certifications when Captain Trujillo stopped her. I was amazed she had the audacity to get involved. "You can't put something in your training file unless the department allows you to take a training course, Sergeant Bailey." How many times will I have to hear that? "Well, I hope you're not gonna stop me. That would be a big mistake on your part, Captain." She didn't respond, so I made my point. "Captain, I took this

### The Fix; I am Somebody; A National Problem

training on my own time. They're certified law enforcement classes. If those certificates don't go in my training file, someone will have some explaining to do." My expression was dead serious, something rare for her to experience from me. I was waiting for her words to come out like, "How dare you," or something. Captain Trujillo stood there with those cogs turning in her head, speechless. I left with a few parting words. "I'll be back to check and make sure those papers have been placed in my file. Have a blessed day."

I walked to the corner store to chat with a few folks I knew. On the way back to my car, I realized I left my keys on the receptionist's desk. What greeted me when I walked into that office, no one could have planned better. There they were, D.C. Franks and Captain Trujillo both looking at my certificates. If only I had a camera. They were both visibly upset and uttering my name as I came in. A childhood cartoon came to mind, "Trapped like two rats in a trap ... CURSES." I guess I'm a comedian at heart, I admit it. I politely smiled, with a hint of seriousness, "Excuse me. I hope I'm not interrupting." They both looked up. "I'm sorry, I forgot my keys." I reached over and grabbed my keys while they both stood there in silence. I turned and walked out. Don't tell me there isn't a God, and he's dark-skinned too! The Guardians had always figured those two were working hand in hand against us. And it looks like we were right. Trujillo had to have called Frank's right after I left the training academy.

Any doubt I wasn't qualified would be those hard core officers who wouldn't change their minds, even if they could. I didn't take the SWAT training to prove Franks, or anyone else wrong. I took it because I was denied an opportunity. No one was going to keep me from what I was entitled to. Proud of my accomplishments, it was time to return to Guardians business.

The complaints of white officers abusing people in the community were mounting. It wasn't at the level we'd seen when the K-5 was running amuck, but it was prevalent. There was an increase in complaints of racial profiling the

## No Black Heroes

city had failed to address. Sadly, the use of the "N" word was still being reportedly used by officers. All this, plus African American officer numbers were diminishing in Bridgeport, like the national trend. It was a sad time, and police departments nationally couldn't have cared less.

The once slightly diverse department we had was becoming nonexistent. Without a more diversified department, we saw an increase in black kids being arrested for minor offences such as trespassing, loitering, and disorderly (for playing their music too loud). The cycle of minor arrests was sure to hurt those kids by keeping them from getting good jobs in the future. Their chances of becoming police officers were definitely going out the window. The Guardians needed to be more visible, to counter the increase in racial profiling we were experiencing. But another problem was apparent; we didn't have enough members like we had in previous years.

While going over a few ideas at home, Doc Hill called me. "Mr. President, you need to look at the Connecticut Post." I hung up and grabbed the newspaper. There it was in black and white, "Bridgeport Police Officer Involved in Love Triangle Shoots at Innocent Victims in Marina Village Housing Project." Officer Brian Bains was having an affair with a Bridgeport police detective who happened to be married to a Connecticut state trooper. The papers said the state trooper and Officer Bains confronted each other over the trooper's wife. What in the world was it, *All My Children*? The soap operas had nothing on us.

I had to read it again. It had to be some kind of mistake. The papers said Officer Bains had become so enraged over his mistress' husband's confrontation, he went to Marina Village and shot at over a half dozen people, including a high school student. The community was outraged over the senseless shooting by an officer. The Bridgeport NAACP President Craig Kelly asked a very poignant question, "Why did this officer feel comfortable shooting at people in our community?" I was sure Craig didn't want anyone's neighborhood to be shot up, but he just wanted to know

### The Fix; I am Somebody; A National Problem

why Bains felt comfortable taking his frustrations out on the black community? To add insult to injury, Bains was still on the job, getting paid while the state mulled over his charges. Something was very wrong in Bridgeport.

Not too long afterwards, a second report of abuse came in. Officer Jeff Huntsman choked a woman in booking; not once, not twice, but three times, while she was in handcuffs. The victim, Cherise Trotter had been talking trash to Huntsman and paid the price. She was arrested for interfering with police. That's the catch-all charge police customarily use when a citizen crosses the line. I took a look at Huntsman's police report. A handcuffed woman was choked and not one line was in the report about it. His version was ridiculous. He said Trotter stuck her tongue out, and he thought she was going to spit, so he turned her around, several times. That had to be the lamest excuse involving abuse I had ever heard. We were all sure Huntsman was going to be fired. I couldn't wait to see the DVD from booking.

My head was spinning; unlawful shootings by our officers, cops choking people in cuffs, and things were getting worse by the day. Before anything else went down, I filed my paperwork on the SWAT disqualification in federal court. D.C. Franks was soon served with papers. I could count on one thing; in 27 years under the federal court system, the city never admitted there was a race problem in Bridgeport. They would deny it again. It was the most perfect imperfect city in the United States of America.

The department was dragging its feet on both Officers Huntsman and Bains' cases. Mid-level and upper supervision were tasked with the beginning stages of the investigations, and interestingly, both cases were being stalled. The union was doing what it did best; standing up for their officers even when they knew both were clearly wrong. The union was as consistent as the city, no wrong could be found in police misconduct or racial issues. If you keep protecting cops when they're wrong, then America is gonna eventually say, "Enough is enough!"

**No Black Heroes**

The union took things to a whole new level, unheard of before. First, we were hearing the same old line about how Officer Huntsman had to control his prisoner. The union took it one step further. They said, "Wasn't it the supervisor's place to stop any confrontations in booking?" The union was blaming another officer to save one? I had to know who they were throwing under the bus. How convenient, the supervisor on duty happened to be a black sergeant, Sergeant Donald Milton.

Still trying to make sense of it all, the announcement came; Mayor Fabrizi had picked a new chief of police. He would be the second African American chief appointed to the Bridgeport PD, Chief Brian Norwood. Bells went off in my head. It was too obvious. The city wanted to get rid of the oversight and Judge Clendenen in the worst way. I could hear the opening statement in court, "We have hired two African American Police Chiefs. It's been 27 years of progress. There is no basis for the federal court to remain."

Chief Norwood had a fancy reception before taking over the department. The Guardians attended in numbers, but something wasn't right. Our new chief seemed stand-offish. I was hoping it was a case of nerves, but I had a sinking feeling. Curious, I made a few calls to the New Haven Guardians. It was not what I was expecting to hear. "We were hoping you guys got Norwood. Good luck with him. All I can tell you, Bailey, is he doesn't consider himself one of us."

It was going to be interesting to see what Norwood was really all about. I watched as he settled in. It was disappointing to see how detached he was, like Guardians weren't there. I invited him to our events, but he was consistently a no-show. We held a fundraiser for the community at the Holiday Inn in downtown Bridgeport. Through his secretary, he declined, citing a previous engagement. Funny, we were all outside that night taking a break, when guess who drove by, Norwood. Guess New Haven Guardians had pegged him right.

### The Fix; I am Somebody; A National Problem

A call came in that I wasn't expecting from my down-low union buddy, Officer Billy Rice. He kept me up on any union backroom deals. "Just thought you should know Bailey, some of my best friends are black!" "Bill, cut it out. What's up with you?" He had me laughing. Bill was one of the few white officers who didn't agree with how black officers were being treated at the police department. He called to let me know the union had just voted to send money to Attorney Karen Torre. Torre was the attorney representing a group of white firefighters opposing black firefighters in New Haven. I had heard about that case, but before criticizing the union, I thought I'd call the New Haven Firebirds to see just what it was all about.

The New Haven Firebirds said Attorney Torre had filed with the Supreme Court on a reverse discrimination claim. The city of New Haven wanted to throw out the promotional test results on the firefighter's lieutenants exam, due to the negative impact it would have on minority firefighters. It was before the Supreme Court.

The police union had no right to use my dues to fight for anything other than Bridgeport police business. They'd crossed the line time and time again. I confronted the outgoing union president Mr. Short "Caca" himself. "Mr. President, did the union agree to send money to Attorney Karen Torre of New Haven? Isn't she's fighting African American firefighters? What's that got to do with us?" He remained self-righteous in his arrogant silence, as if I had no choice but to accept what they'd done. "That's it, I'm resigning from the union." The little troll just sat there, like he was rooted in a tree stump, sure I couldn't resign.

I sent the union my formal resignation papers, and word spread like wildfire. Sergeant Bailey quit the union. "I didn't know you could do that." One by one, officers asked me how I could resign and remain on the job. It wasn't surprising, the union ignored my resignation request. I then sent copies of my resignation to the Right to Work Foundation in Virginia, with a second notice to the union. That time the union was told what would happen if they did not honor my request. The Right to Work Foundation was prepared to file in court on my behalf, at no cost. The union was livid.

Things got intense for me. It started with comments from hardcore union members who spoke under their breath in passing. I responded with a few choice words of my own. Then the long hard, cold stares and silent treatment came. Intimidation was apparently the accepted way to treat someone fighting for what they believed in. For the time being I ignored their childish antics and stood firm.

As Guardians president, I focused on my membership joining the community when there were events in the city. We were at community cookouts, church events, church services for police, and community cleanups in the projects. The Guardians were moving towards being a household name in Bridgeport. More importantly, we were helping our city.

Guardians also began to fellowship with various minority organizations throughout the state, including all the Connecticut branches of the Guardians. Word was getting around about our efforts. We were building relationships by networking with organizations that faced similar struggles Guardians had. My logic was simple, strength in numbers, and good friends. It was my belief that once the court was eventually removed, we could only move forward with other organizations by our side.

Surprisingly, the notice from federal court on my hearing with D.C. Franks arrived earlier than expected. That's when I received word from Bill, my mole in the union. How in the world did he know so much about what was going on? Bill told me the city, union, and upper management at the police department agreed to shut SWAT down right in the middle of their training. He said the union agreed to go along with it "unofficially" to get back at me for resigning. They all figured it would stop my case from going forward.

It was surely a surprise when Attorney John Williams answered their slew of motions. They were expecting me to

### The Fix; I am Somebody; A National Problem

continue on my own as I had in the past. There was no doubt the city would do all it could to protect D.C. Franks. He messed up so badly, they had no choice. Attorney Williams had earned a reputation nationally when it came to civil rights cases. We arrived to court early and Franks was already in the hallway, waiting. He had his usual cocky look on him. I spoke pleasantly to him, while figuring the case wasn't going to take long. What he had done was just too blatant.

The same city that was trying to end the federal court oversight brought in a private law firm to defend Franks. The lead Attorney William Wenzel was assigned to defend him. Amazingly, Bridgeport had shelled out millions over the years in its efforts to remove a court process meant to have things fair for all officers. The tax dollars they spent had me reeling. Why couldn't the city just do what the court was there for and treat all officers equally? It would cost them much more before it was all over. One thing was certain; they couldn't afford to lose this case.

The first question asked at the hearing was why the Bridgeport Police Department canceled the SWAT team. The city curiously admitted the SWAT selection process was flawed. This was a strategy I had not seen before. They weren't admitting any wrongdoing, just that mistakes had been made. Of course none were due to racial issues, according to them. Brilliant strategy, blame it on the process.

They called their first witness "Mr. Mistake" himself, Franks. He had a lot of nerve. He told the court he didn't say "I wasn't qualified." What he told the court was that he had said "I was not as qualified" as the other officers. So much for integrity! He then told Judge Clendenen my five shootings was a concern to the interviewing panel. I was above the curve in shootings, according to him. This was the only time I could ever think of that an officer's experiences with armed confrontations was a negative for SWAT consideration. Franks made it a point to emphasize that I didn't come dressed properly for the interview process, compared to the other candidates. Judge Clendenen was not impressed with Franks' testimony.

Attorney Williams countered about my shootings, "Was Sergeant Bailey ever disciplined or found to have done anything improper in his numerous shootings, that were considered the basis for his disqualification?" D.C. Franks' response was long in excuses with the ultimate answer being no. They changed direction and tried to make a valid claim that their goal was to have officers with previous military experience for SWAT. Attorney Williams chimed in, "Oh, you mean like Officer Brian Bains who made number one on your SWAT list? He was ex-military. Didn't he get drunk and shoot up a public housing project recently?" You could see a sea of red faces in the court with Franks' standing out from the rest.

Then came the question everyone was waiting for. "Deputy Chief Franks, even though a white officer was on vacation during the interview process, and that same officer didn't have the time on the job to take a position in SWAT, isn't it true you selected him anyway?" His answer was so ridiculous all Judge Clendenen could do was look at him out of the corner of his eyes. "The panel felt that Officer Jersey's professionalism was so well known to the department that he was qualified for the SWAT team." Attorney Williams smiled. "So even though he didn't have the time required to apply for SWAT, and missed the oral interview, the panel felt he should be on the team?" Franks didn't answer the question. Williams asked a few more questions. "Were the members of the panel all white Deputy Chief Franks? And is it a fact their votes on the perspective SWAT candidates weren't written down? It was all a verbal kind of thing? Is that correct?" "Yes." "Your honor, I have nothing further."

Next, Williams called me to the stand. He had me explain to the court why I was dressed in sweats during the interview. I informed the court what happened that day, and about my illness. I then talked about my five shootings that were all deemed appropriate. And you best believe

## The Fix; I am Somebody; A National Problem

Judge Clendenen was not pleased when I informed the court that my personnel file had gone missing. He knew that was no coincidence, with the SWAT selection process taking place at the exact same time.

I testified about my previous SWAT training, and the Blackwater SWAT course I had just taken. I proudly told the court about the SWAT commander's course qualifying me to lead a SWAT team as well. Judge Clendenen was seen taking notes. I was sure the city's decision to shut down the newly formed SWAT team backfired. Judge Clendenen asked a few questions, clearly not fooled by the city's latest ploy, or excuses.

The last question had me thinking long and hard. I knew the answer but had to make sure people understood me clearly. Their question was if I would be willing to go through the new SWAT testing process under Chief Norwood. He was in the early stages of forming a new SWAT team. To my complete astonishment, Norwood was going to allow D.C. Franks to oversee the new SWAT team selection process again! Norwood knew full well what Franks was all about, yet he selected him anyway? Suddenly, I had an uncontrollable urge for my favorite snack, Oreos.

"Sergeant Bailey, would you be willing to reapply for the new SWAT team?" I chose my words very carefully. "Your Honor, with all due respect, **no**! I earned my position on the team the first go-around. And for the Chief to allow Franks to be involved in the next SWAT team process is an insult. That tells me a lot about him. No thank you." Judge Clendenen had a pleasant expression in response to my answer. The hearing was then concluded.

The ruling came down shortly thereafter. The words that stood out in the decision were crystal, "Sergeant Bailey's first burden of proof was to establish a prima facie case of discrimination. Sergeant Bailey did so." It went on to say 'Deputy Chief Franks' thin and conflicting excuses for his failure to recommend Sergeant Bailey to the SWAT team was troubling. Preferential treatment was afforded to Officer Jersey."

This was the first case that identified a supervisor from the Bridgeport Police Department with discriminatory behavior. It was a major blow to Franks and perhaps the city. He would be forever linked and identified as someone who treated blacks discriminatorily. The court also ruled on my refusal to participate in the second SWAT team process. I knew by declining to take part in the second series of tests, it would prevent me from being awarded damages. I couldn't have cared less. It wasn't about money, it was the principle. I had a ruling that I wouldn't have traded for all the tea in China, Britain and Hong Kong.

The city fought like hell to have the ruling vacated. I made one thing clear to Attorney Williams. "Whatever it costs, whatever it takes, no matter how much I have to spend, that ruling has to stand." I was ready to pay any amount needed to maintain Franks' new title for what he really was. Several months later, after repeated attempts from the city, the ruling stood.

Back at the police department, many officers including those who didn't care much for me, were shaking their heads. They had to comment, "Wow Sergeant Bailey, you beat him. You beat Deputy Chief Franks." Some had heard that at the hearing I put Chief Norwood down for his feeble attempts to make Franks look blameless. My answer to them was simple, "Just because someone is black doesn't mean they represent black people."

After the court ruling I turned my attention back to the union. They were dragging their feet on my request to resign, and continued to take union dues. I was finished with their defiance. They would understand a judge. The Right to Work Foundation received notice from me and took them to court. It cost the union a lot of money and certainly hurt their arrogant pride. They ultimately conceded and let me out.

## The Fix; I am Somebody; A National Problem

It was a time for change. I needed the Guardians, as a group, to resign from the union. If I could convince them to leave, we would become an organization known not to be toyed with. Once the union saw members, and more importantly dues, going out the window, they would be more receptive to our rights. I was sure of it.

I called an emergency meeting. As expected, the membership needed time to think about it. They were afraid, and I completely understood why. Their questions were, "How long would it be before the union would get back at us? If we quit, will they really fight for us, even though the law requires them to?" They didn't want to be put in that position. Could I blame them?

Before concluding the meeting, the membership was told I contacted the Reverend Al Sharpton in New York. With all the issues going on, I wanted to do something to get the city's attention. What we were experiencing was a national problem. It was time to push that envelope. I didn't tell the membership why he was coming, right away. I wanted those rumors to fly, and they did.

The city got wind that Sharpton was coming to town. They figured I invited him to expose what they were doing to us. The city was feeling the heat of Sharpton's impending arrival, so I saw no need to tell them the real reason he was coming. Let 'em sweat.

Some of the Guardians were concerned about Sharpton. They even questioned how I knew him. It was no secret I had been assigned to provide security for Sharpton years earlier by the East End Baptist Church where he was a guest preacher. After the assignment, he and I spoke and took a few pictures. Sharpton was controversial but had America's attention when it came to the struggles of African Americans. What many overlooked was that he was an excellent preacher too.

Truth be told, Sharpton was a good speaker and draw for any event. The truth was he was coming to help us raise

## No Black Heroes

money for students in Bridgeport. He was going to be the keynote for our yearly awards banquet. We were about to honor members of the community and Guardian police officers. The proceeds would be used for children's school supplies. With the banquet in the planning stages, all that was left was to observe the reaction the city would have, thinking Sharpton was coming for Norwood and company. And it was enjoyable.

As Guardians president, I still had more pressing issues to deal with. The Guardians attempt at getting more minority officers on the job was failing. Future black candidates were being excluded at an alarming rate. During the selection process, it was always the same excuses, "They didn't pass the polygraph, they didn't pass the background check, or they had a record," usually a minor offense. It was shameful to have a class of 30 recruits with only one or two African Americans, if that.

I spoke to Mrs. Rosa Correa of the Civil Service Commission. She was a member of the panel that heard the appeals of police candidates excluded during the hiring process. She couldn't tell me about each candidate but suggested I do some checking on the majority of rejections. What I discovered was an overabundance of denials due to minor traffic violations, not having steady employment, bad credit, and smoking marijuana within five years or less of the police tests.

I thought about the rejections. It seemed absurd to exclude prospective candidates from a police position because of bad credit, or not having steady employment. Not having a job was something statistically blacks experienced higher than any other race. How were you going to maintain good credit if you couldn't find a job? I would've been excluded on that one, years ago, myself! The traffic ticket exclusion was a far worse policy. I mean come on, can anyone say "Racial profiling?" The majority of people being stopped in America were blacks! We were rejecting people on the basis of a system that tolerated racial profiling? Frankly speaking, the policy on marijuana did make sense.

## The Fix; I am Somebody; A National Problem

It never ended. Denise from my church called after completing the testing process for police officer. She told me the psychiatrist rejected her because she was a single parent. I almost fell off my chair when she told me that. His thought process was, how could she be an officer, as a single parent, if an emergency came up? I thought it was a joke. "No Brother Bailey, he rejected me because I'm a single parent." "Denise, I don't know if your rejection appeal can be based on your being a woman, or being a single parent. I know one thing, he's wrong." I told her to call Attorney Thomas Bucci to take care of it. There was no doubt she was going to get paid on that one. Did the city hire the guy because he was cheap? Or were his marching orders to exclude certain individuals when he could? The elimination process was exhibiting an institutionalized system of rejection for blacks we had heard was ongoing nationwide. Sadly, Bridgeport was apparently a member of that club.

As I got off the elevator on the third floor, I spotted Chief Norwood, the union president, and D.C. Franks in deep discussion. Their sudden silence was deafening. It was time to rock the boat a bit. "I hope you will all come to the Guardians awards banquet. The Reverend Sharpton will be our guest speaker." Not one word from them. I gave them a pleasant smile as I walked by.

With me confirming Sharpton coming to town, many officers dared to ask why. "Oh, it's just a community event." It was the truth, but it drove the rumors to new heights. That's when I received a call from Police Commissioner David Hall. He was the newly elected president of the board. Commissioner Hall made it a point to check with Guardians to see how things were going. He was the only one in that position who did. Anything he could do on racial issues, he would address, and then some. Curiously, his intervening at times seemed hard for him. I wasn't exactly sure why, at the time. "Sergeant Bailey, I want to meet with you to discuss a few things. Will you meet with me and a few important people from the city?" "I would be honored, Commissioner."

## No Black Heroes

At the meeting, several from the community were in attendance, including Chief Norwood. That was a first. He never took the time to meet with us before. The meeting was a large contingent of African Americans with concern on their faces. Commissioner Hall began to speak, "Sergeant Bailey, we are concerned about why you have the Reverend Sharpton coming to Bridgeport. That's why we asked to meet with you." Although I knew who was really worried, I asked Commissioner Hall why anyone would be concerned about the Reverend Sharpton. Always direct, Commissioner Hall said, "That's why we're here."

Everyone looked disturbed, except Chief Norwood. He was busy looking busy, toying with his cell phone. "Commissioner, the Guardians have an enormous amount of racial concerns with the Bridgeport Police Department. As the Guardians President, I have my hands full." Chief Norwood looked up from his phone to say he didn't cater to any one group of people, and he thought that he'd made that clear on his arrival. He had a brazen tone as he professed he wasn't going to apologize for his position on the Guardians. My words were sharp, "I'm not asking you for anything, and don't want your apology, alright?" Commissioner Hall interrupted, "Sergeant Bailey, we're concerned about your reasoning behind Reverend Sharpton coming here." I decided to end their worries. "Commissioner, he is coming here to promote my organization and our community event, nothing else." The chief suddenly decided it was time to leave, got up and excused himself.

After Norwood left, I spoke more directly, "I know Chief Norwood's father, and he's a great man. I don't understand his son. He seems offended by the Guardians. We can't speak to him about racism or equality?" I summed up the meeting by telling everyone we didn't want anything from Chief Norwood. "Commissioner, all we were looking for from the Chief was someone to level the playing field." I made it clear that was something we were not going to get under Norwood's command. With that, Commissioner Hall concluded the meeting. He felt more confident knowing we were

## The Fix; I am Somebody; A National Problem

not bringing Sharpton to Bridgeport to go after Norwood or the department.

Breathing heavily, Commissioner Hall pulled me to the side. He absolutely stunned me when he confided he was dying from cancer. I tried to give him some spiritual uplifting by telling him he didn't have the right to say when he would leave, and that God would say when his time would come. Ever the unwavering one, "Well, when God comes, I want you to do me a favor." Hall was a good man, and I was curious as to what he needed from me.

Commissioner Hall was aware about the ruling against Franks, and he was very disturbed by it. He found it unconscionable to have someone in a command position do the things Franks had done. I was in awe that Commissioner Hall cared so much about a discrimination matter. With hardly any strength left in him, he wanted to make sure I would address it on his behalf, with his fellow commissioners. He then requested a second favor, that I visit him at Arlington cemetery when he passed away. If only Americans could have heard the sincerity of his last plea to me. The man was dying of cancer, and he was worried about race issues in the department!

The night of the awards banquet came. Yvette had made the arrangements for food, tickets and programs, and I handled the awards and money. We were honoring Bishop Kenneth Moales Sr. and Bishop J.C. White for their community involvement. Both had built two significant places of worship in Bridgeport that greatly benefited the community. We also honored the first black principal of Harding High, Carol Birks, and the first black councilwoman of Stratford, Emma Brooks. We thought it was important to honor several eighth-grade students for "most improved" in academics. We needed to know our kids, so the future has a chance.

The banquet was held at Mario Testa's restaurant. Testa was the Democratic town chairman for Bridgeport. He was considered a kingmaker for mayors and such in the city. He had no problem with Sharpton at his place. I think his comment was "Bring him on." It was ironic that Reverend Sharpton was about to speak at a place where so much political maneuvering had taken place.

Sharpton arrived and asked that I meet with him in the restaurant's office. He asked straight out, "Sergeant Bailey, I know we spoke on the phone, but how deep do you want me to go." "Reverend Sharpton, I'd like the community to know about police in this country, the Guardians, and what we as a community need to do in coming together." "Thank you, Brother Bailey, I'll get that point across."

He sat with all the honorees, until it was time to speak. People were ecstatic to see him. I asked if he was ready, and he walked confidently to the podium. Not a person in the restaurant made a sound. His opening statement set the tone, "When Brother Bailey asked me to come and speak today, I had no reservations about speaking to you on behalf of the Bridgeport Police officers. You see, it's not that I don't like the police. That's simply not true. What I don't like are the bad ones." Every officer there stood up and gave him a round of applause.

The community was in amazement at his speaking abilities. He didn't come to point a finger, or criticize anyone. He came to bring our community together. Sharpton showed a side many were not aware of, or what the media never acknowledged; he cared. By night's end, the Guardians were on the lips of every community member in Bridgeport. The churches spoke about our event, and even city officials had nothing but praise for Sharpton and our banquet. The kids who were honored, hung out with Sharpton, and took pictures with him. It was the proud moment I had yearned for, the Guardians were recognized as an asset to the community.

I had accomplished what I set out to do, get close to our community and make a difference. The money we took in was used to buy school supplies for children and food for the homeless. The membership was proud and holding

## The Fix; I am Somebody; A National Problem

their heads up, with more attending our meetings than ever before. Guardian members that we honored accepted their certificates with pride and had them placed in their personnel files. We now had one significant advantage in our struggle towards equality, a community that supported us, and we them.

Marvin Gaye said it best, "What's goin' on?" The news broke on the criminal case for Officer Brian Baines, which had now stretched into two years running. His case went to trial and a jury found Baines not guilty of the most serious charges, opting for a lesser charge of reckless endangerment. When someone tries to kill people, I'd be willing to gamble that person would be headed to prison. I had to wonder who was on that jury and if they even cared what took place in an inner-city project.

The community was outraged. Baines, who had shot randomly at residents in the project, was sentenced to one year in jail. Hold up! Let's rewind that. His sentence was actually suspended. Officer Baines would not have to serve any time. Many found it hard to believe that anyone, especially a cop, could get away with such outlandish conduct. Black officers were saying it best, "If that were one of us we would be under the jail." I countered with my own wit, "Haven't you heard, the prison population in America is all us. We own the joint!"

Back at the department, the rumors were mounting about Chief Norwood. He hadn't even been the chief two years and was fast becoming a hated man with all officers, black and white. Why? Then came the call I thought was a joke, someone broke into and urinated in Chief Norwood's house! Not sure if it was true or not, I contacted Wendell Randolph from city yard. He said the city sent him and a few workers to repair Norwood's home. Chief Norwood's car had been keyed, and trash had been thrown around his front yard, too. His door and its framework had to be repaired. Wendell confirmed what I had heard.

## No Black Heroes

The inside scoop on Norwood's problems came from my contact Billy, who was still connected with the union. It seemed Chief Norwood had refused to honor a grievance the union won. The ruling from arbitration said he had to shut down a special unit he started when he first arrived. He flat-out refused to honor the grievance award. Those guys were hardcore union cops. They hated me for resigning from the union, but they hated Chief Norwood more, for ignoring their award.

I actually felt sorry for him. He was still a fellow officer, so I went to see him. "Chief, the Guardians will give you protection if you need it. What's going on with you isn't right and we don't support it." He seemed surprised by my offer but declined. When he first arrived, I tried telling him that as long as we could all remember, there were significant racial issues to be addressed at the BPD. He wouldn't listen. Doc Hill commented, "Norwood hung out with these white boys. Now look what they're doing to him. He never invited us to any of his cookouts. That's what he gets!" "Wow, Doc. Hope I don't ever make you mad at me."

Meanwhile, Mayor Fabrizi's term came to an end. He didn't seek reelection, opting to go back to teaching. According to the news, his problems with drugs were over. The new mayor voted in was Bill Finch. Just about the time Finch arrived, without so much as a hint, Chief Norwood resigned! He took a chief's job in Richmond, Virginia. I believed he'd had enough, after experiencing the hate from the officers he chose to surround himself with. He did say to me before leaving that white officers were so threatening to him at a union golfing event, he was certain some of them were mouthing the word "nigger" as he drove in. I wasn't surprised by his assertion.

Soon after Norwood's departure, rumors surfaced that D.C. Franks was being considered for the chief's position. Over my dead body, and his too, if need be. As the Guardians president, my duties were clear; we could not allow Franks to be in charge of the department. I contacted Mayor Finch and requested a meeting with him. I provided

## The Fix; I am Somebody; A National Problem

him the court ruling that chastised Franks' handling on matters pertaining to black officers. That same week, I received a letter from the mayor informing me Franks was not being considered for the position of chief. The city decided to appoint someone as the interim chief until they could appoint someone permanently. Deputy Chief Joseph Gaudett was chosen. Gaudett came on the job with me, and it was still our hope, after so many chiefs, that he could turn things completely around on racial issues. So far, no one else had.

The National Black Law Enforcement Officers were back in touch with the Guardians with some discouraging news. A census was conducted and police departments around the country were experiencing a rise in racial incidents with their officers, as well as a severe shortage of black supervision. As a nation, there seemed to be a lack of appreciation for, or push for, diversity in our police departments nationally. To add more insult to injury, there was an increase in terminations of black officers. Reportedly, many were dismissed on frivolous charges.

Then the news we all feared would come one day, did. Officer Christopher Dorner of the Los Angeles Police Department (LAPD) turned into national news. Dorner was a black officer who asserted the LAPD refused to investigate his complaints of racism and police abuse by white officers. Dorner believed the LAPD unjustly terminated him because of his complaints. An enraged Dorner declared war on the LAPD, targeting various members of the police department. The news reported Dorner was responsible for four murders and three shootings resulting in serious injuries. Most of the victims Dorner sought out were police and their families.

Officer Dorner was the subject of the largest manhunt in LAPD history. In the end, he died in a fire, a cabin fire where he had been hiding. He burned to death during a raid meant to capture him. Authorities later reported he died of a self-inflicted gunshot wound. Officers who spoke

## No Black Heroes

about Dorner said there was no way the LAPD was going to capture him. He was to be taken out on site.

Black officers in Bridgeport heard about Dorner but were reluctant to speak on it. With so much hate circulating, my curiosity got the best of me. I was curious to know how they felt, and asked a few, to get some insight on their perspectives. One officer said it best, "Dorner's actions were shameful but almost expected." He obviously identified with how Dorner's frustrations turned to rage. Evidently, the constant exposure to biased treatment of African American officers was taking its toll.

It was a bit alarming. Some officers felt Dorner's shootings were, in a way, a sense of vindication. None of them were happy about the loss of lives, especially considering the injuries to police and their families. Obviously, that was not the answer to a national problem. The consensus was, "We complain and complain, but they never listen!" To me, they accurately implied; Dorner was partially the result of the ignorance and denial embedded in police departments nationwide. One officer, obviously livid, spoke out with a vengeance, "Maybe this will force people to see what's goin' on here and what cops like us are really going through!" The Dorner saga gave America something to think about, but for how long? The question was, "Will it happen again?" I prayed it wouldn't.

Chapter 26

# COURT IS OUT; UNION DECEIT; HOPE?

The department announced they were having a lieutenant's test. The Guardians started holding study groups again to prepare for the test. With the years waning and only two black captains left in the department, Captain Roderick Porter offered to tutor us. He questioned, role played, and tested us weekly. I knew it was important to climb in rank, so we all studied hard.

The test was a two-day process. Many of the African American Sergeants who took the test were waiting for the results. A few weeks later, the announcement came. Five of us were in the top 15 on the list. "Congratulations Bailey, you're going to be a lieutenant." "Thanks Captain Porter, we did it thanks to you."

Happiness was then greeted with disappointment. A once reliable means of addressing discrimination abruptly came to an end. The federal court, which had dealt with 30 years of discrimination at the Bridgeport Police Department, was a few months away from ending its oversight.

## No Black Heroes

The union, city, the Hispanic Society, and a new group of detectives called by many the "White Six" had done their damage. The court was completely overburdened with motions and a conglomerate of groups attacking the process. They finally won out.

The city made a public statement that the federal court had cost the taxpayers millions of dollars in court intervention. What the taxpayers didn't hear was that money was spent fighting a process that shouldn't have been necessary to begin with. What's more, the city could have embraced the changes recommended years before, to address the problems that only got worse. What had Guardians snickering were new claims the "White Six" made insisting they had been harmed by reverse discrimination, over the years. They alleged that, under the Remedy Order process, the federal court catered to black officers, costing them money, positions, pain and suffering.

I called a special Guardians meeting to inform the membership we were close to the end. Everyone was furious. They wanted to keep fighting, as did I, but it was just a matter of time. In a moment of boldness, the Guardians membership signed a petition in the form of a motion. We notified the court that the union had intentionally interfered in the court process, undermining our quest for equality. Acknowledging our displeasure, at that point, I knew it was too little too late.

I was certain the union would retaliate. A few days later, we received papers. The union was seeking monetary sanctions. They wanted us to pay them for our taking a stand? We understood their intention; they embodied a group of vicious dogs hell-bent on keeping us in our place. How I wished every officer in America could have seen what happened to us because we chose not to bow down to them. This was the very union that was supposed to represent **all** officers.

The union's antics were meant to divide the Guardians. Not about to back down, I personally filed a motion request-

## Court is Out; Union Deceit; Hope?

ing protection from them. They responded with a second motion demanding we withdraw our complaint, and in return, they would withdraw theirs. The nerve of the union was absolutely ludicrous. What next, perhaps they'd have us bend over! Even so, the Guardians still refused to resign from the union. "If you want to get their attention, quit. Money talks."

I reviewed the additional motions they had filed and saw no need to respond. Judge Clendenen was extremely wise and would see right through their Gestapo tactics. He was not about to grant any sanctions against us for exercising our right to be heard. Back at the department, I continued to stand my ground peering through those hard, cold union faces. Too bad there were no more locker room visits to settle our differences. I would have loved to get a bunch of them down there.

Captain Chapman called with more bad news. "Bailey, the housing unit is shutting down. We ran out of federal funds." He wanted to know if there was somewhere I would prefer to be assigned. "Yeah Capt, the union office." I told him how sorry I was about the community detail ending when so many people needed us. He let me know how proud he was of my making a difference in a place no other officer had committed to. He was aware of the union attacking Guardians too. "Bailey, I just want you to know, we appreciate what you're doing. Guardians know what a strain this has been on you and your family. We're proud of what you've done." "Thanks, Captain."

The federal court called an informal hearing with the union, Hispanic Society, Attorney Wenzel for the city, and the Guardians' law firm Koskoff and Beider. Attorney Torre was there representing the "White Six." I was in attendance to observe the end of an era. The court made its announcement and ordered additional suggestions for improvements, before it would remove itself from the department permanently.

## No Black Heroes

As expected, the complaints filed by the union against Guardians were ignored. The court proceeded to deal with other matters. The first order of business was the notification that all outstanding complaints by Guardian members were to be closed out. They would not be heard. I guess they had to cut the cord somewhere, knowing it was a never-ending story. Judge Clendenen, who had dealt with 30 years of complaints, orders and rulings, was thanked for his service. Although he was always met with resistance, he remained firm in his commitment to opportunities on behalf of all officers, no matter their color.

Judge Janet Bond Arterton oversaw the closing of the court oversight. The Hispanic Society made their way out of the hearing without comment. Attorney Karen Torre, of course, was stomping around making a lot of noise about her clients, and the demands for justice. The court knew what she really wanted, to go back 30 years and make a mockery of the process. On that note, Guardians happily conceded an end to the court intervention. We took great pleasure in knowing the closeout undermined Torre's ambitions and kept the "White Six" from being paid. Judge Arterton calmly ignored Torre's rants. Her few moments of fame were over. Happy trails.

At the conclusion of the court process, I was called back to speak before Judge Arterton. She asked about my thoughts on the Remedy Order being removed from Bridgeport. Attorney Betsey Edwards was there for the city and objected to my speaking. Over her objections, Judge Arterton wanted to hear my position on the court ending the process that addressed racism for so many years.

"Your Honor, thank you for allowing me to speak here today. First of all, I would love to see the court remain at the police department. We still have so many problems facing us. But the truth is, after 30 years of court intervention, the Bridgeport Police Department never really changed. That tells me one thing, no matter how long the court remains, our racial problems are something that just won't go away, at least not in my lifetime, Your Honor." I paused,

## Court is Out; Union Deceit; Hope?

and then continued, "I say that because at 50-some years of age, this is a problem that I've seen since childhood, and it remains to this day. With that being said, how can we expect the Bridgeport Police Department to change what society has failed to do in a lifetime? It's time for us to work out our differences on our own, if we can. That is my hope, Your Honor. Thank you."

Attorney Edwards was surprised to hear those words from someone who fought so intensely with the city over the years. Judge Arterton looked over the bench at me, "Judge Clendenen was right. He said you were very forthright and honest. It was an honor to have you speak here today as this longstanding proceeding comes to a close." I looked at Judge Arterton, knowing it would be my last time in her court, "Thank you, Your Honor for all this court has tried to do for the city of Bridgeport." Sadly, that was it, and it had come to an end.

As part of the agreement to end the federal court oversight, the city agreed to provide money to the Guardians for recruitment. In addition, a new position was created to help the department improve on racial issues. They were to hire an assistant chief. The other stipulation was the city would promote a few more minority lieutenants to the rank of captain, from the existing list.

They had two minority lieutenants on the list the city could promote. It was comical, they selected Lieutenant Rivera. He, like Captain Trujillo, professed that he would not use his being Latino to climb in the ranks. It was no coincidence they were best buds. Lieutenant Rivera, who reportedly denied his heritage for God knows how long, suddenly became a humble Latino again. It was a miracle!

It was sadly no surprise the city stopped short of making Lieutenant Daniels a captain. He was the very next one in line to be promoted. The community was in an uproar over his not being promoted, but there was nothing we could do. Shrewdly, the city kept certain officers from applying for the new assistant chief position the court ordered. A new requirement was implemented; anyone applying for the position had to have a certain amount of time on the job at the rank of captain or above. Most departments nationally allowed lieutenants to apply for command positions, but not Bridgeport. The message was clear, "We don't want Daniels or soon-to-be-appointed-to-lieutenant Bailey to even think about applying."

Captain Porter was the only one who could have taken the test, but he would have lost his time towards his pension if he did. Captain Chapman, to my surprise was retiring. In the end, they chose Captain Lynn Kerwin to fill the position of assistant chief. The city touted they fulfilled its obligation to the court by promoting a minority by way of a female. Hey, we didn't have a problem with Lynn, she was a wonderful person. It was how the city manipulated what it agreed to in federal court.

The union was ecstatic they'd been a part of removing the federal court oversight. Their attorney sent me a letter of confirmation which was not the norm. I considered it an unprofessional cheap shot that deserved a response. I remembered how infatuated he was with Attorney Torre the last day of court. She had just won a Supreme Court decision for the white firefighters in New Haven. Obviously, the union attorney behavior was a result of her sudden stardom. So it was payback time. "Attorney Frampton, I received your letter, which was unprofessional, at best. While on the subject of professionalism, may I point out yours? It was embarrassing to see you all over Attorney Torre like she was some kind of rock star. You were so close to her at times, I thought you were going to trip over her shoelaces." The rest of the letter was intended to point out one thing, he should stop contacting me. And he did.

My promotion to lieutenant was days away. Assistant Chief Kerwin (A.C.) recommended me for a position over Tactical, working with the FBI. Captain A.J. Perez, who was running Tactical, loved the idea, and so did D.C. Armeno who oversaw the division. A.C. Kerwin returned to let me know the chief thought it was a bad idea. I figured D.C.

## Court is Out; Union Deceit; Hope?

Franks was behind the chief's denial, still licking his wounds over his loss to me in court. No matter, my solace was that ruling. Franks would never be a chief in Bridgeport, or anywhere else.

A.C. Kerwin returned, "Sergeant Bailey, we have an opening in professional standards. You could have your own command if you want it." "No problem Chief, I would be honored to work for you." My promotion was that Friday, and the next Guardians meeting would be my last as their president. "It's been a challenging two years. We had two community awards banquets; the Reverend Sharpton was our guest speaker, cookouts, scholarship drives, and several fundraisers. We fed the homeless, and bought children school supplies and toys for Christmas. I hope I did you proud. I want to thank all of you for allowing me to serve as your president."

They tried to convince me to run again. I had to decline, after having gone through so much. Oddly, at the meeting was a small assembly of officers who nominated Officer Amos Thomas for Guardians president. It was curious how he came out of nowhere, and with a contingent in tow, he was seeking the presidency. One month later, he and his people were elected into office. Thomas sudden ascending into office was well-planned. I had a bad feeling about it.

The news that had circulated the next day was ridiculous, but not unexpected. Officer Jeff Huntsman received a written warning for choking a woman in booking. What's the penalty for shooting an unarmed man, a day without donuts? I had some unfinished business to take care of as the outgoing president of the Guardians. Huntsman's penalty was on my list of things to do.

Before I could make an appointment to see the chief on the Huntsman dilemma, A.C. Kerwin called me into her office. Kerwin was tasked with minority issues and police abuse, and was very upset. She handed me the DVD on the Officer Huntsman choking incident and asked me to review it. What I saw made me sick to my stomach. He was clearly

## No Black Heroes

strangling a woman, and had to be pulled away from her three times. I returned the DVD, gave Kerwin my opinion, and thanked her. He should have been referred to the Board of Police Commissioners for what he did, period.

There was no doubt that a huge miscarriage of justice had taken place. Huntsman's case lingered for well over a year, and all he got was a written warning? To keep from exploding, I joked aloud by the union office door, "Who reviewed Huntsman's DVD, Ray Charles?" I then went upstairs to Chief Gaudett's office and asked to speak with him. He looked concerned; my reputation wasn't the best when it came to those in command.

First, I thanked him for allowing me to work with him. I told him I'd always be upfront with him. He then looked at me with some concern. So I got to the point, "Chief, Huntsman received a written warning for choking a woman in handcuffs. Not to mention, his case was delayed for over a year. And we both know a written warning only stays in an officer's file for a year, and then it's removed. It will be like it never happened. That's not right, chief." He told me the Huntsman matter was handled by someone else before it got to him. I needed to drive home a point. I told him, when I was younger, I'd been beaten; choked and left unconscious by an officer at the very spot Trotter had been abused by Huntsman. You could see his shock at what I was telling him. I had hoped my point was made, "When does it end?"

Chief Gaudett apologized for what happened to me. "It's not your fault, Chief. That was years ago." I repeated my disapproval of the Huntsman matter then changed the subject. I wanted him to know I'd be meeting with the FBI. He was curious about the meeting but simply said I should be careful. We concluded the meeting with me telling him I'd do all I could towards making a difference in the department.

I met with FBI Special Agents Parcels and Kassnow at the Bridgeport office. They seemed curious as to what I had

### Court is Out; Union Deceit; Hope?

to say. One of my last commitments to the Guardians was to inform the FBI of what it was like working at the Bridgeport Police Department. More precisely, what was going on there. Guardians felt the place was out of control. I laid it all out for them.

I began by telling them about the beatings minorities suffered at the hands of officers. The K-5 was no longer in existence but their legacy continued with other irate cops. Agent Parcels was given the dates, times, and names of officers we felt were hurting our community. We discussed five officers who got into a brawl at a bar in Stamford where a civilian got hurt. To my surprise, they knew about it, which caught me off guard. I wondered what else they were looking into, and if they could do something about the problems we faced.

I then discussed a case involving Officer Dan Peters who was involved in a traffic accident while intoxicated. Officer Peters left the scene of the accident and called his girlfriend, Sergeant Ann Cotton. "Agent Parcels, several officers were accused of making the accident look like it was a stolen car, under Sergeant Cotton's directions." The whole thing had all the markings of an insurance scam meant to protect Peters' drunk driving. The police department seemed to be sitting on it. I then told them about Sergeant Cotton, who from all accounts, was the catalyst behind the attempted coverup.

It was important Agent Parcels understood why Sergeant Cotton was a concern. He was informed officers had nicknamed her the Black Widow, and why. The rumors were she got her name from sleeping around in the department, then destroying the person she had slept with. "Agent Parcels, Guardians couldn't care less who this woman sleeps with. However, we are concerned with her taking over an entire shift by her possibly seducing lieutenants, captains, and God knows who else on the job." Her own fellow officers were giving me information, upset in how she had been treating black officers under her command! That was our real concern. Her sudden rise in power, coupled

417

with the reports of mistreatment shortly thereafter fueled even more speculation on her new title, "The Black Widow." It was important Guardians made an official report with the FBI, in case we had to take matters further. The city just seemed to maintain a blind eye on our concerns.

I was about to conclude the meeting when it turned in a different direction. They began to ask me questions about Deputy Chief Honis. He had been suspended from the department while an investigation was taking place. Another officer had implicated him in an old murder case. Officers mentioned something about a coverup. I really didn't have any information on it, other than what I had heard. We discussed some old tales that had lingered since before I came on the job. It was said Honis hated prostitution early in his career and had murdered a few of the girls. It was all speculative, spy story stuff to me.

Unsure of how much they knew, I informed them on how the rumors came about; Officer George Lawson. The news reported that Officer Lawson informed the court he was investigating Honis on the murders of several prostitutes when he was framed for his involvement in drugs, then fired. It was a long time ago, and to my knowledge, no one came anywhere close to proving Honis had murdered anyone. But the rumors made good for, "What if some day we find bodies in his yard?" kind of stuff.

The problems the membership was concerned about had been reported. I got up, shook the agents' hands, and they gave me their cards. I sent notice to the Guardians about the meeting with the FBI and wished them well with their new president. I still had concerns about the new incoming regime, but my obligations as their president had all been fulfilled.

Chapter 27

## Cops Gone Wild; Hey Nigger; A Human Skull

A week hadn't gone by since my meeting with the FBI when the news started coming in. Officer John Rose was leaving the Bridgeport Police Department because of the Black Widow. I couldn't believe it. Rose had just been hired! He told the guys on the job he had to leave because Sergeant Cotton called his wife and told her what they had done. Adding insult to injury, Officer Rose and his wife were trying to work things out and happened to be shopping at the mall when Cotton saw them and started a fight with his wife. I tried to talk him out of resigning, but he said he had to leave or lose his wife.

The Black Widow struck again. The stories were intensifying. Her fame had grown to sleeping with married man, and especially those in command. Sleeping with supervisors actually made sense, because no one could challenge her authority. Clearly, any married man who sleeps around would want things quiet, and that would go double for police supervisors. Cotton was a skilled manipulator. She was even heard saying how she felt forced to spend time with

## No Black Heroes

certain ranking officers. She had that "victim of sexual harassment" complaint angle down pat. It was no wonder they refused to confront her abuse of authority.

Let's see. Officer Huntsman choked a woman in handcuffs, nothing. Officer Peters was in a drunken driving accident, and then it was covered up, again nothing. Oh yeah, officers sleeping around with each other, nothing. And last but not least, Officer Rose was forced to resign due to a sergeant who would not leave him and his wife alone; nothing, *nothing*, **nothing**! No one would've believed how the place operated, at times I didn't.

It was time to concentrate on a new chapter in my life. I was determined to move up in the chain of command. It was a goal most said was impossible for me. Officers laughed when I told them someday I'd run my own department. The question was, who would hire me after all the lawsuits and complaints I filed? I was still determined.

The time had come. I was sworn in as a lieutenant and celebrated with Yvette. My daughter Ashley pinned the badge on me. Curiously, Ashley looked a bit pale and tired. She hadn't been around for a while, so I figured it was as she had said, a case of nerves. It was hard to believe I was a lieutenant assigned to my own office in Professional Standards. Time had taken its toll, and created not-so-fond memories of the things I'd confronted in my career. It was a time most officers on the job knew nothing about my confrontations. And those who came on with me were winding down, looking to retire. Imagine my surprise; new officers were looking up to me. One even came by the office and took my picture. "What's that for?" "Hey lieutenant, no one will ever believe you're inside on a desk job." "Wise ass." We both laughed.

The phone rang, it was Officer Rod Duvall. "Lieutenant Bailey, we need your help in patrol. The Black Widow is making life miserable for us, especially the minority officers. I'm offended by her conduct." Officer Duvall said Sergeant Cotton was a regular at disrespecting black officers. He said

## Cops Gone Wild; Hey Nigger; A Human Skull

she was constantly putting them down and scolding them. "Lieutenant, please don't let her know I called you."

I did some checking and was amazed to learn Cotton was taking the shift commander's personal police SUV the entire shift. No one drove the commander's SUV but him. But there she was cruising around the city and giving orders over the radio like she owned the joint. Was she doing him, too? If she was, I hoped she closed her eyes at least. When it came to the word ugly, that guy was considered uuugly.

The next day, I was about to look into more accusations about Sergeant Cotton when the bad news arrived. One of our officers involved with Cotton shot and killed himself. Officer Tom Ricks committed suicide. The gossip was that Ricks found out Sergeant Cotton had been cheating on him. Others were saying Cotton just had a kid, but it belonged to another cop, not Ricks. Officers were upset and blamed her for Ricks' death. All you could hear was, "Fucking Black Widow, she killed him."

Officer Ricks was a good cop and friend. How I wished I could've spoken to him before he took his life. Amazingly, the funeral turned out to be an event few would have expected. I thought I'd seen it all. We were there to pay our respects to a fellow officer when a fight broke out. Officer Dorothy Kims was at the funeral yelling at Sergeant Cotton, and right over Rick's coffin! The argument drifted away from his coffin towards the door. I mean come on, how disrespectful can you be on such a sad day? Officer Kims was outside the funeral home, but you could still hear her, "Stay away from my husband, bitch. Why would you want him? He's not a cop! You killed Ricks. That's not good enough for you?" Kims was telling anyone who would listen how the Black Widow was spinning her web outside the police department. "It's not enough you fucked all the cops? Now you want the husbands of your fellow officers too? Should I hide my dog next?" I quietly walked out of the funeral home after saying a prayer. It was a most shameful way of burying one of our own.

## No Black Heroes

After the funeral, officers were openly calling Sergeant Cotton the Black Widow, and some things I didn't care to repeat. When she returned from her hiatus, if she heard about the title, it didn't seem to bother her. She continued to run the shift like before, as if she owned it. To my disbelief, rumors had surfaced again. She had more officers lined up to date her! What in hell was wrong with those guys? Why would you sleep with someone you knew would be calling your wife? Perhaps they considered Cotton a challenge, like taming the beast or something. To me it was just plain stupid. I called my son and told him to hide. He couldn't figure out what my joke was all about.

Officer Katie Wright called. Things were getting worse. Sergeant Cotton had just talked down to her in front of all the officers. "Lieutenant Bailey, I asked Sergeant Cotton a question. She told me to shut up, not to ask her anything and to get out on the road." Officer Wright said she felt totally disrespected. I knew for a fact no one dared talked down to Katie. She was a well-built female athlete who took great pride in being respected by others. When I say well built, I mean someone who could kick a big man's butt without breaking a sweat. Sergeant Cotton picked the wrong person to mess with. "Lieutenant Bailey, if she keeps it up, she's going to need a medic." Officer Wright made it clear she was going to knock Sergeant Cotton out. "Wright, calm down. I'll look into this. I hear the department is about to bring her up on charges for the Officer Peters accident turned car theft thing. If that turns out to be an insurance scam, she may be finished here anyway." Katie was blunt, "I can't take much more of this witch. She better get her ass out of here."

I asked Officer Wright if anyone else heard Sergeant Cotton talk down to her. She said Officer May did. We all knew May well, that was a dead end. She talked a good game about white officers this, that, and what she would do. Truth be told, she was not about to step up to the plate on race issues. In all my years there, she had never taken such a stand. We needed someone who would support Wright's version of what happened, otherwise she had no case.

## Cops Gone Wild; Hey Nigger; A Human Skull

The next day, Officer Wright called again. She said the Black Widow was in lineup telling all the officers, "When you have a problem, you bring it to me. If you don't, then all I can say is you will have problems with me." Katie said Sergeant Cotton was looking directly at her when she made her little speech. Wright wondered if I had told anyone she called me. "No, I didn't." That's when Katie said something I knew she was capable of, "If she keeps it up, I'm going to put her ass down hard." Her frustrations were obviously setting in.

Disgusted, Katie told me something even I had trouble digesting. "Hey lieutenant, just so you know, the Black Widow wore a pink t-shirt at lineup. It had writing on it that read, 'Snitches gets Stitches.'" "Are you telling me Sergeant Cotton wasn't in uniform at lineup? And she made those remarks looking at you, while wearing a t-shirt with a threat on it?" Officer Wright's response was more than I could digest. "Yes Lieutenant. And for the record, Deputy Chief (D.C.) Pol Hong was there too. I saw a huge problem evolving. Everyone knew D.C. Hong had a reputation of hating black officers, and some say a thing for Sergeant Cotton.

I asked Katie to contact our new Guardians president, Officer Thomas. He needed to know what was going on, and of Sgt. Cotton's outlandish behavior. It was obvious Hong was going along with anything Cotton wanted. I mean come on, wearing a pink t-shirt to lineup? She evidently had full control over Hong. Please, somebody tell me she didn't sleep with him too. Jesus, have mercy.

Lieutenant Tom Lula was highly respected by all his officers, and a good friend. He was upset with the way Sergeant Cotton had been treating black officers as well. You knew you're in trouble when "your own" don't like what you're doing. What Tom told me next really confirmed what I already believed; it was Comedy Central rather than a police department. "Bailey, you won't believe what happened the other night. Sergeant Cotton said she was hungry for some White Castle hamburgers. So D.C. Hong jumped up and ran to his police car. He took Cotton to White Castle in New York!" Insanity! Tom said not only did they go for hamburgers in New York, but they had the nerve to bring a bag back to patrol, in case anyone wanted some. Lula's next comment was pretty much what I suspected, "That's how desperate and stupid Hong is for a woman's attention." I was bent over in laughter, "Thanks, Tom. I'm on this."

The Office of Internal Affairs (OIA) knew about the trip to New York in a Bridgeport Police vehicle and was conducting an investigation. It took no time for them to conclude it. D.C. Hong and Sergeant Cotton were not going to face department charges. I asked for the OIA report under the Freedom of Information Act. OIA determined there was no policy in place to address what they did. Great, I'll call my wife, take a police car and head to New York to catch a show and dinner. It's what I thought would be appropriate after reading that ridiculous report.

I called our newly elected Guardians president and asked if he could formally inquire about OIA's investigation. Officer Thomas said he would, but I never heard back from him. To make matters worse, Hong had been notified by someone in City Hall that I had requested the reports of his New York trip with Cotton for burgers. It was well known that Hong was someone who never took time to meet with any African American officers under his command. He hated us, and didn't seem to care much for Latinos either. The Hispanic Society made it clear they couldn't stand him either. I had no doubt he would be coming after me for inquiring about his trip to New York.

I called Thomas again, "Officer Thomas, you're our president. You really need to address several issues on behalf of the membership. Our black officers are under attack by the likes of the Sergeant Cotton, D.C. Franks, Hong. It's important we at least challenge them, so they don't keep attacking us." Officer Thomas had been the Guardians' president for several months. So far, he had been a no-show on anything we asked of him. He always said he was "working on something," but he never said what. Rumors

### Cops Gone Wild; Hey Nigger; A Human Skull

were flying amongst the membership he thought of himself as the most intelligent Guardians president ever. He always talked about his accomplishments, or how well he handled something. Problem was, we hadn't seen him do anything he claimed to have done.

I made the decision to meet with Mayor Finch, since Officer Thomas was a silent entity of sorts. During the meeting, we discussed Officer Wright's complaints and how the department was not taking out-of-control officers' behaviors seriously. I asked about the investigation regarding Sergeant Cotton and the accident turned car theft involving Officer Peters. He said it was still under investigation. After our meeting, I mailed a two-page report to him. It chronicled what we had discussed, including Sergeant Cotton wearing a pink t-shirt with the logo "Snitches get Stitches" at lineup, and her intimidation tactics with Officer Wright. In it, I also hypothetically asked him how D.C. Hong and Sergeant Cotton could cross state lines, to New York for lunch, on taxpayer dollars.

Not long afterwards, the news broke. Five officers were being charged for faking a car theft and using their positions as police officers to cover up a hit-and-run accident. Sergeant Cotton was the primary focus of the investigation. Regrettably, other officers had been ill-advised by her and faced departmental charges as well.

True to form, Hong came around with that look on his face. He reminded me of a spoiled brat looking to cause trouble the first chance he got. If looks could kill, I would've been a goner. I'm sure he thought I had forced the city to bring Sergeant Cotton up on charges. Truth was, it was something the Chief had OIA pursue. I just made sure the process wouldn't be postponed like so many cases before. Sergeant Cotton needed to stop harassing Officer Wright and other officers, with Hong looking the other way.

As always, when and if I had chance encounters with Hong, I'd speak to him with professionalism. "D.C. Hong, good morning." He'd turn his face abruptly and continue to walk, without saying a word. "Unprofessional little kamikaze." I think he heard my comment, turning back my way quickly. I kept walking, knowing the target was focused squarely on my back.

It had been several months of hearings for Sergeant Cotton and the other officers. While in patrol checking on rumors, I heard the guys talking up a storm. At first, I thought a decision had been handed down. "Hey Lieutenant, have you heard?" They were all smiles and excited about it. "Lieutenant Bailey, Detective Larry Shamus has a side job, he's a male escort. He's on a dating site advertising himself as Lorenzo the Hot 'N' Hung!" They were so proud to have a fellow officer working as an escort. One guy said he was going to contact Shamus. That was the job for him. I looked a little closer at the article. "Hey guys, did you read this? This advertisement is for men." "**What?!!!**" They all scrambled over to read the rest of the article. "Who's gonna retire and work as a gay escort?" Silence had taken over. There was no doubt that Shamus was going to face departmental charges for working an escort service. Gay or not, it was not a side job we were allowed to have. A few weeks later, he was gone. There was always something going on at the P.D.

Then the big news, the ruling came down. Sergeant Ann Cotton was ultimately suspended without pay and demoted to patrol officer. The Board of Police Commissioners decided she used her position inappropriately to help her boyfriend Peters with what should have been a simple accident report. Instead, she directed officers to make it look like a car theft. The other officers received various suspensions without pay, but far less than what she received.

When Sergeant Cotton returned, officers smiled to her face but secretly continued to despise her for Officer Rick's death. They wished she had been fired for what happened to him. A few people she trusted and confided in informed me she believed I was responsible for her suspension. I'm sure Hong also put that notion in her head after he found out I had checked on their White Castle caper. The good news was she had to hang up her pink t-shirt.

The case that was the insult of all insults to Guardians involved Officer Paul Patrick, a union representative. The membership called it to my attention. His problems were serious. He told the police department he was on union business quite a bit that year. During a routine check, it was discovered he had been on vacation during the times he should have been on union business. He missed about 100 days. Another officer had done the same thing years earlier but missed far less than Patrick. She was fired. I was sure he was going to face the same fate.

Officer Patrick was a close friend of the new union president, Sam Bowers. According to many who hated his mannerisms, Officer Bowers was an overweight slouch who took no pride in his appearance. He wore grubby clothes, was always disheveled in appearance, and his teeth always looked yellow-stained, with bits of food scum. His smile was not for the faint of heart. Bowers reveled in his new authority as King Muckety–muck. His real claim to fame was in his helping those he favored. Officer Patrick was from all accounts his buddy. So wrong or right, he was going to go all-out for him.

Officer Bowers' logic when helping his friends was frightening. Here's how he played Officer Patrick's drama. Another police officer had been out of work several months due to the death of a child. Chief Gaudett gave him time off to grieve, without taking vacation or holidays from him. We all heard about it and thought it was a kind gesture from the chief after such a devastating event. We also felt it showed great police management. In an effort to protect Officer Patrick, unofficial threats surfaced. If Officer Patrick were penalized for his misconduct, the union would expose the chief's kindness for the officer who had been out grieving. They used the compassion of the chief to protect an officer who stole 100 days from the city. The inside scoop said Bowers was threatening to use the race card, too. The officer who had been out grieving for his child happened to be

## No Black Heroes

black. It was a second time the union had thrown an officer under the bus for another, and both times those officers happened to be black! In the end, Officer Patrick's case died quietly. We never heard anything else about it. Upset, my petty side wanted to mail a toothbrush to Bowers with a detailed note on what he should do with it.

I called Officer Thomas again, and it was the same old line, "I'm very close to having something that will rock this place for the Guardians." He had said that so many times before. Why didn't he just record that and hit play? It had been over a year and Officer Thomas hadn't done a thing. There were no more awards banquets, no cookouts, no toy drives, or Thanksgiving turkeys for the poor. The membership was beginning to call him Officer "Tom," short for Uncle Tom. "Howza can I helps yaz, Boss?" It was how most of us felt. He made a mistake by speaking to my good friend Bill, my covert union buddy. Bill came back to let me know, "Lieutenant, Officer Thomas talked about you and the Guardians like you guys were stupid or something. He kept putting you guys down, saying you guys always complain and can't stand up for yourselves. What's up with your president?" "Bill, I haven't a clue, but thanks for looking out."

Time was flying, Carwin had long since retired and Ted did so a few weeks before. His niece Officer Tresha Parks stopped by my office to speak with me. You could tell Tresha was Ted's family. She meant business when it came to Guardians' affairs, and she wasn't afraid to stand up. "Lieutenant, did ya know Officer Thomas, our so-called Guardians president, spends a lot of time at City Hall?" My worst fears popped into my head. Could he be the one bought and paid for?

Here's where it got a bit interesting. Officer Thomas took the Sergeant's exam and was promoted. What got my attention was his transfer to CAD, the Command Dispatch Center. There was no notice of an opening for a supervisor in CAD as there always had been in the past. What's more, how did a newly appointed Sergeant get that assignment?

## Cops Gone Wild; Hey Nigger; A Human Skull

Usually, a bid would be put out and the assignment filled by seniority. The move reminded me of one of those special assignments D.C. Franks and Captain Trujillo hid from us to take care of one of their own. Strangely, the union didn't say much about it either.

The word floating around the department was Sergeant Thomas had been specially trained and the only one qualified to take the CAD assignment. Thomas had been in patrol since before I could remember. When and where did this class in emergency protocol come from? You could bet your last pair of panties Franks and Trujillo didn't send him.

Under Sergeant Thomas' lack of leadership, the Guardians were on the way down the tubes. Sergeant "Tom" was apparently taking care of himself. He had no intention of filing any complaints against anyone on behalf of the Guardians. He was in CAD making tons of money in overtime. Guardians were fresh out of federal court with no way to fight the racial problems that were mounting again. White officers who hated the court oversight and Judge Clendenen were feeling their oats. The comments were getting louder and louder, "Who the Guardians going to run to now? Judge Clendenen isn't here to take care of ya." To top it off, no one was coming to the Guardians meetings any longer. We had become a do-nothing organization.

"*Hey nigger*, get the fuck out of the street." What? What was that? The phone rang before I could finish my thought. Did I just here the "N" word over the police radio? Detective "Doc" Hill was on the phone. "Bailey, did you just hear that? Someone said the "N" word over the radio!" I leaned back in my chair, was that the new wave of things to come?

The whole city must have heard it. "Should we call Sergeant Thomas?" Hell to the no! Why call him? Unless it was about overtime, forget it. I told Doc I'd call dispatch and asked a CAD operator if they had monitored the last transmission. The office phone rang just as I hung up from Doc. "Lieutenant Bailey, it's me, John." "Lieutenant Cusack, how

429

## No Black Heroes

can I help you kid?" "Ron, can you come downstairs? I need to talk to ya." "Sure, I'll be right there." I had a feeling John was going to tell me who had used the "N" word. He was pretty much on top of everything in patrol.

I ran downstairs and could see he was visibly upset. "John, what's wrong?" I thought he was upset over what everyone heard on the radio. I never would have guessed, in my wildest dreams, what he was about to say. "Ron, I was the one who used the "N" word just now." I couldn't believe my ears. Lieutenant Cusack was a highly respected supervisor, by all officers on the job, especially black officers. He had always treated us with respect. I knew John was a kidder; so I figured it had to be a joke. Standing next to him was Lieutenant Robert Gibbons. If someone had said he had used the "N" word, now that would've made sense. I laughed, "John, you're kidding me, right?"

He tried to explain what happened. He said he was driving his police car to an emergency call when this kid just nonchalantly walked in front of his car. John had to slam on the breaks to keep from hitting the kid, who was intentionally taking his time. When John rolled down the window, the kid said to him, "What up, my nigga?" I was waiting to find out how the "N" word got transmitted over the radio. John said he yelled back at the kid, "Who you calling a nigger?" He told me just as he leaned over to speak to this kid his radio got keyed by accident on the car door handle. He said it caught the words "nigger" just as he spoke. I looked at John stunned. I'd known him since he first came on the job and had served under his father before him. "John, I just don't know why you'd even think to repeat that word." You could see the disappointment in him. "Whatever the department does we have no control over. But I can safely say Guardians will not be coming after you. You've always been great with us and the community. We can only wait and see what the chief will do." He thanked me and said he was sorry.

John figured I had influence over the Guardians and that could be something the chief would take into account.

## Cops Gone Wild; Hey Nigger; A Human Skull

Captain Porter called to let me know the investigation was given to D.C. Hong. Rod was low-keyed but steadfast in supporting the organization. His tutoring was the main reason so many of us made rank. Wait! All I could think was D.C. Hong aka "Mr. White Castle" was doing the investigation? What a joke. Guardians were fairly certain that Hong wouldn't ignore the seriousness of an officer calling someone the "N" word knowing how African Americans felt about it. I was not convinced.

A week later, his recommendation was sent to Chief Gaudett. Now get this, D.C. Hong recommended that Lieutenant Cusack receive a written warning for calling a kid a "nigger." I had heard Chief Gaudett saw Hong's recommendation and plopped back in his chair so hard he almost fell to the floor. The Guardians wanted Hong brought up on charges for his ridiculous recommendation. It was a great idea but wouldn't fly. Besides, we had do-nothing Guardians president Sergeant Thomas. As always, when things hit the fan, he was nowhere to be found and wouldn't answer his phone.

Chief Gaudett was aware NAACP president Carol Vermont was very disturbed by what happened. The news reports reflected that the community was concerned about the use of the "N" word by a police supervisor. Our membership, on the other hand, had mixed feelings about Lieutenant Cusack. Most of us actually hoped he would make out alright. The Chief had to consider all factors. Then the announcement came, Lieutenant Cusack was suspended for two weeks without pay and removed from the SWAT team. Compared to other towns where officers were fired for using racial slurs, the discipline was considered light! As expected, the Guardians didn't contest it.

John confided he wasn't upset at being suspended for two weeks. He was really disappointed over being removed from SWAT. "John, listen to me. Let it go. If you ever had to shoot an African American while in SWAT, what do you think would be the first thing to come out in the news? White officer who used the "N" word shot and killed a black

## No Black Heroes

man. You're better off not being there." John knew I was right, but I figured he would have tried returning to that unit, if given the chance.

I was beginning to regret taking the supervisor's position and leaving TNT. I missed the drug work and team spirit. But sometimes things can go your way. I received a call from my informant, Franklin. I named her after Benjamin Franklin whose face is on the $100 bill. Franklin was the only person in the history of the Bridgeport Narcotics Division who was always one hundred percent right on anything she gave us. Her info resulted in drug seizures every single time, but she would work only for me.

"Franklin, what's up, girl?" "Bailey, there's some shit going on at Madison and George Street. Your boys in TNT can't get in, but I can." I asked if it was weight. She said it wasn't a lot of drugs, but more along the lines of something weird going on there. "Girl, what you talking 'bout?" "Let's just say I'll make the buy and you can go see for yourself." She was talking in riddles, but hey, she had never let me down before.

All the judges knew about Franklin's successes and would sign a search warrant with her name on it without hesitation. I got permission from command to take Madison Avenue out. "Lineup." "Welcome back, Lieutenant." "Glad to be back. The target tonight is 230 Madison Avenue, right across from Columbus School." We discussed who should be in the house when we hit it and what kind of drugs should be there due to Franklin's buys. We copied the money we gave Franklin and recorded the serial numbers to prove we bought drugs from within the house. We figured the money would still be in there because the hit was going to be just a few hours after the last buy.

We drove single-file to the target, jumped out of the cars and walked at a quickened pace in line formation to the house. We hit the door with a battering ram at 2:00am. Boom! "Down, Down, Down!" Once inside, everyone was put down on the floor and the rooms cleared. We snaked our

## Cops Gone Wild; Hey Nigger; A Human Skull

way single file through the entire house, room by room. If someone was in a room, the lead officer would take him down, and the next officer in line took over the point position. Then came the words a commander wants to hear on the set, "Secure, secure, secure." Once all rooms were cleared, everyone we put down in the house was handcuffed and seated. Officers were assigned to keep watch while we began the search of the house.

I sat at the kitchen table with Aileen Cooney reading her Miranda Rights. Strangely cooperative, she told me what was in the house and where. When we talked about the basement, that's when things suddenly went south. She stood up from her chair, "You can't go down there. If you do, it'll be at your own risk. Don't go down there." She had been telling me everything, but turned crazy over the basement. I figured the mother lode was down there. "Miss Cooney, please sit down."

The search warrant was for the entire apartment, including the basement, and it wasn't what she wanted to hear. I quickly got up, heading for the basement door. Ms. Cooney was adamant, "Don't say I didn't warn you." Oddly, the basement access was in the kitchen. Old houses in Bridgeport were sometimes a mystery in their design. We descended down the stairs, curious about what got Ms. Cooney so riled up. Close to the bottom step I could smell the stench. It was an aroma not too many officers had experienced. "Heads up TNT, dead guy." We lit up the basement with our flashlights and were greeted with several inscriptions on the walls. Officer Eddie Rivera was behind me, "What the fuck is this?" I looked closer. The markings were inscribed in blood. But whose? After enduring the horrible smell, we finally found the light switch and flipped it on. "Whoa, what in the ...!"

Ms. Cooney yelled out, "Don't go in that locked room. You'll be sorry if you do." Then I figured it was some kind of a setup. She was telling us not to do something, so we would? We were all looking at a large, solid door with a padlock. There were clear, blood-soaked marks on it, too. In my

## No Black Heroes

30 years, I'd never seen anything like it. I kicked the lock and the latch snapped, "Hey Lieutenant, you still got moves, yo." We opened the door, with guns drawn, and I stood there, stunned. "For the love of God ..."

The two Hispanic officers behind me leaned over and peered into the room, cautiously. They stopped right where they were. "Hey Lieutenant, no offense, we can't go in there." They both headed back upstairs. Eddie moved closer and looked in. "Hey Lieutenant, do you mind if I go back up too? I can't go in there either." "Sure Eddie, no problem. I can do this." I turned back and just stood there, in total bewilderment.

As I gazed in sheer astonishment, you could hear one of the officers upstairs in the bathroom, vomiting. In the middle of the room was a dusty, crusted-over, black kettle. On top of it was a human skull. There was an alligator head and goat's head in the pot. A stick protruding from the pot had a snake wrapped around it. The feathers all around the kettle added to the eeriness of the scene. The pot was full of blood, and there were strange white markings scrawled on the floor. Glasses of wine were placed in several spots near the kettle. The stench was horrendous.

I calmly walked back upstairs and sat down with Ms. Cooney. She looked surprised, as if I should have died in the basement. I sat there for a moment, silently staring at the floor. The scene was imprinted in my mind, replaying. The rest of the team waited in anticipation, to hear about what could be severe enough to cause an officer to be bent over a toilet bowl. Politely, I informed Ms. Cooney I meant no disrespect. She had a right to believe in anything in this world, and I supported that. But I had to ask her poignantly, "Who in the hell does

Santería, brujería, or satanic ritual. What next?

### Cops Gone Wild; Hey Nigger; A Human Skull

that head in the kettle belong to? Are you for real?"

The team members who had remained upstairs looked at me like we just entered the Twilight Zone. They couldn't believe my question. "Lieutenant, did you say "head," a human head?" Cooney looked at me and wouldn't say anything else. At first, I thought the head must have belonged to a body dropped on Seaview Avenue some time ago. The case was memorable, and I had always wondered about it. I mean really, how many people went around the city of Bridgeport collecting heads? The department hadn't identified the headless body because his hands were chopped off. We couldn't print the poor soul, and his DNA didn't give us a clue about who he was.

After regaining my senses, I made sure we didn't violate the limits of the search warrant and called Judge Sullivan. "Your Honor, I know it's late, but we need another warrant signed. We just found a human skull." Judge Sullivan said nothing. It took a while for him to speak. "Say again, Lieutenant" "Your Honor, we just found a human head, a skull." Silence again. "Your Honor, are you still there, sir?" "Lieutenant, it sounds like you said your team just found a human head. That's not funny at this hour." "Your Honor, it's no joke." Judge Sullivan seemed to wake up. "Jesus, Jesus Christ Lieutenant. Okay, I'll make coffee for your guys. Come over when you're ready."

We couldn't search the house without the proper description of what we were looking for, body parts! The warrant was typed and signed. Funny, not one Hispanic officer would go down into that basement. Eddie told me the markings were from Santería, a Cuban African-based religion, and the name Santería sounded familiar. Then it dawned on me; I had heard about testimony Frankie Estrada gave. He cut the throat of a goat in P.T. to protect himself from the police. Jesus, I hope these people didn't murder someone to keep us out. If they did, it didn't work!

By the end of the night, we seized drugs, money, a gun, and the human remains. The next day, the news was all

## No Black Heroes

over the department. Front-page news, "Drug Raid Uncovers Skull, Blood In Ritual." Several news channels asked for a comment. "When we found it, I wasn't sure what we had. I can say this much, I've never seen anything like that before, in my entire career." The news ate it up.

Later, I was told the skull had been sent to the Yale School of Anthropology in New Haven. A few months later, a student at Yale, Annie Le, was murdered in the very research building it was rumored the skull had been kept. She was murdered by lab technician Raymond Clark, her body stuffed in a wall. Clark had no explanation for why he murdered Annie Le, which made the whole thing that much stranger. The connection only fueled the Santería thing. Rumors or tall tales, who knew?

For weeks, the guys kept calling me at the office, to make sure I was still alive. I wasn't sure if they were joking. It was obvious a few of the Latino officers were concerned about the skull and its meaning. It seemed they were waiting for me to fall off the face of the earth. "Hey, Lieutenant Bailey, all jokes aside, do you think that girl at Yale died behind that skull?" "Will you guys cut it out?"

This whole thing actually brought back a memory on rituals, Kojak. He was considered a major cocaine dealer who believed deeply in the occult. We raided his house and he too was like Ms. Cooney, cooperative and courteous. We searched for hours with no luck. I clearly remember a figurine of a woman on the living room floor. It was right there staring at us for hours. When I looked closer, Kojak, like Cooney, suddenly spoke up, "Bailey, it's bad luck for you to touch that." Going with my instincts, I lifted it up. "Take him out of here!" Under the statue was a kilo of uncut cocaine. Word on the streets was I'd been cursed by the voodoo magic. My friend Gloribel who practiced the occult, countered the curses just in case, lighting candles, blowing alcohol into the flames, and things I couldn't begin to mention.

### Cops Gone Wild; Hey Nigger; A Human Skull

I returned to TNT and thanked the guys for one last fling. "It was great working with you guys, even with the in-house graveyard Halloween stuff. I had a blast." "No problem Lieutenant, anytime. We were glad to have you back. Besides, none of us was going to touch that skull." "You guys are nuts, be safe."

Chuck Wilson of the National Association of Black Law Enforcement Officers (NABLEO) called. I was becoming the older mature voice for the African American officers. It wasn't my most comfortable suit. He wanted to know why the Bridgeport Guardians were no longer a part of the National. "Chuck, Sergeant Thomas is the Guardians' President. He's not doing anything from what I've seen." I told Chuck that Thomas wasn't pursuing any complaints filed, was ducking the membership, and was a regular at the mayor's office. Perhaps Sergeant Thomas withdrew the Guardians from NABLEO, because the National would've inquired on some of his peculiar actions, and inaction.

Chuck changed the subject and pleasantly surprised me; he said NABLEO was going to honor me with a Lifetime Achievement Award at the national banquet. He informed me that Senator Richard Blumenthal sent an official citation of recognition in my honor. "The NAACP, and Congressman Jim Himes, had just given me a community award, now this?" It isn't often you get honored by a senator and congressman in so many months." "Hey Bailey, you worked hard and deserve it."

Back at the department with the federal court gone, people like Hong and Franks were taking advantage. Although I was no longer the Guardians president, members were desperate for someone to step up on their behalf. Even one of the police commissioners had resigned and said he had enough. The news reported Commissioner Thomas Kanasky resigned from the Board because the city was ignoring the history of minority officers and the federal discrimination lawsuits from previous years. I had no doubt Commissioner Kanasky was referring to previous cases that had been stalled or buried compared to minority officers'

**No Black Heroes**

cases. You would think after so many years at some point, the department would try to change a wound that had not healed.

Chapter 28

*Brother Bailey, you will have two
miracles coming. Let's pray on this.*
—Bishop J.C. White

## EDUCATION; CANCER; TWO MIRACLES

Working late one night I noticed Chief Gaudett's office lights on. No one should have been in his office that late. I walked in to check, and there he was typing away. "Chief, is anything wrong?" He looked at me and smiled. "Lieutenant Bailey, I'm working on my degree. Some of the classes are online. While you're here, let me ask you, why aren't you going to school?" I looked at him a bit confused, "Do what?" Then he said something I'll never forget, "Lieutenant, you can do this, you can be a police chief." He told me he was a bit envious of the city of Hartford because it was a chief-producing machine. He wanted the same for us and said I needed to think about taking classes.

I left his office thinking long and hard about what he said. I had always thought about going back to school someday but loved working the streets. I talked to Yvette, and of course, she said, "Why not? You paid your dues; it's time you looked at something for you." At 57 years of age, should I go back to school? I wasn't too sure about it, but Yvette insisted it was never too late.

## No Black Heroes

I looked for a program that wouldn't conflict with my schedule and lucked out in finding a weekend program just across the state line in Massachusetts. Springfield College offered a bachelor's degree program in human services that would take about two years to complete. It was actually a degree in community, just what I needed on my resume. I was about to do something I hadn't done before; finish school.

My first class was called Core One. It was about racism in America. There was no surprise in my getting an "A" in that class! Still, I found it difficult at times to attend. I thought a lot about the community and wished I could've been there and more involved. I was working as a Lieutenant in professional standards, still working out at the Tae Kwon Do school, and involved with the Guardians. Truth be told, I needed to excel in school if I was going to be more productive and move forward in my life.

Life had been a series of ups and downs, but the next words I heard proved that to be right. "Ronnie, you know I love you, right?" "Yvette, what's wrong?" She began to cry. "Ronnie, I have breast cancer. I'm sorry." I just stood there thinking, God, not my wife? What had me speechless was when she told me, she admitted that she had kept it to herself for months. With only five weeks left before her surgery, she had no choice but to tell me. "You're sorry for what? Why'd you keep this to yourself?" Her response left me dumbfounded, "You're doing so well in school. With your fighting the department too, I didn't want to burden you."

My first reaction was one of anger; she did something she'd never done before, hid what could turn out to be a life-altering event that could change both of us, especially her, forever. Then I realized I had to step up and be the husband she would so desperately need. Still reeling and hurt, it was time for me to slow things down and help her meet this thing head-on. I'd seen many an officer on the job who had faced cancer; their ordeals were unpredictable and devastating to the toughest of them. I wanted Yvette to smile, and I was heartbroken for her. I wanted to make one

## Education; Cancer; Two Miracles

of my silly remarks so she'd laugh. That day, I didn't have one.

My first thought was to drop out of school, but Yvette wouldn't have it. She said I had to keep going. To lessen her burdens we hired someone to clean the house on weekends so she could take it easy. I also took on more of the household chores such as cooking, shopping, washing clothes, and any of her errands were mine, I insisted. We had many adjustments to make while I prayed for her.

Praying! I made a beeline for my pastor, Bishop White. He had seen me though all my trials and victories. It was Bishop who kept me in prayer and faith my entire career. With all I had come through, Bishop was always there to give me strength and blessings, through God. I had no doubt he was going to see me through this too. "Bishop, my wife has breast cancer." He invited me into his office and looked at me as if I had no need to worry. Then he calmly closed his eyes and reflected for a moment. We discussed a few things, and then he told me something I never expected. "Brother Bailey, you will have two miracles coming. Let's pray on this." He'd never been wrong before. I was curious, "Two" miracles? But I accepted and believed.

About two weeks before Yvette's operation, I was having lunch when it happened. Suddenly I became lightheaded and couldn't catch my breath. My heartbeat was erratic. Something was very wrong, but I had to remain calm. I drove myself to the Bridgeport Hospital emergency room. On the way there, I received a call from my daughter and answered calmly, thinking she might be the last person I would ever speak to. I was careful not to scare her and told her I'd call back. Boy, if she had only known.

At the hospital the nurse took my pulse. I knew I was in trouble when the nurse went from calm to a high-pitched voice asking for a stretcher. Her frozen smile was unnerving. "I'm in trouble." The nurse gave the usual "You'll be fine." speech. That joker-like smile she had said otherwise. I was placed on the stretcher and rushed into the operating

# No Black Heroes

room. My heart was running three times faster than it should have. Perhaps I really was a mental case like people had said. I was still calm for some unknown reason.

The physician removed my shirt and asked if I had just eaten. He wanted to shock my heart but couldn't if I had. Thank God for lunch! He asked if it had ever happened before. All those years, I thought the skipping was a temporary side effect from being in a shooting. He asked about my first one. "My first shooting was in '87, Doc." Curious, he wanted to know how many I had been involved in. "Five, not counting the three dogs I shot on raids." He looked down at me and shook his head in disbelief. "Just so you know Doc, the palpitations happened in all five shootings, but would stop a little later" "Mr. Bailey, have you been under any type of stress lately?" Before I could answer, he joked, "I would have heart issues too, if people were shooting at me."

His next comment had me thinking I was done. "Officer, we're going to stop your heart." "You're going to what!" "Don't worry Mr. Bailey, you'll be fine." That's when I wished I had skipped lunch. I would have preferred being shocked instead of that. They injected me, and sure enough, I was lying there wide awake and my heart stopped. "I better not curse, I won't be able to explain to God if those were my last words." The entire emergency room was filled with laughter. All I wanted was for that bad boy to start up again, and it did, thank God.

The procedure didn't work and my heart returned to the irregular beats. He wanted to try it one more time. I agreed reluctantly but wasn't looking forward to it. One more joke, "Hey Doc, I do have a gun on me. If you mess up, it could be a sixth shooting." They all laughed and stopped my heart again. "Hey, can we please not do that again?" By then the specialist had arrived. She calmly injected me with another drug and bam, my heart was right back in rhythm. "Okay, do you have that in a pill so I can get back to work?" There was more laughter, but I was serious. They all thought it was great to see someone calm under such circumstances.

## Education; Cancer; Two Miracles

I was referred to a heart specialist, Dr. Murali Chiravuri. He was considered one of the best in the field on heart irregularities. Once they released me, I booked off sick for the day. Trying to keep up my sense of humor, I was thinking of calling retired Chief Irving. I could let him know I had booked off sick. I bet he wouldn't have disappointed and would have responded by bringing me up on charges! Fact was, I was worried for Yvette. I couldn't tell her what happened. She had enough to deal with. I had to remain strong for her. She needed to know I would see her through this thing called cancer.

I went to see Dr. Chiravuri in Stratford. After the examination, he was frankly surprised. "You've had this problem since 1987. How were you able to manage it for so long?" "Doc, it would act up for a while, I'd hit my chest, hold my breath, calm myself, anything so it would go back to normal. This was the first time I almost lost consciousness and couldn't breathe." The good news was the procedure he was going to do was considered minor. It was something recently developed that wasn't available back in the day, an ablation. He wanted to do it immediately. "Doc, I have to wait. My wife has breast cancer and is having her operation in two weeks." He understood and said to call the moment I was ready. "Lieutenant Bailey, go slow until we can fix this."

The day of her surgery, I drove her to the hospital with my books in tow. School was a major effort for me, knowing what Yvette was going through. I promised to continue with my studies, but man what a struggle. Yvette's sisters were also there waiting. The operation lasted four hours before the physician came out and told us the operation was a success. The entire tumor had been removed and her breasts were reconstructed. Yvette was sitting up in a special chair, still high from the drugs. She asked why this was happening to us. I cracked a joke, "What do you mean us? By the way, the doctors were fooling around with you while you were asleep. Sexual things." Yvette choked on the water she was sipping, producing a slight silent laugh.

## No Black Heroes

She had a long recovery ahead of her. Once home, one of the tasks was to remove the fluids that had built up in her breasts. The tubes ran from inside her breast to small sacks. The sacks were suctioned and emptied out daily, and I had no problem doing it. I felt honored to help her through the recovery. Her sisters seemed at ease knowing I would not let Yvette down.

A few weeks later, we were at her doctor's office, nervous about what the tests revealed on the tumor and lymph nodes they removed. We had been told many times, the lab was still testing the material. The results would determine the road she would have ahead of her. Neither would be easy, but I didn't want to see her go through chemotherapy. I could only sit there thinking about Bishop White and what he had said to me, the two miracles. If her lymph nodes were affected, or the tumor aggressive, we didn't know what the outcome would be. Finally, we were told she'd require radiation treatments, but no chemo. She would have to endure monthly shots, medications, and regular physician appointments for at least five years. But the physicians assured us she was cancer free. Truth be told, I put my faith in God and trusted in what Bishop White had said, "Two miracles."

Once Yvette was a little better, it was time to tell her what had happened to me. She wasn't happy about me not telling her right away. "Look who's talking. It was more important for you not to worry. It's a minor procedure, not a heart transplant. I'll be fine. Besides, Bishop has already prayed on this." I tried to cheer her up with the news I was maintaining all A's in my classes. Her smile was short but congratulatory.

The day of the operation Yvette seemed strong. I was glad to see her doing so well. At the operating center, they walked me in and laid me on a table, wrapped up in some sort of rubber blanket. I was told they were going to use low types of current or something like that, and I had to be insulated. Dr. Chiravuri said they were going to run two wires from my groin up to my heart. They had to find the area

## Education; Cancer; Two Miracles

that was causing the problems. Once they found it, they were going to, in simple English, burn it. He said not to worry because I wouldn't feel a thing. He explained that the area of the heart causing the problem should be very very miniscule in size. The procedure was scheduled to last about an hour. I went to sleep with a prayer.

Yvette was obviously very worried while pretending she wasn't. What should've been an hour operation turned into four. I was in recovery when Dr. Chiravuri came in to speak with us. "Lieutenant Bailey, I've done this procedure on hundreds of patients. Your heart should have had a defect the size of a pinhead. Instead, we found a one-inch-long area. I've never seen anything like that before, in my entire career. I cannot believe you were able to live a normal life all these years." Oh my God, the second miracle Bishop spoke of. It was right there staring me in the face. He said not to worry and that I could go home. I looked at Yvette thinking to myself, 'Two miracles'. We were both going to be just fine!

I called Bishop White and thanked him for his prayers. "Brother Bailey, you have always been a blessing to this church. God will always be there for you. I love you." The next day I went jogging. My wife, of course, thought I was nuts. I had no fears, because I knew God was with us. He always had been. On my return to work a few days later, I reported to Chief Gaudett who looked surprised. He told me I had been in his prayers. I thanked him for his kindness and went back to my duties.

Chapter 29

## Hangman's Noose/Shot in the Back

My return to work was a far cry from what I had expected. I was completely beside myself with the revelation that someone had left a hangman's noose by Sergeant Joann Meekins' car. It was thought the noose was in retaliation for Joann contesting the lieutenant exam results. She had contested its fairness and impact on black sergeants. We had a group of minority sergeants on the top end of the list, but a larger pool of black sergeants were further down and wouldn't make rank. She felt more African American sergeants should've placed higher on the list, and that the test was faulty.

Some were saying Joann's car was targeted because she was the wife of Ted Meekins, founder of the Guardians. Others said she planted the noose in the hopes of bringing the federal court back to the police department. You didn't have to be a genius to figure out who was saying that. It was ridiculous to think the court would return to monitor the police department. After 30 years, there was no way the court would return.

## No Black Heroes

The FBI was called in to investigate. A grand jury was also convened to inquire into the racial implications of a hangman's noose placed within the boundaries of a police department. It was like old times when I first came on. The hate was so obvious between the races, it was stifling. The rope was just another piece of the sordid legacy of the BPD, a repeat of what Lieutenant Daniels went through years earlier. It wasn't a white thing, but an all-of-us thing. We just couldn't get along.

Joann was exercising her rights. Hell, her challenging the lieutenant exam could have possibly affected me. I wasn't calling her on the phone complaining. I was so tired of what my father, myself, and so many others before had gone through. When would America stop placing so much importance on color? There was no doubt, passing the torch of hate has perpetuated ignorance, nationally.

Any officer thought to have had anything to do with the noose near Joann's car could expect to testify before the grand jury. I was subpoenaed and expected as much. I had been vocal on discrimination my entire career, so my history alone made me a suspect. And it was foolish for me not to think certain officers didn't tell the FBI I had a lot to gain by placing that rope on Joann's car. They all thought we were trying to bring the court back, because racial tensions were worse than ever before.

The grand jury held their investigations in New Haven, Connecticut. I was led into a large jury room by a marshal. That's when the questions began. What was my name, rank, time on the job, and had I known why I was called. The early questions were pretty much a picture of who I was for the grand jury. That's when they honed in, "Lieutenant Bailey, how many complaints have you filed in federal court on discrimination?" "Six sir, and I won them all." "Why did you tell me that, lieutenant?" "So you'd know I didn't just file frivolous complaints. My complaints were substantiated in court."

## Hangman's Noose/Shot In the Back

Then came the question I was waiting for. "Did you want the federal court to remain at the Bridgeport Police Department?" "In a perfect world, I'd say yes. But the problems we have won't go away, even if the federal court remained, it wouldn't matter."

Normally, jurors can't ask questions, but this was the Grand Jury. The process was different from normal standards of court. They were entitled to ask questions. A juror wanted to know why I felt no one could change the racism at the Bridgeport Police Department. He had a facial expression of scorn for some reason. I paused, and looked directly in his eyes, "Sir, some people don't think black officers will ever measure up. The truth of the matter is we, all of us, black and white; we're all linked to racism in this country! So the federal court returning can't fix this. We have to."

The juror looked as if my answer annoyed him. That sort of honesty can have that effect on people. I knew that because I was experiencing the "same behavior" back at the police department. Then the moment of truth came. The advocate for the grand jury walked over to me and said DNA evidence had been found on the rope. He wanted me to provide the court with my DNA, but that I was under no obligation to provide it. My answer more than surprised him. "Of course you can have it. Anything you need is fine with me." That's when things got a little curious. He repeated his assertion, "Lieutenant, you don't have to give us anything. It's entirely up to you." I wanted to make something crystal clear to that entire jury. "Sir, I have nothing to hide. I didn't do it, so you can have anything you want." With that, I was done. On the way out, I took note that the juror who asked me all those questions looked visibly upset. Maybe he was someone who had problems with honesty. Maybe he was one of the problems.

In the hallway, the State Police were waiting. They swabbed my mouth with a Q-tip, got their sample, and I went home. If I were a betting man, I'd have to say there wasn't any DNA taken from that rope. My gut told me it was

## No Black Heroes

a ruse to see who would be reluctant to provide a DNA sample. That would've been an indicator of someone with something to hide. It didn't matter one way or the other to me. I didn't do it.

Months later, the grand jury concluded their investigation. They couldn't determine who left the rope on Sergeant Meekins' car. What did happen was a negative turned into a positive. Joann and Ted petitioned the state of Connecticut to enact a law on such hateful things as a hangman's noose. As a result of their fight, Connecticut was the first state to make it a crime to place a noose in any manner meant to intimidate. It had become, by law, a hate crime.

If you could believe it, the department was on a new downward spiral after the grand jury. White officers were complaining that upper management was allowing the Guardians to run the department, even though the federal court was no longer monitoring. Guardians had made rank in good numbers, and we were making decisions and enforcing the rules. Some officers didn't like it, so they were using the color theme over and over again.

Then came the rumors. The department should've been filmed for reality TV! Word circulated that Chief Gaudett was allowing Sergeant Thomas to work all the overtime he wanted. It was rumored that Guardians were to be pacified through their president. Those rumors were perpetuated. Thomas was a top wage earner, making more money than the mayor! It wasn't enough we had someone leave a noose and had accusations made about black supervisors overstepping their authority, now this. Actually, I believed officers were right and someone was bending over backwards for Sergeant Thomas. But it was someone in City Hall, if you asked me.

What should have been our real concern was Assistant Chief Kerwin retiring. She told me she was packing it in. I had watched her try so hard to make a difference, only to be rebuffed at every turn. The color thing was so deeply rooted a nuclear blast would not have been able to end it.

## Hangman's Noose/Shot In the Back

Kerwin retired to the dismay of all Guardians except one, Thomas. He couldn't have cared less, while making his overtime. Shamefully, after her bouts of ill treatment, Lynn was gone.

The city did a so-called national search. Dave, Rod and I didn't bother to apply. We knew there would have been a stipulation to keep us out again, so why bother? After their lengthy national (wink, wink) search, they selected James Nardozzi as the new assistant chief. He was a resident from a nearby town. Dave asked, "National search?" We lost faith in our hopes for someone to come make a difference. Besides, we knew what the new assistant chief's agenda from City Hall would be, cut the overtime.

Chief Gaudett was surrounded with the likes of D.C. Hong, Franks, Captain Trujillo and their supporting cast. They made recommendations the chief signed off on. Could things get any worse? Our exclusion from any additional training, assignments, and the intense scrutiny towards anything we did was intolerable. I wasn't sure if Gaudett was at fault. The command staff is supposed to look out for things like morale, abuse, racism and overtime issues. They had his ear, we didn't. It surely didn't help having Sergeant Thomas, the silent minority, underrepresenting us.

Although disappointed, I looked ahead. I was determined to finish school and move on. We had been shut out of so many things so many times. But what the heck. Let me try again. There was an opening for a lieutenant or above in rank to attend the FBI management school. It was a given that if you were sent to that school, your chances of becoming a chief were solidified. It was my second time applying, and I was denied again.

Lieutenant John Sweetwater was chosen. My disappointment wasn't in not being chosen to attend; it was in Lieutenant Sweetwater being chosen again and again. How many schools was the guy going to get? He had just gone to the PERF School for police management in Boston, and now the FBI school? He attended two management training

## No Black Heroes

schools within a year? "Take care of your own" had new meaning. To cope with the unfairness of it all, I enjoyed a humorous thought. If only Chief Gaudett knew Sweetwater was constantly trashing him to others as incompetent, the Mayor's pet, and stupid. And this was the Chief's choice for the PERF and FBI schools?

I was through trying to make sense of the police department. I completed my degree at Springfield College, obtaining my bachelor's in under two years. I graduated Summa Cum Laude and was the 2012 Grand Marshall to lead my class. I immediately registered with the University of New Haven for my master's degree. After doubling up on classes, I graduated 14 months later with a Master's in Public Administration. This was something the Bridgeport Police Department couldn't deny me. I needed to get away from what had caused me so much pain.

Could I cross the color barrier into police management? The odds were against me. Police Chiefs in America were members of an exclusive white owned and operated club. The feather in my cap that could catapult me to a chief's position was the FBI police management school. Surprisingly, a third opportunity for the FBI school came up. I applied as a joke, haphazardly, hoping it wouldn't be my third exclusion.

This time it was Lieutenant Mark Straubel who was granted the training. Mark was a good friend, and I was happy for him. As always, there was no explanation given for him or any of the other officers being chosen. Mark apologized, knowing about my constant exclusions from special supervisory training, and the FBI school. "Hey man, it's not your fault. Don't worry about it."

With so many against the Guardians, and a do-nothing Guardians president; it was the 1950s show we were experiencing. Our numbers were low, and police management was taking care of their own. The community was feeling it, and it wasn't just in Bridgeport. As a nation, we were seeing a disconnect between the police and their communities. I

## Hangman's Noose/Shot In the Back

knew it would only get worse, but I had hoped my prediction was wrong. I'd experienced the Civil Rights Movement during my teenage years. You can only keep people marginalized for so long.

One more class and I would be gone. The department offered a police management class at Sacred Heart University. Some said the department offered the class so no one could gripe about not being chosen for the FBI school. I took advantage of the opportunity to augment my schooling, nonetheless. Six months later, I almost "died" at the management class graduation. Look who was chosen class valedictorian, none other than Lieutenant Sweetwater! Was he being spoon-fed or what for a chief's job? Like the movie said, "Feed me Seymour, feed me."

My resume was very impressive, but would it be enough? I began to look for opportunities when the bad news arrived. D.C. Hong was reassigned to my division in an effort to make improvements. Great! Was he going to bring the Black Widow along too? I couldn't get a break. If he got on my nerves, I'd bring him a bag of White Castle hamburgers as a gift. It was a nightmare in the making. The guy hated blacks, especially me. Now I had to answer to him? His claim to fame was his talent at getting a person upset into having an outburst, and then he'd nail the officer. I could only hope he was up on his martial arts. If he pushed me too far, "Buddha," as many had called D.C. Hong, and I were going to hold an exhibition. I smiled a bit; he did look like a short potbellied Buddha figurine.

I got up early with the intention of beating Hong to work. Before leaving, I thought I'd catch up on the news. It was not what I wanted to hear. "Breaking news, Bridgeport Police Lieutenant Robert Dukes shot an unarmed black man in the back, killing him." The news said Dukes told authorities the man was reaching for something, and Dukes fearing for his life, shot him. The only thing found on the guy was a cell phone.

## No Black Heroes

I came from the streets; I knew how the 'hood worked. What person in his right mind, and never mind being black, would confront a police officer with a cell phone? What was this guy supposedly doing, reaching for his phone to call Mom? "Hey Mom, I'm running from the police. Is dinner ready?" Give me a break. That "I feared for my life" line was wearing thin in America. Did Dukes shoot that man because he was afraid, or was he looking for that badge of courage to impress his buddies? "To protect and serve," Dukes may have missed what we were supposed to be about.

The Guardians were talking about how a few months earlier, Lieutenant Dukes had done the same thing. He chased someone for a minor offense, emptied his gun at the guy, claiming, "He feared for his life." As expected, no gun was on the suspect that time either. Luckily, Dukes missed his opportunity previously to make headlines. But this time was his shining moment. He shot and killed a man armed with a cell phone. He was now a proud member of the "I had to do it" club. No wonder many of us joked he was kin to KKK figure David Dukes.

I told a few at the department my thoughts on Lieutenant Dukes and his shootings. It was only a matter of time before it would get back to him, and that was my intent. It was taboo to criticize another officer's shooting, but hey, I wasn't Bridgeport PD's favorite son anyway. He needed to know Guardians thought of him as a glory hound, and a coward for shooting at an unarmed man.

Sure enough, I saw Dukes a few days later. His look said it all. I smiled and said hello to gauge his reaction. He turned his head and walked away. Yep, someone told him what I had said. Let me push him a bit for good measure. "Good, if you're looking the other way, at least I won't get shot in the back." I could hear his shoes slide to a stop. I turned the corner of the hallway, slightly bent forward ducking from the shots about to come. You had to have a sense of humor at the BPD!

## Hangman's Noose/Shot In the Back

On a serious note, there had been a movement of sorts in America for some time in answer to the officers' shootings of unarmed men. The reports of outbursts and pockets of resistance across the nation were swelling. The decades of resentment, mistrust, and hate associated with so many unarmed people killed by police, officers across the nation could end up paying a heavy price. I didn't want to see that, and hoped I was wrong. But officers like Dukes was one of the reasons why policing in America was becoming the center of attention.

Chapter 30

## Cops on Drugs; The Struggles

When I came on the job in 1983, with the assistance of the court we were able to bring close to 100 black officers to the Bridgeport Police Department. Approximately 29 years later, we were down to about 42, and steadily dropping. With a force of 450 cops, 100 were Hispanic and the rest white. This was the norm in police departments across the nation. Was this really 2013?

Sergeant Thomas was assigned to the recruitment drive for the police department. Everyone at the PD was sure it was all about overtime, or we were certain he would not have signed on. I watched his recruitment efforts carefully. He went to a few churches, hung out at the malls, passed out a few flyers, and spent a lot of time at lunch, selling his "I'm the best thing since sliced bread" nonsense. His recruitment drive for minority candidates was not what it could have been.

For me it was a painful time. My son Ronnie had been in and out of jail several times for probation violations. He hated the police and what they stood for. It hurt when he informed me the correction guards spit in his food because he refused to bow down to them. Toiletries were sold at five times what they really cost, or more. His tormentors were scared and took great pleasure in doing things to him, but from a distance when he was locked down. "Ron, you got to stay out of that place." He said he was done and would change. The system he told me of was all about incarceration, and money spent at the expense of the families.

His little brother and my youngest son Brandon, also hated the police. The cops were stopping him constantly, giving him tickets for asking why he'd been stopped. The neighboring town's police department took great pleasure in hassling him. He was young, black, and refused to shut his mouth, making him an easy mark. He would ask me why he couldn't ask a question of them, "Because they have authority, even if they misuse it. You have to play the game, son. I'm sorry," "Why can't they be like you, Dad?" He had a right to speak up if he felt he was being treated unfairly. But that opened the door for what he was going through. The police hated to be challenged and made you pay for it if you did.

I was looking at what I hoped would be my final few years at the BPD. There was one item that needed tending to, D.C. Hong. This was a person on a mission. His sole existence was about getting back at me. Knowing my stance on respect, Hong did everything he could to violate the one thing I had commanded, my dignity. He started by giving me assignments that belittled my position. I challenged his senseless behavior in writing. I pointed out that I was a lieutenant, and not a patrol officer to be assigned menial tasks. To rile him, my cousin dropped by the front desk of the department, in a suit, posing as a board member of the NAACP, asking for me. Hong of course heard about my meetings with the NAACP and promptly canceled those little extra duties.

He tried keeping close tabs on me, the micromanagement approach. I would disappear for hours at a time, re-

## Cops on Drugs; The Struggles

fusing to answer his calls. When he confronted me, I'd pretend to be answering my phone, speaking with community leaders. As expected, the impatient little guy would storm off. He tried speaking down to me, but that gave way to just the right responses. "Hey D.C., you should try to "measure up" and be professional." I would look him up and down while speaking, eyeballing his shortness in height. I was *his* nightmare. Here he came again! "Little Buddha" never gave up. "Lieutenant Bailey, the rumor around the water cooler is you're going to be transferred soon." It was a feeble attempt to elicit a response. I let him know how curious it was that he hadn't been there a minute, and suddenly, I was being transferred and out the door. I walked away from him, smiling.

I reported to my immediate supervisor Captain Robert Sapiro what Hong was doing and what he said. My reports over the next few months were about Hong's poor, and at times, demeaning behavior towards myself and other officers under his command. Of course, copies of those reports were sent to Hong too. The ultimate insult to him was how I communicated it in a professional manner. That really infuriated him.

Never one to give up, Hong tried another tactic, reviewing my hours. He wanted to know why I was leaving work early. So I called Captain Sapiro to remind him I had permission from the chief to leave early. Yvette was still facing struggles, due to her cancer treatments. I had to be home with her. I kept Hong in the dark on that, it was none of his business. I even took comp. time off so no one could say anything, even though the chief kindly said I could take whatever time I needed for Yvette.

Even with all the stress in my life, I continued to fulfill my duties. The Bridgeport Police random drug testing system for officers needed improvement. Somehow, officers knew when their names were on the list, the months they were to be tested. To stop the leaks, I started picking up the list at the company, instead of receiving it by mail. If you're going to drug test people, they shouldn't know that you're coming. Duh!

The very first month under the new system, two officers tested positive for drugs. The union was complaining that I somehow tampered with the test! No one could tamper with the test, and they knew that. The company administered the test. I simply made the arrangements. But I could see where it was headed. The union was going to protect its officers at any cost. It wasn't going to happen at my expense.

The next month, I called patrol to have Officer Jason Ross report for drug testing. As soon as he was notified, he booked off sick. I ordered two officers to go to his house to have him return, with the understanding that his drug test would be considered a fail if he didn't. He returned, but before we could test him, he began vomiting all over the floor. I called for an ambulance, which took him to the hospital. John Whelan was the test administrator for the company. He chucked and called me over. "John, what's so funny?" He said we needed to get some lettuce and cucumbers for a salad. What was he talking about? "Lieutenant, all we need is some oil to go with the vinegar, for our salad." Then it dawned on me. There was a strong odor of vinegar coming from the floor. Roth went home and drank vinegar to interfere with the test results. All it does is make a person sick, nothing more.

Not long after Officer Ross went to the hospital, union president Bowers showed up. He had his usual angry pitbull look. As an architect of intimidation, he stormed in, demanding to know what happened. Bowers wasn't happy with my version of what Ross had done. "Ross left the department supposedly sick, went home, and drank vinegar. Smell it, that's not Mr. Clean on the floor. That's the reason he threw up."

As for Ross, I knew what it was all about and I sympathized with him and understood his troubles. Not long ago, he was involved in a shootout. I'd seen the effects of officer-involved shootings before. I was sure that having experi-

## Cops on Drugs; The Struggles

enced a shooting had pushed him over the edge. He must have had problems dealing with it and eventually turned to drugs. I took no pleasure in failing Ross on the drug test. He tried skipping, and my hands were tied.

I informed the union in writing that he failed the drug test, for not appearing when ordered. They were furious and hinting that I had an axe to grind with the union through its members. A good cop was on drugs and needed help. Their response was to deny he had a problem and blame it on my conduct. The department and union together could have helped Ross. Instead, he was told to deny he had a drug problem. Just before he was about to go before the Board of Police Commissioners, he retired. It was a sad time for me, personally. Ross was a friend we could've helped.

The next officer to test positive for drugs was Officer Benedict Eden. He was a member of the drug enforcement unit, and a long-time Guardians member. When he tested positive, the whole department was in shock. The union couldn't use the white thing, that's for sure. What Eden did next amazed even me. He told the department I was responsible for his failed drug test. He filed a sworn affidavit, with the union in tow, asking for the test to be thrown out, and for me to be reassigned.

Bowers was behind that crock, no doubt. He didn't like the fact that I was catching officers on drugs. He sure as hell was incensed that I didn't jump as he came a-huffing and puffing my way. It was extremely disappointing having Eden, a so-called friend, come after me the way he did. His true colors had been exposed. He couldn't stand up and take responsibility for his actions. The name Benedict fit him well. He was a classic example of why black officers in America were failing; take care of you, and everyone else be damned.

I found it amazing that Officer Bowers was doing what whites in positions of authority had done for centuries before; use us against each other. It was a practice passed down centuries ago by Willie Lynch. His manifesto told how

## No Black Heroes

to control your slaves. He declared that slavery could be maintained for 300 years or more, pitting blacks against blacks. It was the ultimate control tool. Little did Lynch know how right he had been.

The department conducted a formal investigation at the request of the union on my allegedly tampering with the drug test. I asked Bowers one question, "If you believe Officer Eden is not using drugs, then you must believe I keep drugs on hand for tampering with the tests. Which one is more believable, Bowers?" It was the first time his fat ass had nothing to say.

Another officer failed the drug test, and the union was livid. Officer Brian Span was called in for testing and got sick. Come on guys, Ross already tried that! Span drove himself to the hospital complaining of poisoning. Supposedly, someone put something in his coffee. Lieutenant Ray Masek was in command of patrol and was not buying his story. He was in the process of shutting down the eatery Span claimed had poisoned him. One of the sergeants got a hold of Span to let him know what was going on. His poisoning suddenly became a case of heat exhaustion! Heat exhaustion? It's 55 degrees out! Bowers was informed that Span automatically failed the test for not showing up. He went into his stomping act again. Boy, give a guy a little authority and look what ya get; a foot-stomping man-child!

The succession of failed drug tests had Chief Gaudett concerned. He ordered me to test the entire TNT drug unit. Eden's failed test was an indication that something was wrong over there. I showed up unannounced, with Tony, another test administrator. We tested all the officers, and it was no surprise Officer Fred Sykes tested positive for drugs. Officer Eden had told me months earlier about Sykes' drug problem before he himself had failed. "Brother Bailey, Sykes is on crack. That's for real." And these guys were in a unit that at one time was the best of the best. Boy how times had changed.

## Cops on Drugs; The Struggles

With another failed drug test, the pressure was on to have me removed from professional standards. Officer Sykes followed Officer Eden's, "Lieutenant Bailey tampered with my test" nonsense. Cops on drugs and I'm the problem? Contrary to wishful thinking, I didn't have a stash of cocaine at my home to tamper with drug tests.

Bowers and Hong stood by with great anticipation, hoping Gaudett would remove me from my position. Officer Sykes tried to add more fuel to the fire by making the accusation that I had made fun of him and was giving him threatening looks. What do I look like, Bowers? It was time to remind those fools of whom they were messing with.

I wrote a report to the Chief advising him that if Officer Sykes couldn't come to terms with his addiction, he should be referred to the Board of Police Commissioners as unfit for duty and forced to retire. Officer Sykes and the union were sent copies of my report. It brought about a huge silence from Sykes and Bowers. Good, shut up.

D.C. Hong wasn't about to give up that easily, though. He spread rumors that Gaudett wasn't pleased with my work. Hong's insinuations got back to me, of course. I figured he was hoping I'd do something stupid in response to his manufactured gossip. With all I had been through during my career, I was not about to stoop to his level. I couldn't if I wanted to. I wasn't going to let Hong entice me into staining the last chapter to my career. I had plans for Hong's persistent attacks.

As if that weren't enough, my daughter Ashley had been sick for months. We couldn't figure out what was wrong. She had become so distant, we barely knew her anymore. I'd drop by evenings to visit her, but she was never home. During the days, she constantly slept. My worries were extended, because she had no job that I knew of. Yet curiously, she had expensive clothes, took daily trips to the beauty salon, and she was driving a newer BMW. Her excuse was her boyfriend was paying the bills.

## No Black Heroes

Soon the hints came that Ashley was working the clubs, but doing what? Confronted, she finally admitted working as a bartender, and at times a hostess. Ashley's beauty had men crazy for her. I could see the hostess gig due to her ability to manipulate men. Still, I felt uncomfortable with her new job. Something wasn't right, and her health was worsening. "Ashley, this is not a life for you. My mother always said, 'You're the company you keep.' The clubs, alcohol, drugs. There's no future in that. What about your health?" Her lifestyle had to be affecting her health, and she was getting worse.

To my dismay, she moved out of her mother's place into her own apartment. Where was all the money coming from? How could she afford so much working a few hours on weekends? I was speaking to her on the phone. She seemed unusually upset and suddenly, in a fit of rage, hung up. Ashley had never disrespected me in her entire life. I drove straight over to her apartment.

She refused to answer the door. "Ashley, open the door or I'll break it down, now!" Slowly, the door opened. She was half dressed and looked like someone had beaten her. On the floor were mounds of trash, like she hadn't cleaned up in weeks. My worst fears had me hoping this was a bad dream. Someone wake me up. She was barely able to stay awake. The only thing keeping her conscious was her pain. She was crunching the covers with what little strength she had.

With no way of avoiding the inevitable, she confided in me. Ashley had been using over the counter pills and prescriptions drugs to manage her pain. The doctors couldn't figure out what was wrong with her. She was having severe migraine headaches, stomach problems, and was always exhausted, to the point she admitted passing out several times. That explained the bruises and marks I'd see occasionally on her. I had a sinking feeling about the clothes, car, and how she bought them. With so much going on, and the fact she and I had drifted apart over the years, I focused on her health issues.

## Cops on Drugs; The Struggles

I took her to the hospital looking for answers. "Dad, it's a waste of time. Been there, done that." She was right. It was just as she said. They would give her a prescription and tell her to follow up with her physician. She was in such excruciating pain she could hardly walk. My worst fears took over. Was Ashley hooked on painkillers, or was her unknown illness the catalyst for all the prescriptions she was given so readily. Eighteen years in drug enforcement, I had seen only the flip side of what drugs were all about, misery. What Ashley said next had me brokenhearted, "Dad, why does God hate me? What I ever do to him?"

Unable to maintain her apartment, Ashley moved in with us, but things had changed from the days she was little. She and Yvette for some reason had grown apart and seemed to hate each other. They had their own interpretations of each other, Yvette was the evil stepmom, and Ashley was Dad's manipulative little girl. They both had it wrong. All I ever wanted was a family. One thing was for certain, my hopes for a family pulling together had long since passed.

A few months later, Ashley moved back to her mother's, never to return. Angry at the world, she turned her hatred on me. She even kept our grandson away from us. There were so many unanswered questions. I couldn't fathom Ashley's underlying hate for us. Sadly, when she moved out, it was the last time I'd speak to or see my little girl. Reclaiming what I could of myself, I thanked God for all I had in this life, and continued on as best I could.

Chapter 31

## CONCLUSION NO ONE SAW COMING

The new assistant Chief Nardozzi was passing by and stopped to introduce himself. We had a long talk about policing, race, and even the effects of the federal court before its exit. I found it a pleasure to see someone looking to change the negative atmosphere of the BPD. It was my hope that he could make some changes before I was gone.

D.C. Hong was more desperate than ever to get at me and assigned a second supervisor to oversee my duties, Captain Robert Craw. I was the only lieutenant at the department who answered to two captains, Captain Craw and Captain Sapiro. Hong was not pleased with my reaction. "D.C. Hong, it's a real pleasure to answer to Captain Sapiro and Craw, both professionals."

I immediately informed Captain Craw of all I had gone through with Hong. He was given copies of everything detailing Hong's underhanded tactics. For extra measure, I notified Hong of my disclosures to Captain Craw. He was not a happy camper, knowing Craw was aware of everything. As expected, Captain Craw voiced his displeasure of Hong's antics. Craw was always a matter-of-fact kind of supervisor I admired. He always called it like he saw it, but spoke up to whomever, no matter what.

Everyone at the department was pleased with my work except Hong and Bowers. With drug use by officers down, my focus turned to the abuse of the sick policy. The use of the department's unlimited sick time was out of control. Officers had been out of work for months, and in some cases, years at a time. I couldn't think of a single job in America where you could stay out a year or more and get paid. I had no idea it had been going on, but it was about to end.

I assumed informing the union of the problem would be a good start. It was the few who could ruin it for everyone else. The officers with cancer, or other crippling illnesses, needed unlimited sick time, not the ones who stayed home to collect. Bowers maintained his usual stance that his officers had unlimited sick time, so leave them alone. I was trying to help keep a benefit any one of us might need someday. If things stayed the way they were, the unlimited sick time was going out the window at contract time.

I started going to sick officers' homes to check on them. The department physicians were requested to examine any officers who had been out more than three months. That was my cut-off. The union was up in arms, saying I had no right. After a Board of Police Commissioners meeting where they accepted my new parameters, it hit the newspapers. Everybody was up in arms over the news report, blaming me for the press. I didn't call them! Captains Craw and Sapiro, on the other hand, were ecstatic about my efforts, but not Hong.

With no other way to get at me, Hong utilized Craw's position in his little scheme. He ordered me to make reports to Captain Craw anytime I took off work to take care of Yvette. In addition, he ordered me to walk any department paperwork over to City Hall daily, instead of using the email sys-

## Conclusion No One Saw Coming

tem, like all the other supervisors. He even walked by my office frequently, to check on my whereabouts.

I decided to be more aggressive in keeping Hong at bay. I kept my door shut, so he wouldn't know if I was in my office. All my phone calls were forwarded to the answering service. Hong's constant calling my office was just another ploy to check on me. He never had anything worthwhile to say. I refused to take part in anything considered a harassment tactic. He didn't like it and I didn't care. On occasion, I blew him a kiss to show my defiance. What was he going say, my blowing him a kiss was affectionately insubordinate? Enough was enough.

The final showdown came over a report I gave Assistant Chief Nardozzi. The report detailed Hong's constant harassment. I couldn't believe "Buddha's" nerve, calling me in his office with Captain Craw in tow. "Lieutenant Bailey, I am aware you gave a report to Assistant Chief Nardozzi reporting my behavior as unprofessional. Is that correct?" "If you are aware of it, then why are you asking me that?" That comment went over well. He was shaking in anger. "I need an explanation, Lieutenant Bailey." Oh boy, he's straining his voice. My response was borderline madness, "You're not entitled to an explanation, but I will enlighten you." I paused for a moment. "D.C. Hong, when I speak to you, it's with respect. You, on the other hand, don't act in the same manner. I'm very disappointed in you. You're supposed to be a professional." Then came the Mona Lisa-like smile he would have when he had no words. It looked to me like all the air had been let out of his bubble. I looked down at his hands to see if he was going to reach for his gun. My words were extremely insulting to someone who thought of himself as a superior officer. He was anything but superior.

His comeback was sarcastic, "Lieutenant Bailey, I find you to be Machiavellian in your behavior." I sarcastically responded back, "Tupac, right? I didn't know you were into rap." Hong was trying to insult me and assumed I didn't understand his so-called fancy words. He was trying to insult me by inferring I was devious and unscrupulous. What

## No Black Heroes

an idiot. I was about to let him have it when Captain Craw intervened. "Deputy Chief Hong, I think you're upset and not listening to Lieutenant Bailey. He is not asking you to be his friend. He just wants you to be professional in dealing with him as a coworker." He looked at Captain Craw, disgusted with his comment. His response was dull, "Duly noted." He then stormed out of the office without saying another word. Why is he leaving? This is his office.

"Captain, you didn't have to say anything to Hong. I don't want you to get in trouble over me." "Lieutenant Bailey, you were right. He was way out of line." "Captain, thanks so much, but please be careful. Hong is relentless and unforgiving. I don't want you to suffer because of me." Captain Craw smiled and touched my shoulder as he left the office.

It was a confusing time. The Guardians president never acted on any of my complaints, but here was Captain Craw, a white supervisor, defending me. I was sick and tired of it all; it was time to get out of Dodge. First, I needed relief from Bowers and Hong. And I knew just what to do. It was sure to enrage both of them, but there was no other way. I could no longer work under the conditions they put me in.

I filed a second report with A.C. Nardozzi detailing all of D.C. Hong's comments, harassment, and insulting behavior from day one. The anchor to my complaint was in having Captain Craw support my position. To shut Hong down once and for all, I filed a discrimination complaint with the Commissioners on Human Rights and Opportunities (CHRO). It wasn't a complete surprise when Hong booked off sick. Should I go to his house to ask for a physician's note? That would've gone over well!

I was on a mission and my next stop was CAD to see Sergeant Thomas. I had resigned from the Guardians and he wanted to know why. I kept my reasons vague on purpose, "I had to, Amos. There are some things I can't discuss right now but it's for the good of the organization that I resigned." The whole department was in shock. The truth was

## Conclusion No One Saw Coming

that I was embarrassed to be a part of something that was becoming a lot of nothing. The Guardians was not the organization I joined years ago. I also wanted to distance myself from Sergeant Amos Thomas. Something about his coziness with City Hall and being the Guardians president made me uneasy.

Knowing the nature of the beast, I bought a digital camera that looked like a clothes hook. I spruced up my office and placed it in a location to film any movement. I'm not surprised. I knew it! When Hong returned from his "illness," he was recorded going into my office after-hours. He was looking though my papers and messing with my computer. That explained why my paperwork had been missing from the office and the computer was performing poorly. Tinker Bell was messing with it. Not sure I had a right to film in the department, I held onto it for added insurance. Luckily, the CHRO complaint kept Hong at bay. His skulking around at a distance was the result of that complaint. It would buy me time for my next move.

Next, I contacted Attorney John Williams. I informed him that union president Bowers was pushing to have me removed from my position under false accusations. His assertions of drug tampering and constant attacks had to stop. I needed Bowers shut down. After explaining to Attorney Williams about all the union had done, he responded, "Lieutenant Bailey, when do you want me to file?" I needed to send Bowers a clear message immediately. He was served papers that week.

Monday's news was the union had an emergency meeting with a select few of Bowers' cohorts. Word was he was furious, but worried. They were asking members to do anything to get back at me. If they crossed the line, the next step would be a retaliation claim in court. I was on my way out, but under my terms, not theirs.

Officer Bowers wasn't one to give up easily. Bill, who was still deep in the union, said Bowers was intending to use Officer Eden somehow. I felt bad for Eden, who was still

## No Black Heroes

battling his addiction. Stupid me, I was worried about him, yet he was obliging Bowers. Bill said Bowers was intending to work that black on black angle using Eden.

Bowers upped the ante; Bill said the union turned to Officer Debbie Price for help. I didn't see that one coming. Officer Price was fired for abuse of the unlimited sick time. She stayed out of work over a year, without providing one single physicians note. She even told her supervisor she wasn't coming back to work until she felt like it. The Board of Police Commissioners fired her, and of course she blamed me. Price filed a complaint with the Equal Employment Opportunities Commission. The complaint implied I hated black women and it was the reason she was terminated. Bowers' black on black-led charge using Price and Eden was devious. His arsenal now included two black officers making racial claims. Guess he really studied Willie Lynch's manifesto well.

I used a textbook maneuver to shut the union down once and for all. Information was leaked that I was close to arresting a few cops for drug use. An additional rumor was circulated that my informants helped me get information on several officers, including two I already caught before. Police are often like old gossiping women. They all ran with the rumor, maintaining their distance like I had leprosy or something. From their reactions, I had to wonder how many more cops were on drugs.

It was time to test one last theory. Was Sergeant Thomas really an Uncle Tom like everyone was saying? He seemed disturbed about me returning to speak with him. "Sergeant Thomas, the union has been planning some under-the-table stuff to get at me. I have taped conversations of what they were planning. His response was very interesting. "Lieutenant, won't you get in trouble for recording someone's conversation?" "Not if it's leaked from an unknown source to the news." I asked him to look out for me and thanked him for his time. Let's see if homeboy is what they say he is.

## Conclusion No One Saw Coming

I walked out of Sergeant Thomas' office and down the hall. After counting to 10, I walked back to his office but stood just outside his door. "Hey Bowers, Bailey was just here." That's all I needed to hear. Thomas was in cahoots with the union president? If only Thomas knew I used him to get Bowers off my back. Wow, Officer Bowers and Sergeant Thomas were working behind the scenes together. Who was using whom?

Racism had risen to new heights in the department. It truly developed into a system of systematic hate over the years, and from all sides. It was mostly black against white, but there were a few complaints of gender, too. The city compounded the problem even more. They devised a plan to address racial complaints in their attempts to keep things in-house. Good luck with that. Any discriminatory complaints were to be evaluated by the City Attorney's Office before they could proceed further. Great! The city, during its entire 30 years under court oversight, never admitted to one case of discrimination. They were going to evaluate racial complaints for merit? We would have had a better chance hitting Powerball, if you asked me.

I began filling out applications for employment. It was time to leave the city of Bridgeport. My first application was with the East Haven Police Department. I had read in the papers about East Haven PD officers abusing the Latino community. The Justice Department was investigating their department. I thought it would be a great opportunity for me to make a difference as their chief, so I applied.

As expected, they hired Chief Brent B. Larrabee who had been brought in by the Mayor of East Haven months earlier. The selection process was humorous at best. Chief Larrabee was a member of the very consulting firm that was conducting the search for the next East Haven chief. There was no surprise in that pick.

I called Chief Ronell Higgins of the Yale New Haven Police Department. Chief Higgins was surprised I was looking to continue my career elsewhere. "Lieutenant Bailey, if you

## No Black Heroes

want to be a police chief, you have to go 50 miles one way or the other. There are no opportunities in Connecticut." Chief Higgins was a friend and mentor to up-and-coming leaders. He was one of the few looking to promote African American leadership. I wasn't sure if he meant no opportunities in Connecticut or no opportunities for men of color in Connecticut. But I heeded his 50-mile radius recommendation.

I did some research before applying again and discovered something very disturbing. The state of Connecticut has 169 cities and towns. With all the police departments in the state, only three had African Americans who held the title of Chief of Police. It was an insult to see such disproportionate numbers in leadership positions. I looked a bit deeper into the dismal outlook of black leadership and noticed the Connecticut Police Chiefs Associations were at the forefront in assisting cities in their selection process for prospective new chiefs. Was everyone in a position of authority of the opinion that we weren't qualified to lead a police department? Maybe the Justice Department should be my next stop. The numbers in Connecticut begged for it.

I happened to see an opening for Chief of Police in Massachusetts. It was a long drive, but perhaps my chances were better there than in Connecticut, just as Chief Higgins suggested. It was a three-hour drive but my options were limited. Forty-six applicants applied, but after three interviews, a presentation, and a lengthy discussion with an interview panel, I was selected Chief of Police. After all that had happened to me over the years, I had that new beginning I desperately needed. No way was I going back to the department pumping my chest with those "How ya like me now" comments. I had nothing to prove and opted to leave quietly. The ones who tried to hold me back all those years would see a man leaving with dignity, and integrity.

The first person I told after Yvette was Dave. He was the one who inspired me to climb the ranks and excel. It was killing him to keep my secret. He wanted it to be a day of bragging rights in lineup. His reaction was classic Dave.

### Conclusion No One Saw Coming

"It's gonna to be good to let these fools know we can make it without their help." Lieutenant Daniels was passionate about his blackness. I was proud to have served with him and hoped he would enjoy the announcement. Of course Ted Meekins needed to know, too. Who in their right mind could leave him out? He was the one who restored my faith in cops, and who mentored me during my career. He was proud and speechless. Speechless was a first for him.

Just before my impending departure, I told Chief Gaudett. My duties on the third floor were essential to his command. Fondly, I remembered his challenging me to get my degree, as I began to thank him for his encouragement. He seemed concerned and puzzled. "Chief, I wanted you to be one of the first to know I'm retiring. I'll be leaving for a position as a chief in Massachusetts. He scared the absolute mess out of me. Chief Gaudett stumbled back holding his chest and plopped down in his chair. "Ron, I can't believe this. I'm speechless. Oh my God. This is wonderful." "Chief, are you alright? I just wanted to say thanks, not give you a heart attack. You had a vision. Well I'll be the first one under your command to be a chief." He was the first one to formally say it, "Chief Bailey, all I can say is congratulations. This is wonderful news." I asked him if he could keep it quiet until I was gone. He understood and kept it mum.

I had about four weeks left to get my affairs in order. I was getting my office ready for the next person when I heard a tap on my door. It was Sergeant Thomas. "Lieutenant Bailey, I need a favor." Wow, he must be desperate to ask me for something. "Bailey, Assistant Chief Nardozzi cut my overtime. He's considering transferring me out of my assignment. I've filed a complaint against him." I shouldn't have been surprised with what he said to me next. He somehow knew I was leaving. I surmised Sergeant Thomas found out from someone in the benefits office that I put my papers in. We all knew he had connections in the mayor's office.

## No Black Heroes

What came out of his mouth next was an absolute mind-blowing shock. He asked me to write a report for him with details of Nardozzi's racist ways, as he put it. "Bailey, Chief Nardozzi is a racist. He hates black officers. You know that." He kept saying over and over, "If you could write a report supporting me, it would really help me out." Sergeant Thomas then hinted at my reputation for honesty. I tried to tell him what he wanted me to do was wrong; he wasn't listening. That's when he took it to another level. "Hey Bailey, you know he's a racist, come on. You could write a report and everyone will believe you. You're known for telling the truth." Thomas wouldn't take no for an answer. He wanted to use my honesty to reinforce his complaint. Even when I told him Assistant Chief Nardozzi had asked me to contact Judge Clendenen so he could speak with him about discrimination in the department. Thomas' mind was made up. "Bailey, I really need you to do this for me. You know how this place is, and Nardozzi." He summed it all up by reminding me that I'd be leaving anyway so why not write it.

Thomas then played on my past struggles and asked that I reflect on the police department and how they treated me over the years. He said I didn't owe them a thing. All I could do was respond to him and hope he would let it go. "Don't do this, Amos. How could you do something like that knowing it wouldn't be right?" He smiled and said he was sure I could think of something to write, and to let him know.

Over the next few weeks, Thomas made it a point to remind me about the report he needed. I had never seen him so much before! Is this what we had come to as black officers, do whatever it takes to win? It was certainly a rough closing chapter to my career.

It was a few days before I left for good. I drove by the TNT office to take one last look. Inside, I took a long look at all the unit citations displayed on the wall. My name was conspicuously missing from all of them. Thousands of drug arrests, five shootings, six lives saved, and the department

## Conclusion No One Saw Coming

had erased my existence. My exclusion was meant to be the ultimate insult, by someone. I went by the training academy and took a look at the class plaques. I was on two of them, 1983 and 1987. The 1987 plaque referred to me as Wild Bill Bailey. Was I crazy back then, or what? Maybe still!

Yvette thought I was crazy. She felt I should've taken a few weeks off before starting a new job. I'll never forget, it was a Sunday night and I was shutting my door to the office for the last time. I thought long and hard about the community of Bridgeport. My thoughts drifted to my children. Had I given my life to Bridgeport, sacrificing them? Two had been arrested several times, one in and out of jail his entire young life. I had a daughter who wanted nothing to do with me. Would she ever be right again? I should have been there for them. I failed my family for a place that hated me. Would the city ever truly realize what they had done to me and my family?

My thoughts turned back to how the Bridgeport Police Department had wronged me for 30 years. Officer Thomas' words were resonating louder in my head. "Why not get back at them, Bailey? They have it coming for what they done to you." Yeah, I didn't owe them anything having been treated like dirt. All I had to do was label one person to get even with the whole damned place for what they'd done to me. Thomas' last remark really hit home, "Bailey, they all take care of their own. We need to take care of ours."

I made my way to the bottom of the stairs with a few folders in hand. On the ground floor, I paused. Sergeant Thomas' words were still in my head "What did I have to lose?" Tired, I closed my eyes for a moment, then looked up inadvertently at the plaque on the wall in the lobby. A Bridgeport police officer killed in the line of duty gave the ultimate sacrifice, his life. I realized that I had, in all sincerity, given my life as well. And look at how they had treated me all those years. I shook my head, knowing my final answer to Thomas was the correct one. My integrity wasn't for sale, it never was. I turned and walked out of the Bridgeport Police Department for the very last time.

## No Black Heroes

The next day, I started my three-hour drive to Massachusetts. All I could think of was how God had been so good to me during all my struggles. I figured by then Dave was making the announcement in lineup that I had retired to take a new position as chief.

Yup! It was my phone. Dave must have told them I was gone. Just before I arrived at my new office, there was a text message from a number I didn't recognize. And it read, "I just heard you got a job as a police chief. If that's really true then you will know what to do with this." Under those words was a picture of a slender white man, his face shielded, holding his penis!

# Afterword

My story should have given you insight into how things really are for African American police officers in this country. It's frightening to realize that my writings and predictions were made well before the national eruption of awareness that began in Ferguson, Missouri. I'm thankful to see that all Americans are upset in what they are now witnessing.

Speaking of Ferguson, Missouri, it has a population of 65% African Americans. Yet the police force of Ferguson, as of this writing, has 53 officers in its ranks. Only three are black. The shooting death of Michael Brown was a tragedy and almost destined to happen, under those circumstances. What is extremely troubling is that after his death, someone burned his father's church down. Do we hate each other to such an extent that it's come to that?

I ask you to reflect for a moment on Michael Brown, Eric Garner, Omar Edwards and Cornel Young Jr, all who lost their lives to police officers. I can just imagine you asking

## No Black Heroes

yourselves, "Who are Omar Edwards and Cornel Young Jr?" They were two African American police officers shot and killed while off duty by white police officers. They called it friendly fire, a mistake. Here is what shocked me; I cannot find any history of a black officer shooting a white officer under such circumstances, ever. We are an at-risk race due to the color of our skin, and that includes African American police officers.

A recent study, "Task Force on 21st Century Policing" was conducted by experts from across the country. It calls for better police training, true community policing efforts from top to bottom, and a diversified police department that reflects its community. Having the person who scored high on the police exam is not necessarily the best person for a given community. And it's not about color; it's about equal representation and culture. I implore all of you to read that report.

African Americans are seeking to be a part of the law enforcement community and our judicial system. They are met with resistance, and ever-changing rules. Yet by our very existence we are the majority that supports a judicial system through incarceration. With seven million in our corrections system nationally, 63% are minority. Our inadequate representation in police departments plays a role in the issues we are faced with today. If police departments do not change now, the price will be regrettable later. The days of civil disobedience are here and magnifying.

The federal court was tasked with addressing discrimination at the Bridgeport Police Department and remained for 30 years! That by the way is a national record. During that entire time, the city of Bridgeport never truly admitted there was a problem with regards to discrimination. In comparison, the Justice Department today has interceded in numerous police departments across this nation for exhibiting the same problems Bridgeport ignored for so many years. This should tell you something about the issues we are facing. And many still don't want to talk about it, and surely won't admit to it!

# Afterword

There is another problem propelling racism and therefore affecting policing in America. The unequal class system has kept the poor dependent on menial work and pay not fit for a family to live on. The results of this unbalanced system are communities plagued with crime, drugs, and poverty. The American dream has millions living on the streets, homeless and often hungry. This is not how the richest country in the world should set the example.

There will be those of you who will say black people have choices and can better themselves. Our system of education doesn't support that belief. There is a severe lack of quality educational opportunities for all children in America. Inner cities across our nation lack the proper resources and support mechanisms in education, unlike those in more affluent communities. The Brown vs. Board of Education Supreme Court ruling of 1954 called for equal education. Clearly that didn't happen.

The title *No Black Heroes* is not just mere words to represent this book. Someone had to point out that black policing in America is a constant struggle. From the beginning, we as a race have been tainted. America needs to understand our heroes portrayed in the movies are nothing like Superman or Captain America. We were given heroes such as Blade the black vampire and Hancock, the alcoholic superhero. Even Spawn was a pseudo superhero from hell! Are these the best images we can muster? Perhaps, one day we can borrow one of America's superheroes. I have often toyed with the idea that Batman, the master of disguise, is actually a black man. Wouldn't it be amazing to have a superhero crime fighter of color with superior intelligence, a master of martial arts, and a figure who cares about people more than himself?!

I also submit to you the Black Lives Matter movement is a culmination of denied opportunities and frustrations, years in the making. I mean seriously, if someone challenges gay or women's rights, there are united movements formed with professional athletes, actors, politicians and society at large, and rightly so. But Black Lives Matter has

## No Black Heroes

been met with criticism and denial. Black people have been struggling for equal rights for centuries, and we are still being excluded and denied our proper place in society.

In conclusion; I must point out for those who confront the police, talk down to them, blame and disrespect the men and women in blue, you are wrong! Don't condemn an entire group by the actions of a few. If you do, then aren't you guilty of the very thing so many complain of today, stereotyping? We need to support the officers who do care. They deserve your respect and support. The corrupt ones will fall soon enough, they always do. So please take the time to tell an officer you appreciate what they do. Kindness can only have a positive effect. Yes, I expect you to be better than we are.

# Afterword

*Hope.*

*The one thing we all need to move forward, together.*

Blessings,

William "Ron" Bailey

In remembrance of my son

William Ronnie Bailey III
October 1, 1982—May 23, 2016

Ron Bailey III,
my first-born son.

Ron and his son, Ron Bailey IV.
There is hope!